ONE TEXT, A THOUSAND METHODS

BIBLICAL INTERPRETATION SERIES

Editors
R. Alan Culpepper
Rolf Rendtorff
Ellen van Wolde

EDITORIAL ADVISORY BOARD
Mieke Bal • Phyllis A. Bird
Erhand Blum • Ekkehard Stegemann
Vincent L. Wimbush • Jean Zumstein

Number 71

ONE TEXT, A THOUSAND METHODS

Studies in Memory of Sjef van Tilborg

Edited by

Patrick Chatelion Counet and Ulrich Berges

 **PRESS**

Atlanta

Copyright © 2005 by Koninklijke Brill NV, Leiden, The Netherlands

This edition is published under license from Koninklijke Brill NV, Leiden, The Netherlands, by SBL Press.

All rights reserved. No part of this work may be reproduced or transmitted in any form or by any means, electronic or mechanical, including photocopying and recording, or by means of any information storage or retrieval system, except as may be expressly permitted by the 1976 Copyright Act or in writing from the publisher. Requests for permission should be addressed in writing to the Rights and Permissions Department, Koninklijke Brill NV, Leiden, The Netherlands.

Authorization to photocopy items for internal or personal use is granted by Brill provided that the appropriate fees are paid directly to The Copyright Clearance Center, 222 Rosewood Drive, Suite 910, Danvers, MA 01923, USA. Fees are subject to change.

Library of Congress Control Number: 2016942918

Printed on acid-free paper.

CONTENTS

Preface   vii
Frontispiece   viii
Introduction   1
  Patrick Chatelion Counet

PART 1: OLD TESTAMENT

1. The Violence of God in the Book of Lamentations   21
   Ulrich Berges

2. Obdurate Short-Sightedness in the Valley of Vision: How Atonement of Iniquity Is Forfeited (Isa 22:1–14)   45
   Willem A.M. Beuken

3. One Day, Three Days, and Forty Days in the Book of Jonah   65
   Erik Eynikel

4. Psalm 69: A Composition-Critical Contribution   77
   Alphonso Groenewald

5. A Struggle with God: Poetics and Theology of Psalm 35   97
   Matthijs Kronemeijer

6. Isaiah's Roles: The Unity of a Bible Book from the Perspective of the Sender-Role   115
   Archibald L.H.M. van Wieringen

7. Cognitive Linguistics and Its Application to Genesis 28:10–22   125
   Ellen van Wolde

8. "Hearing Voices While Reading": Isaiah 40–55 as a Drama   149
   Annemarieke van der Woude

Part 2: New Testament

9. Resolving Communication Disturbances in Luke 12:35–48 through Narratology   177
   Andries van Aarde

10. No Anti-Judaism in the Fourth Gospel: A Deconstruction of Readings of John 8   197
    Patrick Chatelion Counet

11. What on Earth (or in Heaven) Is a Resurrected Body? The Outline of a Historical-Anthropological Answer   227
    Pieter F. Craffert

12. Acts 8:26–40: Philip Baptizes the Ethiopian: Narrative and Pragmatic-Linguistic Aspects   255
    Detlev Dormeyer

13. The Rhetorical Analysis of Galatians: Is There Another Way?   275
    D. Francois Tolmie

14. Style Criticism and the Fourth Gospel   291
    Gilbert Van Belle

15. Intertextuality: Traces of Mysticism   317
    Huub Welzen

Part 3: Biography and Bibliography

Sjef van Tilborg: A Short Biography   351
   Ulrich Berges and Patrick Chatelion Counet

Bibliography of Sjef van Tilborg   356
   Patrick Chatelion Counet

Index   361

PREFACE

This book should have been a *Festschrift*, a surprise to our dear friend and colleague, Professor Dr. Sjef van Tilborg (MSC), who was going to be 65 on the 10th of April 2004 and who would retire a few months later as professor of the New Testament of the University of Nijmegen in the Netherlands.

Sjef died, unexpectedly, on the 22nd of May 2003. This was a severe shock. He had been preparing for his farewell conference on the theme "In Search of Other Worlds," a day with lectures on minimal music, astronomy, film, and Zen Buddhism. Sjef would end the day with a lecture on Death Threats in the Apocalypse.

It turned out otherwise. This book is still a *liber amicorum* but also an *in memoriam*, dedicated to the memory of Sjef van Tilborg, who was a great scholar, a concerned pastor, and a remarkable and fine human being.

The editors would like to thank the persons and institutions that made this book possible. Van Tilborg belonged to the Missionaries of the Sacred Heart—Missionarii Sacratissimi Cordis (MSC). We thank the congregation in the person of Dr. Ton Zwart (MSC) for their generous support to this book. We also received financial support from the Faculty of Theology of the University of Nijmegen. We thank Dr. Gian Ackermans, who proofread the manuscript conscientiously. We owe many thanks to Marije Bijleveld (MA), Lara Hanssen (MA), and Hendrik Jan Bosman (MA) who did a splendid job on the layout. Antonio Sison (MA) corrected the English translation of some texts. A special word of thanks is due to Fons Meijers (MSC) and Prof. Dr. Peter Nissen, who have supplied detailed information for the biography of Sjef van Tilborg.

We thank the many contributors to this volume. Sjef would have been eager to study the articles and to discuss the results with us. We will miss his comments, his radical Christian insights, and, above all, his intense presence.

Nijmegen, the Netherlands,
March 24, 2004

Patrick Chatelion Counet
Ulrich Berges

Sjef van Tilborg, MSC (1939–2003)

INTRODUCTION

Patrick Chatelion Counet

Idee des Todes

Der Engel des Todes, der in gewissen Sagen Samael heißt, und mit dem, wie berichtet wird, auch Moses ringen mußte, ist die Sprache. Er kündigt uns den Tod an—was sonst tut die Sprache? Aber ebendiese Ankündigung macht es uns schwer, zu sterben. Seit unvordenklicher Zeit, seit Anbeginn ihrer Geschichte liegt die Menschheit mit dem Engel im Kampf, um ihm das geheimnis zu entreißen, daß er bloß ankündigt. Aber aus seinen knabenhaften Händen läßt sich nur die Ankündigung zerren, die er uns ohnehin zu überbringen kam. Der Engel hat daran keine Schuld, und nur wer die Unschuld der Sprache erfaßt, begreift auch die wahre Bedeutung der Ankündigung und kann—vielleicht—lernen zu sterben.

Giorgio Agamben[1]

Biblical exegesis nowadays is characterized by a proliferation of methods. S. Moore speaks of a double paradigm shift; since the nineteen-seventies, there has been a methodological shift from diachronic to synchronic methods, and an epistemic shift from modern to postmodern thinking.[2] The two are connected and that is why J. Dunn's definition of the new criticism as "the flight from history" is only partly correct.[3] The shift from diachronic to synchronic methods involves a transposition not only from the historical context to the world of the text (from history to story), but also from the text to the process of reading (from author to reader) and even from the constitution of meaning to the reflection on methods (from interpretation to methodology). Its relation to historical critical methods can define the new

---

[1] G. Agamben, *Idee der Prosa* (Übersetzung aus dem Italienischen—*Idea della Prosa*, 1985—von Dagmar Leupold und Clemens-Carl Härle), Frankfurt am Main 2003; p. 139.

[2] S. Moore, *Literary Criticism and the Gospels. The Theoretical Challenge*, New Haven-London 1989; p. 130. See also P. Chatelion Counet, *John, a Postmodern Gospel. Introduction to Deconstructive Exegesis Applied to the Fourth Gospel*, Leiden etc. 2000; pp. 104–19.

[3] J. Dunn, *Jesus Remembered* (Christianity in the Making, Vol. 1), Grand Rapids, Michigan/Cambridge-U.K. 2003; pp. 67–97.

criticism only partly.[4] For the greater part, it has to be considered as a phenomenon in itself.

1. *The Methodological Shift: A Thousand Methods!*

The shift from diachronic to synchronic exegesis, as described by Moore, does not involve the end of historical critical research. Far from it. As it seems, the orientation on the history of the development of texts in the field of the exegesis of the Old Testament, as well as the research of the "historical Jesus" in the field of the New Testament, are never-ending stories. The new criticism does not replace the old methods, but goes incompletely different ways. In fact, there is no competition and—it seems necessary to say so—nothing to be afraid of.[5]

Most of the diachronic instruments developed through historical critical research—Source Criticism, Form Criticism, Redaction Criticism, Composition Criticism, etc.—are history-oriented; one understands the text as the outcome of a historical development. Diachronic instruments are devised to reconstruct the production of texts; the want to discover the *pre-text*. The success of these methods turned out to be tremendous as the "discovery" of the sources of the Pentateuch and the Synoptic Gospels—to mention only two colossal results—unquestionably shows. The research goes on.[6]

---

[4] According to D. Clines and J. Exum, to those engaged in the newest of the "new" literary criticisms—feminist, Marxist, reader-response, deconstructionist, and the like—even stylistics, rhetorical criticism, and structuralism and other formalist criticism are no longer "new"; D. Clines & J. Exum, "The New Literary Criticism," in J. Exum and D. Clines (eds.): *The New Literary Criticism and the Hebrew Bible* (11–25), Sheffield 1993; here p. 12.

[5] See the reaction of J. Ashton who calls the method of deconstruction "the work of the devil"; ironically enough, he takes over the deconstructive insight that texts try to hide their textuality in order to create the illusion of truth and reality: "The Fourth Gospel is not only an instance of the Gospel genre, but also a reflection upon it" (J. Ashton, *Understanding the Fourth Gospel*, Oxford 1991; pp. 502/513 and p. 434).

[6] Notable in the new diachronic studies is the interest in interpretive communities and (first) readers. This applies to Old Testament studies as well as to New Testament studies; to mention just a few from the recent studies: B.E. Reid, *The Transfiguration: A Source—and Redaction-Critical Study of Luke 9:28–36*, Paris 1993; M.P. Knowles, *Jeremiah in Matthew's Gospel: The Rejected Prophet-Motif in Matthaean Redaction*, Sheffield 1993; B. Repschinski, *The Controversy Stories in the Gospel of Matthew: their Redaction, Form and Relevance for the Relationship between the Matthean Community and Formative Judaism*, Göttingen 2000; J. Vermeylen, *La loi du plus fort: histoire de la rédaction des récits davidiques de 1 Samuel 8 à 1 Rois 2*, Leuven etc. 2000; J.A. Wagenaar, *Judgement and Salvation: The Composition and Redaction of Micah 2–5*, Leiden etc. 2001; A. Groenewald, *Psalm 69: Its Structure, Redaction and Composition*, Münster 2003.

As distinct from the orientation on the historical production, synchronic instruments developed through literary critical research—semiotics (post-) structuralism, narratology, intertextuality, reader response criticism, etc.—are text-oriented; one tries to explore the text, not as the result of a historical process, but as the point of departure for a reading process. Synchronic methods are devised to reconstruct the *present* text and its reception. Although rather new, literary criticism has already yielded some classical studies.[7]

Are the diachronic and synchronic approaches compatible? Scholars argue about the primacy of the different methods. Some say that "the experience of reading the text," the synchronic approach, is "more important than understanding the process of its composition," the diachronic approach.[8] Others say "every study [of a biblical text] ... must contribute something to the realisation of the book" and its *Sitz im Leben*.[9]

Scholars who reflect on the question of compatibility orientate mostly on the results of different methods and not on the methods themselves. Thus, their view that they are compatible relies on the mutual application; it is the answer to another question. To give an example, this answer is comparable to the application of insights from psychology to space technology. Taking in account certain theories of behaviorism, longer space travels can be made more successful, but this does not turn psychology and physics into compatible methods. Like the common intention to make a car drive better does not make the instruments to replace a tire interchangeable with the instruments to repair cylinders, so the fact that one aims at the same target (the explanation of biblical texts), does not turn diachronic and synchronic exegesis as compatible methods.

The real question of compatibility concerns the methods of research, not their results. Even if the results are compatible or interchangeable, this says nothing about the methods and approaches. In his introductory

---

[7] See R.A. Culpepper, *Anatomy of the Fourth Gospel. A Study in Literary Design*, Philadelphia 1983; R.M. Fowler, *Let the Reader Understand. Reader-Response Criticism and the Gospel of Mark*, Minneapolis 1991; E. Conrad, *Reading Isaiah*, Minneapolis 1991; G. Aichele (et al.); E.A. Castelli (ed.), *The Postmodern Bible: The Bible and Culture Collective*, New Haven etc. 1995 (seven "postmodern" areas of engagement are organized here: reader-response, structuralism and narratology, poststructuralism, feminism, and rhetorical, psychoanalytic, and ideological criticism; the book is presented as if there is no "author" but only a collective).
[8] Culpepper, *Anatomy of the Fourth Gospel*, p. 5.
[9] Ashton, *Understanding the Fourth Gospel*, p. 476.

article on the volume *Synchronic or Diachronic?*,[10] J. Barr makes the interesting remark that synchronic studies are not anti-history and can not be anti-history because "historically [a biblical text] meant what it meant synchronically in the relevant biblical time."[11] But if synchronic studies are not anti-history how then does the synchronic differ from the diachronic? Barr states that the term "synchronic" is used more as a sort of metaphor than as an exact account of the proposed shift from a "historical" paradigm to a "literary" one;[12] in this he is not entirely correct. Indeed, the term "synchronic" describes orientation on literary approaches, but it points also to an important new objective that is not anti-historical but rather a-historical. Barr correctly refers to F. de Saussure for whom the difference was not between non-historical and historical, but between system and element.[13] This observation has far-reaching consequences for the distinction between the methods—maybe farther than Barr would like; it shows the incompatibility of the synchronic and the diachronic. Synchronic research focuses on systems, *the paradigmatic*, as de Saussure says, while diachronic research focuses on elements within those systems, *the syntagmatic*. Diachronic methods are oriented towards historic and verifiable elements *in praesentia*; synchronic methods are orientated towards ideas *in absentia*.[14] The red pottage of Jacob offered to Esau, the siege of Jerusalem in 701 B.C.E., and the Babylonian Captivity are diachronic in the sense of syntagmatic elements that can be presented as objects in time and space. Against this, the idea of desiring an object—pottage or birthright, the capture of a city, or the return from captivity—belongs to the synchronic in the sense of a paradigmatic system beyond time and place.[15] De Saussure offers the example of a column in a temple. It is connected to the architrave,

---

[10] J.C. de Moor (ed.), *Synchronic or Diachronic? A Debate on Method in Old Testament Exegesis* (papers read at the ninth joint meeting of "Het Oudtestamentisch Werkgezelschap in Nederland en België" and "The Society for Old Testament Study" held at Kampen, 1994), Brill-Leiden etc. 1995.

[11] J. Barr, "The Synchronic, the Diachronic," p. 2 (in: *Synchronic or Diachronic?*, see note 10).

[12] Barr, "The Synchronic, the Diachronic," p. 9.

[13] Barr quotes the English translation of *Course de linguistique générale*, "The Synchronic, the Diachronic," p. 6.

[14] F. de Saussure, *Cours de linguistique générale* (Édition critique préparée par Tullio de Mauro), Paris 1990; pp. 170–75.

[15] Cf. A. Greimas, *Du sens. Essais sémiotiques*, Paris 1970; in his scheme of "actants," Greimas places the striving for an object on the axis of desire (p. 249ff.).

which it supports; this is a syntagmatic relation that has its specific importance in time and place—removing the column could have disastrous consequences for the temple. But if one notes that this column is a Doric column, then it evokes a mental comparison with other orders (Ionic, Corinthian, etc.), thus with elements that are not presented in space; this relation is associative or paradigmatic—changing your opinion about the artificial design is perhaps disastrous for your achieved ability in the field of classical architecture but not for the edifice as such.[16] To explore syntagmatic or paradigmatic relations, one needs completely different instruments.

If researchers of the diachronic and the synchronic point to compatibility, they mostly refer to the harmonization of results, not of methods. To give a few examples from again the volume *Synchronic or Diachronic?*, E. Talstra, who defends "and" instead of "or" between the synchronic and the diachronic, asks nevertheless in which order one would have to apply them; he thinks that synchronic analysis has procedural priority over diachronic analysis.[17] In the same volume, R. Carroll chooses the diachronic reading as the preferred reading because only a diachronic approach can explain the contradictions and discrepancies in a text (here Jeremiah); synchrony is "a holistic reading" and hence renders the contradictions and discrepancies "unresolvable."[18] These are two opposed understandings of the relation between synchronic and diachronic methods that show two things: the diachronic and the synchronic are separated in respect to: (1) the instrumental reach (procedural priority) and (2) the field of research (they handle different problems). To keep to the point of contradictions: a diachronic approach considers a contradiction as an indication of redaction and looks for further elements to prove this idea; these elements are of a *syntagmatic* nature in the sense that they constitute the materials of a historical reconstruction. A synchronic approach considers the contradiction as an expression of a systematic structure and looks for further ideas to underpin this structure; these ideas are of a *paradigmatic* nature in the sense that they constitute the construction in which the contradiction appears as a manifestation.

---

[16] De Saussure, *Cours*, p. 171; for paradigmatic (which will be an important term in later structuralism) de Saussure uses the term "the associative."
[17] E. Talstra, "Deuteronomy 9 and 10; Synchronic and Diachronic Observations," pp. 188 and 207 (in: *Synchronic or Diachronic?*, see note 10).
[18] R.P. Carroll, "Synchronic Deconstructions of Jeremaiah; Diachrony to the Rescue," p. 50 (in: *Synchronic or Diachronic?*, see note 10).

Like D. Clines we would like to deconstruct the categories "diachronic" and "synchronic" as a false "binary opposition."[19] However, after two hundred years of an unchallenged procedural priority of historical critical methods, the appearance of a new criticism works as deconstruction in itself. Since the nineteen-seventies, the hegemony of the one over the other has come to an end and it is no longer evident which is the privileged term in the dominant culture; this is deconstructive enough. A further deconstruction, holding the idea that the diachronic is essentially synchronic and vice versa, cannot be made; at least not on the methodological part of the difference (later on, we will amplify on the details of Derrida's deconstruction of the epistemic difference). Even Clines is far from denying the methodological distinction or even arguing that it is a bad one. We endorse his viewpoint that the categories of "synchronic" and "diachronic" are names for segments of a spectrum rather than the labels on the only two pigeonholes for all that goes in the name of biblical scholarship.[20]

The broadest term to collect the different methods is hermeneutics. A first dichotomy can be made by discerning between a hermeneutics of production (the diachronic search for syntagmatic elements) and a hermeneutics of reception (the synchronic search for paradigmatic elements). In their "diagram of biblical interpretation," Soulen and Soulen take the well-known distinction between the world behind the text ("whence"), the world of the text ("what/what about"), and the world in front of the text ("whither"), to spread the different methods over three partly overlapping columns.[21] Diachronic studies reach from the "whence" to the "what," synchronic studies from the "what" to the "whither". Both sorts of methods can take in account their mutual *results* so that, dependent of the status quaestionis, one can speak either of synchronic oriented diachronics (question: how came the final text to its present form), or diachronic oriented synchronics (question: what is the meaning and function of the final text).[22] Creative crossings, in the sense that the borders of the *methods* are

---

[19] D.J.A. Clines, "Beyond Synchronic/Diachronic," p. 67 (in: *Synchronic or Diachronic?*, see note 10).

[20] Clines, "Beyond Synchronic/Diachronic," p. 52.

[21] R.N. Soulen & R.K. Soulen, *Handbook of Biblical Criticism*, Louisville etc. 2001³; p. 235.

[22] Cf. U. Berges, "Sion als thema in het boek Jesaja: Nieuwe exegetische benadering en theologische gevolgen," in: *Tijdschrift voor Theologie*, 39 (1999) 118–38; esp. 119–20.

crossed in an eclectic and anarchistic way, are a postmodern endeavour that until now seldom has been undertaken.[23]

2. *The Epistemic Shift: One Text?*

The "all sail, no anchor" character of today's methodology in exegesis is said to be counterbalanced through the orientation on the one biblical text as the safe haven of all analyses. But since the early nineteen-seventies this is exactly the question: can or may we speak of "one text" in a non-problematical way? There are two reasons to deny the fact that the bible is "one text." The first one has to do with the text as a stable signifier, the second one with the text as an incomplete sign.

The bible doesn't exist as a signifier. Editions like the *Biblia Hebraica Stuttgartensia* or the *Novum Testamentum Graece* are necessary constructs because of the absence of autographs. The necessity of these editions shows that the idea—that the biblical text is "one"—is not a fact but a decision. In addition, the different canons of the bible in Jewish, Roman-Catholic, Reformatory, and Orthodox traditions make even more clear that the idea of "one text" is based on decisions. This means that the object of exegesis, with every new edition of Nestle-Aland or Kittel, is in a state of flux. It makes the Saussurian dream of a stable object, as the base for a linguistic science, groundless.

The absence of a stable signifier opens an epistemological abyss[24] that is deepened by the notion that texts are incomplete signs. M.-A. Tolbert tries to explain the phenomenon that parables, even if investigated

---

[23] Attempts to realize such crossings are described by D. Carr as a "pivotal role" between synchronic and diachronic methods, D. Carr, "Reading Isaiah from Beginning (Isaiah 1) to End (Isaiah 65–66): Multiple Modern Possibilities," in R.F. Melugin and M.A. Sweeney (ed.): *New Visions of Isaiah* (188–218), Sheffield 1996; here p. 217. Against the combination of synchronic and diachronic readings is E.W. Conrad who takes over the idea of J. Noble that diachronic readings are based on a "Quotation-Theory" (the text is formed through the verbatim incorporation of original documents) while synchronic readings are based on "Resource-Theory" (the author used his sources as a resource to draw freely ideas, characters, themes, etc. without being tied); E.W. Conrad, "Prophet, Redactor and Audience: Reforming the Notion of Isaiah's Formation," in R.F. Melugin and M.A. Sweeney et al. (306–26); here pp. 309–10.

[24] Moore, *Literary Criticism*, p. 128.

by the same method, are interpreted so divergently.²⁵ She looks for an explanation not in the methods—because identical methods can lead to different interpretations—but in the form of the parable itself. Her ideas can be transferred to texts in general. Tolbert points to the *open* character of parables and explains this from a rhetorical model that considers the parable a (persuasive) metaphor. She states that the parable is an *incomplete* metaphor. The entire parable serves as the vehicle (or comparatum), but the tenor (the comparandum) is absent: "The need to complete the [metaphorical] movement in the parable by supplying a tenor is the impulse behind parable interpretation."²⁶ The open character of parables necessitates interpretation: "The meaning of the parable (...) lies partially outside the story itself in the interaction of text and context, whatever that context may be."²⁷

This vision on parables as incomplete metaphors is a useful concretization of Derrida's concept of *écriture* as an open text. Our suggestion is to understand "text" according to Tolbert's ideas as absolutely "open." Texts must be seen, not as incomplete metaphors, but as incomplete signs.²⁸ (1) Just as a parable is a vehicle without tenor, so the biblical text is a signifier without signified. The biblical text is an *incomplete* sign because of the absence of signifieds. (2) Texts are linked intertextually with other texts. (3) Texts are connected to various associations of the interpreter. The (contextual) movement always brings the text to new situations and ever-changing new contexts. Derrida calls this process re-contextualization; the refolding to one's own situation is the way in which the interpreter becomes the implied reader of the text. However, also the context of the interpreter is in constant evolution.

The epistemic shift that evolves from these considerations about texts as incomplete signs is twofold. (a) The idea of meaning becomes problematical. And (b) the difference between diachrony and synchrony comes into question.

---

²⁵ M.-A. Tolbert, *Perspectives on the Parables. An Approach to Multiple Interpretations*, Philadelphia 1979; pp. 45–49.
²⁶ Tolbert, *Perspectives on the Parables*, p. 45.
²⁷ Tolbert, *Perspectives on the Parables*, p. 49.
²⁸ De Saussure defines "sign" as the connection between a "concept" (signified) and an "acoustic image" (signifier): "Nous proposer de conserver le mot *signe* pour designer le total, et de remplacer *concept* et *image acoustique* respectivement par *signifié* et *signifiant*" (*Cours*, p. 9).

2.1. *The Absence of the Signified (Meaning)*

If texts are incomplete signs—Derrida gave his famous adage "Il n'y a pas de hors-texte"[29] to this insight—meaning becomes insecure. De Saussure struggled with the idea of negative differentiation: the dependence of signified and signifier. In speech or "discourse" (*parole*), the sign is negatively determined: it receives meaning from what it is not (from other signs). In the system of language (*langue*) the sign is positively determined: it is itself (not influenced by users or semantic differences). De Saussure did not prove this; it was a postulation.[30] In his concept of sign the referent (or object) disappears (figure 1). From the sign-triangle of the Stoa (the connection between 1. a real thing with 2. its sound or signifier and 3. its intelligible thing or signified), he cuts away the corner with the "external real thing" (τὸ ἐκτος ὑποκειμενον).[31]

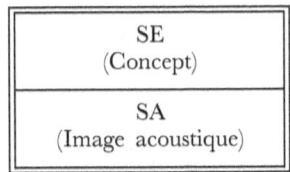

Figure 1. *De Saussure's (two-dimensional) concept of sign*

What remains is the relation between the signifier and the signified; these belong together like the two sides of a sheet of paper.[32]

Derrida denies that we ever possess a signified which is not simultaneously also a signifier. The sheet of paper on de Saussure's table gives the impression of a meaningful underside but when we turn the page over, we are again confronted by a signifier (see figure 2).

---

[29] J. Derrida, *De la Grammatologie*, Paris 1967; p. 227.
[30] De Saussure, *Cours*, pp. 45 and 166. The explanation why de Saussure did not want his pupils to publish his lectures, has to be sought in his disappointment in failing to find a stable structure for linguistics.
[31] I.e. the *object* (τυγχάνον) or "real" thing; cf. Sextus Empiricus, *Against the Logicians* (Loeb Classics) London etc. 1967 (II. 1,11–12). The concept of the Stoa is used by many modern authors as the basis for their concept of sign; cf. C.K. Ogden and I.A. Richards, *The Meaning of Meaning*, London (1923) 1966 (p. 11); E. Fischer-Lichte, *Bedeutung: Probleme einer semiotischen Hermeneutik und Aesthetik*, München 1979 (pp. 40–44).
[32] De Saussure, *Cours*, pp. 89, 144, and 166.

Post-structuralism, as Robert Young says, "involves a shift from the signified to the signifier; it fractures the serene unity of the stable sign."[33]

Figure 2. *Derrida's (one-dimensional) concept of sign*

To give an example, the signifieds of the signifier "Messiah"—let's say that possible signifieds of Messiah are "redeemer," "Son of Man," "liberator," "eschatological Prophet," "Christ," or simply "Jesus"— turn out to be themselves signifiers: "redeemer means . . .," "Son of Man means . . .", etc. In theology, as has been sufficiently proven by all the Quests in the historical-Jesus research, even "Jesus" is a mere signifier.[34]

2.2. *Deconstruction of Diachrony and Synchrony*

Derrida presents a criticism of the distinction between diachrony and synchrony in various places in his writings, namely, as of a more encompassing criticism of De Saussure's ideas on *langue*, and *parole*. Structuralism presupposes that language as a system (*langue*) contains all the structures used by a particular expression of language (*parole*).[35] The syntactic, semantic, and pragmatic structures of the language system are recognizable in every expression of language.[36]

For *post*structuralist critics, these structures are constructs and the idea of a *langue* that contains all these structures is an *idée-fixe*. The *langue* is not a transcendental reality, something that enables the use of language; the reverse applies. Stating that a *langue* exists independent of the *parole* and even as its prerequisite *is* using language. This in itself simple conclusion has a deconstructive effect. It makes the distinction between language *system* and language *use* ineffective and *indécidable*: the language system can only manifest itself in the written or spoken word (Derrida's *écriture*); presentation of a *langue* can only

---

[33] R. Young (ed.): *Untying the Text. A Post-Structuralist Reader*, Boston etc. 1981; p. 8.

[34] "Que le signifié soit originairement et essentiellement (. . .) trace, qu'il soit *toujours déjà en position de signifiant*, telle est la proposition en apparence innocente où la métaphysique du logos, de la présence et de la conscience, doit réfléchir l'écriture comme sa mort et sa resource"; Derrida, *De la grammatologie*, p. 108.

[35] De Saussure, *Cours*, pp. 36–39, 141–43, and 193–97.

[36] For a classification of semiotics in syntaxis, semantics, and pragmatics, see Ch. Morris, *Foundations of the Theory of Signs*, Chicago 1938.

happen via the *parole*. This thought is found in Derrida's idea that nothing precedes the *écriture*,[37] as well as in Wittgenstein's idea that meanings do not exist in a preconstrued system, but that they develop in and through the use of language.

With that, the distinction between diachronic and synchronic approaches to the text also comes into question. Derrida's ideas about iterability and recontextualization[38] make it clear that texts are layered and fragmented in their synchronic appearance too. He shows that a text that is supposed to form a synchronic unity (supposed, because its components possess thematic, linguistic, and semantic similarities) ultimately consists of layered and fragmented meanings. This is the case, not because of a diachronic breaking up of the text in documents, pretexts, and fragments which are written in different times or come from different traditions, but because of layers which are present in the components themselves.[39] The hypothesis of diachronic fragmentation reinforces the observed synchronic fragmentation. Conversely, however, it remains the question whether the observed synchronic fragmentation can be a confirmation of the lack of diachronic unity. Synchronic fragmentation (dissemination) is always present. The argument that a text must be diachronically layered because of its lack of unity fails because of this essential synchronic dissemination, which in itself carries the diachrony (in the sense of being layered) of language as such. This means that, in the end, there is no clear cut between diachronic and synchronic stratifications.

3. *A Threefold Epistemic Shift*

Derrida's deconstruction of diachronic and synchronic stratifications does not affect the pluralism of methods, it affects the way of thinking, and brings about not a methodological but an epistemic revolution.

---

[37] Derrida rejects the possibility of reducing signifiers to a metaphysical presence (the Logos): "L'extériorité du signifiant est l'extériorité de l'écriture en général et nous tenterons de montrer... qu'il n'y a pas de signe linguistique avant l'écriture" (*De la Grammatologie*, p. 26).

[38] See J. Derrida, *Marges de la Philosophie*, Paris 1972 (on iterability: p. 375); and J. Derrida, *Limited Inc*. Paris 1990 (on recontextualization: p. 252).

[39] Derrida explains the synchronic stratification through the idea that signifieds always appear in the form of signifiers; the signified is not at rest in a signifier but is always itself a new signifier (*De la Grammatologie*, p. 108).

One of the most far-reaching consequences is the insight that we do not control language—the *écriture* which is a web of written and spoken (and unwritten and unspoken) entity of signs, forever in the making—but that language is in control of us. This insight marks the shift from hermeneutics to posthermeneutics, from structuralism to poststructuralism, and from modernism to postmodernism.

(1) *Pragmatics: from historical hermeneutics to posthermeneutics* Derrida's insights re-instate pragmatics (in the sense of Ch. Morris's relation between signs and users). In historical-critical hermeneutics, as well as in structuralism, the person of the researcher may be of no importance. Since the nineteen-seventies, the subject of understanding regained a new role through reader-response criticism. The posthermeneutical re-instatement, however, does not assign most power to the reader (*intentio lectoris*)[40] but emphasizes the working of play, *différance* and dissemination. Language and texts (the *intentio operis*) have a manipulating and playful influence on their users who fail to master this game. Rather than a flight from history, postmodern (posthermeneutical) exegesis—that takes interest in historical (first) readers—is a reaction to the search for historical pre-texts, and the absence of the subject. But against the traditional hermeneutical view, the power of the understanding subject is overruled by the uncontrollable forces of the *écriture*.

(2) *Referentiality: from structuralism to poststructuralism* Whereas in structuralism the referent disappeared behind the search for systems and structures, *post*structuralism re-instates referentiality. The corner that de Saussure took away from the sign-triangle of the Stoa (the "real thing") returns, but in a special way. Poststructuralist critics affirm that exegesis does not (re)present the referent but, at most, gives witness to it. The referent is not simply the undifferentiated "reality," but is a trace (Derrida) of something figural (Lyotard) that escapes any system of (re)presentation.[41] The figural, "thing *manqué*," is heterogeneous to the "textual"; at the same time it is constitutive for referentiality ("it is about something"). Reference and designation are

---

[40] Cf. U. Eco, *The Limits of Interpretation*, Bloomington and Indianapolis 1990; Eco tries to restrain the role of the reader ("the universe of literary studies has been haunted during the last years by the ghost of the reader," p. 46); the protection against over-interpretations lies in the *intentio operis* (p. 52). According to Derrida, however, the work won't give much protection, because of the *disseminatio operis* (*Marges*, p. 392).

[41] J.-F. Lyotard, *Discours/Figure*, Paris 1971; p. 75.

essential elements of language which, however, cannot be seen as effects of the system or the *langue* because they cannot be expressed as in opposition to this language system. More simply said, "that it is about something" is heterogeneous to "what is said."[42] A consequence for biblical exegesis is that the interpreter has to reflect constantly on the tendency of signifiers to present the unpresentable. This must sound familiar to biblical scholars and interpreters of the Word of God, whose task it is, from the beginnings of exegesis, to give witness of the unpresentable.

(3) *Multi-interpretability (dissemination): from modernism to postmodernism* In modern hermeneutics the aim of understanding is progress. The goal of a "Horizontverschmelzung" is a better understanding ("besser Verstehen").[43] Knowledge is considered as a tool to control our world.[44] Against this "Zielstrebigkeit" of the predominantly German hermeneutics,[45] *post*modernism (predominantly French) holds the idea of uncontrollable perspectives, polysemy, and dissemination. Parting of the idea that exegesis has to reveal a transcendental truth is a consequence for biblical exegesis of this principle of multi-interpretability.

4. Conclusion

All in all, the postmodern epistemic shift is characterized by a radicalization of the "Reflexion auf eigenes Tun." To a certain extent E. McKnight is right in identifying poststructuralism and postmodernism with "reader-oriented exegesis."[46] A complete identification is too restrictive, but in emphasizing pragmatic aspects over syntactic

---

[42] Lyotard, *Discours/Figure* p. 14; see about the "figural," B. Readings, *Introducing Lyotard. Art and Politics*, London 1991; pp. 3–52.

[43] H.-G. Gadamer, *Wahrheit und Methode. Grundzüge einer philosophischen Hermeneutik*, Tübingen 1960; pp. 282 and 289.

[44] Habermas distinguishes between three interests of knowledge (technical, practical, and emancipatory); the technical interest intends to rule instrumentally the "objectivised external world"; J. Habermas: "Erkenntnis und Interesse," in H. Albert and E. Topitsch (eds.): *Werturteilstreit* (334–53), Darmstadt 1971; here pp. 342–43).

[45] About this confrontation between German (Gadamer, Habermas, Frank) and French philosophers (Derrida, Lyotard, Marion), cf. Ph. Forget (Hrsg.), *Text und Interpretation. Deutsch-Französische Debatte mit Beiträgen von J. Derrida, Ph. Forget, M. Frank, H.-G. Gadamer, J. Greisch, und F. Laruelle*. München 1984; see also D. Mitchelfelder and R. Palmer (eds.), *Dialogue and Deconstruction. The Gadamer-Derrida Encounter*, New York 1989.

[46] E. McKnight, *Postmodern Use of the Bible. The Emergence of Reader-Oriented Criticism*, Nashville 1990²; pp. 60–62.

and semantic aspects, it shows that from now on exegesis cannot be practiced without reflection of the exegetical subject on his or her interpretative community (S. Fish), his or her ideological perspectives (Sj. van Tilborg), and his or her epistemic "Vorverständnis" (J. Derrida). It leads to the challenge that biblical scholars have to explain what they seldom explain: what methods they use (and why), what their aim is in analyzing a certain text, what the boundaries are of the possibilities to say plausible things on this particular subject, and what their epistemic point of view is.

"For deconstructionist critics there is no text, only infinitely different interpretations," says Dunn in his review of postmodern exegesis.[47] Again, he is only partly correct. For deconstructionist thinkers there is no outside-text ("pas de hors-texte"), the referent is a problem and the (reading) subject is a problem. And, indeed, an interpretation does not put an end to the understanding of a text. For deconstructionists there is not "one text." Texts—even when read for the first time—carry the understandings, presuppositions, and "Vorverständnisse" (the interpretations) of the reader. To become aware of all these interpretations, data, and impedimenta that one brings into the reading process, belongs to the rather new task that the postmodern epistemic shift demands.

5. *One Text, a Thousand Methods*

This book, dedicated to the memory of Sjef van Tilborg, brings together a variety of methods. These methods are not the subject of theoretical considerations only. The request of the redactors to the contributors of this volume was to concentrate on a (favorite) method, applying it—after a short introduction—to a specific text. The contributions are divided in two sections, Part One on the Old Testament, Part Two on the New Testament—as mentioned above, there is considerable doubt on the existence of "one text."

5.1. *Part One: Old Testament*

In the opening article of the first part, Ulrich Berges takes his point of departure in an *ideological-critical approach* that van Tilborg had once

---

[47] Dunn, *Jesus Remembered*, p. 96 (our emphasis, *red.*).

applied in his monograph on Matthew 5–7.[48] Through an analysis of the theme of violence in the book of Lamentations, Berges criticizes the ideology of a notion of God that is free of any contradiction; he considers the image of a "soft" and always loving God, as part of the human wishful thinking and even idolatry.

Willem Beuken uses a *semantic analysis* to criticize some historical-critical insights, such as the hypothesis that the "Sitz im Leben" of Isaiah 22:1–14 is the festive atmosphere following the relief of Jerusalem in 701 B.C.E. Through strict semantic analysis and "close reading," Beuken shows that Isa 22:1–14 has created his own (hi)story. Several occurrences between the siege of Jerusalem in 701 and the downfall of 586 form the mourning situation in which the readers are transferred.

The instrument of *intertextuality* is used by Erik Eynikel who goes on the search for narrative time and symbolism in the book of Jonah. The indications of time in Jonah possess a symbolic value, as has been reported in previous literature; the question here is how to apply them to the context of Jonah. This intertextual quest takes the reader to various kinds of contemporary literature.

Composition-criticism is the method used by Alphonso Groenewald to describe the redaction-critical development of Psalm 69. Through this method, we concentrate on the positioning of a certain text in a cluster of texts (Psalm 69 in the Psalter). Composition criticism goes beyond the boundaries of redaction criticism that focuses mainly on specific redactional elements within a text. Groenewald, however, explains the "aktualisierende Einschreibungen" (the hand of redactors within Psalm 69) against the theology of the redactors ("the theology of the poor") who tried to make Psalm 69 suitable for a cluster of Psalms. The composition of the Psalter causes the redactional "Fortschreibung" of existing texts.

Poetical analysis is the focus of Matthijs Kronemeijer's article on the prosodic arrangement of Psalm 35. The approach is purely synchronic and takes its point of departure in the idea that the Psalm is a prayer. Close to the ideas of J. Fokkelman, Kronemeijer divides the Psalm in 74 verses of which 10 are tricola, and of which the 15 strophes are coupled to form stanzas. In composing the psalm, the poet used this structure to create a palindrome.

---

[48] Sj. van Tilborg, *The Sermon on the Mount as an Ideological Intervention*, Assen etc. 1986.

Archibald van Wieringen takes up *reader-oriented exegesis* and he applies it in a rather original way. For his analysis of the "chain of calls" in Isaiah 40:1-11, van Wieringen concentrates not on the receiver's pole but on the sender's pole. From the several headings in the book of Isaiah, he concludes that one has to distinguish between an (unnamed) implied author, the discursor/narrator Isaiah, and the character "Isaiah." These different roles of Isaiah have their influence on the communication with the implied reader(s). In his conclusions, van Wieringen compares these communication functions with those in Luke's Acts of the Apostles.

In her article on *cognitive linguistics*, Ellen van Wolde shows how the theory and method of cognitive linguistics explicitly deal with the development of a mental picture in the text. Van Wolde applies the method to Genesis 28:10-22, by reconstructing the existence of two mental images in this text. These images reveal two conflicting concepts of God. The reconstruction enables the reader to construe a mental representation of Genesis 28 in which the conflict gets a function.

The question that concerns Annemarieke van der Woude is whether Isaiah 40-55 can be called a drama. In Isaiah research, she distinguishes four drama approaches: a liturgical, a theological, a theatrical, and a literary one. Van der Woude uses the concepts of "drama" and "dramatic text" as they are formulated within *drama criticism*, to answer this question. She argues that Isa 40-55 is not a drama to be performed, but a drama to be read. Several examples taken from Isa 40-55 illustrate her point.

5.2. *Part Two: New Testament*

In the opening article of the second part, Andries van Aarde applies *narratology* to Luke 12:35-48. His introduction in the method of narrative exegesis concentrates on the narrator's choice to describe the character internally or externally. By analyzing the temporal aspects in his passage, van Aarde makes clear that the narrator in the double narrative of Luke-Acts uses one ideological point of view. It concerns the knowledge of the "mystery" which demands responsibility from the part of the insiders. Through Peter and Paul, the narratees of the communication, and through "pauses" in the narrative, the implied reader is "informed" how to resolve the disturbances that cause these pauses. In line with the notions of van Tilborg, van

Aarde shows that narrative exegesis needs not disregard the historical situation within which a particular text communicates.

Deconstruction and *narratology* are the methods applied by Patrick Chatelion Counet to John 8, and especially to the interpretations of this passage as anti-Judaism. He analyzes the communication of "Jesus and the Jews" on the story level, "John and the Jews" on the narrative level, and "the readers and the Jews" on the level of enunciation. This analysis involves a threefold deconstruction (story, narration, and context) of two objects. On the one hand, a deconstruction of the Christian anti-Judaic interpretations of John 8, on the other hand, a deconstruction of the text itself—the presumed opposition between Jesus' (John's) theology and that of the Jews is reduced to oppositions in Jewish theology itself.

Through *historical-anthropology* Pieter Craffert tries to answer the question from what material a "resurrected body" is made. Focusing on Jesus' resurrected body, Craffert commentates on several interpretations that try to close the gap between ancient and today's perspectives by ethnocentric and anachronistic strategies. Introducing the social-scientific interpretation of anthropology, he undertakes a threefold analysis: of the subject's cultural system (i.e., ancient texts), of the interpreter's cultural system (i.e., modern-day perspectives), and cross-cultural comparisons. In his conclusion he recognizes the "cycle of meaning" of ancient people that can open our modern eyes for their living reality of souls, immortals, and resurrected bodies.

Detlev Dormeyer uses *narrative and pragmatic linguistics* for an interpretation of Acts 8:26–40. He differentiates three text elements, the external text-form, the content, and the pragmatic intention. These levels return in his interpretation of the nine narrative sequences of the large biographical apophthegm of Philip in Acts. Dormeyer makes several analogies for the meeting of Philip and the eunuch: with the Greek-Roman novel of love, with other meeting-stories, and with the idea of mental imaginations. This brings him close to van Tilborg's interest in Philostratus' *Imagines*, and in his conclusions he paints a "picture" of the missionary of Philip between the skylines of Jerusalem and Gaza.

As the title of his article already announces ("Is there another way?"), François Tolmie does not present a "classical" *rhetorical analysis* of Paul's Letter to the Galatians. With R. Anderson and P. Kern, he refutes the hypothesis that Galatians is either a sample of classical rhetoric or that it could be interpreted in the light of ancient rhetorical textbooks. Instead of applying an ancient rhetorical model to Galatians, Tolmie attempts to reconstruct Paul's rhetorical strategy from the text itself. He concentrates on two sections of Galatians (1:1–5 and 1:6–10) in order to identify the dominant rhetorical strategy. Of course, this is a first step in a proceeding project.

In his article on *intertextuality* and mysticism, Huub Welzen describes one of the methods used in the Christian tradition for spiritual readings of biblical texts, the *lectio divina* as developed by Guigo II in the 12th century. Welzen connects this *lectio divina* to intertextuality as a linguistic re-creation of archetexts through the mystic's own experience. Examples to show the effects of these intertextual and mystic transformations are taken from Gregory of Nazianzus, John of the Cross, and Hildegard of Bingen, especially the prologue to her "Liber Scivias." The biblical echoes in their works show that the struggle of these mystics, with the ineffability of their experience, is shaped by biblical tradition.

PART 1

OLD TESTAMENT

CHAPTER ONE

THE VIOLENCE OF GOD IN THE BOOK OF LAMENTATIONS

Ulrich Berges
University of Nijmegen, the Netherlands

One of the main theological thoughts in the life and work of Sjef van Tilborg is that of divine חסד "chesed," which can be translated with a variety of terms such as loyalty, faithfulness, kindness, love, or mercy.[1] The term occurs frequently in the Hebrew Bible (245 times) and is especially prominent in the Book of Psalms (127 times). It is not found in the priestly stratum of the Pentateuch and in Ezekiel; it also occurs less frequently, but nonetheless, in texts which are full of theological significance in the other prophetic books. In spite of the exilic disaster, the divine faithfulness is emphatically stressed, as in the case of Joel 2:13: "Return to Jhwh, your God, for he is gracious and merciful, slow to anger, and abounding in steadfast love, and relents from punishing."[2] This definition of the inner qualities of the God of Israel[3] has its literary origin in the self-proclamation of Jhwh to Moses in Ex 34:6–7: "Jhwh (is) Jhwh, a God merciful and gracious, slow to anger, and abounding in steadfast love and faithfulness, keeping steadfast love for the thousandth generation, forgiving iniquity and transgression and sin, yet by no means clearing the guilty, but visiting the iniquity of the parents upon the children and the children's children, to the third and the fourth generation." Without analyzing the so-called "Gnadenformel" in detail, it can be no doubt that God's love and kindness are accompanied with his anger and his readiness to punish the guilty.[4] This *coincidentia oppositorum* is strengthened by the fact that in texts referring to the

---

[1] D.J.A. Clines (ed.), *Dictionary* Vol. III (1996) 277–81; see G.R. Clark (1993).
[2] See Is 54:8.10; 55:3; 63:7; Jer 9:23; 16:5; 31:3; 32:18; 33:11; Os 2:21; 6:6; Jon 4:2; Mic 6:8; 7:18.20.
[3] See the Jewish tradition of the 13 middot, the 13 "measures"/"qualities" of God (cf. in the NT: Lk 6:36; Jn 1:4–16; Jam 5:11).
[4] See esp. H. Spiekermann, *Steadfast Love* (2000) and R. Scoralick, *Güte* (2002).

"Gnadenformel," the elements "slow to anger" (ארך אפים) and "abounding in steadfast love (רב־חסד) [and faithfulness] (ואמת)" are always used side by side (Jona 2:13; 4:2; Ps 86:15; 103:8; 145:8; Neh 9:17).

Taking into account the importance of divine chesed in the Hebrew Bible, it is not by chance that in the third chapter of the Book of Lamentations, just in the middle part of that central chapter, God's "steadfast love" (חסד) occupies a prominent position, once again in opposition with or in addition to his capacity to cause enormous grief: "The steadfast love of Jhwh never ceases, his mercies (רחמיו) never come to an end" (3:22). "Although he causes grief, he will have compassion (רחם) according to the abundance of his steadfast love" (3:32).[5] This sapiential instruction is placed not in the mouth of somebody whose life is secure and protected, but is pronounced by *the* protagonist (הגבר) who experienced cruel affliction under the rod of God's wrath. God himself has driven him into darkness without light, has turned his hand against him, has broken his bones, has shut out his prayers, ambushed him like a beast of prey, set him as a mark for his arrows, filled him with bitterness, and sated him with wormwood (Lam 3:1–21). The change of attitude within the protagonist in Lam 3:22–39 is not caused by the fact that Jhwh *has* changed his destiny but by the fact that the afflicted person keeps hoping that God *will* show his compassion again. This act of hope is not followed by a "happy end" but by a further description of hardship and tribulation (Lam 4 and 5) leading to the final petition that God (!) should change his attitude of fierce anger: "Restore us to yourself, Jhwh, that we may be restored; renew our days as of old—unless you have utterly rejected us, and are angry with us beyond measure" (5:21–22). The hope in God's chesed is not the last word in the Book of Lamentation, as though it were the final solution in a life full of grief (cf. Jam 5:11), but it is presented as a crucial attitude enabling the believers to endure divine negativity.

The following presentation of God's violence in the Book of Lamentations is designed to criticize the often too one-sided view of divine love.[6] This does not mean that God's love and wrath are placed in one and the same order, as if he would act in a totally arbitrary

---

[5] Detailed analysis in U. Berges, *Klagelieder* (2002) 198–208.
[6] See H. Spiekermann, *Gottes Liebe* (2001) for stimulating articles on divine wrath and love.

manner, and would not be attentive to human petitions.[7] But it is a reminder that God's behavior is bound neither to human expectations nor to ethical standards of modern western societies. Thus, this contribution in memoriam of Sjef van Tilborg is to be seen as an ideology-critical approach that he himself had once applied in a monograph on the Sermon on the Mount. The critical voice is now directed, not against the ruling class, as it was in the case of the study of Sjef, but against those in church and theology who want to defend a notion of God that is free of any contradiction.[8] The image of a "soft" and always loving God is part of the human wishful thinking and has to be qualified as idolatry.[9] The prohibition of material representations of Jhwh in the Hebrew Bible[10] does, in this sense, also extend to mental representations. The Torah does present Jhwh in quite a number of different ways, a fact that should not be underestimated.[11] The complexity of God's love and wrath results not the least from the biblical dynamic to promulgate Jhwh as the only true God, thus absorbing the main characteristics of the Gods in the various surrounding panthea. It is just in the aftermath of the exilic disaster that the theological reflection about the belief in Jhwh reaches one of its peaks in the formulation of Is 45:6b–7: "I am Jhwh, and there is no other. I form light and create darkness, I make weal (שלום) and create woe (רע); I Jhwh do all these things."[12]

At this point, one can appreciate the enormous influence of the exile with all its negativity on the perception and notion of Jhwh. What happened to Israel and Jerusalem/Zion with the temple was

---

[7] R. Scoralick, *Güte* (2002) 129: "Die Gottesprädikationen versuchen einen Mittelweg zwischen den Extrempositionen zu steuern. Jhwh ist in seinem Verhalten nicht berechenbar, aber er ist verläßlich treu auch über Brüche hinweg. Der Kontext verdeutlicht die fundamentale Zugewandtheit als Ansprechbarkeit und Anrufbarkeit JHWHs für Israel und wird damit zum Handlungsmodell in zukünftigen Krisen."

[8] What he stated in regard to his own study also applies, *mutatis mutandis*, to this contribution: "The intention is not to replace as much as to question certain topics. A different perspective can bring to light shades of meaning in an identical text which till now have not been given enough attention"; Sj. van Tilborg, *Sermon* (1986) 1.

[9] M. Görg, *Der "schlagende" Gott* (1996) 100: "Der schlechthin gefällige Gott ist der Bibel fremd."; idem, Der un-heile Gott (1995); S. Krahe, *Ermordete Kinder* (1999).

[10] C. Dohmen, *Bilderverbot* (1987); cf. Ex 20:4.23; 34:17; Lev 19:4; 26:1; Dtn 4:16–18.23.25; 5:8; 27:15.

[11] In this context, the hypothesis of K. van der Toorn, *Iconic Book* (1997) 229–48 does play a role: he states that the veneration of divine images in the ANE-context is replaced in Israel by the veneration of the Torah.

[12] W. Groß, *Das Negative* (1992) 34–46.

not outside God's reach, but had to do with his all embracing competence to do good *and* evil! This conclusion also brings forth a positive aspect: because Jhwh is the cause of everything, he too has the power to change the situation of exile and destruction. Because he can destroy he is also able to heal! But to hold Jhwh responsible for good *and* evil creates a new severe problem: what is the inner relation/the intrinsic connection of good and evil in Jhwh?[13] Many questions remain: Is it enough to affirm that God's love is simply much stronger than his anger?[14] Is God's wrath nothing more than a single drop in the ocean of this steadfast love? What is there to say about God's love if somebody experiences nothing else than this single drop (of his wrath) like the sufferer in Ps 88? Even if the sufferer in Lam 3 is right to affirm that Jhwh does not afflict "from his heart" (Lam 3:33), he acknowledges that God afflicts innocent persons like him.[15]

1. *Jhwh's Wrath and Violence in the Hebrew Bible*

According to R. Schwager who made known the theory of René Girard[16] to a broader public of exegetes and theologians, there are more than six hundred places in the OT where nations, kings, or individuals are depicted to act violently against each other.[17] Nearly one thousand times, it is affirmed that Jhwh smashes, destroys, and kills peoples, nations, or individuals.[18] Approximately one hundred times, it is stated that the God of Israel ordered the death of human persons.[19] Some exegetical publications of the last two decades are discussing the issue of divine violence[20] but surprisingly enough, only

---

[13] According to the priestly tradition (Gen 1,1–2,4a), God created everything good but he did not create everything; the chaotic elements like the chaotic waters (tehom) and darkness were pre-existent to divine creation; see W. Groß, *Das Negative* (1992) 36: "Gott hat zwar alles gut, aber er hat nicht alles erschaffen."

[14] Thus Huub Oosterhuis in an interview in the Dutch journal, *VolZin* from 18.10.2002, 7.

[15] See from a contemporary Jewish perspective N. Gillman, *Sacred Fragments* (1990) 187–213: "Suffering: Why Does God Allow It?"; very stimulating W. Brueggemann, Theology (1997) 359–72 ("Ambiguity and the Character of Yahweh") and 373–99 ("Yahweh and Negativity").

[16] R. Girard, *La violence et le sacré* (1972).

[17] R. Schwager, *Sündenbock* (1986) 58.

[18] R. Schwager, *Sündenbock* (1986) 65.

[19] R. Schwager, *Sündenbock* (1986) 70.

[20] See N. Lohfink, *Gewalt* (1983); Idem, *gewalttätige Gott* (1987); E. Noort, *Geweld* (1985); M. Girard, *Violence* (1987); M. Vervenne, *Satanic Verses?* (1991); Idem, *Violent*

few exegetical monographies are written on that subject.[21] It would be worthwhile to check all the biblical passages and to arrange them according to a sort of typology and to find out about their diachronical relationship. But also without this, it is safe to affirm that Jhwh has a quite impressive record of violence. A passage from Is 63 must suffice to underline this aspect of divine behavior: "I have trodden the wine press alone, and from the peoples no one was with me; I trod them in my anger and trampled them in my wrath; their juice spattered on my garments, and stained all my robes (v. 3). I trampled down peoples in my anger, I crushed them in my wrath, and I poured out their lifeblood on the earth" (v. 6).

Every so often in the Hebrew Bible, the motif of God's violence is linked explicitly to the theme of divine wrath and anger.[22] It is interesting to note that God's wrath is still absent in the book of Genesis; it is not even mentioned in reaction to the sinfulness of mankind (transgression in Eden, Cain, flood, tower of Babel, Sodom and Gomorrah, etc.). In the Hebrew Bible, God's wrath does come in the context of Israel's deliverance from Egyptian oppression (Ex 4:13–14; 15:7) and it is in the aftermath, and as a consequence, of the Sinai covenant that this concept starts to play a decisive role in the history of Jhwh with his people. As kingly ruler who freed his people from the power of Pharaoh, Jhwh punishes severely the trespasses of the covenant obligations (see Ex 22:21–24; Num 25:1–5; Dtn 1:26–36; 11:17; 29:22–28).[23] During the journey through the desert towards the promised land, the divine fits of anger are numerous because of the sinful and stubborn behavior of his people: "And Jhwh's anger was kindled against Israel, and he made them wander in the wilderness for forty years, until all the generation that had done evil in the sight of the Lord had disappeared" (Num 32:13; cf. "golden calf" Ex 32). The Deuteronomistic School evaluated the whole history of Jhwh with Israel in the light of God's legitimate anger (Dtn 31:17.19; 32:16.19.21–22; Jos 7:1.26; 2 Kings 17:11.17–18; 23:26; 24:40).[24] That

---

Imagery (2003); E. Zenger, *Gott der Bibel* (1994); R.N. Whybray, *Immorality* (1996); H. Häring, *Ploegscharen* (1997); K.-S. Krieger, *Gewalt* (2002).

[21] W. Dietrich and C. Link, *Dunklen Seiten Gottes* (2000).

[22] See C. Westermann, *Boten* (1981); G.A. Herion, *Wrath* (1992); W. Gross, *Zorn* (1999); R. Miggelbrink, *Zorn Gottes* (2000); R. Miggelbrink, *Zornige Gott* (2002).

[23] Herion, *Wrath* (1992) 994.

[24] The same is true for extensive parts of the prophetic literature: Jes 5:25; 9:11.16.18.20; 10:4.5.6; 54:9; Jer 4:4.8.26; Ez 7:3.8.12.14; Hos 11:9; Mi 7:9.18; Zef 2:2.3; 3:8; Nah 1:2.

anthropopathic presentation depicts Jhwh more as a God of necessary *pathos* than of emotional or even irrational passion: "it seems not to be an essential attribute or fundamental characteristic of Yahweh's *persona* but an expression of his will; it is a reaction to human history, an attitude called forth by human (mis)conduct."[25] This concurs with the opinion of Lactantius, the Christian philosopher of the early 4th century who states in his famous writing "De ira dei" that God's anger is a necessary part of his *imperium* and *dominium*.[26] Without his fierce anger there wouldn't be any cultic reference ("religio esse non potest ubi metus nullus est," De ira dei 11.15) and God wouldn't be taken seriously because he could not stop the transgressions of the evildoers. God's wrath is seen as a necessary instrument to prevent the earth and her inhabitants from falling into chaos and anarchy. Therefore, the concept of divine wrath in the Hebrew Bible can be judged as a precursor of the legitimate political power (protestas, not violentia).[27] But this solution does not solve all problems because intermingled with his legitimate wrath, one can observe at times a deep emotional frustration on the part of God who sees his love rejected: "How can I give you up, Ephraim? How can I hand you over, O Israel? How can I make you like Admah? How can I treat you like Zeboiim? My heart recoils within me; my compassion grows warm and tender. I will not execute my fierce anger; I will not again destroy Ephraim; for I am God and no mortal, the Holy One in your midst, and I will not come in wrath" (Hos 11:8–9; cf. Gen 8:20–22; Is 54:6–10). God's legitimate pathos to reestablish his dominion over his people and his emotional passion are not always distinguishable in a clear-cut manner. Much of Jhwh's passionate anger grows out of a frustrated relationship which leads on his part to discontent, aggressiveness, and finally to aggression.[28]

In this context, it is interesting to observe that only in *one* of the seven individual laments which speak of God's anger (Ps 6; 27; 30; 38; 77; 88; 102) is the divine passion said to be caused by human

---

[25] Herion, *Wrath* (1992) 991.
[26] De ira dei 23,14: "ubi ergo ira non fuerit, imperium quoque non erit. deus autem habet imperium, ergo et iram, qua constat imperium, habeat necesse est."; see the critical text-edition of Chr. Ingremeau, *Lactance* (1982); furthermore R. van den Broek, *Lactantius* (1993).
[27] J. Assmann, *Herrschaft* (2000) 53–61.
[28] M. Girard, *Violence* (1987) 161–64 who uses the categories of A.J. Greimas, *Colère* (1981/1983).

sinfulness (Ps 38:4–5.19). In all the other cases, the individual stands totally helpless and at a loss about that divine aggression, praying that God might turn away from his wrath (Ps 6:2; 27:9). No reason lies at hand to justify that kind of divine aggression (Ps 77:10–11; 88:7–8.15–19; 102:11). Similarly, in the Book of Lamentation, the wrath of Jhwh is never explicitly linked to human sinfulness (Lam 1:12; 2:1.3.6.21.22; 3:1.43; 4:11; 5:22); nevertheless, the culpability of Israel and the justification of God's punishment are clearly affirmed several times (Lam 1:8.14.18.22; 2:14.17; 3:42; 4:6.13.22; 5:7.16). This does not hold true for Job who suffered under God's wrath (Job 19:11) without having committed anything to deserve such a fate. Neither divine passion, nor pathos, is responsible for Job's fate, but God's bet with Satan (Job 1–2), obscuring the image of Jhwh's ethical credibility.

In not a few passages, the dark sides of the God of Israel are put forward: his fight all night long with Jacob (Gen 32:23–33), his attempt to kill Moses (Ex 4:24), his slaughter of Uzzah whose only fault was to have tried to prevent the ark from falling to the ground (2 Sam 6:6–7), or the massive killing of seventy thousand people because of *one* trespass of David (2 Sam 24:1–16).[29] With all these in mind, it wouldn't be difficult to write a "chronique scandaleuse" of Jhwh in the Hebrew Bible.[30]

2. *Jhwh's Wrath and Violence in the Light of the Ancient Near Eastern Context*

The negative characteristics of Jhwh—as well as the positive ones—have to be seen in the light of the notions of Gods and Goddesses in the Ancient Near East (ANE). In the Myth of Atrahasis, the Storm-god Enlil leads an alliance of divine destruction in the form of a flood against humanity because the Gods were exceedingly disturbed, especially at night, by the noise of the multiplied inhabitants of the earth (ANET 104–106). In the Epic of Gilgamesh, the same Enlil is full of wrath against the hero Utnapishtim because he escaped the mass destruction produced by the flood. When the latter finally offered a sacrifice to the Gods, a gesture which had saved his own

---

[29] 1 Chron 21,1 attributes it to a incitement of Satan against David.
[30] See P. Volz, *Dämonische* (1924); M. Weber, *Aufsätze III* (⁸1988) 137–40.

life, they smelled the sweet savor and crowded like flies about the sacrificer. Then the Goddess Ishtar declared solemnly:

> Ye gods here, as surely as this lapis upon my neck I shall not forget,
> I shall be mindful of these days, forgetting (them) never.
> Let the gods come to the offering;
> (But) let not Enlil come to the offering.
> For he, unreasoning, brought on the deluge
> And my people consigned to destruction. (XI, 160–169; ANET 95)

This line of argumentation is set forth by Ea, the God of wisdom, who reproached Enlil:

> Thou wisest of gods, thou hero,
> How could thou, unreasoning, bring on the deluge?
> On the sinner impose his sin,
> On the transgressor impose his transgression! (XI, 178–181; ANET 95)

The many parallels to the biblical flood story are striking: When Jhwh smelled the pleasing odor of Noah's offering after he had survived the flood, God said in his heart: "I will never again curse the ground because of humankind, for the inclination of the human heart is evil from youth; nor will I ever again destroy every living creature as I have done. As long as the earth endures, seedtime and harvest, cold and heat, summer and winter, day and night, shall not cease" (Gen. 8:21–22). The negative-destructive *and* the positive-motherly characteristics, which in the Gilgamesh Epic are distributed over several Gods, are integrated in the biblical flood story into the one and only Jhwh. This is what makes his personality so complex.[31]

In the Egyptian myth of the destruction of humanity, the elderly Re who detected a rebellion on earth against him and sent his eye, the Goddess Hathor-Sekhmet, to slaughter the rebellious ones. But she is so pleased with her task of destruction that Re has to resort to a ruse to prevent her from killing all humans. He mixed a kind of red stuff into her bier so that it looked like a huge quantity of blood that covered the land she was about to destroy. Hathor-Sakhmet swallowed it and got drunk so that she couldn't complete her work of destruction (ANET 10–11). This myth, which was composed at the end of the Amarna-period, was a reaction of the religious politics of Echnaton

---

[31] See N.C. Baumgart, *Umkehr* (1999); N.C. Baumgart, *Flut* (2003) 30–36.

and his totally positive world-view in which the Sun disc Aton made disappear all chaotic elements. The myth of the destruction by Hathor-Sakhmet re-affirms chaos and negativity and leads to a more differentiated, realistic world-view.[32]

In Canaanite mythology (KTU 1.2 I 30–45), the Storm-god Baal smites the emissaries of Yamm to whom he must submit according to the decision of El, the head of the pantheon. Baal is so enraged that he has to be restrained by Anath/Ashtoreth, the consort of Baal (TUAT III/6, 1122–1124; ANET 130). After his short presentation of these and other ANE deities, G.A. Herion concludes: "In these and other ANE myths, gods and goddesses are anthropomorphized so vividly that it is often possible to describe (even in some psychological detail) their idiosyncracies and personal characteristics. In the mythological texts, their anger often seems a natural extension of their personalities."[33]

This is much less the case with Jhwh, who at times even regrets his anger. The god of Israel has violent characteristics, but these are not determined by his anger (cf. Lam 3:33; Ez 18:23; 33:11; Hos 11:9; 14:5). Contrary to other ANE depictions of divine wrath, the anger of Jhwh is never politically exploited by kings or others in power.[34] It is not the violence of Jhwh in the Bible, as such, which is remarkable, but the fact that he rages so often against his own people:[35] "Therefore thus says Jhwh Zebaot, the God of Israel: I am determined to bring disaster on you, to bring all Judah to an end" (Jer 44:11).

In the prophetic literature, and only there, the characteristic of a violent God finds its expression in the formula "day of Jhwh" (יום יהוה)[36] or "day for Jhwh" (יום ליהוה).[37] In the oldest text of this

---

[32] H. Sternberg-el Hotabi, *Mythos* (1995) 1018–19; A. de Jong, *Re* (1993) 95–105.
[33] G.A. Herion, *Wrath* (1992) 992. He goes on showing that the ANE deities don't act only according to irrational passion but in cases of cultic sacrilege and broken oaths, also according to rational pathos (992–93).
[34] G.A. Herion, *Wrath* (1992) 993: "In other words, in the Bible no political entity ever profits from the wrath of Yahweh."
[35] N. Lohfink, *Unsere neuen Fragen* (1989) 101: "Der grausamste Gott des alten Orients war vielleicht Assur. Aber er wütete gegen andere Völker, nicht gegen sein eigenes Volk. Jhwhs Eifersucht dagegen ging fast bis zum Mord an der Geliebten."
[36] Is 13:6.9; Ezek 13:5; Joel 1:15; 2:1.11; 3:4; 4:14; Amos 5:18bis.20; Obad 15; Zeph 1:7.14bis; Mal 3:23.
[37] Is 2:12; Ezek 30:3; Zech 14:1. See H. Spieckermann, *Dies Irae* (1989) 194–208; B.M. Zapff, *Prophetie* (1995) 66–105 (Lit!).

tradition, the prophet Amos criticizes the idea that the day of Jhwh would be a day of peace and happiness: "Alas for you who desire the day of Jhwh! Why do you want the day of Jhwh? It is darkness, not light; as if someone fled from a lion, and was met by a bear; or went into the house and rested a hand against the wall, and was bitten by a snake. Is not the day of Jhwh darkness, not light, and gloom with no brightness in it?" (Amos 5:18–20). In Zephaniah this "dies irae, dies illa" (cf. Zeph 1:15) is explicitly linked to Jhwh's judgment on his own people, especially against those in Jerusalem who think that God is not actively involved in history: "At that time I will search Jerusalem with lamps, and I will punish the people who rest complacently on their dregs, those who say in their hearts, 'Jhwh will not do good, nor will he do harm'" (Zeph 1:12).

3. *Divine Wrath Against Jhwh's Own People as Medium of Historical Intervention*

That Jhwh's wrath rages against his own people is remarkable but by no means exceptional in the light of ANE-texts. Very close to the biblical concept of Jhwh's wrath against his own people comes the inscription of the so-called Mesha Stone (ANET 320–321). There it is written that the Israelite king Omri could humble Moab for a long period of time because the God of the Moabites, Chemosh, had been angry with his land (כי יאנף כמש בארצה) (cf. 2 Kings 3:4–5). Around 830 B.C.E. Mesha succeeded once again in making Moab independent from Israelite rule and this is declared to have been possible only because Chemosh had changed his negative attitude, comparable to the appeasement of Jhwh's wrath (cf. Judg 2:14; 3:8; 10:7–8; Ps 104:40–42). According to the inscription of Mesha, the king of Moab, the Israelite king had to surrender the town of Jahaz, which he built for himself as military base in the occupied territory because "Chemosh drove him out before me" (וינרשה כמש מפני). The groundbreaking study of the Swedish scholar B. Albrektson made clear that divine influence on historical events was not at all a prerogative of Jhwh but was commonly shared also for other deities in the ANE.[38] Thus, the national catastrophe of Agade is attributed in

---

[38] See B. Albrektson, *History* (1967) 101: "The affinity of the Moabite Stone to

the sumerian text "Curse of Agade" (ca. 2000 B.C.E.) to the wrath of the storm-god Enlil because of the foregoing destruction of his temple by the defiant king Naram-Sin.[39] Enlil's anger led to the occupation of the land by the ruthless Gutians who brought nothing but death and devastation: "The valiant lay on top of the valiant, the blood of the treacherous flowed over the blood of the faithful (line 189–190; ANET 650)." The same is true for the depiction of Enlil in the Sumerian Lamentation over the destruction of Sumer and Ur:

> Enlil, the shepherd of the blackheads, this is what he did—
> Enlil, in order to destroy the righteous houses, to decimate the righteous.
> To set an evil eye on the sons of the righteous, the noble—
> On that day Enlil brought down the Guti from the mountain-land,
> Whose coming is the Flood of Enlil, that no one can withstand.
> (lines 71–75; ANET 613)

The natural phenomena of storm and flood stand for the foreign military forces, which overpowered the Mesopotamian cities[40] at the end of the Ur III period (ca. 2000 B.C.E.): "These historical city laments describe the destruction of particular cities and their important shrines. They attribute the cause of this destruction to the capricious decision of the divine assembly. Once the decision is made, it is irrevocable. After the chief gods and goddesses abandon their cities and shrines, the poems narrate the onslaught of Enlil's storm, a metaphor for the military attack of the enemy. Another typical characteristic of these laments consists of the portrait of the weeping goddess who bewails the destruction of her city."[41]

In the "Plague Prayers of Mursilis" (ANET 394–396) the Hittite king (1339–1306 B.C.E.) tried to get rid of a terrible plague which afflicted his country. The plague was caused by the anger of the Hattian Storm-god over the faults of the king's father: "I know for certain that the offence was not committed in my days, that it was committed in the days of my father. But, since the Hattian Storm-god is angry for that reason and people are dying in the Hatti land, I am (nevertheless) making the offerings to the Hattian Storm-god,

---

Hebrew accounts of Yhwh's dealings with his people in history is thus striking, but nothing unique or exceptional."

[39] See also K. van der Toorn, *Sin* (1985) 56 and the whole of chapter 4: "The Wrath of the Gods. Religious Interpretation of Adversity and Misfortune."

[40] Lament over the destruction of Ur; Lament over the destruction of Sumer and Ur; Nippur-Lament; Eridu-Lament, and Uruk-Lament.

[41] F.W. Dobbs-Allsopp, *Weep* (1993) 13.

my lord, on that account." Very prominent is the element of divine anger in the so-called Mesopotamian city-laments. Only because of the anger of the Gods and their leaving the shrine (cf. Lam 2:7), mythologically speaking, can a city be destroyed: "A defeated people preferred to attribute their loss to the anger and subsequent abandonment of their own gods rather than to the power of the victor's gods."[42] Such is the case in the lamentation over the destruction of Ur (ANET 455–463) where the Goddess Ningal bewailed bitterly the attack of her shrine: "Verily Anu has cursed my city, my city verily has been destroyed; verily Enlil has turned inimical to my house, by the pickaxe verily it has been torn up. Upon him who comes from below verily he hurled fire—alas my city has been destroyed; Enlil upon him who comes from above verily hurled the flame."

In the Book of Lamentations, Jhwh raging (cf. 1:5.12–15.21; 2:1–9.17.21) against his own city and temple is very much depicted in resemblance to the storm-god Enlil, who was responsible for the destruction of the Mesopotamian cities: "In essence, then, Yahweh conceived as the divine warrior who goes into battle on the 'day of his anger' forms a fitting analog to Enlil conceived as the destructive storm who comes 'on that day.'"[43]

In his Babylon-Inscriptions, Esarhaddon (681–669 B.C.E.) motivates the terrible destruction inflicted by his father Sancherib (705–681 B.C.E.) upon the Mesopotamian capital in the year 689 B.C.E. and the deportation of the statue of Marduk to Assur, which incurred the wrath of the chief-god. According to Esarhaddon, who doesn't mention the name of Sancherib, the anger of Marduk was kindled by the social, political, and cultic abuses in Babylon.[44] The concept of divine wrath is clearly used in a political strategy to justify the ruthless destruction of Babylon and its temples by his father Sancherib.[45] Only because Marduk again took compassion over his destructed capital city of Babylon, he himself turned around the signs indicating the length of the disaster (60+10 years), resulting in the much shorter period of 11 years (10+1).[46]

---

[42] F.W. Dobbs-Allsopp, *Weep* (1993) 45–46.
[43] F.W. Dobbs-Allsopp, *Weep* (1993) 65.
[44] R. Borger, *Inschriften* (1956) 13: "Da ergrimmte der Enlil (Herr) der Götter, Marduk; um das Land niederzuwerfen und seine Bewohnerschaft zu verderben, sann er Böses." See also R. Albertz, *Exilszeit* (2001) 48.
[45] W. Mayer, *Zerstörung* (2002) 11–12.
[46] K.R. Veenhof, *Geschichte* (2001) 268; see also the Babel-stela from Nabonidus (555–539 B.C.E.).

The parallel with the destruction of Jerusalem one hundred years later lies at hand: it is by the wrath of Jhwh, because of the sinfulness of his capital city, that he orders a foreign nation to destroy his city and to deport the population for the length of seventy years (Jer 25:12; 29:10). As Marduk designates a foreign king (Esarhaddon) as his *servant* to rebuild Babylon and to restore his cult there, Jhwh orders the Persian king Cyrus to do the same for Jerusalem (Is 41:1–5; 44:28; 45:1).[47]

The counterpart of divine wrath as instrument of historical intervention is divine tenderness. This can be seen in the basalt stela of Nabonidus (ca. 556–539 B.C.E.): "The princely Marduk did not appease his anger, for 21 years he established his seat in Ashur. (But eventually) the time became full, the (predetermined) moment arrived, and the wrath of the king of the gods, the lord of lords calmed down; he remembered (again) Esagila and Babylon, his princely residence."[48]

Such a hopeful turn of the divine decision is also known in the Mesopotamian city laments, which all end in a positive way (especially evident in the Nippur-Lament). The wrath of the Gods is appeased and friendly words are heard again. The broken ramparts, city walls, houses, and temples will be rebuilt; the social order will be reestablished, and the country shall prosper again.[49] Contrastingly, in the Book of Lamentations, such positive notes are completely missing and one must turn to the opening words of Deutero-Isaiah to hear about Jhwh's decision to finish his punitive measures against Juda and Jerusalem: "Comfort, comfort my people, says your God. Speak tenderly to Jerusalem, and cry to her that she has served her term, that her penalty is paid, that she has received from Jhwh's hand double for all her sins" (Is 40:1–2).

---

[47] M. Albani, *Der eine Gott* (2000) 86–87, note 342. See also the prophecy of Marduk (*TUAT* II/1 65–68) from the time of Nebukadnezar I (1124–1103 B.C.E.) in which Marduk decides to go into exile to Elam and to return from there (cf. Is 40:9–11).

[48] *ANET* 309; *TUAT* I/4, 407.

[49] This positive turning point has to do with the "Sitz im Leben" of the city-laments. They were mainly used by the occasion of the rebuilding/restoration of the city—or temple walls.

4. *Wrath and Violence of Jhwh in the Book of Lamentations*

There is no other book in the Hebrew Bible where the wrath and the violence of Jhwh are depicted in such gloomy colors than in the scroll of Lamentations. In Lam 1:12–16, he behaves as an enemy against Zion. The classical constellation in the biblical lament-genre is significantly changed because Zion does not ask for help from Jhwh in the face of her enemies, but she speaks to the passersby about God's infliction on her (יגה) (cf. 1:5).[50] The personified city as mother of her inhabitants plays the role of the city-goddesses in the Mesopotamian city-laments.[51] As the city-goddess had to endure the wrath of the upper Gods, so Zion/Jerusalem had to bear the anger of Jhwh (Lam 1:12; 2:1.21.22). His fierce anger went as fire into her bones, he spread a net for her feet, turned her back like a hunted animal. Jhwh bound her transgressions into a yoke and handed her over to those she could not withstand; he rejected all her warriors and young men and trodded the wine press (cf. Is 63:1–6; Joel 4:13) against the virgin daughter Judah whose children were desolate. In his violence, Jhwh acts very much like the storm-god Enlil to whom much of the destructions in the Mesopotamian city-laments is attributed. The language of the Psalms according to which the evildoers pursue the just with the net as if they were hunting a wild beast (Ps 35:7; 64:6; 140:6; 142:4), applies here to Jhwh himself. He is no longer the one who frees from the net (Ps 25:15; 31:5; 124:7), but the one who hunts his own people (cf. Hos 7:12). In the metaphors of fire, net, and yoke, Zion underlines her desperate situation because Adonai acts as an enemy against her young men (1:18; 2:21; 5:13.14), and calls for an assembly to slaughter them: "The feast metamorphoses into a grisly spectacle in which Jerusalem's mighty warriors become sacrificial victims instead of joyful celebrants."[52] With Jhwh acting in such a cruel manner, no consolation is available (1:2.9.16.17.21).

The concept of divine wrath dominates the whole second chapter of Lam (2:1.2.3.4.6.21.22) where Jhwh is again depicted as an enemy (אויב) (2:4.5.22) who collaborates with Zion's enemies (2:3.7.16.17). Once again, it is ironically stated that the day of Jerusalem's destruc-

---

[50] N.C. Lee, *Singers* (2002) 115: "the expected distinction between Yhwh and the enemy (as in lament) is collapsed: *Yhwh is likened to the enemy.*"
[51] U. Berges, *Klagelieder* (2002) 110–17.
[52] F.W. Dobbs-Allsopp, *Lamentations* (2002) 69.

tion was a feast (מועד) for the winners (2:7) called in by Jhwh himself (2:22). Unlike in the first chapter, the focus in the first half of Lam 2 lies in the destruction of the political entities such as king, rulers, priests, and prophets in Zion and Juda, with special emphasis on the fate of the Jerusalem temple. Walls, gates, ramparts, and palaces of the city are destroyed by divine intervention and only at the end of this description is attention paid to the population in the form of the elders and maidens mourning in the dust, wearing sackcloth with their heads bowed down to the ground (v. 10). The cruel fate of the population is further highlighted at the beginning of the second half of this chapter (2:11–13) when the poet loses control over his emotions as he watches children who are dying in the arms of their mothers: "My eyes are spent with weeping; my stomach churns; my bile is poured out on the ground because of the destruction of my people, because infants and babes faint in the streets of the city" (2:11). But that's not enough; like a reporter on the battlefield, he focuses on the fainting and starving children. Thus, he witnesses their last words: "They cry to their mothers, 'Where is bread (grain) and wine?' as they faint like the wounded in the streets of the city, as their life is poured out on their mothers' bosom" (v. 12). This is a very touching scene: not often does the OT show the last minutes of the victims of violence and war. Here, it does—the bosoms of the mothers become the grave of their children![53] These are very dangerous pictures and politicians in our day try to avoid by all means that such scenes be shown in the news editions. The so-called *imbedded reporters* are just not allowed to report such scenes! Where does that reluctance come from to cover in full the *real reality* of war? Because the images of dying children tell the real truth, not the truth of the powerful, but that of the innocent victims!

5. *Zion's Critique of and Protest against the Violence of Jhwh*

In the Hebrew Bible, there are voices that dare to confront Jhwh with his own destructive passion, which can't be legitimated by his pathos for justice and for the punishment of the evildoers (cf. Abraham

---

[53] A. Berlin, *Lamentations* (2002) 73: "The picture is made more moving by having the children expire in (or faint into) the bosom or lap of their mothers—the primary site of babies' nourishment and protection (cf. Num 11:12)."

in Gen 18:22–33). In those places where rational, i.e., theological, justifications become insufficient to explain God's wrath and violence, these critical voices come to be heard. One of these voices belongs to mother Zion: where God's punishment reaches innocent children, she dares to criticize his action. It is the poet who invites her to do so: "Let tears stream down like a torrent day and night! Give yourself no rest, your eyes no respite! Arise, cry out in the night, at the beginning of the watches! Pour out your heart like water before the presence of the Lord! Lift your hands to him for the lives of your children, who faint for hunger at the head of every street" (2:18–19). The culpability of Jerusalem and her prophets is strongly affirmed (2:14.17). There is no question about the right of Jhwh to punish the sinful city and her leading class (cf. Is 1), but the violence employed against her was totally out of proportion. Even and just in his anger, Jhwh remains bound to his own standard of justice and ethical behavior.[54]

In very dramatic words, mother Zion holds Jhwh himself responsible for all her grief (2:20–22). She addresses him as the real cause of her suffering and that of her children: "Look, Jhwh, and consider! To whom have you done this? Should women eat their offspring, the children they have borne? Should priest and prophet be killed in the sanctuary of the Lord?" (v. 20). The fate of the starving children stood already at the center of 2:11–12, but the situation gets even more dramatic: in vv. 11–12 the offspring had asked in vain for food, in v. 20 the women consume their own dead children.[55] The wrath of Jhwh did not stop in front of innocent children and mother Zion confronts him with his deeds. First of all, she wants to catch his attention: "Look, Jhwh, and consider!"[56] The situation very much resembles a confrontation between a female victim and her male aggressor, who should come to acknowledge the enormous pain he caused. God himself should see and consider "*to whom*" (למי) he did (עוללת) all this, i.e., to her children (עוללים) (2:19.20; cf. 2:11): the

---

[54] Thus, the statement of W. Groß, *Zorn* (1999) 63 has to be modified: "Einen gerechten Gott kann man in dieser Hinsicht, unter der er gerecht ist, nicht anklagen; im glühenden Zorn vollzieht der gerechte Yhwh wohlbegründete Strafe."

[55] "Teknophagie" as punishment or curse: Lev 26:29; Dtn 28:53–57; cannibalism in Jer 19:9; Ezek 5:10; 2 Kings 6:28; for further examples see A. Berlin, *Lamentations* (2002) 75–76.

[56] The Dutch translation (*Willibrord 95*) does not translate these two imperatives: "Heer, hebt U ooit iemand zo behandeld?"

literary pun between God's action (olalta) and the innocent victims (olalim/olelim) is very sharp. The question "to whom have you done this" (לְמִי עוֹלַלְתָּ כֹּה) is answered: to the עֹלֲלֵי טִפֻּחִים, the "children of birth," i.e., "the new-born children."

In contrast to Jhwh, who has apparently lost control over his passion in his fierce anger, mother Zion does not lose her composure but speaks in clear cut words: "There is none of the hair tearing, skin gouging, or loud hysterics that comprise the conventional literary portrayal of mourning women (and goddesses) in antiquity. Nor do we even meet the broken and spent persona who concluded the previous poem."[57] The lament is voiced in critical terms against the one who slaughtered her infants in the streets, and a parallel is drawn with priest and prophets being killed in the sanctuary (2:20c). At first view, the death of the temple officials seems to be an anti-climax, but the parallel with the dying children has to be taken seriously. Like mothers who have lost their children, Jhwh loses his cult-personal. The perversion of mothers eating their children stands parallel to God who did not prevent the killing of priest and prophet in the sanctuary. As the motherly bosom symbolizes warmth and nutrition, the sanctuary stands for prosperity and life. Thus, the center of life has become a deadly trap (cf. 2 Chr 24:21).

In the following v. 21, mother Zion intensifies her critique of Jhwh's actions; in a very unusual way she confronts him with his criminal deeds: "The young and the old are lying on the ground in the streets; my young women and my young men have fallen by the sword; in the day of your anger you have killed them (הָרַגְתָּ בְּיוֹם אַפֶּךָ), you have slaughtered (טָבַחְתָּ), you did not pity (לֹא חָמָלְתָּ)." That Jhwh acts *without showing mercy* is never stated in the Psalms or in other prayers in the Hebrew Bible, but is well known from the prophets, especially from Ezekiel.[58] It affects the fate of the individual (Job 6:10; 16:13) as well as the life of the community (Lam 3:43).

In Lam 2:21c, Zion underlines Jhwh's violence three times: "*you* have killed, *you* have slaughtered, *you* didn't pity" (cf. 2:4). Another word-play is that between the verbs טבח (to slaughter) and טפח II (to give birth,[59] v. 20.22). Jhwh had killed and slaughtered without

---

[57] F.W. Dobbs-Allsopp, *Lamentations* (2002) 99.
[58] Ez 5:11; 7:4.9; 8:18; 9:5.10 (positiv: 36:21); Jer 13:14; 15:5; 21:7; Jes 30:14; Zech 11:6.
[59] According to D.J.A. Clines (ed.), *The Dictionary of Classical Hebrew* III, Sheffield 1996, 373.

pity those children mother Zion had given birth to and had raised up. Thus, God is not less cannibal than the mothers eating their own children.⁶⁰ The motif of mothers consuming their offspring is reused in Lam 4:10: "The hands of compassionate women have boiled their own children; they became their food in the destruction of my people." The perversion of the mother-child relation is stressed by the characterization of the mothers as "compassionate" (רחמניות) referring to the root רחם which indicates among other things the "motherly womb" (cf. Gen 20:18; 29:31; 30:22) and in the plural form "tenderness/compassion" (Gen 43:30; 1 Kings 3:26; Am 1:11; Zech 7:9). Just as those women, once full of love for the offspring in their womb, were forced to boil the dead corpses for their own consumption.⁶¹ It seems not to be by chance that immediately after this cruel picture, the tetragram occurs for the first time in the fourth chapter (4:11), double linked to the motif of divine wrath: "Jhwh gave full vent to his wrath; he poured out his hot anger, and kindled a fire in Zion that consumed her foundations." Like the mothers [in Zion] who boil their offspring, Jhwh consumes (אכל) the foundations of Zion. What kind of future lies ahead if such things happen? Do loving mothers remain the same after having consumed their children? And does Jhwh remain the same after his destruction of the beloved foundations of Zion (cf. Ps 78:68–69; 87:1)? A fundamental difference between the mothers in Zion and Jhwh has to be noted: *they* were forced to do what they did because *he* did not restrain his wrath but completed (כלה) his anger (cf. Ezek 5:13; 6:12; 7:8; 13:15; 20:8.21). Should Jhwh not have been obliged to restrain his wrath in the face of dying children and the cannibalism of their mothers? Why didn't he act according to the way he himself had urged the aggressors of Israel to act (cf. Is 10:5–15;⁶² Jer 25:8–14; 50:15–18; 51:20–26)? As instruments of divine wrath, foreign nations shouldn't have misused their power for disproportional destruction (Zech 1:15) as it is to be seen in the case of Babylon: "I was angry with my people, I profaned my heritage; I gave them into your hand, you showed them no mercy (לא־שמת להם רחמים); on the aged

---

⁶⁰ A. Berlin, *Lamentations* (2002) 76: "God who slaughters his people is no less cannibal than the mothers who eat their children."
⁶¹ For further details and intertextual relationships, U. Berges, *Klagelieder* (2002) 249–51.
⁶² See W.A.M. Beuken, *Jesaja 1–12* (2003) 281–87.

you made your yoke exceedingly heavy. You said, 'I shall be mistress forever,' so that you did not lay these things to heart or remember their end" (Is 47:6–7).

Despite the fact that the poet of Lam 4 re-uses the motif of the dreadful fate of the innocent babes from Lam 2, he doesn't take over the harsh critique on Jhwh's behavior. This omission has to do with the fact that the literary device of Zion's personification is restricted in the Book of Lamentations to the first two chapters. In the third chapter, one finds the voice of an enigmatic I-figure, "I am one who has seen affliction under the rod of God's wrath" (אֲנִי הַגֶּבֶר רָאָה עֳנִי) and in the last two chapters the collective voice of the survivors becomes prominent. This shows that the possibility to address Jhwh in such a harsh and critical manner is linked in Lam to the personification of Zion. Contrary to the *geber* in Lam. 3:22–33, the literary figure of Zion didn't find a way out of her distress. She accuses God of having killed her children, of having slaughtered them without pity on the day of his wrath (Lam 2:21c). That God is able to kill belongs to his dark side (cf. Gen 20:4; Ex 4:23; 13:15); his deadly aggression is directed towards foreign nations (Is 14:30; Am 2:3; Ps 135:10; 136:18), as well as towards his own people (Am 4:10; 9:1; Ps 59:12; 78:31.34.47). When Zion criticizes him that he not only killed but slaughtered (טבחת) without mercy (לא חמלת) (2:2.17.21), her critique exceeds other instances of divine violence (cf. Ez 21:15.20.33). The verb "to slaughter" is normally used for the killing of animals for human consumption (Gen 43:16; Ex 21:37; 1 Sam 25:11). When it is used metaphorically for killing humans, it points to the cruelty of the action (Jer 48:15; Ps 37:14). Like the great slaughter of Edom (טבח גדול) (Is 34:6; cf. Babel in Jer 50:27; 51:40), Jhwh slaughtered Zion's infants.

In contrast to the end of the other four songs in Lamentations, there is no positive element whatsoever at the end of this second song. All motherly care with which Zion nourished her children had been in vain, because "those whom I bore and reared my enemy has destroyed" (טִפַּחְתִּי וְרִבִּיתִי אֹיְבִי כִלָּם). Against the plural (LXX: ἐχθρούς, Peschitta und Targum), one should maintain the singular reading of the MT because "my enemy" points to Jhwh himself. What the poet had expressed earlier in a comparison, God *like an enemy* (כְּאוֹיֵב) (Lam 2:5; cf. "like a foe" in 2:4; כְּצָר), Zion expresses in a direct statement. That Jhwh converts himself into an enemy of his own people is also affirmed in Is 63:10, as reaction to the disobedience of Israel: "therefore he became their enemy; he himself fought against them" (וַיֵּהָפֵךְ לָהֶם לְאוֹיֵב הוּא נִלְחַם־בָּם).

The severe critique of mother Zion that Jhwh turned into a merciless enemy who killed her innocent children is the dramatic finale of the first two chapters of the book of Lamentations. Jhwh, the God of Israel, has turned into the slaughterer of his own people.[63] Zion's critique and protest remain without answer from Jhwh—as her children didn't get an answer to their plea for bread and wine (2:12).

6. *Some Concluding Remarks*

After having presented some of the "satanic verses" in Lamentations and their interpretation in the light of the Ancient Near East and innerbiblical traditions, an exegesis understood as theological discipline can't avoid asking questions about the consequences for the theological reflection. At this point the discussion with other theological disciplines would be of great value. Thus, these concluding remarks are nothing more than a first attempt in that direction.[64]

The heretical temptation to exorcize the dark sides of Jhwh, his wrath and negativity out of a Christian notion of God, hasn't lost any of its attraction since Marcion in the 2nd century C.E. These negative texts are often judged as "pre-christian," "unchristian," or "less than Christian"; their only function is to show why Jesus Christ, the full manifestation of God's love and tenderness, had to come.[65] But the rejection by the early church of Marcion and his heretical splitting up of the positive and negative sides of God should be a constant reminder for Christian theology.[66] It remains doubtful if the differentiation between "opus dei alienum" (cf. Is 28:21) and "opus

---

[63] See K.M. O'Connor, *Lamentations* (2002) 41–43.

[64] With gratitude to the members of the Faculty of Theology at Nijmegen who participated in a symposion-session on Lamentations on 22.05.2003, the day our colleague and friend Sjef van Tilborg departed from us.

[65] See some examples of that negative attitude in E. Zenger, *Vengeance* (1996) 13–23.

[66] This also holds true for the systematic reflection on religions in general, see J.-P. Wils, *Dialectiek* (2002) 111: "Religies leren ons niet hoe te leven in een wereld zonder geweld, maar hoe te leven met en ondanks geweld. Zij kunnen dit leren omdat zij een—in de letterlijke zin van het woord—oorspronkelijk weten bezitten omtrent geweld. Omwille van dit weten zijn religies zowel overlevingsbedreigingen als ook overlevingspraktijken."

dei proprium" leads to the right direction.[67] It seems to be more true that the acceptance of God's wrath and violence functions as a precondition for the possibility to keep a clear notion of God's chesed, his love and tenderness. The acceptance of divine wrath makes it unnecessary to accept the thought that Jhwh acts violently against innocent people *out of love*. This turn in the relationship between aggressor and victim leads to disastrous consequences for the psychological well-being of believers because it forces them to declare themselves guilty of unknown trespasses (cf. Job and his critique of his friends). Such a perversion is comparable to structures which are at work in cases of child abuse committed by parents: in his terrible pain the mistreated child holds on to the hope that his parents act out of love and that what happens is only because of his own fault.[68]

Instead of this wrong path, the wisdom-inspired reflection of the geber in Lam 3 leads into the right direction, i.e., "to hold and affirm conflicting and contradictory truths without eventually surrendering either."[69] At the end of the reflection, which grew out of the endurance of the wrath of God, it is stated: "For Jhwh will not reject forever. Although he causes grief, he will have compassion according to the abundance of his steadfast love; for he does not willingly afflict [not out of his heart] or grieve anyone" (Lam 3:31–33).

Two points are important to note: firstly, that Jhwh does not reject *forever*, and secondly, that he does not afflict *out of his heart*. That means that Jhwh's wrath does belong to his characteristics and that his image is not determined by it.

It is the hope to see and experience, once again, God's chesed, which stands behind the laments of Job, Zion, the geber, and the petitioner of Ps 88.[70] The biblical protest against Jhwh, who acts in contradiction with his own ethical standards, is not rooted in a cultural disapproval of a violent God,[71] but in the hope to experience

---

[67] E. Jüngel, *Offenbarung* (1984) 92: "Wir halten also fest: opus dei alienum und opus dei proprium laufen nicht beziehungslos parallel nebeneinander her, sondern das Werk zur Linken Gottes ist immer bezogen auf das Werk zur Rechten Gottes. Gott tötet, *damit* er lebendig macht. Luther kann auch sagen: Gott annihiliert, *damit* er aus dem Nichts neu schaffe."
[68] A. Miller, *Mistreated Child* (1991) 124.
[69] F.W. Dobbs-Allsopp, *Lamentations* (2002) 120.
[70] See U. Berges, *Schweigen* (2003).
[71] At this point, the discussion with systematic theology would be fruitful; cf. G. Essen, *Geloof* (2002) 79, who asked himself if one can accept a God who acts immorally?

his benevolence again. The sapiential reflection of the geber in the center of the Book of Lamentation, to keep hoping of God's chesed despite of all grief inflicted by him (Lam 3:22–24), does not present the solution of the problem of divine negativity, but the internal motivation to protest against it. Thus, the Book ends with the question to Jhwh if he will keep on with his anger or if he will make a full turn in favor of his people: "Restore us to yourself, Jhwh, that we may be restored; renew our days as of old—unless you have utterly rejected us, and are angry with us beyond measure" (Lam 5:21–22). The same is true in Ps 85, a psalm which was very dear to Sjef van Tilborg, in which the petitioner affirms God's negativity but also gives voice to his most intimate desire: "Show us your chesed, Jhwh, and grant us your salvation" (Ps 85:8).

Bibliography

Albani, M., *Der eine Gott und die himmlischen Heerscharen. Zur Begründung des Monotheismus bei Deuterojesaja im Horizont der Astralisierung des Gottesverständnisses im Alten Orient* (Arbeiten zur Bibel und ihrer Geschichte 1), Leipzig 2000.
Albertz, R., *Die Exilszeit. 6. Jahrhundert v. Chr.* (Biblische Enzyklopädie 7), Stuttgart 2001.
Albrektson, B., *History and the Gods. An Essay on the Idea of Historical Events as Divine Manifestations in the Ancient Near East and in Israel* (CB.OT 1), Lund 1967.
Assmann, J., *Herrschaft und Heil. Politische Theologie in Altägypten, Israel und Europa*, München 2000.
Baumgart, N.C., *Die Umkehr des Schöpfergottes. Zu Komposition und religionsgeschichtlichem Hintergrund von Gen. 5–9* (HBS 22), Freiburg i.Br. 1999.
——, "Die große Flut und die Arche" in: *BiKi* 58 (2003) 30–36.
Berges, U., *Klagelieder* (HThKAT), Freiburg i.Br. 2002.
——, *Schweigen ist Silber—Klagen ist Gold. Das Drama der Gottesbeziehung aus alttestamentlicher Sicht mit einer Auslegung zu Ps. 88* (Salzburger Exegetisch-Theologische Vorträge Bd. 1), Münster 2003.
Berlin, A., *Lamentations* (OTL), Louisville 2002.
Beuken, W.A.M., *Jesaja 1–12* (HThKAT), Freiburg i.Br. 2003.
Broek, R. van den, "Deus habet imperium, ergo et iram: Lactantius over de toorn van God" in: A. de Jong (ed.), *Kleine Encyclopedie van de Toorn* (Utrechtse Theologische Reeks 21), Utrecht 1993, 29–42.
Brueggemann, W., *Theology of the Old Testament. Testimony, Dispute, Advocacy*, Minneapolis 1997.
Clark, G.R., *The Word Hesed in the Hebrew Bible* (JSOT.S 157), Sheffield 1993.
Clines, D.J.A. (ed.), *The Dictionary of Classical Hebrew Vol. III*, Sheffield 1996.
Dietrich, W., Link, C., *Die dunklen Seiten Gottes. Bd. 1: Willkür und Gewalt*, Neukirchen-Vluyn ³2000 (1995); *Bd 2: Allmacht und Ohnmacht*, Neukirchen-Vluyn 2000.
Dobbs-Allsopp, F.W., *Weep, O Daughter of Zion: A Study of the City-Lament Genre in the Hebrew Bible* (BibOr 44), Rome 1993.
——, *Lamentations*, Louisville 2002.
Dohmen, C., *Das Bilderverbot. Seine Entstehung und seine Entwicklung im Alten Testament* (BBB 62), Frankfurt a.M. ²1987.

Essen, G., "In het geloof schuilt een boosaardig beginsel. Is de God van Jezus een gewelddadige God?" in: P. Valkenberg (ed.), *God en geweld*, Budel 2002, 65–89.
Gillman, N., *Sacred Fragments. Recovering Theology for a Modern Jew*, Philadelphia 1990.
Girard, M., "La violence de Dieu dans la bible juive: approche symbolique et interpretation théologique" in: *ScEs* 39 (1987) 145–70.
Girard, R., *La violence et le sacré*, Paris 1972.
Görg, M., *Der un-heile Gott. Die Bibel im Bann der Gewalt*, Düsseldorf 1995.
——, "Der 'schlagende Gott' in der 'älteren' Bibel" in: *BiKi* 51 (1996) 94–100.
Greimas, A.J., *De la colère. Étude de sémantique lexicale* (Documents de recherche vol. 3, no. 27. Groupe de recherches sémio-linguistique, CNRS), Paris 1981; repr. du sens II. Essais sémiotiques, Paris 1983, 225–46.
Gross, W., "Zorn Gottes—ein biblisches Theologumenon" in: W. Beinert (ed.), *Gott—ratlos vor dem Bösen* (QD 177), Freiburg i.Br. 1999, 47–85.
——, "Das Negative in Schöpfung und Geschichte: Yhwh hat auch Finsternis und Unheil erschaffen (Jes. 45,7)" in: W. Gross & K.-J. Kuschel (eds.), *"Ich schaffe Finsternis und Heil!" Ist Gott verantwortlich für das Übel?*, Mainz 1992, 34–46; repr. in W. Gross, *Studien zur Priesterschrift und zu alttestamentlichen Gottesbildern* (SBA 30), Stuttgart 1999, 145–158.
Häring, H., "Ploegscharen omgesmeed tot zwaarden (Jo. 14,10). De wortels van het geweld in de religie" in: *TvT* 37 (1997) 265–90.
Herion, G.A., *Wrath of God* (Anchor Bible Dictionary Vol. 6), New York 1992, 989–96.
Ingremeau, Chr., *Lactance. La colère de Dieu* (Sources Chrétiennes 289), Paris 1982.
Jong, A. de, "Als Re vertoornd is" in: A. de Jong (ed.), *Kleine Encyclopedie van de Toorn* (Utrechtse Theologische Reeks 21), Utrecht 1993, 95–105.
Jüngel, E., "Die Offenbarung der Verborgenheit Gottes. Ein Beitrag zum evangelischen Verständnis des göttlichen Wirkens" in: K. Lehmann (ed.), *Vor dem Geheimnis Gottes den Menschen verstehen. Karl Rahner zum 80. Geburtstag*, München 1984, 79–104.
Krahe, S., *Ermordete Kinder und andere Geschichten von Gottes Unmoral*, Würzburg 1999.
Krieger, K.-S., *Gewalt in der Bibel* (Münsterschwarzacher Kleinschriften 134), Münsterschwarzach 2002.
Lee, N.C., *The Singers of Lamentations. Cities under Siege, from Ur to Jerusalem to Sarajevo* (BIS 60), Leiden 2002.
Lohfink, N. (ed.), *Gewalt und Gewaltlosigkeit im Alten Testament* (QD 96), Freiburg i.Br. 1983.
——, *Der gewalttätige Gott des Alten Testaments und die Suche nach einer gewaltfreien Gesellschaft* (JBTh 2), Neukirchen-Vluyn 1987, 106–36.
——, *Unsere neuen Fragen und das alte Testament. Wiederentdeckte Lebensweisung* (Herder TB 1594), Freiburg i.Br. 1989.
Mayer, W., "Die Zerstörung des Jerusalemer Tempels 587 v. Chr. im Kontext der Praxis von Heiligtumszerstörungen im antiken Vorderen Orient" in: J. Hahn (ed.), *Zerstörungen des Jerusalemer Tempels. Geschehen—Wahrnehmung—Bewältigung* (WUNT 147), Tübingen 2002.
Miggelbrink, R., *Der Zorn Gottes. Geschichte und Aktualität einer ungeliebten biblischen Tradition*, Freiburg i.Br. 2000.
——, *Der zornige Gott. Die Bedeutung einer anstößigen biblischen Tradition*, Darmstadt 2002.
Miller, A., "The Mistreated Child in the Lamentations of Jeremiah" in: A. Miller (ed.), *Breaking Down the Wall of Silence: To Join the Waiting Child*, London 1991, 114–26.
Noort, E., *Geweld in het Oude Testament. Over woorden en verhalen aan de rand van de kerkelijke praktijk* (Ter Sprake 28), Delft 1985.
O'Connor, K.M., *Lamentations and the Tears of the World*, New York 2002.
Scoralick, R., *Gottes Güte und Gottes Zorn. Die Gottesprädikationen in Ex. 34,6f. und ihre intertextuellen Beziehungen zum Zwölfprophetenbuch* (HBS 33), Freiburg i.Br. 2002.
Schwager, R., *Brauchen wir einen Sündenbock? Gewalt und Erlösung in den biblischen Schriften*, München ²1986.

Spiekermann, H., "Dies Irae. Der alttestamentliche Befund und seine Vorgeschichte" in: *VT* 39 (1989) 194–208.

———, "God's Steadfast Love. Towards a New Conception of Old Testament Theology" in: *Bib* 81 (2000) 305–27.

———, *Gottes Liebe zu Israel. Studien zur Theologie des Alten Testaments* (FAT 33), Tübingen 2001.

Sternberg-el Hotabi, H., *Der Mythos von der Vernichtung des Menschengeschlechtes* (TUAT III/5), Gütersloh 1995, 1018–37.

Tilborg, Sj. van, *The Sermon on the Mount as an Ideological Intervention. A Reconstruction of Meaning*, Assen 1986.

Toorn, K. van der, *Sin and Sanction in Israel and Mesopotamia. A Comparative Study* (SSN 22), Assen 1985.

———, "The Iconic Book. Analogies between the Babylonian Cult of Images and the Veneration of the Torah" in: K. van der Toorn (ed.), *The Image and the Book. Iconic Cults, Aniconism, and the Rise of Book Religion in Israel and the Ancient Near East*, Leuven 1997, 229–48.

Veenhof, K.R., *Geschichte des Alten Orients bis zur Zeit Alexanders des Großen* (ATD Ergänzungsreihe Bd 11), Göttingen 2001.

Vervenne, M., "'Satanic Verses'? Violence and War in the Bible" in: R. Burggraeve & M. Vervenne (eds.), *Swords into Plowshares. Theological Reflections on Peace* (Louvain Theological & Pastoral Monographs 8), Louvain 1991, 65–126.

———, "Violent Imagery in the Hebrew Bible: Satanic Verses or Anti-metaphors?" in: K. Kiesow & Th. Meurer (eds.), *Textarbeit. Studien zu Texten und ihrer Rezeption aus dem Alten Testament und der Umwelt Israels, FS P. Weimar* (AOAT 294), Münster 2003, 523–44.

Volz, P., *Das Dämonische in Jahwe*, Tübingen 1924.

Whybray, R.N., "The Immorality of God. Reflections on Some Passages in Genesis, Job, Exodus and Numbers" in: *JSOT* 72 (1996) 89–120.

Weber, M., *Gesammelte Aufsätze zur Religionssoziologie III* (UTB 1490), Tübingen 1921; ⁸1988.

Westermann, C., "Boten des Zorns. Der Begriff des Zornes Gottes in der Prophetie" in: J. Jeremias & L. Perlitt (eds.), *Die Botschaft und die Boten, FS H.W. Wolff*, Neukirchen-Vluyn 1981, 147–56.

Wils, J.-P., "De dialectiek van de Verlichting en de logica van het geweld" in: P. Valkenberg (ed.), *God en geweld*, Budel 2002, 90–111.

Zapff, B.M., *Schriftgelehrte Prophetie—Jes 13 und die Komposition des Jesajabuches. Ein Beitrag zur Erforschung der Redaktionsgeschichte des Jesajabuches* (FzB 74), Würzburg 1995.

Zenger, E., "Der Gott der Bibel—ein gewalttätiger Gott?" in: *KatBl* 119 (1994) 687–96.

———, *A God of Vengeance? Understanding the Psalms of Divine Wrath*, Louisville 1996.

CHAPTER TWO

OBDURATE SHORT-SIGHTEDNESS IN THE VALLEY OF VISION: HOW ATONEMENT OF INIQUITY IS FORFEITED (ISA 22:1–14)

Willem A.M. Beuken
Catholic University of Leuven, Belgium

Iucundus homo qui miseretur et commodat (Ps 111 [112], 5 Vulgate)
In ineffaceable remembrance of Sjef van Tilborg

1. *Translation*

22:1 The oracle concerning the valley of vision.
    What is the matter with you now
      that you have gone up,
      all of you, to the roofs?
2   You, usually full of shouts,
      tumultuous city,
        exultant town!
    Your slain are not slain with the sword
      or dead in battle.
3   All your rulers run away together,
      without the bow they were captured.
    All who were found in you were captured,
      though they tried to flee far away.
4   Therefore I say:
    "Look away from me,
      let me weep bitter tears.
    Do not labor to comfort me
      for the destruction of the daughter of my people."
5   Truly, it was a day of tumult
      and trampling and confusion
        for the Lord Yhwh of hosts
    in the valley of vision,
      of lifting up a cry
        and of screaming to the mountain.

6	Elam lifted up the quiver
	  with chariots and horsemen,
	    and Kir uncovered the shield.

7	It came to pass
	  that your choicest valleys were full of chariots,
	    and the horsemen took their stand at the gates.

8	He took away the covering of Judah.
	  On that day you looked
	    to the weapons of the House of the Forest,

9	and the breaches of the city of David— you saw that there were many. You collected the waters of the lower pool,
10	and you counted the houses of Jerusalem, and you broke down the houses to make the wall inaccessible.

11	You made a reservoir between the two walls
	  for the water of the old pool.
	But you did not look to him who made it,
	  or have regard for him who fashioned it long ago.

12	The Lord Yhwh of hosts called on that day
	  to weeping and mourning,
	    to baldness and girding with sackcloth.

13	Yet behold, joy and gladness,
	  slaying oxen and killing sheep,
	eating flesh and drinking wine.
	  "Let us eat and drink, for tomorrow we die."

14	But the Lord Yhwh of hosts has revealed himself in my ears:
	"Surely there will be no atonement
	  of this iniquity for you
	    till you die,"
	says the Lord Yhwh of hosts.

2. *Account of the Translation*

vv. 2b–3 The microstructure of these three verse lines is so perfect that any changing of the text is to be dissuaded (Bosshard-Nepustil, *Rezeptionen* [1997] 45):

2b חללים	לא	חללי־חרב	ולא מתי מלחמה
3a כל־קציניך	נדדו	יחד	מקשת אסרו
3b כל־נמצאיך	אסרו	יחדו	מרחוק ברחו

The first line, a negation, speaks about the slain warriors while the second and the third line, positive statements, speak about the captives. With regard to the latter ones, two groups are distinguished: "all your rulers" (v. 3a) and "all who were found in you" (v. 3b). Both were captured (אסרו), but the first group had indeed fled (נדד, "to flee without a purpose"; cf. ThWAT V, 247 [W. Groß]), the second one only tried to flee as far as possible (ברח: with an aspect of furtiveness; cf. ThWAT I, 779 [J. Gamberoni]). The distinction is only clear if we interpret the suffix of נמצאיך as a *genitivus locativus*: "all who were found in you" (cf. LXX: ἐν σοί; Watts, 279; instead of a *genitivus partitivus*: "all of you who were found" [RSV]).

By itself, the meaning of מקשת (translated "without the bow") is open: (1) "by the bow," i.e., by the archers; (2) "without the bow," i.e., not in battle: either the enemies did not need to use their bows or the victims had no chance to use their bows (Alexander, 380–381). Given the metaphorical meaning of the bow as the military power of a people, the latter interpretation is more likely. The rulers did not unfold strength in the face of the enemy (cf. v. 2b: "not slain with the sword"; Josh 24:12; Jer 49:35; Hos 1:5.7; 2:20; Am 5:2; Ps 44:7; 46:10; 76:4; courtesy Matthijs de Jong, Rijksuniversiteit, Leiden).

The last word of v. 3, ברחו, is interpreted as a *perfectum de conatu*: "they tried to flee far away" (Delitzsch, 266). From the linguistic point of view, the sentence can be translated as "they had fled from afar," i.e., from the countryside to the city of Jerusalem. The external parallelism with v. 3ab, however, suggests that מרחוק, as מקשת there, stands for a place of idle security, i.e., "(to flee) far away." Just as the bow did not help, so the attempt to reach a remote place was in vain (cf. Alexander, 380; Oswalt, 403). מרחוק permits this interpretation (cf. ThWAT, VII, 492 [L. Wächter]: "Die separative Bedeutung der Präp. *min* kann in der Verbindung *merahôq* abgeschwacht sein...vgl. Ex 2:4; 20:18.21; 1 Sam 26:13; 2 Kön 2:7; Jes 22:3; 23:7; 59:14; Ps 38:12").

v. 4 In the time perspective, which develops here, the prophet addresses the inhabitants of the distressed city (v 1b; only v 2a contains a retrospective on former times without danger). In this context, v. 4a refers to the present situation: "Therefore, I say" (AB, JPSV, Hitzig, Alexander, Delitzsch, Duhm, Feldmann, Penna, Schoors, Kaiser, Childs; *pace* RSV ["Therefore, I said"], Watts, Oswalt, Blenkinsopp; cf. Joüon-Muraoka [Grammar] 1991, §112–113: "...performative perfect...especially common with verbs of saying: Gen 22:16; Deut 8:19; 26:3; 2 Sam 17:11; 19:30 etc.").

v. 5a This verse opens a section in which the warming-up period for the siege is described: the approach of the hostile army (vv. 5–8a) and the defense preparations of the inhabitants (vv. 8b–11). This period belongs to the past but the disastrous outcome of the siege is now palpable (vv. 1–4). The whole history is called "a day of tumult and trampling and confusion for the Lord Yhwh of hosts." As a consequence, the time perspective is both present and past. Given the fact, however, that this verse opens the retrospective, we translate the nominal sentence in the past tense: "It *was* a day of tumult...."

v. 5b The meaning of v. 5ba (מקרקר קר) is disputed (HALAT 1071). The ancient versions differ too much from MT to be of any help. 1QIsa^a (v. 5b: מקרקר קדשו על ההר; "... his holy place on the mountain") reflects an emendation more likely than the original reading (Kutscher, Language [1974] 281: "The scribe apparently did not realize the connection between this word here [i.e. the hapax legomenon [שוע] and the root [שוע "to cry"]). The common interpretation of MT (RSV: "a battering down of the walls") assumes the root קיר, "wall," to be at stake (already Kimchi and Ibn Ezra; further Alexander, Duhm and the earlier commentators). Another interpretation takes קר and שוע as names of nations in connection with v. 6: "Kir raged in the Valley of Vision, and Shoa on the hill; while Elam bore the quiver in troops of mounted men, and Kir bared the shield" (JPSV). More recently, scholars have found a connection with later Hebrew קרקר, "to cry" (Jastrow, Dictionary [1903] 1427; cf. Taan. 29a) and Ugaritic *kr* in the same meaning (*krt* 120, 222; thus Weippert, Jes 22:5 [1961] 97–99; G.R. Driver, Problems [1968] 36–57, esp. 47–48; Wildberger, 806). Therefore Oswalt (404) translates: "lifting up the shout." This interpretation (in different wording, namely "lifting up a cry") has been adopted here although the following remark deserves attention: "The possibility that מקרקר may be a pilp form from קור I "bore or dig" (cf. Brown, Driver, & Briggs, 881) and קר a shortened form of "a spring, fountain" has hardly been explored" (cf. vv. 9–11; Watts, 278–79: "digging a ditch").

v. 11b In contemporary research, the feminine suffixes of the participles עשיה and יצרה are commonly conceived to have neuter meaning and to refer to the siege described in the foregoing. Accordingly, scholars explain the verse line as denoting Yhwh as "the Lord of history." This interpretation, however, is not unchallenged. Ibn Ezra (38, 100) considered the suffixes to refer to God's "decree" (נזרה; also Vitringa, 867, with reference to Isa 46:11 and 37:26) but this word does not occur in the whole book of Isaiah. Of course, scholars have looked for a feminine noun in the immediate context as a feasible antecedent of the suffixes. Delitzsch (270) rightly noticed that the suffix in עשׂיה could be plural (cf. 54:5) and as such refer to "the walls" in v. 11ba. Yet he takes it to be singular because of the parallel יצרה. Consequently, the resulting meaning is just the same "Jerusalems Strafgeschick." Of old, however, the suffixes have been explained as referring to "Jerusalem," which is mentioned in v. 10 and has been addressed in vv. 1–3.7.8b (2nd p. sg.). The Septuagint favors this interpretation because in this version, the word "city" (πόλις) is added as a plus vis-à-vis MT in vv. 9–10: "They saw that they were many, and that they had turned the water of the old pool *into the city*; and that they had pulled down the houses of Jerusalem, to fortify the wall *of the city*. And you procured for yourselves water between the walls within the ancient pool: but you looked not to him who made it from the beginning, and regarded not him who created it."[1] The Vulgate allows for the same explanation: "et non suspexistis ad eum qui fecerat eam, et operatorem eius de longe non vidistis." Among the medieval Jewish scholars it is Redak who clearly proposes this interpretation: "You did not look toward the Creator, Who made it and established it, and protected it until now from enemies" (Rosenberg, 176). This interpretation survived in some way in AV: "but ye have not looked unto the maker thereof, neither had respect unto him that fashioned it long ago" (cf. Alexander, 384, who combines the two interpretations: "the city or the calamity"). In recent times, it has again arisen (AB: "But you did not look to the city's Maker, nor did you consider him who built it long ago"; Watts, 278, 284; Oswalt, 404).—Our translation intends to keep the problem open. For our interpretation, see under *The Guilt of Short-Sightedness*.

3. *Two Stories behind the Prophecy*

Although the redaction of the oracles against the nations has placed the two parts of ch. 22, vv. 1–14 and vv. 15–25, under one משׂא

---

[1] Theoretically, the suffix could refer to the nearest feminine noun "pool" (κολυμβήθρα), but from the context, this is very unlikely.

heading (v. 1; cf. 13:1; 14:28; 15:1; 17:1; 19:1; 21:1.11.13; 23:1), they can be assigned literary autonomy since they are included by various prophetic messenger formulas (vv. 12.15.25; for the congruence of the two parts, cf. Sweeney, 289–90, 293–94, 298–99). Furthermore, we may assume that the adjunct of place "in the valley of vision" (v. 5) has been lent for the משא heading: "The oracle concerning the valley of vision" (v. 1).

The first part of the oracle evidently consists of an accusation (vv. 1–13) and a verdict (v. 14). The political and military situation referred to in this passage is unclear. Of old, authors have found allusions to the siege of Jerusalem by the Assyrian army at the time of king Hezekiah in 701 but also to the conquest of the city during the reign of king Zedekiah in 586. The former calamity may constitute the background of vv. 8b–11a (cf. 2 Chr 32:2–5.30), the latter that of vv. 2b–3 (cf. 2 Kgs 25:4–7) while vv. 5–7 are applicable to both stories. Quite often, moreover, the festivities on the roofs (vv. 1–2) and the banquet instead of mourning (vv. 12–13) are made into an argument for the interpretation that the chapter describes the common joy after the deliverance of Jerusalem in 701. Yet, there is no mention whatsoever of such a festivity in the three versions of this story (Isa 37:36–37//2 Kgs 19:35–36; 2 Chr 32:22–23).[2]

Medieval Jewish scholars had a preference for a connection with the events of 586 (Rosenberg, 174–76; Hirsch, 139–40), older literary-historical commentators for the siege of 701 as background, also because the next passage, 22:15–25, deals with Shebna and Eliakim, persons who return in the story about that siege (Isa 36:3; 37:2; cf. Hitzig, 254; Delitzsch, 265; Duhm, 157–58; König, 219; Wildberger, 812; Sweeney, 288–302; Blenkinsopp, 333–35). Besides, a minority supposes another Assyrian attack on Jerusalem by Sargon II during his campaign against the Philistines in 711 (Oswalt, 408; Hayes & Irvine [Isaiah] 1987, 277–87; survey Berges [Buch Jesaja] 1998,

---

[2] A wholly different explanation situates the passage in the aftermath of the battle of Kish, in which the Assyrian king Sennacherib defeated the Babylonians (704). The rejoicing city addressed by Isaiah (vv 1–3.7) would be Babylon when it welcomed Sennacherib. In vv. 8b–13 Isaiah would describe the reaction of the people in Jerusalem: instead of repenting they prepared for a siege while enjoying the lull before the storm (Gallagher, 60–74). Although this thorough historical study is able to declare many obscure details in Is 22,1–14, it is unlikely that remote political events form the background of the passage. The two major calamities which happened to Jerusalem (701 and 586) are the first to be considered.

148f.). Nevertheless, it remains a weak point in this interpretation that of Assyria neither the army nor the king is mentioned in this chapter. The last record of Assyria is found in 20:6, the next one in 23:13. (The nearest mention of a military campaign is that of Elam and Media against Babylon [21:1–2.9].)

In recent years, the two interpretations have no longer been considered as irreconcilable. Scholars have come to accept that the situation in view refers to both historical events. An old but neglected explanation contends that the whole oracle is "a generic prediction, a prophetic picture of the conduct of the Jews in a certain conjecture of affairs which happened more than once, particular strokes of the description being drawn from different memorable sieges, and especially from those of Sennacherib and Nebuchadnezzar" (Alexander, 379). Without adopting the qualification "prediction," namely by the prophet, the discussion now concentrates on the redaction history of the passage. This happens in the larger context of the fact that the section of chs. 13–23 as such, it is argued, shows traces of an editing which puts the Assyrian invasion(s) on a par with the Neo-Babylonian overthrow of Judah, in order to elucidate that both punishments belonged to the one plan of Yhwh with regard to Israel and the nations (Oswalt, 408; Clements, 182–87; *id.*, Deliverance [1980] 33–35; Bosshard-Nepustil, Beobachtungen [1987] 42–92).[3] According to another explanation, the dual reference of the passage is not a matter of redactional reworking but of reader interpretation: in the light of a canonical, holistic approach to the Scriptures the narrated event of 701 foreshadows the disaster of 587 (Childs, 159).

4. *Why Going up to the Roofs?*

It is not easy to determine the nature of the people's "looking in the wrong direction" (vv. 8–11) although it is called an "iniquity" (עון) for which there will be no "atonement" (v. 14: אם יכפר). At first sight, these strong theological qualifications are out of proportion to the behavior of Jerusalem's inhabitants as described in the beginning of the passage (vv. 1–2, also v. 13). This sketch, however, is encumbered with the mortage explanation that it refers to the festivities in

---

[3] Bosshard-Nepustil's (55 ff.) interpretation of 22,6 as a later actualization which identifies the city under siege with Babylon is left outside of account here.

Jerusalem after the siege of the city in 701 had been lifted. Yet, in the three versions of this story there is no mention of this exuberance (cf. *The Story*). Moreover, in the predominant exegesis several words in vv. 1–2 have too easily been made to fit this interpretation:

- The term "roof" (גג) points to a place where people (and birds) retire for seclusion (Josh 2:6.8; 1 Sam 9:25f.; 2 Sam 11:2; 16:22; Ps 102:8; Prov 21:9; 25:24) or illegal cult (2 Kgs 23:12; Jer 19:13; 32:29; Zeph 1:5). Only Neh 8:16 speaks of booths erected on the roof of private houses while in Judg 16:27 it is the roof of a temple where the public gather for a popular celebration. In Isa 15:3 and Jer 48:38 roofs are the locality where private mourning takes place (DOTTE I, 1511 [גג]).
- The term "shouts" (תשאות) means basically "vigourous noise" (Job 36:29; 39:7). Only in Zech 4:7 it refers to a celebration rite in connection to the construction of the temple.
- The term "tumultuous" (הומיה) does not specifically refer to joyful cheering but to the combination of noise and movement which is characteristic of any city (1 Kgs 1:41; Isa 5:14; 14:11; 32:14; Ezek 23:42; Job 39:7; Prov 1:21; ThWAT II, 446 [A. Baumann]). As a word for boisterous unrest it occurs in the context of thunder-storm (1 Kgs 18:41), turbulent sea (Isa 17:12; 51:15; Jer 5:22; 6:23; 51:42; Ezek 1:24; Ps 46:4; 65:8), war (1 Sam 4:14; 14:16.19; 2 Sam 18:29; Isa 31:4; Jer 47:3), and cultic gatherings (Jer 3:23; 11:16; Amos 5:23; Ps 42:5).
- It is only the term "exultant" (עליזה) which unmistakably refers to a situation of joy (Hab 3:18; Ps 28:7; 68:5; 96:12; 149:5; Prov 23:16; ThWAT VI, 128–130 [G. Vanoni: "Freudenkundgebung"]). A negative connotation of recklessness, frivolity, and malicious delight is often involved (2 Sam 1:20; Isa 23:12; 32:13; Jer 11:15; 15:17; 50:11; Zeph 2:15; 3:14; Ps 94:3).

In light of these data, it is a moot point whether the attitude of the people against which the prophet takes a stand would be one of merrymaking. Therefore, according to some interpretations, the going up to the roofs does not form part of a celebration. Already Ibn Ezra (98) noticed with regard to v. 1: "Some think, they went up in order to offer incense to the host of heaven, but my opinion is, that they went up in order to see the forces that besieged Jerusalem, as is generally done under such circumstances." It is a common explanation of the Jewish tradition, moreover, to distinguish between the stay on the roofs as a consequence of the *present* calamity and the hustle and bustle which *previously* characterized the city (according to Rosenberg, 173: Rashi, Redak, Ibn Ezra and Lam.R, Proems XXIV; furthermore Hirsch, 139–40).[4] Therefore, JPSV (397) translates: "O you who were full of tumult."

It is quite possible, then, that this time-honored interpretation matches with a finding of the critical research regarding the Hebrew dirge or elegy. A major form which often opens and certainly dominates a funeral poem is the contrast between "now" and "once" (Jahnow, Leichenlied [1923] 99; Berges 2002, 95–96; Labahn, Trauer [2002]). Examples are manifold (2 Sam 1:19.25; Isa 1:21–26; 14:4.12; Jer 2:21; 48:17; 49:25; Ezek 27:32–36; 28:11–19; Lam 1:1; 2:1; 4:1–2). As the dirge in its classical lament is often introduced by the exclamatory "how" (איך, איכה), it merits consideration whether in 22:1 the exclamatory אפוא (AB: "What is the matter with you") performs a similar function (cf. Job 17:15).

In this case, the question is left: what does the initiative of "going up to the roofs" mean? If we have to exclude a festive celebration and take the contextual opposition between "as it used to be" and "as it is now" seriously, going up to the roofs must be related to the sketch of the calamitous situation in vv. 2b–3. These verses depict the utter defenselessness of the inhabitants of the city, and how all life has disappeared from it. It has not come to a regular battle (v. 2b), the leadership has deserted but were not able to save themselves (v. 3a), those found in the city have no chance to escape (v. 3b). In this context, "to go up to the roofs" must stand for an attempt to hide oneself as opposed to the lot of those who are captured in the streets. The social value of the roof as a place where people retire adds to this explanation (cf. above). The story of Joshua's spies at Jericho forms a major confirmation (Josh 2:1–24). At the same time, this going up to the roofs symbolizes the citizens' lack of faith in Yhwh and as such it contrasts with the ascent to the temple in times of distress of which king Hezekiah sets a shining example (37:14; 38:22; cf. the nations in 2:3). Moreover, the overall description of distress in Isa 22 is exemplified by many passages in the book of Lamentations (cf. 1:3–4.12.16; 2:11.13.21–22; 4:8–9. 17–19).

---

[4] It is interesting enough to notice that Alexander (380) is aware of the problem although he solves it by interpreting the joyful excitement of v. 1 in relation to v. 13.

5. *The Core of the Indictment*

The main semantic item of the accusation is doubtless the one that is construed around "to see":

> 8b   On that day you looked (ותבט) to the weapons of the House of the Forest,
> 9a   and the breaches of the city of David—you saw (ראיתם) that they were many.
> 11b But you did not look (לא הבטתם) to him who made it (עשיה), or have regard (לא ראיתם) for him who fashioned it (יצרה) long ago.

The heading of the passage, "the valley of vision," underlines the importance of the topic "to see" for this oracle. It can be summarized as an appeal to the people to pay attention to what really matters: the defense works of the city or Yhwh, "who made it/fashioned it long ago" (v. 11b). We have discussed the problem of what the object of "made/fashioned" refers to: to the calamitous events which have befallen the inhabitants of Jerusalem, or to the city itself (cf. *Translation*: v. 11b).

(a) Adherents of the former interpretation point to the fact that the topic of God's acting in Israel's history exceeds the limits of this prophecy. It can be considered as the very essence of Isaiah's message, both of the historical prophet and of the book which bears his name. Summons to look at Yhwh's work, accusations that Israel does not do so and promises that the blind eventually will see and understand pervade the book of Isaiah. "Geschichte ist der Wirkungsbereich Jahwes" (Wildberger, 825).[5] For the purpose of this message, Isaiah has made creation terminology subservient to his theology of history. In 22:11, this would come to the fore in the terms "to make" (עשה) and "to fashion" (יער).

A survey of passages in which verbs of "to see" occur together with the verb "to make, to do" (עשה) seems to confirm this. The following texts are almost unanimously ascribed to the historical prophet and bear a strong resemblance to 22:11:

> 5:11–12   Woe to those who rise early in the morning, that they may run after strong drink, who tarry late into the evening till wine inflames

---

[5] It is the great merit of Wildberger's commentary on Isaiah 1–39 that time and again he points to this phenomenon.

them! They have lyre and harp, timbrel and flute and wine at their feasts; but they do not regard (לא יביטו) the deeds (פעל) of Yhwh, or see (לא ראו) all the work (מעשה) of his hands.

5:18–19 Woe to those who draw iniquity with cords of falsehood, who draw sin as with cart ropes; who say: "Let him make haste, let him speed his work (מעשהו) that we may see (נראה) it; let the purpose of the Holy One of Israel draw near, and let it come, that we may know it!"

17:7–8 On that day people will regard (ישעה) their Maker (עשהו), and their eyes will look (תראינה) to the Holy One of Israel; they will not have regard (לא ישעה) for the altars, the work (מעשה) of their hands, and they will not look (לא יראו) to what their own fingers have made (עשו), either the Asherim or the altars of incense.

While the two "woe" proverbs generally are ascribed to the historical prophet, there is some discussion about the authenticity of the third text. The redactional term "on that day," the broadened interest in the attitude of humankind towards the God of Israel and the topical change from war (17:1–3.9) to idolatry (17:7–8) lead some scholars to date these verses in the postexilic era (Wildberger, 650–51; Barth, Jesaja-Worte [1977] 207, 289; Blenkinsopp, 303ff.). Others, however, perceive in the universal orientation of these verses a striking resemblance with 2:10–22, a passage which also switches from Judah's lack of respect for their God in a particular political situation to the haughty neglect of Yhwh by humankind. Consequently, they date 17:1–11 as a whole in the period after the Syro-Ephraimite war (732–34), during the warming-up of the new revolt against Assyria (724; Sweeney, 255, 260–61). The dating question does not matter to our investigation. If these verses stem from the redaction, they only confirm that the topic of looking in the wrong instead of the right direction necessarily includes the issue of what Yhwh "does/makes" as opposed to what Israel, yea human beings, "do/make."

For the sake of completeness, we should take into consideration a group of Isaianic texts which express that eventually people will come to see what Yhwh has accomplished in Israel and on earth (18:3; 26:10–11; 29:23; 30:30; 32:3; 35:2). The topic, moreover, is not restricted to chs. 1–39. In chs. 40–66 it returns in the reproachful question whether anyone else has achieved what Yhwh has achieved (40:26; 41:5; 42:19–20; 53:1–2), and in the assurance that some day, people will see and recognize Yhwh's work in their midst (40:5; 41:20; 52:8; 66:14; cf. also the impious challenge of 66:5, familiar to that in 5:19).

(b) In favor of the latter interpretation which assumes Jerusalem to be the object of Yhwh's acting, it should be remarked that the verb "to fashion" (יצר) always has a specified grammatical object with it or an object supposed by the context (cf. the list in DCH IV, 269ff.; in the book of Isaiah, with God as subject: 27:11; 43:1.7.10.21; 44:2.9.10.12.21.24; 45:7.9.11.18; 46:11; 49:5; 64:7; with another subject: 30:14; 41:25; 54:17).[6] The only other text, apart from Isa 22:11, in which the object is not specified is 2 Kgs 19:25/Isa 37:26:

> Have you not heard from long ago? I have done it (אותה עשיתי). From ancient days I planned it (ויצרתיה). Now I bring it to pass that you should cause fortified cities to crash into heaps of ruins (translation of Oswalt, 657).

In this text, the objects of the verbs אותה עשיתי and ויצרתיה are generally considered to refer to the military campaign of the Assyrian king (vv. 26b–27) but here, too, we find an explanation that they refer to Jerusalem: "Have you not heard from afar that I made it in the days of yore? I.e. that I made Jerusalem? And that I formed it? Is it possible that now I brought it that it should be made desolate . . .?" (Redak according to Rosenberg, 298; this is also, according to Alexander, 68–69, the interpretation of Calvin). Although the context does not favor this explanation, its very existence confirms the earlier finding that normally the verb יצר requires a concrete object. This supports the thesis that 22:11b refers to Yhwh's "making/fashioning" of Jerusalem.

(c) If we overlook the results of the preceding semantic inquiry we come to the conclusion that both interpretations of v. 11b have a right to exist. The first clause, "you did not look (לא הבטתם) to him who made it (עשיה)," evokes the developments of the hostile attack on Jerusalem (cf. Lam 2:17: "Yhwh has done what he purposed"). The second clause, "you had no regard (לא ראיתם) for him who fashioned it (יצרה) long ago," zooms in on the fact that Yhwh has devised this same city. This interpretation is not a methodological running with the hare and hunting with the hounds. After all, the calamitous events which have befallen the city and its status as an artefact of God are tied together. From the human point of view it is a paradox, from the faith point of view it is a necessity. Yhwh allows the siege of Jerusalem because the city which he has founded does

---

[6] In 46,11, the object suffix refers to עצתי (Qere), "my counsel," in the preceding half verse (cf. Koole, 3/1, 515ff.; Hermisson, 135).

not meet its purpose, i.e. to be a city of justice and righteousness. This two-sidedness of Yhwh towards Jerusalem is an important topic, not only in the book of Isaiah (1:21–26; 3:1–4:6; 28:14–22; 29:2–8; 30:18–19; 31:4–9; 33:14–24; 54:4–8; 64:7–11) but all through the prophetic books (Jer 6:6–8; 22:7–9; Ezek 16:35–43; Hab 1:6–17; Ps 74; Lam 2; cf. ThWAT III, 937–38 [M. Tsevat]). Moreover, by putting two apparently contradictory deeds (the attack on Jerusalem and its formation long ago) on a par (in the frame of one bicolon), as achievements of Yhwh, the prophet clothes Yhwh's relationship to the city in a bewildering paradox.

In conclusion we can say the following. The short-sightedness of Jerusalem's inhabitants is not that they indulge in festivities and in general do not care for Yhwh. The issue at stake is not Epicureanism versus worship of the deity. Their sinful negligence consists of not perceiving that the deviser of their city himself encourages the enemies to mobilize against it because it does not comply with its particular purpose of being a city of justice. In other words, their guilt has to do with the very identity of Yhwh: "I myself have laid in Zion for a foundation a stone, a massive stone, a cornerstone valuable for a sure foundation. One who trusts will not shake! I will make righteousness the line, and justice the plummet" (Isa 28:16–17; cf. Isa 1:21–26; 8:18; 10:12; Ps 48:9; 74:2; 87:1–2; 102:17; 125:1–2; 127:1–2; 147:2). By way of a comparison, the two-sidedness of Yhwh returns after the exile in the embarrassing message that he who punished Jerusalem is also the one who will restore it (Isa 40:1; 49:14–23; 51:17–52:10; 54:1–8; 60:8–16; 62:1–9).

6. *The Guilt of Short-Sightedness*

The foregoing interpretation facilitates the explanation of the astonishing verdict: "Surely there will be no atonement of this iniquity for you till you die" (v. 14). Its severity is in line with what the current circumstances amount to: "the day of Yhwh" (vv. 5.8.12), but its irreconcilable character is perplexing. A hostile army marched against Jerusalem but the inhabitants did not perceive its significance (vv. 5–7.11). Instead of getting to the heart of the matter, i.e., that "he (Yhwh) took away the covering of Judah" (v. 8),[7] they confined themselves to the surface: an inspection of the defense works and

---

[7] The monocolon form underlines the importance of this statement.

efforts to improve them (vv. 8b–11a). While Yhwh intended the siege to provoke penance (v. 12), it led to banquets (v. 13). As serious an offense as this may be, the fact that forgiveness is beyond the bounds of the possible is bewildering.

For a clear understanding of the matter we must first take a look at the motivation of the debauchery: "For tomorrow we die" (v. 13). This statement is often considered either as calculating resignation in the light of human transitoriness or as cynism in the anxious foreboding that the seizure of the city will entail a vast slaughter. The latter interpretation is more plausible in the light of the adjuncts of time which accompany the sinful statement and Yhwh's corresponding verdict: "for tomorrow we die" (v. 13) and "till you die" (v. 14). The importance of this time factor ensues from the dominating background of "the day of Yhwh." It is also related, however, to the specific nature of Yhwh, "who fashioned it long ago" (v. 11).[8] By accepting imminent death as an inevitable fate, the inhabitants of Jerusalem failed to appreciate YHWH as the one who has devised their city and pledged himself to its permanence (Isa 26:1; Ps 46:6; 48:9; 87:5; 125:1).

In the book of Isaiah, underestimating Yhwh, not only as legislator but first of all as Israel's God who has engaged himself to the welfare of his people, is called "iniquity" (עָוֹן: 1:4; 5:18–19; 27:9; 30:13 [cf. 11]; 33:24 [cf. 22]; 40:2; 43:24; 50:1; 57:17; 59:2.12 [cf. 13]; 64:6.8 [cf. 7]; 65:7). It merits particular notice that v. 14 does not follow v. 11 immediately. The verdict is not motivated by Jerusalem's misunderstanding of Yhwh (v. 11) but in connection with the rejection of his call to penance (vv. 12–13). In other words, "that day" on which the hostile army laid siege to Jerusalem (v. 12 refers to v. 5) was not meant by Yhwh as a retaliation for the lack of deference to himself (v. 11) but as a warning, a chance to restore the broken relationship with him. The subsequent "joy and gladness" instead of weeping and mourning is not an expression of hedonism; it adds up to a repudiation of God's reconciliatory attitude. In this

---

[8] The temporal meaning of מֵרָחוֹק, in connection with the verb יצר (/ עשה), is beyond discussion because the verbs involved do not have the meaning of "coming" or "bringing" as is the case elsewhere (cf. Deut 28,49; Isa 5:26; 43:6; 49:12; 60:4.9; Hab 1:8). Yet, it may be true that the aspect of Yhwh's secrecy, conceived as local distance, plays a role in Isa 22:11 and 37:26 (Wildberger, 805, 808, 951, 955).—The temporal meaning of the expression regards either the past (cf. Isa 25:1; 37:26; Jer 31:3; 45:21 [also 30:10; 46:27; Ps 139:2; HALAT 1134]) or the future (2 Sam 7:19; [Ezek 12:27]; Mic 4:3).

way, the rejection of Yhwh's call to penance (v. 13) raises the lack of regard for "him who made it/who fashioned it long ago" (v. 11) to the second power.

Seen against this background, the judgement comes less as a surprise: "There will be no atonement of this iniquity for you till you die" (v. 14). For a full understanding of this irreconcilable verdict, it should be taken into account that in the Old Testament, either the priest or Yhwh is the agent of atonement but Yhwh is never the direct object of atonement. Atonement is vital for Israel because of its ongoing failures but it is not an act of compensation by Israel itself. It is Yhwh who offers atonement and brings it about (כפר) with Yhwh as grammatical or logical subject: Deut 21:8; 32:43; *1 Sam 3:14*; Isa 6:7; *27:9*; 28:18; *Jer 18:23*; Ezek 16:63; Ps 65:4; *78:38*; 79:9; *Dan 9:24*; 2 Chr 30:18; references in italics hold כפר + עון).

Given this semantic structure of the verb "to atone," the question arises whether or not Yhwh is the logical subject of the passive clause in v. 14: "This iniquity shall not be atoned for you." Two meanings are diametrically opposed to each other. Most scholars consider the passive verb form (יְכֻפַּר pual) as a *passivum divinum*, apparently on the basis of the oath formula "Surely" (אִם), preceded by an exceptional, emphatic introduction ("The Lord Yhwh of hosts has revealed himself in my ears"), and because of the fact that Yhwh is the acting person (v. 12 and v. 14) in this context of "the day of Yhwh" (v. 12 refers to v. 5).[9]

But then again there is the following view: "Im pass. כֻּפַּר wirkt die alte Anschauung (nämlich der 'synthetischen Lebensauffassung') noch nach: Es heißt nicht: Ich (Jahwe) werde euch diese Schuld nicht vergeben; כפר al meint: Das Schuldverhängnis nimmt unfehlbar seinen Lauf, die Schuld wird sich auswirken mit ihrem vollen Gewicht" (Wildberger, 829).

It seems possible to reconcile these opposing views. On the one hand, Yhwh should not too easily be assumed to be the logical subject of the passive clause: "This iniquity shall not be atoned for you." Since the context of the verdict raises the expectation of a strong performative statement with an active verb form, something like: "Surely, I shall not forgive...", the absence of such a clear pronouncement gives food for thought. On the other hand, since it is

---

[9] Janowski, *Sühne* (1982) 133–37; ThWAT IV, 315ff. (B. Lang).

the meaning of the preceding indictment that the inhabitants of Jerusalem pay no attention to Yhwh, in spite of his two initiatives to enter into their visual field ("the day of tumult" [v. 5] and the day of his call to penance [v. 12]), it would be strange if the text suggested that Yhwh leaves it to some impersonal, cosmic order to settle his conflict with the people of the city. If the announcement of the verdict comes as a personal revelation of Yhwh to the prophet (v. 14a), its execution must also be a personal revelation of him, under duress, to the people (v. 14b). Yhwh's standoffish way of speaking in the verdict might stem from an old worldview in which "iniquity" forms an ontological power, but it has also a specific theological impact. It does not openly tag Yhwh as someone who refuses atonement.[10] It makes it possible to interpret the lack of atonement as something which Jerusalem has to blame on itself.

If we understand v. 14 in this way, Yhwh does not stand in the way of atonement for Jerusalem's iniquity. On the contrary, it is the inhabitants of Jerusalem who have rejected first the message conveyed by "the day of Yhwh" (vv. 5–8), next Yhwh's call to penance (v. 13) and, by doing so, his atonement (v. 14). As a consequence, they bring their downfall on themselves because "die Negation der Vergebung ist reale Todesdrohung."[11]

7. *Summary*

"There is no history without meaning and no meaning without history." The editors of the In Memoriam Volume for Sjef van Tilborg have invited contributors to explain one biblical text or passage in the light of this adage. The foregoing study of Isa 22:1–14 has tried to give history its due, all of that and no more than that. The commonly accepted hypothesis that the Sitz im Leben of this passage is the festive atmosphere following the relief of Jerusalem in 701 (cf. Isa 37:36–37) was too much as meant for the history behind the text. We found out that the passage has created its own (hi)story. It forms an amalgam of various calamitous events which befell the city: the siege of 701, the downfall of 586, and other comparable dangers

---

[10] As a matter of fact, there is only one text in the Old Testament in which Yhwh is the subject of the verb "to atone" with a negation, moreover not in a statement of himself but in a plea addressed to him (Jer 18:23).

[11] Janowski, *Sühne* (1982) 117.

to its survival. These occurrences have flown together in one mourning situation into which the readers are transferred: a lament for the city which has been conquered and whose inhabitants are either slain or captured (vv. 1–4).

This creatively arranged story serves as an example of how Jerusalem and Yhwh associated with each other, or rather how Jerusalem failed to come up to Yhwh's expectations, with all the well-known consequences. In this way, history has been made subservient to the embarrassing question: Who is to blame for the ruin of the city and the death of its inhabitants? They themselves or Yhwh? Why was the door shut on atonement?

The answer lies in Jerusalem's double failure regarding Yhwh. First, when on "the day of Yhwh," the hostile army assaulted the city (vv. 5–7), the inhabitants stared in the wrong direction: they inspected the defense facilities but "did not look to him who made it/had no regard for him who fashioned it long ago" (vv. 8–11). They did not perceive that Yhwh allowed the enemies to lay siege to the city *not in spite of* the fact that he had formed Jerusalem long ago but *precisely because* he had done so with a special purpose. Secondly, when Yhwh called to penance in the perspective of the imminent calamity, they did not respond to his warning. Indeed the people drowned it by challenging each other to debauchery (vv. 12–13). The connections of this passage with the story of Isaiah's commissioning cannot be elaborated here,[12] but it should be evident that when Jerusalem's inhabitants fail to perceive who Yhwh really is, and fail, moreover, to listen to his summons to penance, the order with which the prophet Isaiah has been charged comes true:

6:9 Go and say to this people:
"Keep listening, but do not comprehend;
keep looking, but do not understand."
10 Make the mind of this people dull,
and stop their ears,
and shut their eyes,
so that they may not look with their eyes,
and listen with their ears,
and comprehend with their minds,
and turn and be healed.

---

[12] At first sight, two correspondences catch the eye: (1) The basic structure of ch. 6 consists of "I saw Yhwh" (v. 1) and "I heard Yhwh" while in ch. 22, the people "did not look to him" (v. 11) and according to v. 13, did not listen to him; (2) The prophet is granted atonement (6:7), the people reject it (22:14).

We must see the verdict in this light: "Surely, there will be no atonement of this iniquity for you till you die" (v. 14). The wording of the oath avoids suggesting that the inhabitants themselves could have arranged for atonement but refused to do so. The sentence remains loyal to the (non-priestly) theology of atonement: Yhwh is the subject; the people are the object of atonement. The wording also avoids stating that Yhwh refuses to grant atonement. This would be inconsistent with the fact that "he fashioned it (i.e., Jerusalem) long ago" (v. 11). Instead, while respecting the belief that only Yhwh is the author of atonement, the verdict lays the guilt of the fact that it has not come off, even in the sight of death, with the inhabitants. Thereby atonement does not fully disappear from the scene. The readers are left with the question: When will Yhwh's atonement get a new chance? We have to read on, for an answer to this burning issue, to the next text about atonement of iniquity in the book of Isaiah: "Therefore by this the iniquity of Jacob will be atoned, and this will be the full fruit of the removal of his sin: when he makes all the stones of the altars like chalkstones crushed to pieces, no Asherim or incense altars will remain standing" (27:9). The charter of Jerusalem does not allow for the veneration of another god than of "him who fashioned it long ago."[13]

Bibliography

Commentaries on Isaiah (mentioned by name only)

Alexander, J.A., *Commentary on the Prophecies of Isaiah I–II*, Philadelphia ²1875 (reprint Grand Rapids 1976).
Blenkinsopp, J., *Isaiah 1–39* (AB 19), New York 2000.
Childs, B.S., *Isaiah* (OTL), Louisville, KY 2001.
Clements, R.E., *Isaiah 1–39* (NCeB), Grand Rapids 1980.
Delitzsch, F., *Commentar über das Buch Jesaia* (BC III/1), Leipzig ⁴1889.
Driver, G.R., "Isaiah I–XXXIX: Textual and Linguistic Problems" in: *JSS* 13 (1968) 36–57.
Duhm, B., *Das Buch Jesaia* (GöHAT III/1), Göttingen ⁴1922, Nachdruck 1968.
Feldmann, F., *Das Buch Isaias I. Kap. 1–39* (EHAT 14), Münster/Westf. 1925.
Friedlaender, M. (ed.), *The Commentary of Ibn Ezra on Isaiah*, London 1873.
Hermisson, H.-J., *Deuterojesaja. Bd. 2: Jes 45, 8–49, 13* (BK.AT XI/2), Neukirchen 2003.
Hirsch, J., *Das Buch Jesaia*, Frankfurt am Main 1911.

---

[13] I am most grateful to my colleague and old friend Dr. Sean McEvenue (Lafayette, LA, USA) for correcting my first English draft of the article.

Hitzig, F., *Der Prophet Jesaja*, Heidelberg 1833.
Ibn Ezra, s. Friedlaender, M.
Kaiser, O., *Der Prophet Jesaja. Kapitel 13–39* (ATD 18), Göttingen 1973.
König, E., *Das Buch Jesaja*, Gütersloh 1926.
Koole, J.L., *Isaiah Part 3, Volume 1: Isaiah 40–48* (HCOT), Kampen 1997.
Oswalt, J.N., *The Book of Isaiah. Chapters 13–39* (NICOT), Grand Rapids 1986.
Penna, A., *Isaia* (La Sacra Bibbia), Torino 1958.
Rashi, see Rosenberg, A.J.
Rosenberg, A.J., *Isaiah I. Translation of Text, Rashi and Commentary* (Miqra'ot Gedolot), New York 1982.
Schoors, A., *Jesaja* (BOT IX), Roermond 1972.
Sweeney, M.A., *Isaiah 1–39 with an Introduction to Prophetic Literature* (FOTL XVI), Grand Rapids 1996.
Vitringa, C., *Commentarius in librum prophetiarum Jesaiae. Pars Posterior*, Herbornae Nassaviorum 1722.
Watts, J.D.W., *Isaiah 1–33, 34–66* (WBC 24–25), Waco 1985, 1987.
Wildberger, H., *Jesaja. Bd. I: Jesaja 1–12. Bd. II: Jesaja 13–27. Bd. III Jesaja 28–39* (BK.AT X/1,2,3), Neukirchen 1972, 1978, 1982.

Other Works

Barth, H., *Die Jesaja-Worte in der Josiazeit. Israel und Assur als Thema einer produktiven Neuinterpretation der Jesajaüberlieferung* (WMANT 48), Neukirchen 1977.
Berges, U., *Das Buch Jesaja. Komposition und Endgestalt* (HBS 16), Freiburg 1998.
——, *Klagelieder* (HThKAT), Freiburg, Basel, Wien 2002.
Bosshard-Nepustil, E., "Beobachtungen zum Zwölfprophetenbuch" in: *BN* 40 (1987) 30–62.
——, *Rezeptionen von Jesaja 1–39 im Zwölfprophetenbuch. Untersuchungen zur literarischen Verbindung von Prophetenbüchern in babylonischer und persischer Zeit* (OBO 154), Freiburg/Göttingen 1997.
Clements, R.E, *Isaiah and the Deliverance of Jerusalem. A Study of the Interpretation of Prophecy in the Old Testament* (JSOT.S 13), Sheffield 1980.
Gallagher, W.R., *Sennacherib's Campaign to Judah* (SHCANE XVIII), Leiden 1999.
Hayes, J.H., and Irvine, S.A., *Isaiah The Eighth-Century Prophet. His Times and His Preaching*, Nashville 1987.
Jahnow, H., *Das hebräische Leichenlied im Rahmen der Völkerdichtung* (BZAW 36), Gießen 1923.
Janowski, B., *Sühne als Heilsgeschehen. Studien zur Sühnetheologie der Priesterschrift und zur Wurzel KPR im Alten Orient und im Alten Testament* (WMANT 55), Neukirchen 1982.
Jastrow, M., *A Dictionary of the Targumim, Talmud Babli, Yerushalmi and Midrashic Literature*, Philadelphia 1903 (reprint Tel-Aviv 1972).
Joüon, P./Muraoka, T., *A Grammar of Biblical Hebrew I–II* (SubBi 14/I–II), Roma 1991.
Kutscher, E.Y., *The Language and Linguistic Background of the Isaiah Scroll (1 QIsaa)* (StTDJ VI), Leiden 1974.
Labahn, A., "Trauer als Bewältigung der Vergangenheit zur Gestaltung der Zukunft. Bemerkungen zur anthropologischen Theologie der Klagelieder" in: *VT* 52 (2002) 513–27.
Weippert, M., "Zum Text von Ps 19,5 und Jes 22,5" in: *ZAW* 73 (1961) 97–99.

CHAPTER THREE

ONE DAY, THREE DAYS, AND FORTY DAYS
IN THE BOOK OF JONAH

Erik Eynikel
University of Nijmegen, the Netherlands

The book of Jonah uses four indications of time: one day is the duration of Jonah's journey when entering the city; he spends three days and three nights in the belly of the great fish; three days are needed to cross the city of Nineveh; and forty days represents the time period before Nineveh will be turned upside down. Obviously these numbers possess symbolic value. Research on the use and meaning of these numbers has already been reported in previous literature. This paper will focus on these results and will apply them to the context of Jonah. We begin by studying the use of "one day."

The number *one* is most often used in the form of an adjective (cf. its place in Hebrew after the noun). *One day* obviously refers to a short period of time. For example Rebecca says to Jacob after learning of Esau's plan to take revenge: "Flee to Laban my brother in Haran, and stay with him a while, until your brother's fury turns away; ... Why should I lose you both in one day?" Another example is 1 Sam 2:34 where it is announced that Hofni and Pinehas will die in one day. There are many other examples where this expression indicates an unusually short period of time during which an event (mostly catastrophic) will occur. But "one day" in these examples refers literally to "one solar day" and, although unusual, what happens on that day is not impossible or totally unrealistic. Consequently, the indication of time is not purely symbolic; it is the unusual brevity, which adds an extra dimension to a realistic situation. A different picture is found in the prophetic literature and more specifically in Isa where the unusual short indication of time "one day" is part of a totally unrealistic and metaphorical picture: Isa 66:8: "Who has heard such a thing? Who has seen such a thing? Shall a land be born in one day? Shall a nation be brought forth in one moment? For as soon as Zion was in labour she brought forth her sons." The answer to the questions in v. 8 is obviously "no," unless we are witnessing a miracle here. The enigmatic short utterance is an exception to the natural course of affairs and the indication of time is part of the miraculous message: Zion will be delivered in "a miraculously short time."[1]

Let us turn now to examples where "one day" is used with verbs of motion as in Jonah 3:4. There are only a few examples of such use in the OT: beside Jonah 3:4 there is the text of 1 Kings 19:4 (Elijah goes a day's journey into the desert) and Ezr 4:34 "the earth is vast, and heaven is high, and the sun is swift in its course, for it makes the circuit of the heavens and returns to its place in one day." In this example "one day" is certainly a short period of time because the circuit of the heavens is a long distance that the sun completes in only one day, but here again "one day" is literally one solar day, the time necessary for the sun to complete one "revolution."

The text about Elijah in 1 Kings 19:4 is a closer parallel because of the expression: הלך דרך יום (the number "one" in "a day's journey" is absent but must be understood; i.e., הלך דרך יום אחד which is very similar to אחד מהלך יום in Jonah 3:4). Elijah did not go far into the desert before he became discouraged and wanted to die. It is universally recognized that there are many similarities between the story of Jonah and that of Elijah in 1 Kings 19 (Elijah's deathwish in 1 Kings 19:4 and Jonah's in Jonah 4, etc.).[2] However, this parallel use of "one day" has not received the attention it deserved. Elijah did not travel into the desert any longer than one day's journey, neither did Jonah travel further than a one day's walk into the city of Nineveh (although the city was "a three day's journey"). Jonah did not even travel as far as the city center to deliver his prophecy; he stayed at the periphery of the city. Before going into further details I would like to mention the view advanced by D. Marcus in a paper presented at the SBL meeting in Washington, D.C., in November 1993 entitled: "Jonah's Nineveh: the 'Big Apple' of the East (Jonah

---

[1] Another example: Isa 47:9 and most probably also Zech 2:9. Compare also 2 Petr 3:8: "But do not ignore this one fact, beloved, that with the Lord one day is like a thousand years, and a thousand years are like one day." In this text the day indication is obviously symbolic and refers to a very short period of time (for God) in contrast with an extremely long period for men (1000 years).

[2] See for further similarities, e.g., E. Eynikel, "Jonah," in: W.R. Farmer et al. (eds.), *International Bible Commentary*, Collegeville: Liturgical Press, 1998, p. 1151.

3:3)." Marcus adduced cuneiform parallels where the expression "a one day journey" occurs.³ He specifically cites several cuneiform texts where the phrase "a one day's journey" is used to indicate a short journey. Three days, on the contrary, means a long journey, especially in relation to troop movements and military campaigns.

There are indeed references in Sumerian, Accadian, and in the Ugaritic literature where these expressions occur; e.g., in the context of a military campaign: a "one day's march" is a short trip; a "three day's march" is a long journey. Therefore according to Marcus the expression מהלך שלשת ימים in Jonah 3:3 refers to the distance that Jonah must travel to reach Nineveh. So the phrase "Nineveh is a three day's walk" suggests that travelling from Jerusalem to Nineveh is a very long journey. However, for Jonah it was only a short journey, "a one day's walk." To prove his thesis Marcus refers to Elijah, who in the already mentioned passage of 1 Kings 19, travels from Palestine to Mount Horeb in forty days which has to be considered as another example of "a prophetic, athletic top performance." In contrast to the Israelites, who needed nearly forty years, for Elijah to travel from Mount Horeb to the Promised Land was only a short journey away. The problems with Marcus' thesis, however, are considerable: first of all it is never mentioned in Jonah that Nineveh was a distant city. Secondly the expression: "a three day's walk" relates to Nineveh's size. Jonah 3:3 states that Nineveh was "a large city for God," an expression that is considered by most exegetes as some kind of superlative: "a godalmighty big city"⁴ or better as Vawter translates it: "a godawfully big city."⁵ In my view, the size of

---

³ D. Marcus, "Jonah's Nineveh: the 'Big Apple' of the East (Jonah 3:3)," in: E.H. Lovering, Jr. et al. (eds.), *AAR/SBL Abstracts 1993*, Atlanta: Scholars Press, 1993, p. 195. His paper was later published as "Nineveh's 'Three Day's Walk' (Jonah 3:3): Another Interpretation,' in: Stephen L. Cook and S.C. Winter (eds.), *On the Way to Nineveh: Studies in Honor of George M. Landes* (ASOR books 4), Atlanta: Scholars Press, 1999, pp. 42–48.

⁴ J. Day, "The Book of Jonah," in: A.S. van der, (ed.), *In Quest of the Past: Studies on Israelite Religion, Literature and Prophetism* (OTS 26), Leiden: Brill, 1990, p. 34. F. Trible, *Rhetorical Criticism. Context, Method, and the Book of Jonah* (Old Testament Series), Minneapolis: Fortress Press, p. 178, criticizes the view that the expression is a superlative. She states that the expression "great-*le*-God" lends itself to various interpretations: it can mean "so great that it impresses even God" or "divine favour" or the "divine abode." I am convinced, however, because of all the wickedness that was present in Nineveh (Jonah 1:2), that only the first interpretation is correct and that, therefore, the expression can be interpreted as a *kind* of superlative.

⁵ B. Vawter, *Job and Jonah: Questioning the Hidden God*, New York: Ramsey, 1983, p. 105.

the city stands in relation to its wickedness: the larger the city, the more wicked it will be. Therefore explaining "a three day's walk" as referring to the long distance between Jerusalem and Nineveh, as D. Marcus does, does not make much sense. However if the indication מהלך שלשת ימים refers to the size of the city: the statement that Jonah entered the city after only a one day's journey implies that he did not reach the city center. We will come back to this point later; first, however, we need to study the use of the number three in the context of *three days*.

Three is the smallest plural.[6] Three sometimes means "some," for example when the Aramaeans threaten Joash, Elisha orders Joash to strike the ground with arrows. Joash strikes the ground three times. Elisha becomes angry and says: "You should have struck the ground five or six times; now you will strike down Aram only three times" (2 Kings 13:19). It is obvious that Joash struck only three times because "three" is a conventionally complete set. Many other examples can be found in the Prophetic and other Biblical texts where three is used as a conventional plural; to indicate completeness or full effect; three days, travel into the desert are necessary for a pilgrimage to the Lord (Exod 3:18; 5:3); three times a year an Israelite needs to appear before the Lord (Exod 23:17), etc.

When we study periods of time related to the number three, i.e., three years, three months, and three days, we see that they all view "three" as a conventional, considerable lapse of time. Isaiah 20:3 states "Isaiah has walked three years barefoot" while 2 Sam 6:11 notes that the ark stayed for three months with Obed-Edom.

In 2 Sam 24:11-12 David is allowed to choose which punishment he prefers for transgressing the prohibition on the population count: "Seven years of famine; three months fleeing for his enemies or three days of pestilence in the land." David chooses the last option because he prefers to depend on God rather than on men. This example is interesting for our study of Jonah because it shows that "three days" is sometimes the absolute limit of human endurance: "three days" means "to the limit." Another example of this limit is found in the

---

[6] J. Hehn, *Siebenzahl und Sabbat bei den Babyloniern und im Alten Testament: eine religionsgeschichtliche Studie* (Leipziger semitistische Studien 2,5), Leipzig: Hinrichs, 1907, pp. 69-72. B.J. Segal, "Numerals in the Old Testament," in: *JSS* 10 (1965) 2: "For Semites Plurality Begins with the Number 3." See C. Houtman, *Exodus Deel* 1 1:1-7:13 (COT) Kampen: Kok, 1986, p. 75.

plague of darkness: "for three days there was no light" (Exod 10:22–23).

Jonah's stay in the belly of the fish also lasts three days and three nights. Obviously, the above examples suggest that "three days" refers here to "the bitter end." Other examples can be found in Exod 15:22: "They went for three days in the wilderness (of Shur) and found no water" and 1 Sam 30:12 where the Egyptian, whom David and his men found, had been left behind for three days and had not eaten for three days and three nights. According to Jack Sasson[7] this is the only other passage where "three days and three nights" occurs in the OT. He insists (contra Landes)[8] that this phrase refers not so much to the famished state of the Egyptian, but to the long distance between the Amalekites and David, this suggesting that the Amalekites were beyond reach. This would provide additional evidence for the view that "three days" can indicate a considerable distance. To strengthen his claim Sasson adds another example: Judith 2:21, where it is said that Holofernes' troops marched for three days to cover the distance between Nineveh and Bectileh. We, however, cannot help thinking that in 1 Sam 30:14 "he had not eaten for three days and three nights" not only refers to distance but also to an extreme limit of endurance. Esther 4:16, with vocabulary very close to that in 1 Sam 30:17, further illustrates this point: Esther calls upon the Jews to fast אל־אכלו אל־תשתו שלשת ימים. Here the context clearly points to the lapse of time, not to distance, and indicates the outer limits of human endurance. This is also the meaning in Jonah 2:1. The phrase there demonstrates that Jonah is in a very precarious situation. Only the Lord himself can save him. Hos 6:1–2 is very illustrative in this regard: "Come let us return to the Lord; for he has torn, that he may heal us; he has stricken, and he will bind us up. After two days he will revive us; on the third day he will raise us up." This passage is not a perfect parallel to Jonah's

---

[7] J. Sasson, *Jonah* (AB 24B), New York: Doubleday, 1990, p. 153.
[8] G.M. Landes: "The Three Days and Three Nights Motive in Jonah 2:1," in: *JBL* 86 (1976) 446–50. Furthermore, J. Sasson, *Jonah*, pp. 153–54, rightly critiques G.M. Landes' claim (*JBL* 86 (1976) 449), who stated that "three days and three nights" refers to "the time span the fish is assigned to return Jonah from Sheol to the dry land." To Sasson's two counter-arguments: 1) What about the time the fish took to get him there (= Sheol)? 2) We can hardly use (as Landes does) 2:1 as a commentary on 2:7; such an approach risks turning the psalm into a travel guide to hell and back, we would add: "three days and three nights" in Jonah 2:1 refers to the long time that Jonah was in his hopeless situation *in* the fish (symbol of Sheol).

situation because Hosea speaks of "reviving already after two days" but it illustrates how bad Jonah's situation is. Even after three days and three nights Jonah is still in deep trouble. "Deep" is an appropriate adjective here because the fish represents Sheol as the psalm demonstrates. Other examples can be found in the NT (John 11, where Lazarus has been dead for more than three days and Matt 12:10, Jesus himself is raised from the dead on the third day) and in Sumerian literature (Innana stayed for three days and three nights in the land of "no return." Then her messenger starts to cry to Enlil and the other gods to save her).[9]

In Jonah 3:3 we have מהלך שלשת ימים. Here the expression "three days" has a somewhat different connotation.[10] Three days, as we

---

[9] J. Pritchard (eds.), *ANET*, pp. 52–57 (reference on p. 55, l. 169). In the Akkadian version that differs considerably from the Sumerian version the reference to the "three days" is missing; see A. Ungnad, H. Ranke, H. Gressmann (eds.) *Altorientalische Texte und Bilder zum Alten Testamente*, Tübingen: Mohr Siebeck, 1926–1927², pp. 206–7. See further F. Nötscher, "Zur Auferstehung nach drei Tagen," in: *Biblica* 31 (1950) 237–41 (= Id. in: *Vom alten und neuen Testament. Gesammelte Aufsätze* (BBB 17), Bonn: Peter Heinstein Verlag, 1962, pp. 231–36).

[10] D.L. Christensen, "Jonah and the Sabbath Rest in the Pentateuch," in: G. Braulik, W. Gross and S. McEvenue (eds.), *Biblische Theologie und gesellschaftlicher Wandel. Für Norbert Lohfink SJ*, Freiburg-Basel-Wien: Herder, 1993, pp. 48–60, struggles with the reference to "a journey of three days": "what is less clear is how to interpret the reference to Nineveh in Jonah 3:3 as 'a journey of three days'" (p. 51). In his article Christensen develops a suggestion of I. Kikawada and E. Hesse ("Jonah and Gensis 11–1 (sic.)," in: *Annual of the Japanese Biblical Institute* 1 (1971) 3–21), that there is a literary relationship between Jonah and the seven days of creation. He combines "the three day journey" in Jonah 3:3 with the period from the moment that Jonah delivers his message till the end of the story. This time span is, according to Christensen, also 3 days: following speaking his prophetic words in 3:4 Jonah goes outside the city to build his booth (day 1), through the following day when the plant grows that brought Jonah great joy (day 2) till the final day when the worm kills the plant which makes Jonah angry again, followed by the dialogue between Jonah and God (day 3). There the book ends but, according to Christensen, since Jonah was also "three days in the belly of the fish" (2:1) it is possible to detect a 3+3 structure in the book: three days in chapters 1–2 and three days in 3–4. Consequently "the seventh day of 'Sabbath' rest is not included within the structure of the book of Jonah itself, but is to be found in the implied ending to the story. If Jonah listens to God and 'turns from' his anger, he will experience the seventh day as the 'Sabbath rest' of Genesis 1. If not, he will perish." This reconstruction of Christensen is, however, problematic in its own chronology. Jonah entered the city of Nineveh, a one day's journey, but the city was a three days' journey. Later he settled down under his booth *east of the city*, which means that he needed the full three days to cross the city, because Jonah, coming from Jerusalem, came from the west. Therefore we need to count two additional days before Jonah builds his booth. In other words, the "implied ending to the story" does not fall on day 7 but on day 9 if we follow Christensen's argument and then we lose all "implied" sabbatical symbolism that Christensen wants us to accept.

have seen above, can refer to a distance. Because of the combination of שְׁלֹשֶׁת יָמִים with מַהֲלַךְ, this is certainly the case here. The noun מַהֲלַךְ is not used very often in the OT. Apart from Jonah it occurs in Ezek 42:2 and Zech 3:7 where the word means "access or room to walk." In Neh 2:6 Artaxerxes asks Nehemiah: "How long will your journey be and when will you return?" The question refers to Nehemiah's journey form Susa to Jerusalem. The extra-biblical material also shows that מַהֲלַךְ שְׁלֹשֶׁת יָמִים has to be interpreted as a trajectory, a distance from one spot to another, from point a to point b. This excludes certain hypotheses put forward earlier, e.g., that "three days" refers to the time Jonah needs to walk through all the streets of Nineveh. Van der Woude hesitatingly adopts that interpretation when he says that the phrase refers to the time Jonah needs to visit the most important places in the city.[11] Another interpretation that is to be excluded is one that views the phrase in terms of the circumference around Nineveh because מַהֲלַךְ refers to a journey from point a to point b, but these points never coincide.[12] This argument also refutes the assertion that "three days" refers to the time that Jonah needs to visit the city: one day for travelling to Nineveh, one day for doing business, and one day for returning.[13] Moreover Jonah is not sent to Nineveh to negotiate business.

There remains only one possibility: the expression refers to the diameter of the city. The following verse confirms this interpretation: "Jonah began to enter *into* the city"; not around the city. Here we encounter, of course, an urban problem because Nineveh was never such a large city that one needed three days to cross it. Some therefore refer to the so-called Assyrian triangle: between the Tigris and the Big Zab.[14]

---

[11] A.S. van der Woude, *Jona Nahum* (POT), Nijkerk: Callenbach, 1978, p. 45. So also U. Simon, *Jona. Ein jüdischer Kommentar* (Stuttgarter Bibelstudien 157), Stuttgart: Verlag Katholisches Bibelwerk, 1994, p. 112; and Id. *The JPS Bible Commentary: Jonah. The Traditional Hebrew Text with the New JPS Translation*, Philadelphia: The Jewish Publication Society, 1999, p. 28.

[12] That "a three days' journey" refers to the circumference of Nineveh has been suggested because the diameter of Nineveh was never longer than 5 kilometers on the longest side, which means that it was possible to cross the city in less than two hours. But even walking all around Nineveh's city wall (12 kilometers) would only take a few hours.

[13] D.J. Wiseman, "Jonah's Nineveh," in: *Tyndale Bulletin* 30 (1979) 37–38.

[14] See, e.g., L.C. Allen, *The Books of Joel, Obadiah, Jonah and Micah* (The New International Commentary on the Old Testament), Grand Rapids: Eerdmans, 1976, pp. 221–22, who defines Nineveh in the book of Jonah as "greater Nineveh," the

Sasson cites ancient Greek writers (Herodotus 1.191 and Aristotle Politeia 3.5.1276a) who recount that it took three days before the Babylonians in the city center became aware that the Persians had captured the Babylonian city walls. These traditions and evidence in the book of Jonah itself (Nineveh as "a large city," "a godalmighty large city," with its immense population mentioned in 4:11) suggest interpreting the expression as an indication of the immense physical size of Nineveh. We may not, however, separate this feature from the information given in 3:4: Jonah did not enter the city of Nineveh any further than a one day's walk (although the city was "a three day's journey"). Consequently, Jonah did not even go as far as the city centre. Sasson explains this point in his discussion of the verb החל (hi: to begin) in combination with an infinitive. He concludes that Jonah did not even walk a full day before commencing his announcement; instead, he proclaimed his threat to the Ninevites sometime during the first day. Sasson therefore adds the word "hardly" in his translation of 3:4: "Hardly had Jonah begun to go into the city one day...." We have to concentrate now on the words of Jonah to better understand his behavior. These words contain the final indication of time in the book: "Forty more days, and Nineveh overturns" (Jonah 3:4).

We need now to study the use of *four* and its derivatives.[15] Four can convey the notion of completeness as with the four directions of the winds; the four corners of the land (Isa 11:12; Jer 49:36; Ez 7:2; 37:9; Dan 7:2; 8:8; 11:4; Zech 2:11; 6:5); the four rivers in Eden (Gen 2:10–14). But these instances may be the result of Mesopotamian influence. Four and its derivatives in the Old Testament often possess a negative connotation. Especially in Judges chapters 19–21 four plays an important and negative role. The concubine of the Levite is four months away from home (Judg 19:2); the Levite, who went

---

administrative triangle stretching from Khorsabad in the north to Nineveh and Nimrod in the east. But there is no trace in the administrative texts that shows that this whole area was ever called "Nineveh." Moreover, historicizing the indication "a three days' walk" of Jonah 3:4 is completely missing the point. For example, A.H. Ehrlich, *Randglossen zur hebräischen Bibel: Textkritisches, Sprachliches und Sachliches*, vol. 5, Hildesheim: Olms, 1968 (= Leipzig, 1912), p. 269, calculated that Nineveh had a diameter of fifteen times that of London, and that one indeed needed three days to get across it. Where such a Nineveh was situated will always remain an enigma.

[15] For a study of the numeral 40 in the Babylonian, Mandaean, Israelite, and Arabic material, see W.H. Roscher, *Die Zahl 40 im Glauben, Brauch und Schrifttum der Semiten. Ein Beitrag zur vergleichenden Religionswissenschaft, Volkskunde und Zahlenmystik*, Leipzig: B.G. Teubner, 1909.

to get her, stayed four full days in her father's house (Judg 19:4–7); later when it comes to a battle between the Israelites and the Benjaminites, the former raise an army of 40,000 men (Judg 20:17). The 600 Benjaminites that are left after the battle hide for four months among the rocks of Rimmon (Judg 20:47). Later, they carry off 400 virgins from Jabesh-Gilead (Judg 21:12). Many other examples could be cited where the figure four has a negative connotation, but for the sake of brevity we need to concentrate on the number four relating to time as in the above example from Judges 19:4–7. There are more examples of indications of time in connection with the number forty: Goliath challenges the Israelites for forty days (1 Sam 17:16); the rain during the deluge lasted forty days and forty nights (Gen 7). The hegemony of the Philistines over the Israelites lasted forty years (Judg 13:1). Beside these purely negative examples, we can note the ambivalent use of four and its derivatives: Moses stayed for forty days and forty nights without eating and drinking on the mountain (Exod 24:18; 34:28; Deut 9:9, 11). During his second stay of forty days (Exod 34:28) he prayed for the Israelites to keep God from destroying them. He fasted and repented himself rather than imposing such practices on the people and God hearkened to him and did not execute the punishment. Thus, forty in the context of time often has not only a negative connotation but sometimes suggests a new and better future. See, for instance, also Jesus' sojourn in the desert of Judah. Other examples we have cited show a similar picture: a better future lies ahead after the forty days and forty nights of rain or when, after Elijah's journey to the mountain during forty days, he reaches Mount Horeb where God appears to him.[16]

The LXX version of Jonah speaks in 3:4 of *three* days and Nineveh shall be overthrown: ἔτι τρεῖς ἡμέραι καὶ Νινευη καταστραφήσεται (instead of forty days). This is accepted by some as being the original reading because of the other use of "three days" in the book of Jonah: the size of the city ("a three day's journey") and Jonah's three days and three nights in the fish, and also because days seems much too long a period of time.[17] If the Ninevites have forty days

---

[16] J. Krasovec, "Salvation of the Rebellious Prophet Jonah and of the Penitent Heathen Sinners," in *Svensk Exegetisk Årsbok* 61 (1996) 61, only refers to this meaning of the time indication for forty days: "a period suited to a special opportunity, a retreat or fasting." This definition of the symbolic meaning of forty days refers only to the positive connotations of the time indication and misses the negative aspect of four and its derivatives.

[17] S.J. Lawson, "The Power of Biblical Preaching: An Expository Study of Jonah

before their city will be destroyed they still have plenty of time to prepare themselves or to leave town. However, these arguments support the view that the LXX translator changed the number *forty* to *three* and that forty is the *lectio difficilior*. We therefore need to study the verb הפך that Jonah uses to explain its use in combination with of forty. הפך means "to overthrow."[18] It is used in the Qal with the meaning "to destroy": Sodom and Gomorrah and other cities are said to be overthrown,[19] meaning to be destroyed. The words of Jonah can mean then: "Forty more days and Nineveh will be destroyed." This is what the LXX understood: Νινευη καταστραφήσεται. The Vulgate and Targum interpret it similarly. Another possible translation for the niphal of הפך is, however: "reform, to turn over oneself."[20] This was defended already long ago in rabbinical interpretations and by Philo, as Sasson demonstrated.[21] But also Rashi noted that "God strategically used a word about turning around that can itself be turned around and can speak simultaneously of forgiveness and disaster."[22] Sasson himself proposes a third position: הפך is used with deliberate ambiguity, a suggestion, which is found already in the Talmud (Sanhedrin 89b), in medieval Jewish commentaries and many

---

3:1–10," in *Bibliotheca Sacra* 158 (2001) 339, misses this point completely when he writes "he (= Jonah) held forth a brief window of time—forty days—in which the Ninevites could repent."

[18] A.H. Kamp, *Innerlijke werelden. Een Cognitief Taalkundige Benadering van het Bijbelboek Jona*, Hengelo: Selbstverlag: 2002, pp. 174–76, gives a detailed semantic study of the verb הפך.

[19] Gen 19:21, 25; Deut 29:22; 2 Sam 10:3; Isa 20:16; 49:18; 50:40; Am 4:11; Lam 4:6.

[20] See the similarity in the English expressions "to be overturned" (= be destroyed) and "to turn over" (a new leaf) (= to reform, to start anew).

[21] J. Sasson, *Jonah*, p. 234. Cf. also Pseudo-Philo, *De Jona* c. 46 § 186; see Folker Siegert, *Drei hellenistisch-jüdische Predigten. Ps. Philon, "Über Jona, 'Über Simon' und 'Über die Gottesbezeichnung 'wohltätig verzehrendes Feuer,'"* vol. 1 *Übersetzung aus dem Armenischen und sprachliche Erläuterungen* (WUNT 20), Tübingen: J.C.B. Mohr, 1980, pp. 43–44; vol. II: *Kommentar nebst Beobachtungen zur hellenistischen Vorgeschichte der Bibelhermeneutik* (WUNT 61), Tübingen: J.C.B. Mohr, 1992, pp. 211–12; cf. further: B. Ego, "The Repentance of Nineveh in the Story of Jonah and Nahum's Prophecy of the City's Destruction. Aggadic Solutions for an Exegetical Problem in the Book of the Twelve," in Society of Biblical Literature (ed.), *Society of Biblical Literature 2000 Seminar Papers 39*, Atlanta: SBL, 2000, pp. 243–53.

[22] Rashi on Jonah 3:4 in A.J. Rosenberg (ed. and transl.), *The Book of the Twelve Prophets: Translation of Text, Rashi and Commentary*, New York: Judaica Press, 1991, p. 190. Cf. Y. Sherwood, "Cross-Currents in the Book of Jonah: Some Jewish and Cultural Midrashim on a Traditional Text," in: *Biblical Interpretation* 6 (1998) 70; cf. also her *A Biblical Text and Its Afterlife. The Survival of Jonah in Western Culture*, Cambridge: Cambridge University Press, 2000, pp. 177, 266–67.

modern studies.²³ According to Sasson it is only God, certainly not Jonah but also not the Ninevites, who intended הפך to have this meaning. In his omniscient knowledge, God knew all along that the Ninevites would reform; that is why he let Jonah proclaim or predict: "Forty more days and Nineveh will *reform*." However, according to Sasson, the Ninevites understood the word הפך in the same way Jonah did: *to destroy*. They repented because they realized that they were threatened with total destruction. I am convinced that the ambiguity to which Sasson appeals is present in the use of הפך here, but I am not convinced that the Ninevites missed that double understanding. The verb הפך is used elsewhere in the OT to describe someone's inclination: in 1 Sam 10:9 God gave Saul another heart (changed his heart); also Ps 30:12: "you have turned my mourning into dancing";²⁴ and even once in the niphal in Ex 14:5: "The heart of the Pharaoh was changed." I am convinced that in Jonah the Ninevites are well aware of the possibility of their reform, as well as the possible threat that hangs over their heads. But Jonah intended his prophetic words only negatively. That is why he did not announce what God had commissioned him to say in 1:2. God commissioned him to announce that the wickedness of Nineveh has come up before Him.²⁵ Jonah, however, did not mention the city's wickedness; nor did he explicitly mention its possibility of reform. He did not even mention God at all. His intention was to proclaim only unconditional doom. I agree with the many authors who see a sort of sabotage in Jonah's behavior.²⁶ This begins with his fleeing to Tarshish and

---

²³ R. Clements, *The Purpose of the Book of Jonah* (SVT 28), Leiden: Brill, 1975, pp. 24; B. Halpern and R.E. Friedman, "Composition and Paronomasia in the Book of Jonah," in: *Hebrew Annual Review* 4 (1980) 87; D. Stuart, *Hosea—Jonah* (WBC 31), Waco, TX, 1987, 489; P. Trible, "Divine Incongruities in the Book of Jonah," in: Tod Linafelt and Timothy K. Beal, *God in the Fray. A Tribute to Walter Brueggemann*, Minneapolis: Fortress Press, 1998, p. 000; see also Id. *Rhetorical Criticism*, p. 180; Y. Peleg, "'Yet Forty Days, and Nineveh Shall Be Overthrown' (Jonah 4:3). Two Readings (shtei krie'ot) of the Book of Jonah," in: *Beth Mikra* 158 (199) 226–42.
²⁴ See also Ps 105:25; Sef 3:9.
²⁵ This interpretation takes כי as a conjunction introducing indirect speech. כי can, of course, also be a causal conjunction introducing a subordinate causal clause. Since ambiguity is a major feature of the book of Jonah, both usages are probably intended at the same time.
²⁶ Contra J. Krasovec in: *Svensk Exegetisk Årsbok* 61 (1996) 69 who explains Jonah's attitude not as a result of "the sin of stubbornness but by a lack of knowledge." Krasovec argues for this view by referring to Jonah's prayers in chapter 2 (the psalm) and 4:2. But Jonah prayed the psalm for his own salvation out of his situation that can be described as "virtual death." And in 4:2 Jonah's prayer is more

continues in his very short prophecy, uttered only once after travelling hardly a one day's journey into the city. But the Ninevites understood his words in a double way: another day and Nineveh will be overthrown unless it reforms. The use of days, as we saw above, could help them see that alternative: a reference to time often indicates a bad period but can also contain the prospect of a better future, of salvation especially when it is coupled with notions of praying, fasting, etc. (see, e.g., Moses Mt. Sinai). And that is exactly what the Ninevites do.[27]

Conclusion

The four periods of time in the book of Jonah all have symbolic meaning. Comparison with references elsewhere in the Old Testament has demonstrated that "three days" in relation to evil and disaster is often the extreme limit of suffering that a person can endure. Jonah was in the belly of the fish for three days and three nights, that is to the bitter end. A journey of three days refers to a significant distance. A three day's walk in Jonah 3:3 points to the magnitude of the city, but consequently also to the massive evil that existed there. Jonah only travelled as far as one day's walk into the city. One day is a short period of time, and in relation to a journey it refers to only a short distance. Jonah does not enter the city center. He stays along the periphery of the city. There he declares: forty more days and Nineveh will be turned over (destroyed/reformed). When we look at the symbolism of four and its derivatives in the Old Testament we see that they are often used in a negative context, but also may portend a better future. Ambivalence is also present in the verb הפך meaning "overturn" but also "reform," "turn over (a new leaf)." This "double meaning," demonstrated by J. Sasson and others, is crucial in understanding the book's central message. We showed in this paper that the use of "forty days" additionally functions as an ambivalent element used by the author in presenting this message.

---

a lamentation or a complaint about God's mercy. It is very hard to see this as the result of a lack of knowledge.

[27] U. Simon, *The JPS Bible Com.*, p. 29, mentions the possible "double meaning" but calls it dubious because "the narrator does not call our attention to this latent ambiguity: the moral alternation of the Ninevites is expressed in v. 10 by the verb *sh-w-b*, not *h-f-k*." That last observation in fact proves that the Ninevites indeed understood הפך as a call for repentance: שוב. Moreover, if the narrator would have used שוב in 3:4 the second meaning, "to destroy," would be absent.

CHAPTER FOUR

PSALM 69:
A COMPOSITION-CRITICAL CONTRIBUTION

Alphonso Groenewald[1]
University of Pretoria[2]

1. *Introduction*

It has only been a few years since psalm scholarship acknowledged the fact that the canonical Psalter is the result of a complex process of collection as well as redaction.[3] The attempt to explain the present shape of the Psalter is thus a relatively recent endeavor.[4] Since

---

[1] This contribution is dedicated to the memory of the late Prof. Dr. J.H.A. (Sjef) van Tilborg. During my stay of three and a half years in Nijmegen he was more than just a colleague to me: his empathy, friendship, as well as deep concern for my well-being, will always be cherished. I was therefore deeply saddened by his sudden death in May 2003.
[2] This article is published as part of a Post-doctoral Fellowship Programme in the Department of Old Testament Studies, Faculty of Theology, University of Pretoria.
[3] In this regard Janowski (1998:397) infers as follows: "Wie in jüngerer Zeit schrittweise erkannt wird, ist der kanonische Psalter das Ergebnis eines komplexen Sammlungs- und Redaktionsprozesses. In dessen Verlauf wird jeder Einzelpsalm in einen größeren Kontext gestellt, durch den ihm oft ein neuer Sinn und eine zusätzliche Funktion zuwächst."
See also W.S. Prinsloo (1995:466–67): "Soos blyk uit die menigte resente publikasies is die vraag of daar 'n samehang in die Psalmboek is en hoe dié vermeende samehang verklaar moet word, tans 'n brandende vraagstuk in die Psalmnavorsing. Terwyl daar enersyds diegene is wat enige samehang ontken, is daar andersyds diegene wat hulle ernstig daarvoor bemoei om die samehang aan te toon... Dit is verblydend dat die Psalmboek, soos die ander boeke van die Bybel, nou ook al hoe meer as boek gelees word."
[4] In this regard W.S. Prinsloo (1995:459) infers as follows: "In die jongste navorsing word daar egter al hoe meer klem gelê op die feit dat die Psalmboek 'n samehangende literêre geheel is. Daar word aangevoer dat daar getuienis is van 'n redaksionele aktiwiteit wat uitgeloop het op 'n doelbewuste rangskikking van Psalms. Hierdie rangskikking verleen aan die Psalmboek as geheel 'n funksie en boodskap wat groter is as die somtotaal van sy onderdele, naamlik die afsonderlike Psalms. Psalms is nie maar net willekeurig of toevallig naas mekaar geplaas nie, maar die Psalmboek in sy huidige vorm is die resultaat van 'n planvolle ordening. Die Psalmboek, so word dus aangevoer, moet as boek—as samehangende geheel—gelees word."

the enlightenment (*Aufklärung*) psalm scholarship has been carried out with the assumption that the Psalter has no discernible organization.[5]

Currently, however, the final form of the book of the psalms receives more attention and the traditional idea of a somewhat haphazard arrangement is being questioned. This paradigmatic shift is due partly to the fact that the gains of atomistic methods, like form criticism, have begun to diminish.[6] Thus, interest in secondary settings of the psalms, including the literary context of the book as a whole has increased.[7] The emphasis of the reading is thus not on the individual psalm alone, but has shifted to a canonical reading of the individual psalm, i.e., on its respective position in the Psalter and, especially, the significance of its position for its interpretation.[8]

---

[5] Creach 1996:12. Cf. also Howard (1999:332–33): "Until very recently, the Psalter was treated almost universally as a disjointed assortment of diverse compositions that happened to be collected loosely into what eventually became a canonical 'book.' The primary connections among the psalms were judged to have been liturgical, not literary or canonical.... The psalms came together in a haphazard way, and the setting of each psalm in the Book of Psalm ("*Sitz im Text*") was not considered."

[6] Cf. Zenger 1994a:39ff.

[7] Cf. in this regard Spieckermann (1998:145f.): "Primäre Orientierung der Auslegung an der Textebene bedeutet: Orientierung der Auslegung am einzelnen Psalm und am Psalter als Buch. Literarischer Mikrokosmos und Makrokosmos müssen in einem balancierten Verhältnis wahrgenommen werden. Einerseits gäbe es ohne die Mikrokosmen der Psalmen mit ihrer je eigenen Geschichte und Individualität den Makrokosmos des Psalters nicht. Und andererseits ist der Psalter nicht einfach das Konglomerat von 150 Psalmen, sondern eben ein literarischer Makrokosmos, ein weithin überlegt gestaltetes Gebilde, in der kanonisierten Endfassung gleichsam die endgültige Manifestation der einem jeden Psalm innewohnenden Intention, über seine Ursprungssituation hinauszuwachsen und in einem Ensemble von Stimmen dem Gotteslob in seiner ganzen Spannweite und Tiefe Stimmen zu geben. Es ist nicht wohlgetan, die Mikrokosmen der einzelnen Psalmen überwiegend von inhaltlichen Leitmotiven im Makrokosmos des Psalters her zu deuten. Es gibt keine inhaltlichen Gruppen- und Generalschlüssel für die Psalmen, sondern nur Verstehensangebote, die einander nicht ausschließen, vielmehr einander verstärken wollen in der einen Gesamtintention des Psalters, Tehillim zu enthalten und Tehillim zu sein: Lieder aus der Gottesferne und der Gottesnähe und im einen wie im anderen Gotteslob."

[8] Zenger (1999:443–4) puts this assumption into words as follows: "Als wichtigste neue Perspektive beurteile ich selbst den Versuch, die Einzelpsalmen in ihrem größeren literarischen Kontext zu sehen, sei es als Teiltexte einer Psalmgruppe, sei es als Teiltexte des gesamten Psalmenbuches. Um es vorweg und pointiert zu sagen: Es geht bei diesem Ansatz *nicht* darum, das Profil und die Bedeutung des Einzelpsalms zu nivellieren. Das war gerade die Grenze der kult- und gattungsgeschichtlichen Exegese, die weniger am Text selbst als an der 'Welt' hinter dem Text ('Sitz im Leben') interessiert war. Die neuen Perspektiven, die sich ergeben, wenn man den Einzelpsalm im literarischen Kontext eines Teil- bzw. des Gesamtpsalters analysiert und interpretiert, gehen von der Individualität des Einzeltextes aus, bleiben aber nicht bei ihr stehen—weil ja schon die Überlieferung selbst nicht dabei stehenbleiben, sondern die Einzelpsalmen planvoll nebeneinanderstellte oder gar kompo-

Recent investigations of the form of the Hebrew Psalter can primarily be divided into three types: (1) the focus on a specific psalm occurring within its respective contextual relationships;[9] (2) studies focussing on the arrangement of a specific section of the Psalter;[10] and (3) research on the shape of the entire Psalter.[11]

The aim of this article is to contribute to the current debate taking place in this regard. It will focus specifically on Psalm 69 and will endeavor a composition-critical reading of the text of this psalm, i.e., the question regarding the significance for the text's interpretation as based on its respective position in the Psalter.[12]

2. *A Composition-Critical Reading of Psalm 69*

The Psalter is regarded more and more by Old Testament scholarship as the prayer and meditation book[13] of the "small" man (person)—the marginalized—who was critical of the post-exilic temple aristocracy as well as their position of power.[14] The view that the Psalter

---

sitionell/redaktionell zusammenordnete.... Es geht also um eine *zusätzliche* Sinn- und Bedeutungsdimension, die ein Einzelpsalm als Teil des größeren Zusammenhangs, in dem er nun steht, erhält."

[9] To mention but the works of Brunert (1996); Schröten (1995); Weber (1995).

[10] This second approach includes attempts to explain the juxtaposition or order of psalm pairs, groups, and collections. To mention, for example, the works of Barbiero (1999); Cole (2000); Goulder (1982, 1990, 1996); Hossfeld (1998a); Hossfeld & Zenger (1993a, 1993b, 1994, 2000, 2002); Howard (1997); Koenen (1995); Rösel (1999); Schelling (1985); Weber (2001b); Zenger (1991a, 2000); Zimmerli (1972).

[11] This third approach is more overarching and attempts to show that the Psalter in its final form offers evidence of being a single, purposefully edited work. To mention, for example, the works of Creach (1996); Hossfeld & Zenger (1993a, 2000, 2002); McCann (1993); Millard (1994); Niemeyer (1950); Whybray (1996); Wilson (1985).

[12] Lohfink 1988:29–30 and Zenger 1991b:399ff.

[13] Braulik 2003:6ff. See especially Braulik (2003:7): "Knowledge about the Psalter and its popularity is to be explained by the fact that it had been a book of life..., nurturing a personal and individual piety both before and after the beginning of the Common Era.... Modern biblical reasearch has proved that the Psalter is to be understood as a text meant for meditation."

[14] Cf. in this regard Zenger (1999:446): "Die unverkennbare Nähe gerade der jüngsten Teile des Psalmenbuchs zur späten Weisheit macht es sehr wahrscheinlich, daß der Psalter seine Endgestalt im Milieu jener Weisheitsschule erhalten hat, die in gewisser Distanz zur Tempelaristokratie und zu deren hellenisierenden Tendenzen stand und die mit ihrer Verbindung von Tora-Weisheit, prophetischer Eschatologie und 'Armenfrömmigkeit' den Psalter als ein 'Volksbuch' ausgestaltete und verbreitete, das als eine Art Kurzfassung von 'Gesetz und Propheten' (Tora und Nebiim)

functioned as the cultic songbook of the second temple has thus finally been rejected.[15] It is now rather seen as a post-cultic prayer and meditation book which functioned more within the sphere of a private/community piety.[16] No wonder that the supplicants of the psalms did not firstly find their protection in the cult, but rather in the praises of the psalms which ascended to Yahweh, the king of the world, who had established his just rule on Mt. Zion.[17]

This view concurs with conclusions drawn with regard to the redaction-critical development of Psalm 69.[18] It has been established that the last layer (i.e., the cola 32–33b) added to this text—classified as an actualizing inscription (*aktualisierende Einschreibung*)—contains cult-critical statements combined with a "theology of the poor."[19] These cult-critical statements elevate the laudation above the sacrifice.[20] The possibility thus exists that this inscription, which is clearly marked by a theology of the poor, in all probability came from the hands of the same redactors who put together Psalms 69–71.72 in order to form the concluding part of the second Davidic Psalter: in the Davidic Psalter 51–72 the "theology of the poor" occurs for the first time in Psalms 69–71.[21]

---

gelesen, gelernt und gelebt werden konnte. Der Psalter war damals das 'Lebensbuch' v.a. jener Gruppen, die in den Psalmen 'die Armen,' 'die Frommen' und 'die Gerechten' genannt werden. In den Psalmen fanden sie Erbauung, Trost, Hoffnung und Lebensweisung. In den Psalmen begegneten sie dem Gott des Sinai und des Zion—sozusagen ohne 'institutionelle' Vermittlung. Der Psalter war für sie 'Lehrbuch' jüdischer Identität und zugleich 'Sakrament' für die Heiligung des Alltags—außerhalb des Tempels und der Synagogen."

[15] In this regard see Füglister (1988:337): "Die Behauptung, der Psalter sei 'das Gesangbuch des Zweiten Tempels' gewesen, läßt sich somit nicht länger aufrechterhalten." In this regard Zenger (1998b:35) furthermore infers "der Psalter als Ganzer (und im übrigen bereits die meisten Teilsammlungen, die in ihm integriert sind) hat *originär* einen nicht-liturgischen und kultunabhängigen »Sitz im Leben«." See especially Braulik (2003:7): ". . . it is important to realise that, apart from only a few individual psalms, the Psalter has been used liturgically neither in the Second Temple nor in the early synagogue. . . ." See also Füglister 1992:202ff.

[16] Zenger 1999:446.

[17] Berges 1999:15.

[18] Cf. Groenewald (2003:190ff.) for an extensive discussion of the redaction-critical development of this text.

[19] Cf. Groenewald (2003:261ff.) for a discussion of this last textual layer added to the text of Psalm 69 as part of its redactional growth.

[20] In this regard Ro (2002:194) infers as follows: "Das mußte nicht unbedingt eine prinzipielle Ablehnung des Tempels und des Kultes implizieren; zu Aversionen gegenüber den derzeit für den Tempel offiziell zuständigen Kreisen, und zwar wegen deren inkorrekter Kultpraxis, vgl. z.B. Jes 66,3f.; Zef 3,4; Ps. 69:32."

[21] Cf. Zenger (1994b:193): "Die nach 65–68 folgende Komposition der Bittgebete

In the first place, we will focus on the cult-critical statement contained in colon 32. A survey of Psalm 69's neighboring psalms has proven that none of them contains any cult-critical statements.[22] Psalms 65–68—viz. the four psalms preceding Psalm 69—do not belong to the *Gattung* individual complaint songs, but, according to traditional form-critical analysis they are rather to be classified as hymns or hymnic prayers.[23] Furthermore, the motif of the cult is also foreign to Psalms 70–71, which together with Psalm 69, form a cluster of individual complaint psalms (69–71) at the end of book II.[24] Because of the fact that there is no corresponding cult-critical statement(s) in the neighboring psalms, it is necessary to compare it to other psalms which also contain a cult-critical relativization.

There are other examples in the Psalter containing a cult-critical relativization: it furthermore also occurs in Psalms 40, 50, and 51.[25] Firstly, it is important to take note of the respective positions these psalms occupy within the Psalter. Psalm 40 is the second to last psalm in the first book of the psalms (Pss 3–41); concurring with the first Davidic collection (Pss 3–41). Psalm 50, which is the only Asaph

---

69–71 setzt sich einerseits von den vorangehenden Davidpsalmen durch die in ihnen auftretende 'Armenperspektive' ab, die andererseits in Ps. 72 und vor allem im ersten Davidpsalter konstitutiv ist."

[22] The only other reference to the sacrificial cult in this part of the Psalter occurs in Ps. 66:13–15. These verses, however, do not contain a cult-critical statement, but they rather emphasize the fact that the vows made to God in this particular instance also involve sacrifices. According to Tate (1990:150) the reference to burnt-offerings, in connection with the vows, indicates a very serious situation, "a mood of chastened rather than exuberant gratitude, as if to reflect the gravity of the threat that has now been lifted, and the depth of the offerer's debt." The multiple nature of the sacrifices, involving different types of animals, also enhances the element of total dedication and profound thankfulness.

[23] Gunkel and Begrich [1933] 1998:22. With regard to these psalms Hossfeld and Zenger (2000:219) infer as follows: "Seit langem ist die Psalmengruppe 65–68 im Verhältnis zu ihren Nachbarpsalmen aufgefallen. Sie stellt einen Cluster von Hymnen—Dankliedern dar und spricht in Absetzung von der überwiegend individuellen Klage des Kontextes im Wir des Gebetes."
However, with regard to this classification they (Hossfeld and Zenger 2000:214) inferred that the classical *Gattungskritik* has received substantial criticism precisely with regard to the analysis of the hymns. The reason lies in the fact that the hymn, as a conventional form of language, does not really exist: we can merely indicate hymns as a group of texts which have the intention of praising God. Furthermore, they are recognizable through a series of variable and formal indicators, to which we can also add its specific content.

[24] Cf. Zenger 1998a:321.

[25] It should be stated categorically that these texts do not intend to condemn the sacrificial cult in ancient Israel at all; to read them in such a manner is almost certainly to misinterpret them (Craigie 1983:315).

psalm in the second book of the psalms (42–72), occurs between the Korahite psalms (Pss 42–49) and the second Davidic collection (Pss 51–72). Psalm 51 thus introduces the second Davidic collection—ending with Psalm 72. With regard to Psalm 69, it is an acknowledged fact in psalm scholarship that the three Psalms 69–71 form a subgroup within the second book of the psalms; occurring just before the final Psalm 72. Furthermore, conspicuous is the fact that the third book of the psalms (Pss 73–89) commences with a collection of Asaph psalms (73–83).

According to Psalm 40:7–9 the offering of sacrifice (alone) was not enough.[26] These verses refer to the characteristics required of the supplicant, beyond the cultic offerings and sacrifices. It is expected of the supplicant to do the will of God with delight; additionally, he must keep God's *Torah* within his being (heart). In face of Yahweh's *Torah* the supplicant offers him (Yahweh)—instead of the sacrifice—a statement of obedience and subordination (Ps 40:9).[27] The roots of these cult-critical statements were to be found within those groups who held a critical view of the official temple cult as well as the temple aristocracy.[28] In any case, the expansion of an already existing text through the later addition of the verses 14–18[29]—through which the text is identified as a prayer of the "poor and needy" (40:18)[30]—witnesses in this direction.[31]

---

[26] Cf. Ps 40:7.9: "Sacrifice and offering you do not desire... burnt offering and sin offering you have not required... I delight to do your will, O my God; your law is within my heart" (NRSV).

[27] According to Hossfeld and Zenger, "das Tun der Tora ist die »Opfergabe«" (1993a:256). Cf. also Lindström 1994:277.

[28] In this regard Hossfeld and Zenger (1993a:252) infer as follows: "Mit seiner Rede von der »Herzenstora« hebt der Psalm die Gottunmittelbarkeit gegenüber dem Tempel und gegenüber der schriftlichen Tora heraus... Man könnte ihn sich auch als Gebet von Gruppierungen denken, die zunehmend (aus theologischen und aus politischen Gründen) in Opposition zum Machtanspruch der Priesterhierarchie am Tempel traten." See also Zenger 1997:98.

[29] Ps 40:14–18 concurs with Ps 70:2–6. According to Hossfeld and Zenger (1993a: 252–3; 2000:283–4), it is most likely that Ps 70 had already existed independently and only later on was added to Ps 40 as part of the multi-stage redactional process this text underwent. Braulik (1975:221, 268ff.) holds the same opinion. See furthermore Hossfeld and Zenger 2002:406; Weber 2001a:316; Zenger 1997:98.

Compare Naudé (1999;213ff.) for an extensive overview of the different redaction and composition critical proposals with regard to this psalm.

[30] Cf. Hossfeld and Zenger (1993a:252): "Das dürfte, zumal 14–18 ja ein gezielt aufgenommener Text (Ps 70!) ist, nicht als biographische Einzelaussage, sondern als »Gruppenbewußtsein« zu verstehen sein."

[31] With regard to the redactional growth of this text Hossfeld and Zenger (1993a:

Psalm 50—an Asaph psalm—can be divided into three stanzas.[32] Stanza I (50:1–6) forms the introductory passage; the descriptive language is that of a theophany.[33] This stanza is followed by two principal sections (stanzas) which are both in the form of a divine address; both containing cult-critical statements. In stanza II (50:7–15) the divine complaint is not about the absence of sacrifices—on the contrary, there were more than enough.[34] The sacrifices were offered in the wrong spirit: worshipping was supposedly done on the assumption that when the ceremonial act had been performed, it should have been enough. However, the thanksgiving of the heart was missing. Therefore, this stanza outlines the true meaning of sacrifice: sacrifices and burnt offerings are legitimate when they are understood correctly as well as offered in a correct manner.[35] The essence of the whole sacrificial system should rather be seen in the song of thanksgiving (*tôdāh*) offered to God;[36] and together with it the fulfillment of the vow (*ndr*) made to God (50:14).[37] In stanza III (50:16–23) a warning is issued to those whose lives are not in accordance with the covenant stipulations. The true meaning of the law is outlined and reiterated. The concluding verse (50:23)[38] re-emphasizes the point which has already been made in verse 14: the true meaning of the sacrifice

---

252) infer as follows: "... daß der vorliegende Psalm am ehesten durch einen »Fortschreibungsprozeß« zu erklären ist, dessen letzte Phase mit der Einfügung des Psalms in die Teilgruppe 3–41 durch die nachexilische »Armentheologie« zusammenhängt."

[32] For this subdivision see Goulder 1996:38ff. and Hossfeld and Zenger 1993a: 312–16.

[33] Hossfeld 1998b:240. See Schmidt and Nel (2002:256ff.) with regard to theophany as type-scene in the Hebrew Bible.

[34] Goulder 1996:43.

[35] In this regard Doeker (2002:275) infers as follows: "Der Psalm berührt einen anderen Schwerpunkt der Thematik. Ihm geht es in den vv. 7–15 weniger um eine Kritik an der Opferpraxis, als um die Abwehr eines bestimmten, falschen Opferverständnisses und vor allem um die positive Bewertung der Toda." See also Hossfeld 1991:95.

[36] In this regard Hossfeld (1991:95–96) infers as follows: "Die spezifische Kult- und Opferkritik von Ps 50:8–15 wird häufig zu schnell in eine allgemeine Opferkritik eingeebnet. Ps 50:8–15 legt Wert auf die Haltung, mit der das Opfer vollzogen wird und stellt darin mehr Ansprüche als das Opferversprechung von Ps 66:13–15."

[37] Ps 50:14: "Offer to God a sacrifice of thanksgiving, and pay your vows to the Most High" (NRSV). According to Hossfeld and Zenger (1993a:314) it is very important to interpret this verse within its context, and the context criticizes "das Opferverständnis und nicht die Opfer als solche. Er votiert also für die Interpretation von *tôdāh* als Dankopfer und nicht nur allgemein als Lob/Dank."

[38] Cf. Ps 50:23: "Those who bring thanksgiving as their sacrifice honour me; to those who go the right way I will show the salvation of God" (NRSV). Cf. also Hossfeld 1991:96.

is to be found in the offering of thanksgiving (*tôdāh*), as well as walking on the right path where the salvation of God will be revealed.[39]

Psalm 51 also contains a cult-critical relativization. The fact has already been referred to that Psalm 51 was put at the beginning of the second Davidic Psalter (Pss 51–72) by the final redactors of the Psalter. In the verses 18–19[40] it is emphatically emphasized that the merciful action of God will not be received on the basis of sacrifice alone, but on the basis of a "broken and contrite heart." The supplicant who thus offers a "broken spirit" as sacrifice, whether accompanied by burnt offerings or not, can be sure of divine acceptance.[41] According to Hossfeld and Zenger[42] these verses actualize the prophetic cult criticism which, instead of sacrifices, requests obedience to God as well as justice and righteousness to be done.[43] Once again, it must be stated clearly that one should be cautious not to conclude that these verses (Ps 51:18–19) point to a repudiation of cultic worship and that they encourage a kind of spirituality wholly detached from sacrifices.[44] Nevertheless, this psalm does not end with these verses (51:18–19). It is furthermore necessary to briefly focus on the last

---

[39] With regard to the possible dating of this text Hossfeld (1991:101) infers as follows: "Der erste Asafpsalm ... ist von einem Asafsänger ... wahrscheinlich zu Anfang des 4. Jhs. v.Chr. vorgetragen worden."

[40] Cf. Ps 51:18–19: "For you have no delight in sacrifice; if I were to give a burnt offering, you would not be pleased. The sacrifice acceptable to God is a broken spirit; a broken and contrite heart, O God, you will not despise" (NRSV).

[41] Hossfeld and Zenger (2000:54–55) state as follows: "Nicht irgendwelche Gaben die den Geretteten »symbolisieren« sollen, sondern *sich selbst* als den an *Herz* und *Geist* erneuerten Menschen übergibt er seinem Gott."

[42] Hossfeld and Zenger 2000:54. Cf. also Gunkel and Begrich [1933] 1998:287–90.

[43] Cf. in this regard, for example, Hos 6:6 ("for I desire steadfast love and not sacrifice, the knowledge of God rather than burnt offerings"—NRSV); Mic 6:6–8 ("with what shall I come before the Lord ...? Shall I come before him with burnt offerings ...? ... and what does the Lord require of you but to do justice, and to love kindness, and to walk humbly with your God?"—NRSV); Amos 5:21–24 ("... even though you offer me your burnt offerings and grain offerings, I will not accept them; and the offerings of well-being of your fatted animals I will not look upon ... but let justice roll down like waters, and righteousness like an everflowing stream"—NRSV). Compare also Isa 1:11–17 and Jer 7:21–23. We even encounter this line of thought in the wisdom tradition: see Prov 15:8; 21:3.27; 28:9, and especially Sirach 34:21–35:22.

[44] In this regard Leene (1996:70) justly infers as follows: "in that sense this psalm remains within the religious environment in which the Psalter originated: a world in which animal sacrifices were offered." Cf. also Ro (2002:201): "... hier wie dort keine prinzipielle Ablehnung des Tempels, aber Aversionen gegenüber den derzeit für den Tempel offiziell zuständigen Kreisen, und zwar wegen deren inkorrekter Kultpraxis."

two verses as well.[45] Verses 20–21 were most likely added by a later redactor who (re-)interpreted the psalm in terms of Israel's corporate experience. Zenger[46] infers that the concluding verses of Psalms 50 (50:23) and 51 (51:20-1) are inextricably linked to one another: the possibility thus even exists that these verses could be ascribed to the same redactors. A certain tension indeed exists between this part (vv. 20–21) and the first part of the text (vv. 3–19): "Jerusalem (und Zion) ist vorher nirgends im Blick, und die opferkritischen Aussagen von V 18–19 stehen eher in Spannung zur Opfertheologie von V 21."[47] The form of these verses is that of a prayer for the restoration of Jerusalem so that sacrifices could be made on the altar in the temple. And whenever God restores Jerusalem, sacrifices on the altar there will be acceptable to him again.[48] When the redactor thus refers to "right sacrifices" (lit. "sacrifices of righteousness"), he surely has sacrifices in mind in which Yahweh will find the right spirit and which are thus truly symbolic of the supplicant's complete dedication to both cult and ethos.[49]

It has thus become clear that in contrast to the immediate context of Psalm 69 which does not contain any cult-critical statements, it is noticeable that these statements occur in quite strategic places in both book I and II of the Psalter. This supports the assumption that this cult-critical inscription in 69:32 was purposefully inscribed into Psalm 69. It was inscribed by the final redactors not only to write their theology into this text through which they actualized this text for its tradents, but—even more important—it was inscribed into an already existing text in order to correspond to other strategic psalms in these two books (I and II). Psalm 69 thus contains a cult-critical relativization in correspondence to Psalms 40, 50, and 51 which

---

[45] Ps 51:20–21 reads as follows: "Do good to Zion in your good pleasure; rebuild the walls of Jerusalem, then you will delight in right sacrifices, in burnt offerings and whole burnt offerings; then bulls will be offered on your altar" (NRSV).

[46] Zenger 1994b:195. Cf. also Schelling 1985:235.

[47] Hossfeld and Zenger 2000:45. Cf. also Schmidt (1994:357): "V. 18f. wirken mit ihrem plötzlichen Themenwechsel zur Opferkritik zunächst wie ein Anhang."

[48] In this regard Zenger (1997:411–12) infers as follows: "Der Psalm schließt in V. 20–21 mit der Vision von der eschatologischen Erneuerung des Zion ... Das ist die Topik, mit der die nachexilische Theologie, insbesondere die jesajanische Schule, davon träumt, daß Jhwh den Zion zu einem Ort des Heils und der Gerechtigkeit macht—nicht nur für das bedrängte und zerstreute Gottesvolk Israel, sondern für alle Völker."

[49] Cf. Mosis 1992:212, 214.

also contain such statements. By means of these analogous statements the end of book II is thus linked to the end of book I; Psalm 40 is the second to last psalm of book I. Furthermore, by means of these statements the beginning and the end of the second Davidic Psalter are linked to one another. Finally, Psalm 50 is the only Asaph-psalm in book II. Book III (73–89), however, starts with a collection of Asaph-psalms (73–83). By means of these analogous cult-critical statements we encounter in both Psalms 50 and 69, book II is linked to book III.[50]

It has already been stated that the final layer (32–33b), which was added to an already existing text, has been classified as an actualizing inscription (*aktualisierende Einschreibung*). This final layer combines the cult-critical statement (32) with the "piety of the poor" (33ab). This cult-critical statement indeed would have appeased the "poor" (*anāwim*), as they—regarding themselves as the real pious (i.e., the "god seekers")—hold a critical view of the official temple cult with its aristocracy. No wonder that they elevate their praises of the name of God above the sacrifices offered at the temple. The occurrence of this "theology of the poor" in this psalm is of special importance to its composition-critical analysis. Focus will now be placed on the position of Psalm 69 in book II, as well as its relationship to book I.

According to Zenger[51] the first Davidic Psalter (Pss 3–41) is fundamentally characterized by the so-called perspective of the "poor." In the second Davidic Psalter (51–72) we, for the first time, encounter this perspective in the concluding group of Psalms 69–72.[52] It, however, lacks in the Psalms 51–68. Noteworthy is the fact that this perspective is absent in Psalm 53, in spite of the fact that this psalm is a doublet of Psalm 14,[53] which is regarded as a psalm of the poor. It seems to be that the perspective of the poor which occurs in Psalm

---

[50] In this regard Hossfeld (1991:101) infers as follows: "Der erste Asafpsalm 50 mit Theophanie und Jahwe-Rede eröffnet den Davidpsalter 51–72 und nimmt diesen in die Sammlung der Asafpsalmen 73–83 auf. Zugleich steckt er mit höchster Autorität den Rahmen für die nachfolgende Opferkritik vom Grundpsalm 51 ab. Was Jahwe in Ps 50 anordnet, das vollzieht der Beter in der Nachfolge Davids nun im redaktionell bearteiteten Ps 51." According to Cole (2000:137) "the lone Asaphite Psalm 50 performs the identical function with the other Asaphite Psalms 73–83 by putting a frame around the Davidic Psalms 51–71 with 72 within Books II and III."

[51] Zenger 1994b:195. See also Hossfeld 1998a:63.

[52] Cf. Zenger (1994b:193) in this regard: "Die nach 65–68 folgende Komposition der Bittgebete 69–71 setzt sich einerseits von den vorangehenden Davidpsalmen durch die in ihnen auftretende 'Armenperspektive' ab, die andererseits in Ps. 72 und vor allem im ersten Davidpsalter konstitutiv ist." See also Zenger 1998a:321.

[53] Cf. Zimmerli 1972:105.

14:6⁵⁴ has been changed to a perspective of war and persecution in Psalm 53:6.⁵⁵ This conforms well to the assumption that Psalms 51–68 are rather characterized by the perspective of war and persecution.⁵⁶ Psalm 14 belongs to a cluster of psalms of the poor, viz. Psalms 11–14 which conclude the first section of Psalms 3–14 in the first Davidic Psalter.⁵⁷ Roughly speaking, Psalm 53 occurs at the beginning of the second Davidic Psalter (51–72).

It has already been established that Psalms 35–41 form the concluding section of the first Davidic Psalter.⁵⁸ It seems to be that we encounter secondary additions in both Psalms 35 and 40, viz. 35:26–28 and 40:14–18. Noteworthy is the fact that these additions have a counterpart in the independent Psalm 70, which occurs at the end of the second Davidic Psalter. It seems to be that these additions are interdependent on Psalm 70—that would imply that they are later than Psalm 70 and in all probability had this text as *Vorlage*.⁵⁹ According to Hossfeld and Zenger⁶⁰ these additions to these two psalms (35:26–28 and 40:14–18) can be ascribed to a post-exilic redaction of the poor which seems to have been responsible for a reworking of Psalms 35–41. These psalms are now characterized by a comprehensive interpretation of the existence of the poor ("Existenzdeutung des Armen").⁶¹ It is thus clear that the concluding sections of both the first as well as second Davidic Psalter (i.e., 35–41 and 69–72) are characterized by a "theology of the poor."⁶²

From both the poetical as well as the redaction-critical analysis of Psalm 69⁶³ it has become quite clear that the present BHS text of

---

⁵⁴ It reads as follows: "you would confound the plans of the poor, but the Lord is their refuge" (NRSV).

⁵⁵ This text reads as follows: "There they shall be in great terror, in terror such as has not been. For God will scatter the bones of the ungodly; they will be put to shame, for God has rejected them" (NRSV).

⁵⁶ Hossfeld 1998b:63.

⁵⁷ Hossfeld and Zenger 1992:34ff.

⁵⁸ Cf. also Hossfeld and Zenger 1992:23f.

⁵⁹ Cf. in this regard Braulik (1975:221): "Ps 70 bildet somit die Vorform der Verse 40:14–18...." See also Hossfeld and Zenger (1992:32): "... 40:14–18 von jener redaktionellen Hand geschaffen wurde, die ihrerseits Ps 35 so bearbeitet hat, daß auch er nunmehr als ein »Armenpsalm« zu lesen ist, der zusammen mit Ps 40–41 einen übergreifenden Bogen bildet."

⁶⁰ Hossfeld and Zenger 1992:23ff.

⁶¹ Hossfeld and Zenger 1992:34.

⁶² Cf. Hossfeld 1998a:66f.

⁶³ Cf. Groenewald 2003.

Psalm 69 is a comprehensive as well as complex text which is characterized by means of the combination of different kinds of afflictions experienced by the supplicant(s). In the manner affliction is depicted Psalm 69 shares a number of commonalities with Psalms 35, 38, and 41.[64] These psalms also witness to persecution experienced by the supplicant(s). Over and above these references, they also contain allusions to parallel rites of mourning, for example Psalms 35:13–14;[65] 38:7;[66] 69:11a–12b. We can furthermore add the parallel way in which the complaints about the constellation friend-enemy occurs in Psalms 35:11–18; 41:5–11, and 69:9ab. It can thus be inferred that Psalm 69 shares commonalities with strategic psalms in the concluding section of the first Davidic Psalter (35–41), namely, with psalms which appear in the introduction, center, as well as the conclusion of this section.[67] The depiction of affliction which is spread over a few psalms at the end of the first Davidic Psalter, is thus concentrated in one text at the end of book II, namely in Psalm 69.

Psalm 70 is, according to the statement contained in 70:6, *expressis verbis* a psalm of the poor.[68] This short psalm is characterized by two themes, viz. the themes of the enemies and the poor. Both these themes occur extensively in Psalm 69, through which these two texts are closely linked to one another. Psalm 70—which is a psalm of the poor—is followed by Psalm 71 which focusses more on the aspect of old age.[69] When assessing the religious experience underlying this psalm, we are struck by the vulnerability of the supplicant who believed that vicious enemies stalked his every move, but also by his

---

[64] Cf. Weber 2001a:313.

[65] It reads as follows: "But as for me, when they were sick, I wore sackcloth; I afflicted myself with fasting. I prayed with head bowed down on my bosom, as though I grieved for a friend or a brother; I went about as one who laments for a mother, bowed down and in mourning" (NRSV).

[66] It reads as follows: "I am utterly bowed down and prostrate; all day long I go around mourning" (NRSV).

[67] Cf. in this regard Hossfeld and Zenger 1992:26–34.

[68] Ps 70:6 reads as follows: "But I am poor and needy; hasten to me, O God! You are my help and my deliverer; O Lord, do not delay!"

[69] In this regard Hossfeld (1998a:67) infers as follows: "In der Ausführlichkeit, mit der hier auf das Alter Bezug genommen wird, ist Ps 71 im gesamten Psalter einmalig. . . ."

Weber (2001a:322) raises the question whether the occurrences of Ps 71 at the end of book II and Ps 90 at the beginning of book IV (90–106) could reflect a specific redactional intention. Both psalms refer to old age as well as reflect on the life span of mankind; both occur at strategic positions, viz. the transition from one book to another.

exceptional confidence in the divine rescue.[70] The elderly supplicant takes his whole life span into consideration. He, however, especially emphasizes the continual praise of God, which now defines his whole existence. Psalm 71 is closely linked to Psalm 70 by means of the lack of a superscription.[71] This close link between these two texts is also strengthened by means of the connection of several words as well as parallel motifs occurring in both of them.[72] Both psalms refer to the enemies who are pursuing them, and both stress the aspect of shame and reproach when referring to these enemies. Psalm 71, however, is not only linked to the preceding text of Psalm 70, but also to some psalms occurring in the concluding section (35–41) of the first Davidic Psalter. Psalm 71 displays parallels to both Psalms 35 and 38; in any case, also to Psalm 40 since 40:14–18 is related to Psalm 70.[73] The occurrence of these parallels furthermore strengthens the assumption that the concluding section (69–71) of the second Davidic Psalter was intentionally reworked as well as put together by the redactors so that they could form the concluding section of book II, which has clear parallels to the concluding section of book I.

Psalm 72—a royal psalm—concludes both the second Davidic Psalter (51–72) as well as book II (42–72). According to the text of Psalm 72 the sovereign authority unfolds in three different directions:[74] 1) the king as judge and saviour of the poor (72:2–4.12–14); 2) the king as the mediator of blessing for both the land and the people (72:5–7.15–17); 3) and finally, the king as the universal ruler over the whole of the earth (72:8–11). In spite of all the similarities which exist between Psalms 71 and 72, the main link is the theme of the "poor." If we thus consider the concluding colophon in 72:20[75] together with the superscription (72:1—"for Solomon"), it seems to

---

[70] Crenshaw 2001:154.
[71] In this regard Weber (2001a:321–2) infers as follows: "Diese Überschriftslosigkeit, der Umstand, dass manche hebr. Handschriften Ps. 71 zusammen mit Ps. 70 als einzigen Psalm darbieten und die engen inhaltlichen Berührungen dieser beiden Psalmen ... äussert sich darin, dass in der hebr. Überlieferung hinsichtlich Ps 71 ein Schwanken zwischen Eigenständigkeit und Verbindung mit Ps. 70 feststellbar ist." Cf. also Crenshaw 2001:153.
[72] In this regard it can be referred to, for example, the following: the motif of "shame" (70:3f.; 71:1.13.24); "those who seek" (70:3.5; 71:13.24); and the statements on redemption and salvation.
[73] For 71:8 see 40:4; 71:12–35:2.22; 71:13–35:4.26, 38:13, 40:15 = 70:3; 71:19–35:10; 71:24—35:28. See also Crenshaw 2001:153.
[74] In this regard see Zenger 1993:65ff. Cf. also Hossfeld and Zenger 2002:412f.
[75] It reads as follows: "The prayers of David son of Jesse are ended" (NRSV).

be that the elderly David here draws up a royal will for his son Solomon—in the form of a prayer of petition.[76] Thematically it seems that this petition for justice for his son, as well as for his son's kingship, is actually a concretization of the objective which was formulated at the end of Psalm 71 (71:24)[77]—namely while praying to attest to the justice that he had experienced through salvation.[78] The king, as receiver of God's justice and righteousness (72:1)[79] and due to his divine commission, is thus regarded as a medium or agent who is responsible for the concretization and actualization of God's justice— and specifically God's justice to the poor.[80]

---

[76] Hossfeld and Zenger 2000:72. Cf. also Human 2002:665.

[77] It reads as follows: "All day long my tongue will talk of your righteous help, for those who tried to do me harm have been put to shame, and disgraced" (NRSV).

[78] The preceding statements referring to David necessitate some remarks on, as well as clarification of, the "Davidization" of the Psalter. This will, however, not be dealt with in great detail and a few short remarks will suffice (cf. Kleer (1996) for a detailed study of the Davidization of the Psalter). According to Kleer (1996:126; cf. also Zenger 1998c:264ff.) the beginning of the Davidization of the Psalter can be traced back to the identity crisis the Judaeans experienced during the exile. In spite of this, David was still not portrayed as the author or poet of the psalms during this period. The starting point for this motif in terms of tradition history lies in the composition of the books of Samuel. They even portrayed the young shepherd boy David as a gifted musician at his first appearance (Mays 1986:146ff.). But most importantly, the redactors of the books of Samuel presented the David vita in the form of a psalm which was spoken by David (2 Sam 22 = Ps 18). According to Mays (1986:148) this text is the earliest literary evidence of a connection between David and the psalms, and the only specific witness in the David story linked to that relationship. The redactors even let him recite a poem as his last words before his death (2 Sam 23:1–7). This conception of the books of Samuel was the impetus for the explicit, multi-staged Davidization of the Psalter. The notion stemming from the books of Samuel is that it was David who, in spite of being persecuted, still stood under God's protection and composed psalms—whether it be in the conflict with Saul or as the king in confrontation with his enemies and, specifically, when he was on the run from his son Absalom. Kleer (1996:126) infers that by means of the Psalter's Davidization "der Beter is eingeladen, mit David in eine Schicksalsgemeinschaft zu treten, so seine Not zu bewältigen und Hoffnung für die Zukunft zu schöpfen. Thus, to pray and praise through the psalms is to speak the language of those who depend on and trust in the reign of Yahweh. The Davidic connection thus discloses that suffering borne in trust and hope is a suffering that has a place and role in this reign of Yahweh (Mays 1986:155). In turn, David's life becomes an illustration for those who use the psalms of the way in which a life whose hope is in the reign of Yahweh is to be lived. See also Ballhorn 1995:20; Childs 1971:137–50; Füglister 1988:368–84; Hossfeld and Zenger 1996:336–38; Millard 1994:230–34.

[79] It reads as follows: "Give the king your justice, O God, and your righteousness to a king's son" (NRSV).

[80] Human 2002:665f. and W.S. Prinsloo 1999:540. Hossfeld and Zenger (2000:328) define the character of this "justice" as follows: "Im Psalmkorpus selbst wird diese Gerechtigkeit dann zum einen armentheologisch expliziert, was konsequent im

If we once again assess the four concluding psalms of the second Davidic Psalter, the following three characteristics can be emphasized: 1) their relationship to the concluding section of the first Davidic Psalter (35–41); 2) the connection of these four psalms to one another by means of the theme of the "poor"; 3) and finally, the conclusive character they display. It is necessary to pass some remarks on this last feature of these four psalms, i.e., their conclusive character. After the extensive doxology in 72:18–9,[81] the second Davidic Psalter is concluded with a single colophon (72:20). This colophon designates the end of David's prayers of petition and lamentations. This concluding section is characterized by both the compact nature as well as multi-faceted nature of the utterances it contains. It is, however, colored in a distinct manner by means of the specific arrangement of the four texts it contains (69–72). Psalm 69 expresses in a very concentrated manner the diversity of the affliction experienced by the supplicant. This supplicant is simultaneously characterized as belonging to the "poor." Psalm 70—which is *expressis verbis* a psalm of the "poor"—once again focusses on the conflict with the enemies, but simultaneously it spells out confidence in a sure victory over the enemies. Psalm 71 also displays a conclusive character: it portrays the supplicant as the elderly, and specifically as the elderly who reflects on his life which was characterized by affliction and conflict, but also by the sure protection of God.[82] The concluding Psalm 72 identifies the elderly supplicant as the king who recites a prayer for his son—namely, in the form of a sacred royal will. This also implies that these four psalms do not only serve as a conclusion for the second Davidic Psalter, but for the first Davidic Psalter as well. The clear arrangement of these four texts supports the assumption that the single colophon of 72:20 serves as a finale for a unified Davidic Psalter, i.e., for the first (3–41) as well as second Davidic (51–72) collection.[83]

Before concluding this section on the composition of Psalm 69, it is also necessary to refer briefly to the texts preceding this psalm.

Horizont der Armentheologie von Ps 69–71 geschieht, doch nun so, daß der König als Retter der Armen definiert wird."

[81] This doxology reads as follows: "Blessed be the Lord, the God of Israel, who alone does wondrous things. Blessed be his glorious name forever; may his glory fill the whole earth. Amen and Amen" (NRSV).

[82] Hossfeld (1998a:68) formulates this assumption as follows: ". . . der auf ein angefochtenes und zugleich von Gott gehaltenes Dasein zurückblickt."

[83] Hossfeld 1998a:68.

It has already been stated that the four texts which precede Psalm 69, viz. Psalms 65–68, were classified as hymns or hymnic prayers according to the classical form-critical analysis.[84] These texts collectively praise the God of Zion, who conquered the powers of chaos and who filled the whole earth and creation with his life-giving benevolence.[85] Consequently, Psalm 69 is thematically also linked to these texts. Psalm 69 likewise contains the motif of Zion, and namely God who will save Zion, the motif of the whole of creation which will praise God, and furthermore the theme of the struggle against the powers of chaos. According to Hossfeld and Zenger[86] Psalms 68 and 69 are related to one another by means of especially two viewpoints: their image of God and the "theology of the poor." Both texts speak about the God of Israel (68:9.27; 69:7b).[87] They—in unison—emphasize his salvation (68:20ff.; 69:14b.30a) and accentuate his mercy/compassion (68:11; 69:17c). No wonder that his name will be praised with a song (68:5; 69:31ab). The references to the "theology of the poor" furthermore link these two texts together. God rules over the depths of the sea (68:23); this is the place where the "poor" finds himself (69:3a–d.15c–16b). In both texts the righteous are on God's side (68:4; 69:29b). Both psalms contain references to prisoners (68:7; 69:34b). Joy and exultation belong to the privileges of the righteous (68:4), as well as of the "poor" (69:33ab). Those who belong to the enemies and the haters of God (68:2) are specified as the enemies and the haters of the supplicant in Psalm 69 (5a–d.15c.19b).

3. *Concluding Remarks*

We have come to see that cola 32–33b—which were characterized as an *aktualisierende Einschreibung*—were purposefully inscribed into an already existing text. They came from the hands of the same redactors who put together Psalms 69–71.72 in order to form the concluding part of the second Davidic Psalter. In these cola we thus witness the overlapping of two processes in the textual development of Psalm 69, viz. the final stage of the growth of the text (redaction criticism)

---

[84] Gunkel and Begrich [1933] 1998:22.
[85] Sedlmeier 1996:123.
[86] Hossfeld and Zenger 2000:256. Cf. also Weber 2001a:313.
[87] Cf. also Vorndran 2002:247.

which coincides with its positioning at the end of book II (composition criticism) as part of the cluster of Psalms 69–71.[88] It has already been stated that for the first time in the second Davidic Psalter (Pss 51–72) we here encounter a "theology of the poor." These redactors inscribed their theology into the text of Psalm 69 in order to make it suitable for a cluster of texts which would be analogous to the concluding section of psalms (35–41) in the first Davidic collection which is characterized by a "theology of the poor."

Bibliography

Ballhorn, E., "Um deines Knechtes David willen" (Ps 132,10). Die Gestalt Davids im Psalter," in *Biblische Notizen* 76 (1995) 16–31.
Barbiero, G., *Das erste Psalmenbuch als Einheit. Eine synchrone Analyse von Psalm 1–41*. (Österreichische Biblische Studien 16), Frankfurt a.M. 1999.
Berges, U., *De armen van het boek Jesaja. Een bijdrage tot de literatuurgeschiedenis van het Oude Testament*. Inaugural speech 5 March 1999. Katholieke Universiteit Nijmegen.
Braulik, G., *Psalm 40 und der Gottesknecht* (Forschung zur Bibel 18) Würzburg 1975.
———, "Psalms and Liturgy: Their Reception and Contextualisation," in *Verbum et Ecclesia* 24/2 (2003) (forthcoming).
Brunert, G., *Psalm 102 im Kontext des Vierten Psalmenbuches* (Stuttgarter Biblische Beiträge 30), Stuttgart 1996.
Childs, B.S., "Psalm Titles and Midrashic Exegesis," in: *Journal of Semitic Studies*, 16/2 (1971) 137–50.
Cole, R.L., *The Shape and Message of Book III (Psalms 73–89)* (JSOT Suppl.S. 307), Sheffield 2000.
Craigie, P.C., *Psalms 1–50* (Word Biblical Commentary 19), Waco 1983.
Creach, J.F.D., *Yahweh as Refuge and the Editing of the Hebrew Psalter* (JSOT Suppl.S. 217), Sheffield 1996.
Crenshaw, J.L., *The Psalms—an Introduction*. Grand Rapids 2001.
Doeker, A., *Die Funktion der Gottesrede in den Psalmen. Eine poetologische Untersuchung* (Bonner Biblische Beiträge 135) Berlin 2002.
Füglister, N., "Die Verwendung und das Verständnis der Psalmen und des Psalters um die Zeitenwende." In: J. Schreiner (Hrsg.) *Beiträge zur Psalmenforschung. Psalm 2 und 22* (Forschung zur Bibel 60), Würzburg 1988, 319–84.
———, "Die Verwendung des Psalters zur Zeit Jesu," in *Bibel und Kirche*, 47 (1992) 201–8.

---

[88] Hossfeld and Zenger (2000:268) summarize this assumption as follows: "Ps 69 wurde für diese Schlußkomposition vermutlich aus drei Gründen ausgewählt: a) Wegen der Multiperspektivität seiner Notschilderung kann er als Zusammenfassung der in Ps 51ff. gesammelten Klagepsalmen fungieren; b) wegen seiner Verwandtschaft mit Ps 40 als dem vorletzten Psalm der ersten Davidsammlung Ps 3–41 unterstreicht er die intendierte Parallelisierung der beiden Davidsammlungen (vgl. auch entsprechend die Parallelisierung von Ps 70 mit Ps 40:14–18); c) durch sein Interesse am Tempel bzw. am rechten Tempelkult ist der Psalm geeignet, »David« zum Eiferer für den wahren Tempelkult zu machen und so eine Brücke zu der dann folgenden Asafkomposition Ps 73–83 zu schlagen."

Goulder, M., *The Psalms of the Sons of Korah* (JSOT Suppl.S. 20), Sheffield 1982.
——, *The Prayers of David (Psalms 51–72). Studies in the Psalter, II.* (JSOT Suppl.S. 102), Sheffield 1990.
——, *The Psalms of Asaph and the Pentateuch. Studies in the Psalter, III* (JSOT Suppl.S. 233), Sheffield 1996.
Groenewald, A., *Psalm 69: Its Structure, Redaction and Composition* (Altes Testament und Moderne 18), Münster 2003.
Gunkel, H., & Begrich, J., *Introduction to Psalms. The Genres of the Religious Lyric of Israel.* (Mercer Library of Biblical Studies). (Transl. by J.D. Nogalski from the fourth edition of "Einleitung in die Psalmen: die Gattungen der religiösen Lyrik Israels" 1933), Macon [1933] 1998.
Hossfeld, F.-L., "Ps. 50 und die Verkündigung des Gottesrechts" in: F.V. Reiterer (Hrsg.), *Ein Gott eine Offenbarung. Beiträge zur biblischen Exegese, Theologie und Spiritualität,* Würzburg 1991, 83–101.
——, "Die unterschiedlichen Profile der beiden David-sammlungen Ps. 3–41 und Ps. 51–72," in: E. Zenger (Hrsg.), *Der Psalter in Judentum und Christentum* (Herders Biblische Studien 18), Freiburg i.B. 1998(a), 59–73.
——, "Das Prophetische in den Psalmen. Zur Gottesrede der Asafpsalmen im Vergleich mit der des ersten und zweiten Davidpsalters," in: F. Dietrich & B. Willmes (Hrsg.), *Ich bewirke das Heil und erschaffe das Unheil (Jesaja 45,7). Studien zur Botschaft der Propheten.* FS. L. Ruppert (Forschung zur Bibel 88), Würzburg 1998(b), 223–43.
Hossfeld, F.-L., & Zenger, E., "»Selig, wer auf die Armen achtet« (Ps. 41,2). Beobachtungen zur Gottesvolk-Theologie des ersten Davidpsalters," in *Jahrbuch für biblische Theologie* 7 (1992) Neukirchen-Vluyn, 21–50.
——, *Die Psalmen I. Psalm 1–50* (Die Neue Echter Bibel—Lfg. 29), Würzburg 1993(a).
——, "Wer darf hinaufziehn zum Berg JHWHs?: Zur Redaktionsgeschichte und Theologie der Psalmengruppe 15–24," in: G. Braulik *et al.* (Hrsg.) *Biblische Theologie und gesellschaftlicher Wandel.* FS. N. Lohfink. Freiburg i.B. 1993(b), 166–82.
——, "»Von seinem Thronsitz schaut er nieder auf alle Bewohner der Erde« (Ps. 33,14). Redaktionsgeschichte und Kompositionskritik der Psalmengruppe 25–34," in: I. Kottsieper *et al.* (Hrsg.), *»Wer ist wie du, Herr, unter den Göttern?«—Studien zur Theologie und Religionsgeschichte Israels.* Göttingen 1994, 375–88.
——, "Neue und alte Wege der Psalmenexegese. Antworten auf die Fragen von M. Millard und R. Rendtorff," in: *Biblical Interpretation,* 4 (1996) 332–43.
——, *Psalmen 51–100* (HTKAT), Freiburg i.B. 2000.
——, *Die Psalmen II. Psalm 51–100* (Die Neue Echter Bibel—Lfg. 40), Würzburg 2002.
Howard, D.M., *The Structure of Psalms 93–100* (Biblical and Judaic Studies 5), Winona Lake 1997.
——, "Recent Trends in Psalms Study," in: D.W. Baker and B.T. Arnold (eds.), *The Face of Old Testament Studies. A Survey of Contemporary Approaches.* Grand Rapids 1999, 329–68.
Human, D.J., "An Ideal for Leadership—Psalm 72: The (Wise) King—Royal Mediation of God's Universal Reign," in: *Verbum et Ecclesia,* 23/3 (2002) 657–78.
Janowski, B., "Die »Kleine Biblia«. Zur Bedeutung der Psalmen für eine Theologie des Alten Testaments," in: E. Zenger (Hrsg.), *Der Psalter in Judentum und Christentum* (Herders Biblische Studien 18), Freiburg i.B. 1998, 381–420.
Kleer, M., *»Der liebliche Sänger der Psalmen Israels.« Untersuchungen zu David als Dichter und Beter der Psalmen* (Bonner Biblische Beiträge 108), Bodenheim 1996.
Koenen, K., *Jahwe wird kommen, zu herrschen über die Erde: Ps. 90–110 als Komposition.* (Bonner Biblische Beiträge 101), Weinheim 1995.
Leene, H., "Personal Penitence and the Rebuilding of Zion. The Unity of Psalm 51," in: J. Dyk (ed.). *Give Ear to My Words. Psalms and Other Poetry in and around the Hebrew Bible. Essays in Honour of Prof. N.A. van Uchelen,* Kampen 1996, 61–77.

Lindström, F., *Suffering and Sin: Interpretations of Illness in the Individual Complaint Psalms* (Coniectanea Biblica Old Testament Series 37), Stockholm 1994.
Lohfink, N., *Was wird anders bei kanonischer Schriftauslegung? Beobachtungen am Beispiel von Ps. 6* (Jahrbuch für biblische Theologie 3), Neukirchen-Vluyn 1988, 29–53.
Mays, J.L., "The David of the Psalms," in: *Interpretation*, 40 (1986) 143–55.
McCann, J.C. (ed.), *The Shape and Shaping of the Psalter* (JSOT Suppl.S. 159), Sheffield 1993.
Millard, M., *Die Komposition des Psalters. Ein formgeschichtlicher Ansatz* (Forschungen zum AT 9), Tübingen 1994.
Mosis, R., "Die Mauern Jerusalems. Beobachtungen zu Psalm 51,20f.," in: J. Hausmann & H.-J. Zobel (Hrsg.), *Alttestamentlicher Glaube und biblische Theologie.* Stuttgart 1992, 201–15.
Naudé, E., *Psalm 40: één of twee psalms?* Unpublished DD thesis. University of Pretoria 1999.
Niemeyer, C. Th., *Het probleem van de rangschikking der Psalmen.* Leiden 1950.
Prinsloo, W.S., "Die psalms as samehangende boek," in: *Nederduitse Gereformeerde Teologiese Tydskrif*, 36/4 (1995) 459–69.
——, "Psalm 72: 'n verskuiwing van die mistieke na die politieke?" in: *Old Testament Essays*, 12/3 (199) 536–54.
Ro, J.U., *Die sogenannte "Armenfrömmigkeit" im nachexilischen Israel* (Beihefte zur Zeitschrift für die alttestamentliche Wissenschaft 322), Berlin 2002.
Rösel, Ch., *Die messianische Redaktion des Psalters. Studien zu Entstehung und Theologie der Sammlung Psalm 2–89** (Calwer theologische Monographien: Reihe A, 19), Stuttgart 1999.
Schelling, P., *De Asafpsalmen—hun samenhang en achtergrond* (Dissertationes Neerlandicae Series Theologica), Kampen 1985.
Schmidt, N.F., & Nel, P.J., "Theophany as Type-Scene in the Hebrew Bible," in: *Journal for Semitics*, 11/2 (2002) 256–81.
Schmidt, W.H., "Individuelle Eschatologie im Gebet—Psalm 51," in: K. Seybold & E. Zenger (Hrsg.), *Neue Wege der Psalmenforschung* (Herders Biblische Studien 1), Freiburg 1994, 345–60.
Schröten, J., *Entstehung, Komposition und Wirkungsgeschichte des 118. Psalms* (Bonner Biblische Beiträge 95), Weinheim 1995.
Sedlmeier, F., *Jerusalem—Jahwes Bau. Untersuchungen zu Komposition und Theologie von Psalm 147* (Forschung zur Bibel 79), Würzburg 1996.
Spieckermann, H., "Psalmen und Psalter. Suchbewegungen des Forschens und Betens," in: F.G. Martínez and E. Noort (ed.), *Perspectives in the study of the Old Testament and Early Judaism* (VT Suppl. 73), Leiden 1998, 137–53.
Tate, M.E., *Psalms 51–100* (Word Biblical Commentary 20), Dallas 1990.
Vorndran, J., *"Alle Völker werden kommen." Studien zu Psalm 86* (Bonner Biblische Beiträge 133), Berlin 2002.
Weber, B., *Psalm 77 und sein Umfeld. Eine poetologische Studie* (Bonner Biblische Beiträge 103), Weinheim 1995.
——, *Werkbuch Psalmen I. Die Psalmen 1 bis 72.* Stuttgart 2001(a).
——, "Der Asaph-Psalter—eine Skizze," in: B. Huwyler, H.-P. Mathys, & B. Weber (Hrsg.), *Prophetie und Psalmen* (Alter Orient und Altes Testament 280), Münster 2001(b), 117–41.
Whybray, N., *Reading the Psalms as a Book* (JSOT Suppl.S. 222), Sheffield 1996.
Wilson, G.H., *The Editing of the Hebrew Psalter* (SBL Diss.S. 76), Chico 1985.
Zenger, E., "Israel und Kirche im gemeinsamen Gottesbund. Beobachtungen zum theologischen Programm des 4. Psalmbuchs (Ps. 90–106)," in: M. Marcus (Hrsg.), *Israel und Kirche heute. Beiträge zum christlich-jüdischen Dialog*, Freiburg i.B. 1991(a), 236–54.
——, "Was wird anders bei kanonischer Psalmenauslegung?" in: F.V. Reiterer

(Hrsg.), *Ein Gott eine Offenbarung. Beiträge zur biblischen Exegese, Theologie und Spiritualität*, Würzburg 1991(b), 397–413.

———, *»So betete David für seinen Sohn Salomo und für den König Messias«—Überlegungen zur holistischen und kanonischen Lektüre des 72. Psalms* (Jahrbuch für biblische Theologie 8), Neukirchen-Vluyn 1993, 57–72.

———, "New Approaches to the Study of the Psalms," in: *Proceedings of the Irish Biblical Association*, 17 (1994a) 37–54.

———, "Zur redaktionsgeschichtlichen Bedeutung der Korachpsalmen," in: K. Seybold & E. Zenger (Hrsg.), *Neue Wege der Psalmenforschung* (Herders Biblische Studien 1), Freiburg i.B. 1994(b), 175–98.

———, *Die Nacht wird leuchten wie der Tag. Psalmenauslegungen*, Freiburg i.B. 1997.

———, "Das Buch der Psalmen," in: E. Zenger et al., (eds.), *Einleitung in das Alte Testament* (Studienbücher Theologie 1,1), Stuttgart 1998(a), 309–26.

———, "Der Psalter als Buch," in: E. Zenger (Hrsg.), *Der Psalter im Judentum und Christentum* (Herders Biblische Studien 18), Freiburg i.B. 1998(b), 1–57.

———, "David as Musician and Poet: Plotted and Painted," in: J.C. Exum & S.D. Moore (eds.). *Biblical Studies/Cultural Studies. The Third Sheffield Colloquium* (JSOT Suppl.S. 266), Sheffield 1998(c), 263–98.

———, "Die Psalmen im Psalter: Neue Perspektiven der Forschung," in: *Theologische Revue*, 95/6 (1999), 443–56.

———, "The God of Israel's Reign over the World (Psalms 90–106)," in: N. Lohfink & E. Zenger, *The God of Israel and the Nations. Studies in Isaiah and the Psalms*, Collegeville 2000, 161–90 (Translated by E.R. Kalin from *Der Gott Israels und die Völker. Untersuchungen zum Jesajabuch und zu den Psalmen*, Stuttgart 1994).

CHAPTER FIVE

A STRUGGLE WITH GOD: POETICS AND THEOLOGY OF PSALM 35

Matthijs Kronemeijer
University of Nijmegen, the Netherlands

"Searching new worlds" should have been the theme of Sjef van Tilborg's farewell symposium. In this essay to his honor, I will embark on a search, not for a new world, but for hidden beauty in our own old world, the world of our faith. Psalm 35 is part of that world, even if it is an unknown and not much loved part. Its language is difficult and the text appears corrupt. Moreover, the psalm contains some very clear curses and spiteful language that make it unpopular, though not quite unpopular enough to attract the attention of exegetes. I believe that it is worthwhile to draw attention to Psalm 35, not in spite of, but precisely because of, its drama, its rancor and fearful tone. I will try to show that a consistently literary method is the most appropriate way to deal with this sort of text.[1]

This essay will focus on the prosody of Psalm 35, with a few elaborations. Since the literature on Psalm 35 dealing with prosody is very limited, my principal dialogue partner will be the work of *Jan Fokkelman*.[2] Fokkelman is a *literatuurwetenschapper* well known for his work on narrative texts (Genesis and 1–2 Samuel), who has recently turned his attention more to poetic analysis. I will start with a discussion

---

[1] Most of this paper is based on my MA thesis: *Twisten met God. Een exegetische studie van psalm 35*, which I submitted in 2001 to the Catholic Theological University at Utrecht, Netherlands.

[2] There are two long articles by P. Auffret. The oldest is P. Auffret, *Quatre psaumes et un cinquième: étude structurelle des psaumes 7–10 et 35*. Paris, 1992; a reworking can be found in P. Auffret, "Que seulement de tes yeux tu regardes... Etude structurelle de 13 psaumes". *BZAW* 330, Berlin/NY 2003. Then there is one article focusing on a single root in Ps 35:12. J.G. Janzen, "The root *škl* and the soul bereaved in Ps 35." *JSOT* 65 (1995) 55–69. I could not very well use these articles because our presuppositions are contradictory. Fokkelman's treatment of Psalm 35 can be found in J.P. Fokkelman, *Major Poems of the Hebrew Bible*, Volume II, Assen 2000, 134–39.

of the poetics of vv. 1–3 as an introduction to the text and also because the strophic arrangement of the text is peculiar. I will then say some words about the problem of "hate speech" in the Psalms. This is important because of the theological agenda exegetes may have in mind when reading this text. Thirdly, I will explain my understanding of prosody and the technical vocabulary appertaining to it. After that I give my view of the prosody of the Psalm in relation to certain difficulties in the text. As a conclusion, I offer a theory to explain how the different parts of the text fit together.

My approach to the Psalm will be purely synchronic; I believe that the poetic integrity of the text is so great that the assumption of one single author seems by far the most probable. It may be possible to reconstruct an earlier phase of particular passages (and certainly if one does not believe that the final text was composed for actual use), but I do not find this an interesting exercise at all, since there is so much left to be done on the final text.

1. *The Opening*

ריבה יהוה את־יריבי \\ לחם את־לחמי. *O Lord, strive with my adversaries // give battle to my foes.* (JPS translation). The opening verse is programmatic, i.e., it explains in a few words what the text is all about. This stylistic phenomenon is often found in the Psalms and, in many cases, the last verse refers back to the first as a sort of conclusion.[3] In the case of Psalm 35 I would suggest that the opening and closing words were intended to mirror each other: the Psalm then reads as a procession from a fight, ריב, to praise, תהלה, which describes its theme very well.

The root of the opening word is ריב, which means conflict, fight, or struggle. It can refer to a fight either with words or with fists. It is repeated in the last word of the first colon, in the rare form יריבי *yᵉrīvay*. Note the multiple parallelisms in this verse. We find repetition of a root in both the first and the second colon of the verse, in exactly the same positions and with related meanings. Of course

---

[3] See, e.g., H. Beex, *Psalmen in hun originele dichtvorm. Een nieuwe visie!* [sic]. Budel, 2002. Beex has built a poetic theory on the difference between opening/closing/intermediate verses and "strophes." Even if one does not believe in his theory, it is still worthwhile to try to account for his observations.

לחם is stronger than ריב, following the standard pattern "A, what's more, B". Also, a word from the first colon is repeated in the second, the preposition את. The first and second colon both start with an imperative, which is repeated in the following verse in the same places, and in vv. 3a and 3b in the first colon only. Only one word of the first colon is not repeated, the name of God himself, Yhwh. The reasons are clear: no parallel word could be as strong as God's proper name, which should stand at the beginning of the poet's appeal to be heard by God, so any attempt at a parallelism would weaken the verse. Also the second colon should not be too long, for this would slow the poet down before he has even started to speak.

The root ריב reappears in a very sensitive place, v. 23, at the high point of the supplicant's plea for help. Thereby the word establishes itself to a keyword to the text, which is about a vehement conflict anyway. God is asked to fight the supplicant's fight—he has to join him. The fight that is present for him has to be turned upside down.[4] That is what the supplicant asks all along. This reversal motive is something we know well from the Bible. A contemporary example is found in the words of the poet Huub Oosterhuis: 'Zijn woord wil deze wereld omgekeerd / dat lachen zullen zij die wenen // dat wonen zal wie hier geen woonplaats heeft / dat dorst en honger zijn verdreven.'[5] "His (God's) word wants this world upside down, that those who weep can laugh, that those without a home can live here, and thirst and hunger have been dispelled." We can understand now that the text combines a forceful message with poetic complexity and (potentially) spiritual depth. It is with this in mind that I propose to read psalm 35.

2. *Exegesis and Hate Speech*

Above, I gave some arguments why it is hard to appreciate Psalm 35. The text seems to be difficult and some parts repel the reader. Christians who know the high ideals of the Sermon on the Mount will feel the gap at once: Psalm 35 does not show selfless love, or repentance, or forgiveness towards enemies, or contrition towards God, but

---

[4] See also Fokkelman, op. cit., 134.
[5] *Gezangen voor Liturgie* 428; uit H. Oosterhuis, *Aandachtig liedboek*, Baarn 1983, no. 90.

rather the opposites of anxiety, rancor, fury, and spite. I will now briefly offer some suggestions for reading and appreciating the text.

The problem of "hate speech" in the Psalms is a well-known theological problem. It can be approached from different directions, which are by no means mutually contradictory. Erich Zenger has published a discussion of some of the hardest Psalms (unfortunately not Psalm 35), which he analyzed from a biblical-theological perspective.[6] Also, theologians and spiritual authors have written on this problem, notably Dietrich Bonhoeffer, C.S. Lewis, and Kathleen Norris.[7] These authors, different as they are, all reject the exclusion of certain lines or Psalms from use in churches, Bible study or prayer (as what happened, sadly, in the Roman Breviary). Instead, they emphasize the familiarity of the negative emotions that we meet in the Psalms. Any human will occasionally feel angry, frustrated, scared, or spiteful. The Psalms offer a chance to integrate these emotions into a healthy spiritual life.[8]

Psalm 35 can also be approached from this angle—the emotions it describes are all too human and that is what makes them interesting. If, indeed, it is the emotional quality of Psalms that constitutes their value for modern Christians, and not primarily their content or message, this fact has some consequences for exegesis. It means that there is no longer any direct need to look for an uplifting message or thought-provoking theme in the text. Instead, the poetry and, especially, the drama and hyperbole of the Psalms, should be of greater interest to exegetes, since the understanding of these is a precondition for serious and responsible use and study. Drama and poetry Psalm 35 offers in abundance.

Jan Fokkelman frequently complained during his classes about the typical reluctance among theologians to engage in serious literary

---

[6] E. Zenger, *Ein Gott der Rache? Feindpsalmen verstehen*. Freiburg, 1994. English translation: *A God of Vengeance? Understanding the Psalms of Divine Wrath*, Louisville, KY 996.

[7] K. Norris, *The Cloister Walk*, New York 1996 (especially 'The paradox of the Psalms,' 90–107; C.S. Lewis, *Reflections on the Psalms*, London 1958. D. Bonhoeffer, *Das Gebetbuch der Bibel*, München 1940 (*Dietrich Bonhoeffer Werke* 5, with *Gemeinsames Leben*: München 1987).

[8] The Desert Fathers saw the Psalter as a self-contained unity, a complete mirror and field of exercise of human emotion. That is what makes it unique among the books of the Bible. The Fathers also believed that the Psalter does not offer a message different from, or adding to, the message of the Old or the New Testament, but transforms the message of Old and New Testament by its genre, sung poetry. See G. Bader, *Psalterium affectuum palaestra. Prolegomena zu einer Theologie des Psalters* (*HUNT* 33) Tübingen 1996, esp. 114 and 151–52.

study of the texts. Instead, they would focus over-quickly on themes and motives they found spiritually heartening or that suited their convictions, either liberal or orthodox. I share his complaint. In the case of the Psalms (at least) it can now be seen that an approach that is literary in origin, as is Fokkelman's, may form a healthy corrective to this tendency.

3. *Presuppositions and Terminology*

I regard the reconstruction of the original prosody as the inevitable first step in the study of any Psalm. This reconstruction then serves as a basis for the interpretation of single words and verses, and for subsequent research into the history of the text of Israelite religion, composition of the Psalter, or any other matter. Thanks to Fokkelman and others, it is now possible to attempt a more solid reconstruction of the original prosody than ever before.[9]

The working assumption on the text of the psalm is that it is sound and needs no emendation unless it gives no meaning at all. Even the smallest conjunctions (like ו in וְהָרֵק in vs. 3) are of potential value. I have made only one textual emendation to the text: in verse 16-A, I read בחנפי לעגו לעוג *bᵉhanfi laʿagu laʿog*, which will be defended in the next paragraph.

The text naturally reads as a prayer addressed to Yhwh, which was prayed by a single individual, most probably a man. There is no *a priori* reason to doubt that the text is what it seems, a real prayer, though we should not exclude the possibility that it was written as a "fake," that is, intentionally made to look like a prayer, but not intended for real use.[10] But let us suppose it was meant for use. In this case, we should try to imagine a probable place and situation of performance. We cannot know if the context of reading was primarily

---

[9] Fokkelman's treatment of Psalm 35 can be found in J.P. Fokkelman, *Major Poems of the Hebrew Bible*, Volume II, Assen 2000, 134–39.
[10] Cf. for a related discussion E. Zenger, "Der Psalter als Buch." In: E. Zenger (ed.), *Der Psalter in Judentum und Christentum. Beobachtungen zu seiner Entstehung, Komposition und Funktion* (Herders Biblische Studien 18). Freiburg, 1998, pp. 1–57. Similarly: E. Zenger, "Der Psalter als Heiligtum." In: B. Ego, A. Lange, and P. Pilhofer (eds.), *Gemeinde ohne Tempel: zur Substituierung und Transformation des Jerusalemer Tempels und seines Kults im Alten Testament, antiken Judentum und frühen Christentum* (*WUNT* 118) Tübingen 1999, pp. 115–30.

liturgical or juridical, or if the supplicant was supposed to be alone or not. But at least, we may postulate (1) a poet who composed the text, and (2) an intended performer/supplicant who could use it. These may have been one and the same person, but still the distinction is necessary to understand the poetics of the text. As the text was written for maximum audience impact, we may also presuppose that the proper performance required quite a bit of preparation and effort.

We can distinguish different poetical structures in the text. The most important is the so-called prosody of the text, which, in my model, consists of four elements, colon (pl. cola), verse, strophe, and stanza. I will later argue that the text also has two palindromes that interact with the prosodic units. Then there are other poetical patterns and structures that are not directly related to the prosody, such as the repetition of ריב in vv. 1 and 23, and patterns of metaphor.[11] When a rhetorical analysis of the Psalm is attempted, it is not sufficient to take only the prosody as a basis.

Harm van Grol first developed a model of prosody.[12] He has five units: foot, colon, verse, strophe, and stanza. I have omitted the foot. The model can easily be expanded to include either smaller or larger units, and many scholars do so. I have limited myself to these four because I prefer to use only those units that have been demonstrated in the ancient texts.[13] There may still be room for a few of the other units but I am not so sure. The prosodic model as a whole is based on the principle that two, possibly three, and rarely one or four smaller elements constitute a unit one step up. So two or three cola make up one verse, two or three verses one strophe, and so on. It is very well possible that the poets of Israel just regarded this system as a matrix that could be enlarged as their poems required, so beyond the basic units of colon, verse, and strophe we should be careful.[14]

---

[11] I cannot go into them at length in this paper. Most notable are the word fields of shame and honor, of movement, and juridical terms.

[12] H. van Grol, *De versbouw in het klassieke Hebreeuws: fundamentele verkenningen*. Amsterdam 1986.

[13] Authors belonging to the Kamper School (Korpel, de Moor) have done so, with the help of archaeology and philology (e.g., strophe and verse markers in inscriptions and manuscripts).

[14] One should not, obviously, lump together units found in different poems. A long poem may have four-verse or even eight-verse long canticles but that does not imply that such a unit had a character of its own in Hebrew poetics. This psalm suggests the stanza is already a much less stable unit than the strophe. In the intro-

For native speakers of Classical Hebrew the system must have been easy to use and to play with, even for those who were not blessed with strong poetical talents.

Fokkelman uses a larger version of the model. He develops a 12–14-position grid of structural elements which includes sounds, phonemes, morphemes, syllables, words, as well as cantos and canticles, and is derived from the hermeneutical model he used in his work on Samuel.[15] The long model enables Fokkelman to include the proportions of stresses which, according to him, are very carefully distributed in his model. I decided not to indulge in the counting of stresses since this would only make sense if there were agreement on the prosodic structure of the text, which is not the case. Also, I think the model, when expanded, can be potentially misleading at a historical level. Fokkelman considers his work as an exercise of hermeneutics. For him, the extended model is just a tool. He never asks if the model he uses corresponds to the original poetic system that the poets of ancient Israel used. I do ask that question. It is quite possible, even probable, that the Ancient Israelites had a system of poetics quite as sophisticated as those we find in the rhetorical handbooks of the Romans, the Greeks, and the Arabs.

Regarding terminology, I adopt Fokkelman's usage, with a few refinements.[16] I speak of A-, B-, and C-cola to indicate the first, second, and (if present) third colon of a verse. A colon is, by definition, the words spoken between two pauses, with normally two stresses.[17] Two guidelines serve to determine the original cola. The first is to find the most natural way of performing the text with appropriate pauses between cola and verses (the Masoretes are some help here); the second is to establish which reading of the text gives the best overall balance of the verse and/or the strophe.

A verse with two cola is called a dicolon, a verse with three a tricolon. A verse requires a slightly longer breath pause or emphasis

---

duction to his *Major Poems of the Hebrew Bible*, volume I, 20–23 Fokkelman makes a very strange comparison between cola from the Psalms and Job in order to establish what a colon "is." There is a huge difference in genre between Job and the Psalms, and because their poets had different purposes, the cola are different.

[15] Fokkelman, *Major Poems of the Hebrew Bible*, Volume I, Assen 1998, 2–4.
[16] See Fokkelman, *Major Poems of the Hebrew Bible*, Volumes I and II, Assen 1998 and 2000.
[17] See H. van Gorp, R. Ghesquiere, and D. Delabastita, *Lexicon van literaire termen*. Groningen 1998[7], 90.

than a colon; the beginning is always audible. Capital letters indicate strophe types; their potential significance will be shown later.[18] Capital S stands for a standard strophe with 2 verses of 2 cola each. L stands for a "long" strophe with three verses of 2 cola each. E stands for "extended," meaning two verses of three cola each. T stands for a trapezoid, i.e., 3 cola in the first verse and 2 in the second. There is one exceptional strophe (vv. 17–19) construed as 3–2–2, which I will first indicate 1+L and discuss below. In all cases I assume that the length and type of the unit may have some relevance for its effect in the text.[19]

In my view, the strophe is a purely literary unity. Its unity is decided by stylistic figures (parallelism of all sorts) and content only, not by breath pauses and/or the logic of pronunciation. Usually one strophe has only one point to make, which it makes twice, once in each verse; exceptions are strophes 5 (vv. 7 and 8) and 10 (vv. 17–19) where the poet must have wanted to create disruptions to this pattern.[20] The stanza just serves to create greater harmony and regularity in the poem.

4. *A Possible Prosodic Arrangement of Psalm 35*

The following discussion of the prosody of Psalm 35 relies, of course, on detailed study of the text of the Psalm as I have shown, more or less, in the opening treatment of vv. 1–3. In the following the results are only repeated when they play a part in the argument. My approach in this essay has been to compare my reconstruction of the original prosody with those of others and discuss only the differences. However, as I indicated above, there are not so many possible dialogue partners. It makes no great sense to discuss those

---

[18] Regarding strophe types Fokkelman's system is not very precise. He just adds + to his capitals to indicate an extra colon, without specifying where it stands. Also he does not differentiate between two dicola and two tricola.

[19] Referring to the poetical theory of Roman Jakobson could support this further. I am, however, not sufficiently familiar with Jakobson's theory to grasp its significance for Hebrew poetry and its system of parallelism. It is, however, obvious that the effect of an S or L strophe is potentially different from the effect of a T strophe, with verses of unequal length. Think of the Latin poet Ovid, who first used distiches in his light verse and then regular hexameters in his *Metamorphoses*.

[20] See the study by Beex mentioned in note 3 for a different treatment of this phenomenon.

commentaries that do not acknowledge the presence of strophic structures. Their authors' arguments may have some bearing on prosody and stylistic figures, but very often need to be rephrased quite a bit before it is possible to use them. Van der Lugt, who does work with strophes and stanzas, did not discuss this psalm in his 1980 dissertation.[21] This means that Fokkelman is effectively the only possible partner, together with BHS and the Masoretes.[22]

First, a note on textual criticism. Concerning v. 16 I have suggested to read בחנפי לענו לעוג *bᵉhanfi laʿagu laʿog*, instead of לעני מעוג, which seems to make no sense. My proposed reading changes only two consonants and does not affect the order of the text. The repeated absolute infinitive corresponds with the Septuagint, επειρασαν με, εξεμυκτηρισαν με μυκτηρισμον. The prosody of strophe 9 (vv. 15–16) suggests a parallelism between ובצלעי in 15 and בחנפי in 16, so that the word should preferably be left unchanged. A translation such as "stumbling" is possible, and may even give a key to the interpretation of the text. We could think of a "faux pas," a sin or mistake by the supplicant, that is now being exploited by his enemies.

My prosody corresponds with Fokkelman's in all but five instances. First, I regard his 3-C as a separate verse, with two cola, the same as the BHS but more or less against the Masoretes. This turns Fokkelman's first (L⁺) strophe into two S-strophes (vv. 1–2 and 3a–3b). Second, I read שחת רשתם *shahat rishtam* in v. 7 as a separate B-colon (against both BHS and the Masoretes). Third, I read verse 15 as a long tricolon instead of two dicola (with the Masoretes and Septuagint, but against BHS); fourth, I arrange verse 19 with 17 and 18 into one strophe. And finally I consider the invocation *Yhwh Elohay* in 24 as a separate B-colon, as in v. 7, without any support from BHS or Masoretes.[23]

There are two places where Fokkelman and I agree against BHS, vv. 13–14 and 27. In both cases, BHS seems to have problems with

---

[21] P. van der Lugt, *Strofische structuren in de Bijbels-Hebreeuwse poëzie: de geschiedenis van het onderzoek en een bijdrage tot de theorievorming omtrent de strofenbouw van de psalmen* [strophic structures in biblical Hebrew poetry: the history of research and a contribution to the theory concerning the strophic construction of the psalms]. Kampen: Kok, 1980.

[22] Note that in the following, I treat Fokkelman's prosody as if it was intended as a reconstruction of the original prosody, which formally, it is not.

[23] Although the Septuagint translation seems to offer a clue—the words κυριε ο θεος μου—my B-colon, are in some versions attached to the first hemistich and in others to the second.

the long verses proposed by the Masoretes, especially since the preceding verses have very short cola. I do not believe this is a strong argument against the traditional arrangement. The text was created to be performed or at least, to be orally delivered. As has been argued above, the colon exists through the short pause a reader or performer makes between cola. The decision where to make a pause is entirely the reader's; he or she can make it after two words, or after five, just as he or she likes, but one who knows the text well would know how to perform the cola in the most persuasive way. So even if, e.g., my A-colon of v. 27 looks just like vv. 4a or 4b that have two cola (and all have just four words), it is very well possible to read only one colon in 27-A and two in vv. 4a and 4b.

This brings me to the two places where I offer a new division of cola, vv. 7 and 24. In v. 7 I propose to drop the usual transposition שחת רשתם, *shahat rishtam*. The text makes perfect sense when it is read, "a trap with their net," although the meaning is no doubt metaphorical.[24] This is already an argument against the usual conjecture, since no conjectures are necessary when the text is clear.

Secondly, the main purpose of the reading *rishtam // weshahat* is to establish a balance between the two cola. The same can be achieved by reading it as a separate B-colon. In this version the assonance between *li* (end of A-colon) and *nafshi* (end of C-colon) appears much more clearly than in any other arrangement; the same goes for *hinnam* at the beginning of both A- and C-colon. A possible objection might be that in my version the B-colon forms an objective clause to the A-colon. This means that it is an incomplete sentence, a suggestion for the reader to read on. But the same is true for the dicola vv. 4a and 4b, and again the pause between the A- and B-cola could be used for dramatic emphasis.[25] The root שחת is so strong that some drama is obviously intended in v. 7: it is the supplicant's accusation, even if it is phrased metaphorically.

---

[24] I follow M. Dahood to read here an accusative of means. M. Dahood, *The Anchor Bible, Psalms I*. Garden City 1966, 211.

[25] It is an interesting case. In my view, and probably also of those who adopt the conjecture for v. 7, the author of the psalm aimed at creating well-balanced verses. This is my reason to propose a tricolic arrangement. The fact that the Masoretes and other readers do not make a caesura here is no decisive argument to the contrary. The Masoretes probably did not need to enhance the drama of the text by their way of reading; also, if the poet intended two separate cola for stylistic purposes, that does not mean that any reader past or present would have had to perform them as such.

A similar consideration applies to v. 24, where I propose to read *Yhwh Elohay* as a separate B-colon. In vv. 22 and 23 we see the poet/supplicant address God directly four times, once with his proper name Yhwh, and three times with other names. This is indeed the passage where he really wants to make himself heard and there is no better way to achieve this than by addressing God with his proper name. This is also the poet's strategy in v. 24, with *Yhwh Elohay*. For this reason, it would be very strange if the two names for God were pronounced over-quickly. Therefore, a pause for breath and dramatic emphasis is natural. It is no argument to the contrary that the Masoretes do not read a pause here. They pronounced the text differently (as Adonay Elohay) and with no dramatic effects in mind because to them, the text was already holy and a privileged witness to revelation; it did not need any more special effects. Finally, the fact that v. 25 is a tricolon is an argument to arrange v. 24 the same way. Otherwise we would have an oddly formed strophe, but now we have two tricola with regular (short) cola all the time.[26] In my view, these reasons are more than sufficient to arrange v. 24 as a tricolon.

Regarding v. 15, I can see no reason not to retain the reading as tricola proposed by the Masoretes. The Septuagint has the same and the verse makes good sense in this division. Without the difficult נכים (plural of *נכי, beaters or thugs?) the literal repetition of נאספו עלי weakens the meaning of the verse, because it would violate the basic rule for parallelism, "A, what's more, B." The fact that the B-colon is a bit long (12 beats) is no real problem.

I now have to go into my arrangement of v. 19 together with vv. 17–18 into one strophe. All three verses begin with א, which is an alliteration. More importantly, when 17-A is excepted, all three verses contain a chiasmus, with the final element of the A-colon returning in the B-colon (note the double duty of אל in 19-A and -B). Read like this, vv. 17–19 can be defined as a three-point summary of the poet's message. Verses 20–21 can then be understood as a more general elaboration of the message of 19 and as a prelude to the climax of the Psalm, vv. 22–25. (For this, v. 20 כי can be read as "verily," or "truly").

The last issue to be considered now is my arrangement of verse 3 of the BHS into two dicola, which I call 3a and 3b. It seems likely

---

[26] A possible alternative is a reading of the whole strophe as two dicola.

there should be a pause between אמר לנפשי and אני ישעתך, and a four-colon verse would be very exceptional, but maybe this is not enough.²⁷ Part of the problem lies in the division of vv. 1–3 into strophes and stanzas. I have two strophes of each two verses (dicola) and these strophes together make up one stanza. Fokkelman has one strophe of three verses: two dicola and one tricolon. A disadvantage of my arrangement is that vv. 2 and 3a are near parallels, but belong to different strophes. The matter is complicated further by the word סגר *s^egor* of which the meaning is not straightforward. I will first go into this problem.

Usually סגר is translated as "spear" or "lance" following 1QM 5, 7.9; this would give a neat parallelism with v. 2. Another possibility is to read it as it stands, as the imperative of סגר "to enclose, to block." This is also the reading of the Septuagint, καὶ σύγκλεισον. However, this does not say very much. In v. 14 the Septuagint has ὡς πενθῶν καὶ σκυθρωπάζων, "like one mourning and sad," instead of "like one mourning his mother [. . .]." This means that the translator has misread אם "mother" in the original as a preposition אם, and was thus translating the text from a manuscript. Had he known the text, he would have understood the climactic figure friend—brother—mother. So also in the case of סגר he may just have guessed at the wrong vocalization.

A problem with the translation "spear" is that in the Qumran text it seems to mean "haft," which is a bit strange in the context of Ps 35:1–3. In favor of the reading as an imperative pleads that there are very many words in the Psalm with connotations of movement (to meet, to pursue, to fall, to draw forth, to beat down, etc.). "To encircle" could fit into this group. I have a slight preference to stay with "spear" or "lance," but it is hard decision.

Returning to the question of prosodic division: I have the following arguments to count 3b as a separate verse. First, the message of the text requires quite a bit of dramatic emphasis. V. 3b is the climax of the text. God has to pledge himself, which means a lot more than just a display of weapons, and one would not expect this at the end of a verse. It could be logical if the last colon was a natural con-

---

[27] Fokkelman seems not to have thought of the possibility of two strophes, and obviously does not like the possibility of a four-verse strophe or a four-colon verse. So he cannot very well accept a pause. See *Major Poems of the Hebrew Bible*, Volume II, 137, n. 47.

tinuation of the rest of the verse (as in v. 8), but I do not think this could be said for 3-AB since the verse is already parallel with v. 2 after the first two cola. Another argument is the harmony in the strophes. Fokkelman's first strophe is rather oddly formed and he does not explain its internal logic. In the next paragraph, I will argue that the form of a strophe makes a difference to its poetic effect. In this light, it is much easier to account for two simple strophes.

Probably, the best way to shed more light on this problem would be to compare the beginnings of various psalms (especially psalms with programmatic opening lines as this one) and see how they affect the prosodic structure. I cannot do this now. On the basis of what I have done, I would suggest that vv. 1–3 represent an oddly formed stanza, construed *ab/ba* instead of *aa/bb*.[28] A comparison with the second stanza suggests a slightly similar movement from heavy cola to smaller ones and back to heavy ones. There is no reason why two strophes in one stanza could not be construed this way, if this allowed the poet more freedom to present a powerful opening.

5. *The Proportional Arrangement of Cola, Verses, and Strophes*

I will now attempt to describe how the different structural units of the Psalm may fit together. I have found 32 verses, 74 cola, and 15 strophes. Fokkelman has the same number of verses, 72 cola, and 14 strophes. When presented with capitals (a slash indicates a stanza) my division into strophes looks like this:

S S / S S / E L / S / T T / 1+L E / S E / S T

In the passage on terminology, the meaning of the different capitals had already been explained. There are two T's in the middle. Actually, a count of cola shows that the intended middle of the Psalm is indeed between the two T's, since there are 37 cola in the first eight strophes and 37 in the last seven. (This is not conclusive evidence, of course, but a high enough probability.) Even if the two cola 7-B and 24-B are not accepted as separate the symmetry remains, although the change would affect my later argument.

---

[28] Note that the almost complete parallellism of 2-A and 3-A is disrupted by the ו in וחרק, which makes it just a bit more logical to assign these verses to different strophes.

I suggest that the poet used two, and possibly three, palindromes to structure the flow of his text: one or maybe two at strophe level, one at verse level. However, he did not apply them consistently, but allowed for disruptions. If we look at the strophes first, we may imagine a palindrome covering the whole of the poem, with strophes of the same type mirroring each other. It could be described as follows:

$$S\ S\ /\ S\ S\ /\ E\ L\ /\ ^S\ /\ T\ T\ /\ ^{1+}L\ E\ /\ S\ S^{+2}\ /\ S\ S^{+1}$$

The + in superscript indicates extra cola in a strophe. The disruptions in the palindrome pattern are obvious. There are four of them. In the first half it is my strophe no. 7 (vv. 11–12); in the second half there are the extra first colon in strophe 10 (v. 17), the two extra cola in strophe 13 (vv. 24–25), and the one extra in strophe 15, v. 27. If these four passages are taken out for a moment, the palindrome is perfect. And even as the division is now, there is some harmony of proportion, for the disruption concerns four cola in the first half and four in the second half of the poem.

My theory to explain the composition of the Psalm is that the poet did aim to create a palindrome, but decided not to mirror strophe 7 directly. Instead he uses its four cola in places where he needed extra verbal power in the second half of the poem, the three other places I have just mentioned.[29]

This must sound strange. Why shouldn't the poet just have extended his poem where and how he liked? The obvious answer: he valued symmetry and regularity. We need only add that apparently he just did not do so in a dogmatic way. It might be that he thought the text was proportioned quite well as it stands now; he may have considered the palindrome as a device that could help him compose or memorize the poem, but that should not stand in the way of its message.

It still seems strange that strophe 7 (vv. 11–12) does not fit into the palindrome. A solution to this problem lies in the fact that it fits into another palindrome, one that figures not on the strophe level, but on the verse level. When we consider the number of cola in each verse of strophes 7–10 we find: 2-2-3-2-3-2-3-2-2, which is a palindrome again with the central 3 (v. 15) in the exact middle of the

---

[29] Among these three places 17-A stands out because of the exclamation; vv. 24–25 disrupt an all-too-quiet pattern of S-strophes at the high point of the supplicant's appeal for help; and 27-A establishes a slowing-down effect appropriate to the conclusion of the poem.

psalm. The result is that strophe 10 now figures in both palindromes, thereby adding to its unique quality as a turning point in the Psalm.

It is possible to argue for various alternatives to the scheme I had just given. First, it could be argued that strophe 7 does have a parallel in the second half of the poem, namely in 17-A, יהוה כמה תראה. Then we could get the following scheme:

S S / S S / E L / S / T T / 1 / L E / S E / S T

The phrase is clearly separate from the rest of the strophe so that is not a problem, but we get into some terminological confusion now. There is now a strophe-stanza of only one colon, which at the same time belongs to a verse that belongs to a different strophe and stanza; or if it does not belong to the same verse, the second palindrome has to be dropped. Regarding the meaning of the phrase ("Lord, how long will you look on?"), I would like to point to a possible parallel in Ps 22:22, the famous turning point עניתני.[30] This sort of phrase may well have a special place of its own in the prosody of the texts. Another funny aspect of these arrangements is that 12-B, the mirror of 17-A in the palindrome, is extremely short and strong and could be read as an intended parallel.

Another alternative would be to transcribe my strophe no. 10 as TS. It is structured 3–2–2 so it has the characteristics of both the trapezoid and the ordinary S-strophe. This gives the following scheme for the third part of the psalm:

TS E / S E / S T

Or:

T S E S E S T

This structure gives a third palindrome, with vv. 22–23 at the center, verses which are clearly intended as the climax of the supplicant's appeal to God. One should note however that one verse has disappeared in the last arrangement because, obviously, "TS" is only three verses as opposed to the four verses of the S T at the end of the poem.

I am not going to propose a definitive solution as to which alignment best describes the author's intentions, especially because this last palindrome is not very strong. But also, on a different level, we work on paper and the author of the text probably worked only

---

[30] P. Beentjes has argued passionately to read it as it stands, "You have answered me!" In: Marcel Poorthuis (ed.), *Mijn God, mijn God, waarom hebt Gij mij verlaten? Een interdisciplinaire bundel over psalm 22*. Baarn 1997.

from out of his head; as far as we know, he may even have been illiterate. The only thing I want to stress is that we should try to understand how the Hebrew poets thought about their poems and how they conceptualized the different structural units in them.

6. *Conclusion*

My reconstruction of the original prosody can be found on a separate page. I have 74 verses of which 10 are tricola: 7, 8, 13, 15, 20, 21, 24, 25, and 27; these 74 verses form 15 strophes of which 14 are coupled to form stanzas. I suggest that the poet who wrote Psalm 35 did not only aim to create a strong prosodic structure (as Fokkelman argued earlier), but that he also construed two or even three palindromes, one on verse level and one or two on strophe level. How the palindromes should be defined exactly, and how the poet himself regarded them, remains open.

At the level of the rhetorical structure of the poem, my data confirm the existing consensus among commentators that its structure is tripartite. My preferred division is 1–10, 11–16, 17–28 (17-A seems a good marker). The terminology I had developed to describe the different structures could possibly be improved further on the basis of comparison with other Psalms. It would be most interesting to have a good look at the way strophe types, exclamation cola (such as 17-A), and palindromes function there. As a next step, one could try to investigate the inner relations of the Psalter.

It is tempting to further speculate about the intended original context of Psalm 35 (some sort of magic?) but I will not do so now. I remember Sjef van Tilborg telling me about the importance of the concept of ignorance in Buddhism, which for me serves as a warning here even if I do not know precisely what he meant.

It is, above all, the poetic quality of the text that I wanted to show and to defend in this article. Sometimes it seemed to me that the anguished and aggrieved tone of the Psalm could also be understood as coming from the text itself: "Why did you exegetes never want to understand me? Why did you call me corrupt, cut me to pieces, refuse to accept me as the poem I am? May God put you to shame!"

Fortunately, God will fight any supplicant's fight if he asks for it; even though the struggle may often appear a struggle against God. Ultimately, God will be found on the defendant's side.

7. *Psalm 35*

strophe nr			
		לדוד	1
1	לחם את־לחמי׃	ריבה יהוה את־יריבי	
	וקומה בעזרתי׃	החזק מגן וצנה	2
2	לקראת רדפי	והרק חנית וסגר	3
	ישעתך אני׃	אמר לנפשי	
3	מבקשי נפשי	יבשו ויכלמו	4
	חשבי רעתי׃	יסגו אחור ויחפרו	
4	ומלאך יהוה דוחה	יהיו כמץ לפני־רוח	5
	ומלאך יהוה רדפם׃	יהי־דרכם חשך והחלקלקות	6
5	חנם חפרו לנפשי׃	שחת רשתם	כי־חנם טמנו־לי	7
	בשואה יפל־בה׃	ורשתו אשר־טמן תלכדו	תבואהו שואה לא־ידע	8
6		תגיל בישועתו	ונפשי תגיל ביהוה	9
		יהוה מי כמוך	כל עצמותי תאמרנה	10
		ועני ואביון מגזלו׃	מציל עני מחזק ממנו	
7	אשר לא־ידעתי ישאלוני׃		יקומון עדי חמס	11
	שכול לנפשי׃		ישלמוני רעה תחת טובה	12
8	ותפלתי על־חיקי תשוב׃	עניתי בצום נפשי	ואני בחלותם לבוש שק	13
		כאבל־אם קדר שחותי׃	כרע־כאח לי התהלכתי	14
9	נאספו עלי נכים ולא ידעתי	קרעו ולא־דמו׃	ובצלעי שמחו ונאספו	15
		קרע עלי שנימו׃	בחנפי לעגי מעוג	16[31]
10	השיבה נפשי משאיהם	מכפירים יחידתי׃	אדני כמה תראה	17
	בעם עצום אהללך׃		אודך בקהל רב	18
	שנאי חנם יקרצו־עין׃		אל־ישמחו־לי איבי שקר	19
11	ועל רגעי־ארץ	דברי מרמות יחשבון׃	כי לא שלום ידברו	20
	אמרו האח האח	ראתה עינינו׃	ויריחבו עלי פיהם	21
12	אדני אל־תרחק ממני׃		ראיתה יהוה אל־תחרש	22
	אלהי ואדני לריבי׃		העירה והקיצה למשפטי	23
13	יהוה אלהי	ואל־ישמחו־לי׃	שפטני כצדקך	24
	האח נפשנו	אל־יאמרו בלענוהו׃	אל־יאמרו בלבם	25
14	שמחי רעתי		יבשו ויחפרו יחדו	26
	המגדילים עלי׃		ילבשו־בשת וכלמה	
15	ויאמרו תמיד יגדל יהוה	החפץ שלום עבדו׃	ירנו וישמחו חפצי צדקי	27
	כל־היום תהלתך׃		ולשוני תהגה צדקך	28

---

[31] The text of this verse has been amended; the masoretic text reads מעוג לעני.

CHAPTER SIX

ISAIAH'S ROLES:
THE UNITY OF A BIBLE BOOK
FROM THE PERSPECTIVE OF THE SENDER-ROLE

Archibald L.H.M. van Wieringen
University of Nijmegen, the Netherlands

In reader-oriented exegesis, extensive interest in the receiver's pole in the communication exists;[1] concerning the sender's pole, however, the attention given is rather scarce. Nevertheless, this sender's pole contributes to the reader's perception of a bible book's unity to a great extent as well. In this article, I wish to show this aspect regarding the Book Isaiah according to my recent research at the *Katholieke Universiteit Nijmegen*.

1. *Isaiah as Discursor/Narrator*

Headings indicate, as it were, the main structure of a text. This also applies to the Book Isaiah. The headings in Isa 1:1; 2:1, and 13:1 (along with 15:1a; 17:1a; 19:1a; 21:1a.11a.13a; 22:1a; 23:1a) and the absence of any heading in 40–66 after the orientation shift between 39:8 and 40:1 create the main structure in which the text of respectively 1:2–31; 2:2–12:6 and 13:2–14:32; 15:1b–16:14; 17:1b–18:7; 19:1b–20:6; 21:1b–10.11b–12.13b–17; 22:1b–25; 23:1b–39:8; and 40–66 lies. The headings, therefore, create one single discursive text (which is narratively interrupted a few times) with one single communicative sender-instance. This sender-instance plays the role of discursor and is named with the proper name Isaiah in Isa 1:1; 2:1; 13:1.

---

[1] Here, almost the entire oeuvre of Sjef van Tilborg can be enumerated. Theoretically essential was his inaugural speech (van Tilborg 1994). Especially regarding the Gospel of John, the monographs (van Tilborg 1993) and (van Tilborg 1996) have to be mentioned.

In addition to this, the proper name Isaiah occurs as a character in the narrative texts in the Book Isaiah as well.

The distinction between Isaiah as discursor/narrator and Isaiah as character is hardly ever made in Old Testament exegesis: the occurrences of the proper name יְשַׁעְיָהוּ *Isaiah* are usually enumerated without distinguishing their textual role.[2] This may lead to the situation that the absence of the proper name "Isaiah" as from chapter 40 on is used as an argument for the caesura between Isa 39:8 and 40:1.[3]

In chapters 1–39, however, the presence of the proper name "Isaiah" is restricted to a few parts. As discursor/narrator, "Isaiah" only occurs in Isa 1:1; 2:1; 13:1 throughout chapters 1–39, as mentioned above. As a character, "Isaiah" is only present in the narrative parts, namely in Isa 7:3 in the narrative part 7:1–17, in 20:2.3 in the narrative part 20:1–6[4] and in 37:2.5–6.21; 38:1.4.21; 39:3.5.8; in the narrative part 36:1–39:8.[5]

The unity of Isa 1–39, therefore, is not situated at the level of the character with the proper name Isaiah, but at a higher textual communication level, namely the level of the discursor, and, therefore, in the communication to the implied reader, who is indicated to understand all these chapters as a text of the discursor Isaiah.

The text of the headings itself, however, does not originate from the communicative instance discursor, named Isaiah, but stages this instance in the text. This implies that a different instance is responsible for the text of the headings. As a result of this, a communicative setting arises composed of the communicative instance implied author, who is an unnamed, abstract communicative sender-instance, responsible for the headings, and a not-unnamed communicative sender-instance, responsible for the text, which depends on these headings. This communicative situation for Isa 1–39 can be represented as follows.

---

[2] See: Watts (1985), xxvii; Conrad (1991), 34.
[3] See, for example: A. Laato (1998), 45–46.
[4] For some reason, this text-passage is sometimes missing in enumerations of occurrences of the proper name יְשַׁעְיָהוּ *Isaiah*; thus see: Emmerson (1992), 71–72.
[5] Ackroyd (1978), 38; Gosse (2000), especially 5–7, among others, overcome the small number of occurrences of the proper name יְשַׁעְיָהוּ *Isaiah* by emphasizing the semantic thread created by the "theologically" important root ישע *salvation* (instead of *liberation*).

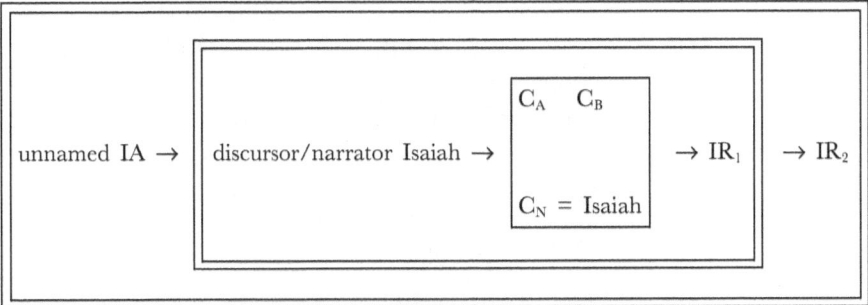

In this diagram,⁶ the section framed by a triple line represents the entire text. An unnamed implied author is responsible for it. Via the headings, this instance delegates its responsibility to a not-unnamed discursor, named Isaiah. This instance subsequently delegates its responsibility for Isa 1:2–31; 2:2–12:6; 13:2–14:32; 15:1b–16:14; 17:1b–18:7; 19:1b–20:6; 21:1b–10.11b–12.13b–17; 22:1b–25; 23:1b–39:8; (and 40–66) to several characters (C_a, C_b, etc.), along with a character (C_n) with the proper name Isaiah, who plays the role of prophet (see the noun הַנָּבִיא *prophet* in 37:2; 38:1; 39:3).⁷ In sum, therefore, the communicative situation (in Isa 1–39) is as follows.

unnamed IA → discursor Isaiah → characters (among which the prophet Isaiah)

Due to the fact that headings are absent in Isa 40–66, no discursor/narrator seems to be indicated for these chapters, at least not with the proper name Isaiah. Even more striking, the proper name Isaiah does not occur at all in Isa 40–66. In what way then can the situation in Isa 40–66 be described?

It is, however, self-evident that there is a discursor/narrator-instance in Isa 40–66 too. Because Isa 40–66 is a discursive text, this instance must be a discursor. With regard to this, Isa 40–66, therefore, is similar to 1–39. Apart from this observation, however, there is more to say about this discursor-instance.

---

⁶ The abbreviation "IA" means "implied author," "IR" means "implied reader," "C" means "character." There are two receiver-instances, one corresponding with the implied author, the other with the discursor/narrator.

⁷ Confer also the noun הַנְּבִיאָה; *prophetess* in Isa 8:3.

The communicative setting of Isa 40–66 is made clear from the outset in the first pericope of this main unit, 40:1–11. In this text-passage, various direct speeches occur, which are connected to each other by differences and similarities in time and in speaker. The main text-linguistic relations can be traced out as follows.[8]

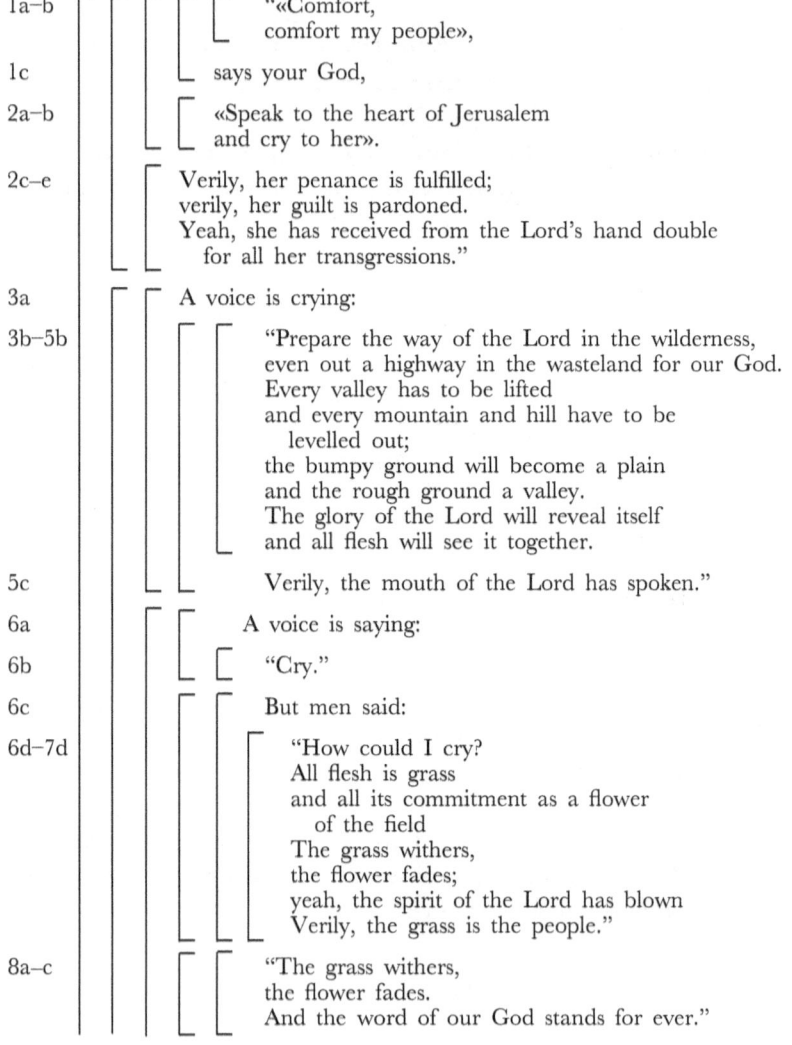

---

[8] See for a theoretical explanation of text-linguistic relations: van Wieringen (1998), 2–11.

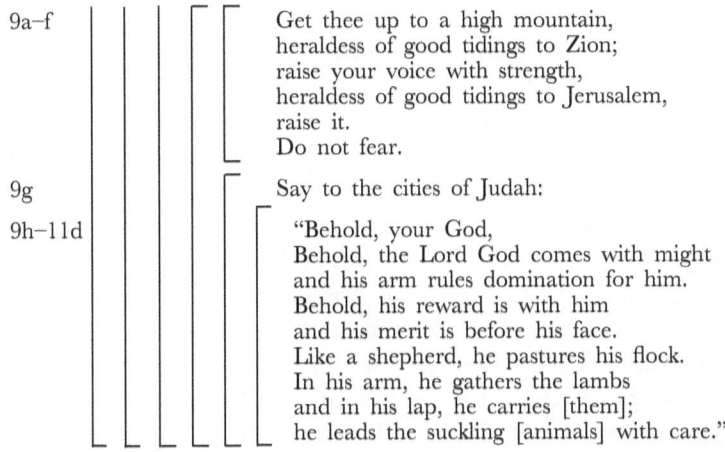

9a–f	Get thee up to a high mountain, heraldess of good tidings to Zion; raise your voice with strength, heraldess of good tidings to Jerusalem, raise it. Do not fear.
9g	Say to the cities of Judah:
9h–11d	"Behold, your God, Behold, the Lord God comes with might and his arm rules domination for him. Behold, his reward is with him and his merit is before his face. Like a shepherd, he pastures his flock. In his arm, he gathers the lambs and in his lap, he carries [them]; he leads the suckling [animals] with care."

Isa 40:1–11 is usually considered to be a chain of calls.[9] Due to the shift in tense between verse 6a אֹמֵר "is saying," a participle, and verse 6c וְאָמַר "said," a *qatal*-form preceded by the conjunction וְ "but," however, the sequence of the direct speeches in the text cannot be equated to the chronological order.[10]

To gain insight into this chain, the direct speeches have to be dealt with. The direct speech by the character אֱלֹהִים "God" (verse 1c) in the verses 1a–b.2a–b, the direct speech by the character קוֹל "voice" (verse 3a) in the verses 3b–5c and in verse 6b, the countervoice direct speech in the verses 8a–c,[11] and the direct speech by the character מְבַשֶּׂרֶת צִיּוֹן (verse 9b) and מְבַשֶּׂרֶת יְרוּשָׁלִָם (verse 9d), the heraldess of good tidings to Zion and Jerusalem, in the verses 9h–11d are not problematic.

Other direct speeches demanded special attention. Firstly, a direct speech is formed by the verses 1a–2e. Verse 1c does not contain the word אֱלֹהִים 'God', but אֱלֹהֵיכֶם "your God." Because of the presence of a second person in the suffix, verse 1c itself is direct speech. The starting point in the verses 1–2 is not that God speaks to a plural addressee to comfort his people, but that a sender-instance says to a plural addressee that God speaks to a plural addressee to comfort his people. In this manner, the discursor becomes manifest in the speaker of verse 1c.[12]

---

[9] Thus for instance: Westermann (1966) 30; Beuken (1979) 15.18.21.
[10] See: van Wieringen (1989), 86.
[11] van Wieringen (1989), 90.
[12] Confer: van Wieringen (1989), 84–85.

In reaction to the call of God, two voices start speaking, in accordance with the plural addressee. The first voice says (verse 3a) in plural to the people on the other side of the desert that, only after a way will have been made through the wilderness and the impassable areas, which separate the people from Jerusalem, can Jerusalem be addressed.

Thereupon a voice (the same voice) speaks (verse 6a) to a singular addressee. This concerns an indefinite subject casting doubt on the possibility to cry, referring to the previous situation of destruction described by grass withering and a flower fading (the verses 6e–7d = the verses 8a–b). Logically it is stated by the same voice as in 6a: although in this manner the situation may be described correctly (the verses 8a–b), God's call remains standing (verse 8c). In sum: the utterance in which an indefinite subject expresses doubts about the call (verses 6c–7d), therefore, precedes the order expressed by the voice saying "cry" in verse 6b, but this doubt is taken away by the same voice in the verses 8a–c.

It can, however, only be understood that an indefinite subject has doubts about the call if the same indefinite subject was previously commanded to cry. This situation only arises when considering the verses 9a–11d as spoken by the voice and spoken to the indefinite subject. In this manner, therefore, the following sequence of events chronologically arises.

	doubts	removal	
first call to cry	about the call	of the doubts	second call to cry
(verses 9a–11d)	(verses 6c–7d)	(verses 8a–c)	(verses 6a–b)

In distinction to the chronological sequence, the textual sequence of the dialogue implies that the identity of the unnamed indefinite subject is revealed to the implied reader just after the doubts of this character are removed. The anonymous indefinite subject develops into the heraldess of good tidings to Zion and Jerusalem.

From the perspective of the development of the identity's revelation, the heraldess of good tidings to Zion and Jerusalem can be considered again from the viewpoint of the verses 1–2. The content of the verses 9h–11d runs parallel to the verses 1c.2c–e to a high degree. In both cases, the speaker of the direct speeches uses the indication אֱלֹהֵיכֶם "your God" (verse 9h and verse 1c). The end of Jerusalem's miserable status corresponds with God's redeeming coming, in which the two issues שְׂכָרוֹ "his reward" (verse 10c) and פְּעֻלָּתוֹ "his merit" (verse 10d) are contrasted with the two issues צְבָאָהּ "her penance" (verse

2c) and עֲוֹנָהּ "her guilt" (verse 2d). In this manner, the text can be understood as being the communicative instance discursor performing in the text in the shape of the character "heraldess of good tidings."[13]

This interpretation implies a parallel structure between Isa 1–39 and 40–66 with regard to the functions of the communicative sender-instances in the text. In principle, both texts are determined by a discursor. This discursor, however, also performs in the shape of a character in the text itself. In Isa 1–39, it is the prophet Isaiah, recognizable by the same proper name. In Isa 40–66, the situation is more complex. A performance in the form of a character is continued in the heraldess of good tidings in 40:1–11 and her continuation in the herald of good tidings in 41:27; 52:7.[14]

This communicative order implies that the discursor with the proper name Isaiah is also present for Isa 40–66, on the one hand, and that the character Isaiah, who performs before the elliptic crisis in the caesura between 39:8 and 40:1, is not present himself afterwards, but takes shape in the heraldess/herald of good tidings.

2. *The Discursor and the Implied Reader*

In contrast to an implied author, the discursor/narrator has the possibility to address the implied reader. This happens in two remarkable texts in the Book: Isa 7:9c–d and 40:1c.

Because of the presence of a second person plural in the verbal forms תַּאֲמִינוּ "you have faith" (verse 9c) and תֵאָמֵנוּ "you stand firm" (verse 9d), supported by other text-linguistic aspects,[15] the verses 9c–d of chapter 7 form a separate direct speech. As a result, the verses 9c–d are a short direct speech of the discursor/narrator directed to the implied reader.[16]

---

[13] Confer also: Fisher (1974); Williamson (1998), 181–82. *Pace*: McEvenue (1997), 214.217 who, in Isa 40–55, sees the position of something as a discursor/narrator made explicit only in the verses 6–7, by reading the verbal form וְאָמַר in verse 6a as a participle female singular with reference to 1QIs^a ואומרה and to the Septuagint καὶ εἶπα—conversely see: Kutscher (1974) 357—and who, by doing so, identifies the voice and the heraldess of good tidings with each other. Confer, however, although within a different context: Beuken (1989), 417.

[14] Confer also: Korpel (1996) 165.

[15] See further: van Wieringen (1998) 63–67; van Wieringen (1998), 89–93.

[16] See also: van Wieringen (1998) 72–74; van Wieringen (1989), 94–95.

In Isa 40:1c, an instance renders a direct speech by making use of a direct speech by itself, using the expression אֱלֹהֵיכֶם "your God." Because of this, the instance speaking directs itself, as it were, to the implied reader without the addressees present in the text.

This implies that in a text in which the character "Isaiah" performs (Isa 7:1–17), the discursor—also named Isaiah—addresses the implied reader, and that in a text in which the character "heraldess of good tidings" performs (40:1–11), the discursor—who, although not explicitly mentioned as such, also has to be Isaiah—addresses the implied reader as well.

In this manner, the implied reader is shaped in the same way in both parts of the Book Isaiah, regarding the content as well as regarding the communicative setting. With regard to the content, an order is given in both situations to believe the word of God. This implies nothing else than preservation, exactly also to Zion and Jerusalem.

Communicatively spoken, a double communication explicitly arises in the text. The order which Isaiah is given as a character to express God's call to the character Ahaz, not to get into a panic, but to keep faith in God (Isa 7:3a–9b), also is the task which the discursor/narrator—also named Isaiah—executes in relation to the implied reader, namely that only faith in God brings relief. The point of Isa 40:1–11 is that, following God's call of comfort, other instances take up this call as well. This continuation in calling, however, not only takes place at the level of the characters, as the voice and the heraldess of good tidings, but also at the level of the discursor/narrator and the implied reader.

3. *Does Luke Have More Communication Functions as Well?*

This double function of "Isaiah" in the Book Isaiah is not a unique construction to guarantee reader-oriented unity in a bible book from the sender-instance's perspective. In other bible books as well, this procedure occurs. Although, in concreto, always realized in a different way, it is typical to almost all the Old Testament prophetic books because of headings which are used.

Neither is this communicative construction absent in the New Testament. It may be most visible in the Acts of the Apostles, although in a form particular to this book. In Acts 1:1, an anonymous "I" presents itself as narrator to Theophilos. Subsequently, a narration arises in the third person. In Acts 16:10, however, a first person plural occurs in the narrator's text for the first time and pops up throughout the entire second part of the Acts of the Apostles (16:6–18; 20:1–16; 21:1–17; 27:1–28:31). The character of the narration, therefore, changes: from a they/he-narration, it shifts to a we-narration. The anonymous narrator "I" becomes one of the characters "fellowmen of Paul."[17] Because of this, an interesting communicative situation arises, in which the narrator himself becomes part of Paul's mission to bring the good news concerning Jesus the Christ to all people, a character's task similar to the sender's function the narrator has in relation to the implied reader.

The great difference with the Book Isaiah is the narrator's anonymity. Nowhere in the Acts of the Apostles is the narrator called "Luke" as the discursor/narrator is called "Isaiah" in the Book Isaiah. A character with this proper name is not present in Acts either. The connection to the proper name "Luke" is from outside of the bible book and may be inspired by the texts Col 4:14; 2 Ti 4:11; Phm 1:24, in which a certain Luke is depicted as a supporter of Paul in the function of character.[18]

Bibliography

Ackroyd, P.R., "Isaiah I–XII: Presentation of a Prophet," in: *Congress Volume Göttingen 1977* (VT.S 29), Leiden 1978, 329–52.
Beuken, W.A.M., *Jesaja deel II A* (POT), Nijkerk 1979.
——, *Jesaja deel III B* (POT), Nijkerk 1989.
Conrad, E.W., *Reading Isaiah* (OBT 27), Minneapolis 1991.
Emmerson, G.I., *Isaiah 56–66* (Old Testament Series), Sheffield 1992.
Fisher, R.W., "The Herald of Good News in Second Isaiah," in: Jackson, J.J., Kessler, M. (eds.), *Rhetorical Criticism (FS J. Muilenburg)*, Pittsburgh 1974, 117–32.
Gosse, B., "L'influence du livre du prophète Isaïe (yš'yhw) sur la présentation du 'salut (yšw'h)' par les cantiques et récits bibliques, et la chute de Jérusalem comme archétype des catastrophes des origines," in: *Henoch* 22 (2000) 3–34.
Korpel, M.C.A., "The Female Servant of the Lord in Isaiah 54," in: Becking, B., Dijkstra, M. (eds.), *On Reading Prophetic Texts: Gender-Specific and Related Studies in Memory of Fokkelien van Dijk-Hemmes* (Biblical Interpretation Series 18), Leiden-New York-Köln 1996, 153–67.

---

[17] As in the Isaiah exegesis, a diachronic approach tries to explain this communicative construction in historical terms only, in which, regarding the Acts of the Apostles, a *Quelle* arises for the so-called *Wir-Berichte*. See for example: Schneider (1980), 89–95.

[18] I am greatly indebted to Drs. Maurits J. Sinninghe Damsté (Amsterdam, the Netherlands) for his correction of the English translation of this article.

Kutscher, E.Y., *The Language and Linguistic Background of the Isaiah Scroll (1 Q Isa^a)* (StTDJ 6), Leiden 1974.
Laato, A., *"About Zion I Will not Be Silent." The Book of Isaiah as an Ideological Unity* (CB.OT 44), Stockholm 1998.
McEvenue, S., "Who Was Second Isaiah?" in: van Ruiten, J., Vervenne, M. (eds.), *Studies in the Book of Isaiah (FS W.A.M. Beuken)* (BEThL 132), Leuven 1997, 213–22.
Schneider, G., *Die Apostelgeschichte. Einleitung. Kommentar zu Kap. 1,1–8,40* (ThKNT 5,1), Freiburg-Basel-Wien 1980.
van Tilborg, Sj., *Al lezend stemmen horen*, Nijmegen 1994.
——, *Imaginative Love in John* (Biblical Interpretation Series 2), Leiden-New York-Köln 1993.
——, *Reading John in Ephesus* (NT.S 83), Leiden-New York-Köln 1996.
Watts, J.D.W., *Isaiah 1–33* (Word Biblical Commentary 24), Waco 1985.
Westermann, C., *Das Buch Jesaja. Kapitel 40–66* (ATD 19), Göttingen 1966.
van Wieringen, A.L.H.M., "Jesaja 40:1–11: eine drama-linguistische Lesung von Jesaja 6 her," in: *BN* 49 (1989) 82–93.
——, *The Implied Reader in Isaiah 6–12* (Biblical Interpretation Series 34), Leiden-New York-Köln 1998.
Williamson, H.G.M., *Variations on a Theme. King, Messiah and Servant in the Book of Isaiah* (The Didsbury Lectures 1997), Carlisle 1998.

CHAPTER SEVEN

COGNITIVE LINGUISTICS AND ITS APPLICATION TO GENESIS 28:10–22

Ellen van Wolde
University of Tilburg, The Netherlands

"Is your mother at home?," I asked the child who answered the telephone. Or should I have said: "Is mummy there?" or "Can I speak to your mum?" I hesitated for a moment. Meanwhile, the child answered, "No, Annie is not at home. Can I give her a message?" O dear, I am lucky, I did not speak to her as if she was a child. I might have said: "My dear lady, could you please let me talk to the person who gave birth to you?" and the child might have become cross and protested loudly: "Sir, you know nothing about my birth or about my genetic origin. Have you never heard of IVF? I shall now give you my mother." Although thus rapped on the knuckles, and justifiably so, I can still maintain that we both referred to the same person, my dear Annie, my beloved friend of the old days. So many women, so many days....

In this example, we get access to the information in a specific way: the selection of ideas, the use of words, the direct and indirect presentation of speech and thoughts, the covert information, such as the difference between the female author of this article and the male narrator in the example, all these aspects allow the reader to build up a mental image of what was said and done in this telephone call. In the end, the reader might only keep in mind something which was pointed at merely implicitly, namely, the presupposed sexual relationship in the past between the speaker and the child's mother and its consequences for the child on the phone. Thus, although the language forms used are functions of their content, the total picture is more than that, because the language activates elements of our pre-existing knowledge and experiences.

Sjef van Tilborg, in his *Imaginative Love in John*, explained the building of such a mental picture in the gospel of John in an impressive way. In this book as well as in his classes, he combined an elaborate and profound knowledge with personal commitment and life experience, so that he enabled his students to weave their webs of meaning in relation to the biblical texts and to develop their lines of meaningfulness in study and life. Therefore, the present contribution will be concerned with a theory and method offered by cognitive linguistics, which explicitly deals with the development of a mental picture in a text. This includes a sketch of some basic concepts of cognitive linguistics and its application to the story of Jacob's ladder in Gen 28:10–22, so that some differences between the standard interpretations of Gen 28 and an interpretation based on cognitive linguistic data will emerge.

1. *Cognitive Linguistics*

It is generally known that language is not contained in dictionaries, but in the minds of the speakers and listeners, writers and readers of that language. Because of this, cognitive linguistics concentrates on language as a result of a cognitive processing. Its starting point is the notion of "concept," which, generally, can be defined as "a person's idea of what something in the world is like" (Dirven and Verspoor 1998:14). More specifically, concepts can relate to single entities, such as the book of Genesis, or to a whole set of entities, such as the concept "world literature." Such concepts, which slice reality into relevant units, are called categories (Taylor 1995). Conceptual categories are concepts of a set as a whole. Whenever we perceive something, we automatically tend to categorize it. For example, when we hear a piece of music, we automatically categorize it as rock music or as classical music or as something else. Thus, the world is not some kind of reality existing in itself but is always shaped by our categorizing activity, i.e., by our human perception, knowledge, and attitude. This does not mean that we create a subjective reality but, as a community, we agree about our intersubjective experiences.

Points of reference in these categories are the prototypes or the prototypical representations of the categories. Prototypicality effects occur not only at the level of meaning but also at the level of referents (cf. Taylor 1995:38–80). For example, when Northern Europeans are asked to name fruits, they are more likely to name apples and oranges than avocados or pomegranates, whereas Southern Europeans would name figs. This also explains why the tree of knowledge in the garden of Eden is generally understood in North West Europe to be an apple tree. However, Gen 3:3–6 only speaks of fruit, without a specification. In his Sistine Chapel painting Michelangelo had to make a choice in order to be able to paint this scene, and he as a Mediterranean painter chose a fig in a fig tree, whereas Rembrandt painted an apple and an apple tree. Both express the prototypical representation of the category fruit in their cultures.[1] Therefore, in order to understand the lexical terms in a text they are to be studied against the background knowledge of a complete cognitive domain.[2] In other words, a cognitive study of lexical terms in a text concentrates on the conceptualization of the historically experienced world as represented in conceptual categories and cognitive domains, which function as a background against which the terms in a text can be understood.

Not only words and their place in the lexicon and cultural domains, but also the syntactic structures are the object of research in cognitive linguistics. Actually, their continuous interaction is central in the studies of Ronald Langacker (1987, 1988, 1991, 1997) and of Giles Fauconnier (1985, 1997, 1998) which form the basis of the present paper.[3] Sentences or predications are the building stones of a text's syntactic organization. Predication is a device to describe an entity by linking it to a predicate which can either be a verb in a verbal predication (or verbal clause) or to a noun in a nominal predication (or nominal clause). From a cognitive perspective, a nominal predication differs from the verbal predication to the extent that in the

---

[1] Another example in the Hebrew bible: when in Job 28:1–10 gold, silver, copper, and iron are mentioned, these metals are, as statistical research of the Hebrew Bible has demonstrated, the most prototypical members of the category of "precious metals" (iron and copper do not belong to the category of "precious metals" by our modern standards, but they did belong to this category in the ancient Near East). Knowledge of this prototypical representation of the category of metals and mining thus offers a significant contribution to the understanding of Job 28 (cf. Van Wolde 2003b).

[2] According to Langacker (1987:147) cognitive domains are contexts for the characterization of a semantic unit.'

[3] Ungerer and Schmid (1996), Dirven and Verspoor (1998), and Allwood and Gärdenfors (1999) offer a good introduction to cognitive linguistics. Langacker (2003) presents an excellent summary of his cognitive grammar. Sweetser and Fauconnier (1996) offer a good introduction to Fauconnier's mental space theory.

former the event is presented as a "thing" or noun, whereas in the latter the event is presented as a temporal relation or "process" (Langacker 1987). In example (1),

(1) He is a doctor, she works as a librarian,

the nominal clause "he is a doctor" indicates that his job is conceived as part of his entity, because in a nominal clause a subject is defined by attributing it to a "setting." First, the selection of the setting as part of a cognitive domain and, second, the subject's placing in this setting have the effect that the subject is conceived as essentially defined by the setting he is part of. On the other hand, the verbal clause "she works as a librarian" indicates that her job is thought of as a temporary business, and the selection of the verbal predicate indicates that the job is not viewed as a setting belonging to a cognitive domain but as a relation limited to a specific time and place. Thus, predication emerges from a continuous interaction between grammatical construction (the syntactic values) and the selection of words that stand out on their cognitive domains (the semantic values), and it always embodies perspective.

This explains why meanings in a text do not reside solely in the inherent properties of the entity or situation described in the text, but why they crucially involve the way in which the author chooses to think about a situation or event and mentally portrays it. Compare, for example, the following two sentences.

(2) Mary got married to Joseph and became pregnant.
(3) Mary became pregnant and got married to Joseph.

These sentences contain the same collection of morphological forms and the same syntactic structure, but the described situation is conceived differently. Hence, these sentences embody different images (as church history can tell you). Cognitive linguistics acknowledges that grammar and lexicon serve an "imagic" function and embody conventional imagery.[4] This imagery also includes the way in which the narrator presents the material from different angles and embeds characters' views and characters' texts in the narrator's text.[5] In reac-

---

[4] The term "imagery" is defined by Langacker (1987:490) as "the ability to construe a situation in alternate ways for purposes of thought or expression."

[5] Follingstad (2001:166–67) explains the different positions of the author, narrator, and character as follows. The author chooses the words and word sequences just as the film director chooses the images and sequences, and he or she is respon-

tion to this, the reader is able to mentally construe a picture of the conceived situation in a certain way.

2. *Perspective*

In biblical studies, literary biblical scholars usually stress the importance of the concept of "point of view," understanding it as a "personal" or "subject-related" vantage point related to a narrator, character, or reader. In cognitive linguistics, this rather vague literary concept of point of view is replaced by the linguistically marked cognitive concept of perspective, which is defined as the "abstract" point of access of information in the text (Follingstad 2001:165). According to Langacker (1987), perspective covers three related notions: prominence, deixis, and viewpoint. In any construal of a scene, certain components are necessarily foregrounded while others serve as reference points for the characterization of the foreground. The difference between "The picture above the sofa" and "The sofa below the picture" is that the first expression locates the picture (figure) with reference to the sofa (ground), while in the second expression the relations are reversed (Taylor 1995:4–5). Or, another example: in "Jacob stayed there for the night, for the sun had set." (Gen 28:11), the first clause is the figure and the reason for this action is presented as the ground, whereas in the reverse order "The sun had set, therefore Jacob decided to stay the night there," the clause about the sun is the figure and Jacob's decision "to stay the night there" is the ground. The second notion of deixis is a familiar one. The demonstratives in "This sofa above the sofa" or "The picture above this sofa," relate to the presentation of a scene from the location of the observer. Also verbs representing a spatial orientation or directionality show a deictic perspective. Finally, the notion of viewpoint is defined as the mental route that a speaker or writer takes in presenting a scene. In the

---

sible for the editing or montage. The narrator presents the material in a way similar to the camera man: the camera eye can shift and show the information from different camera angles. And a camera shot is the kind of picture a camera captures and which is used to tell the story, just as a narrator's text shows a picture from a certain angle or vantage point. The narrator can also represent the characters' view either external to the camera or internal to the camera, so that readers are enabled to share his or her point of view in a way similar to the film shot in which the camera allows spectators to see or feel what the actor sees or feels.

text, which this article opened, the mother was referred to as "your mother," "mummy," "your mum," "Annie," and "my mother," displaying various viewpoint positions. Thus, it becomes clear that all linguistic coding incorporates perspective. The following list of biblical examples, which is not exhaustive, may illustrate this.

- Syntactic prominence as indicated by nominal and verbal predications is present in every text, e.g., in Gen 34:2, "Shechem, the son of Hamor, the Hivite and the chief of the land, saw her," Shechem's actions are described against the background of three appositions (Van Wolde 2003c).
- Syntactic deixis marking directionality by the use of prepositions. See, for example, the difference between "the ladder was set up towards the earth" and "the ladder was set up from the earth" (Gen 28:12, the present paper).
- Syntactic deixis marking orientation through the use of personal and possessive pronouns, cf. Ruth 2:15: "see, your sister-in-law has returned to her people and her gods" in which the possessive pronoun "your" is related to Ruth, whereas the possessive pronoun "her" is related to Orpah, and in which Orpah is perceived as Ruth's sister-in-law and not as Naomi's daughter-in-law (Van Wolde 1997).
- Syntactic viewpoint as indicated by verbal forms, such as the selection of tense, and of indicative or modal verb forms, e.g., the modal verb form in Job 1:1, "Job used to be pious" or "obviously Job was pious" (instead of the indicative "Job was pious") (Kamp 2004).
- Semantic prominence through the selection of words as standing out on a cognitive domain in the prevalent culture, cf. Yri (1998) who showed that the concept of salvation in Hebrew (יָשַׁע) is taken from the domain of conflict, while in Greek it is construed in the domain of health.
- Semantic deixis through the use of a metaphor in which two (or more) conceptual domains are linked and the knowledge of the source domain is extended into an (until then) unconnected other field of experience or knowledge (target domain). This link depends on the mental path from which it is construed, e.g., the use of pastoral metaphors in the Hebrew bible (Van Hecke 1999, 2001).
- Semantic viewpoint by the selection of words, such as the terms used to describe a person, cf. Gen 37:2, in which Joseph is described as a נַעַר; which can be understood as "a lad" or as "a servant" of his brothers (Pirson 1999).

- Semantic viewpoint through the representation of an event or situation by various characters, cf. the representations of the dreams in the Joseph story (Pirson 2002:41–59).

3. *Mental Space and Viewpoint*

Whereas Langacker, in his cognitive grammar, concentrates on the generation or *production* of meaning, which is based on the human ability to mentally construe a conceived situation in alternative ways and thus always involves perspective, Fauconnier (1985, 1997), in his Mental Space Theory, focuses on the *product* of language generation in general and on the study of written texts in particular.

Fauconnier's basic assumption is that "language is a superficial manifestation of hidden, highly abstract, cognitive constructions. Essential to such constructions is the operation of structure projection between domains. And therefore, essential to the understanding of cognitive construction is the characterization of the domains over which the projection takes place. Mental spaces are the domains that discourse builds up to provide a cognitive substrate for reasoning and for interfacing the world" (Fauconnier 1997:34). A mental space is a model that shows "how the information in a discourse is partitioned and accessed and, in particular, which mental space constitutes the viewpoint space from which the information partitioned in other spaces is accessed" (Sweetser and Fauconnier 1996:9 as summarized by Follingstad 2001:161). The following example given by Follingstad (2001:161) can be instructive.

In a James Bond film, the character of Bond impersonates an industrialist named Grey. Another character is Ursula, and she does not know that Grey is really Bond. Now, two people are discussing the film, saying:

(4) Ursula thinks that Grey is handsome.
(5) Ursula thinks that Bond is handsome.

The cognition verb "thinks" is a space builder, that is, "a term which generates a new cognitive domain where information may be processed and accessed" (Follingstad 2001:161). In diagrams 1 and 2, the circle on the left represents the speaker's space external to the film, whereas the circle on the right is Ursula's character belief space (in the film).

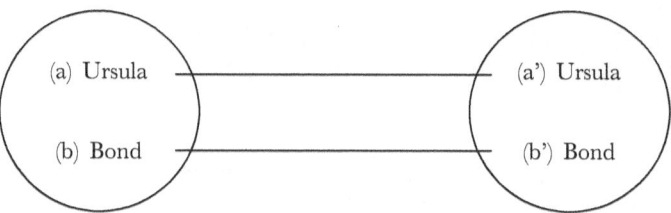

Diagram 1

In the clause "Ursula thinks that Grey is handsome," the speaker describes Ursula's belief and the viewpoint is restricted to Ursula in her belief space only: the capital and bold V, which stands for viewpoint, is placed in Ursula's mental space [**V** with Ursula].

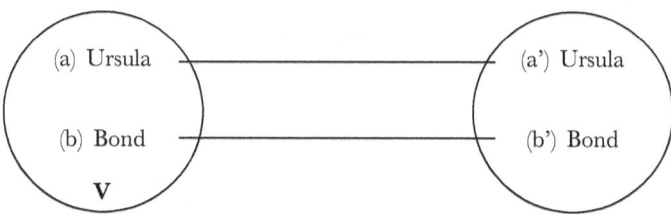

Diagram 2

In the clause "Ursula thinks that Bond is handsome," the reference to Bond shows that the viewpoint is that of the speaker who is describing Ursula's belief. Thus, both clauses (4) and (5) represent a different partitioning of information: [**V** with speaker] or [**V** with the character]. In both clauses, the referent is the same person, viz., Bond, alias Grey, but he is accessed differently.

On the basis of this principle, every text can be studied as to the way it gives access to its information through a series of mental spaces and through a variety of viewpoint positions. Thus, in a narrative text, mental spaces are set up, structured, and linked under pressure from grammar, context, and culture. The effect is a network of spaces through which readers move as the discourse unfolds: starting from an initial space (base space or B), new character spaces (numbered mental spaces or M1, M2, etc.) are generated and structured in various ways (Sweetser and Fauconnier 1996:11).

4. *Perspective in Biblical Hebrew*

Follingstad (2001) showed that Fauconnier's concepts of mental space and viewpoint position can be very helpful in analyzing Hebrew particles.[6] He presented a profound analysis of the particles כִּי, אֲשֶׁר, וְהִנֵּה, and לֵאמֹר, as markers of the location of the viewpoint position.[7] As to the particle כִּי ("because," "for"), he demonstrated that it disconnects the deictic center of the clause from the narrator and moves it to the character's mental space. Thus, כִּי can mark a secondary perception, inference, or semi-indirect thought attributed to a character (Follingstad 2001:192). Actually, כִּי indicates that the viewpoint is shifted to the complement itself, so that "the attributed thought itself is the point of access for information" (Follingstad 2001: 164).

The relative particle אֲשֶׁר ("which," "that") also attributes perspective, but marks the fact that the narrator is the viewpoint from which the complement is constructed. The attention marker וְהִנֵּה ("behold"), on the other hand, grounds the perception to the character as an actual perception and thus expresses that the viewpoint is assigned to the character. Hence, וְהִנֵּה indicates a viewpoint shift, not to the propositional content space (cf. כִּי), but to the character space, and locates the viewpoint in the character space itself and typically implies that the character can actually "see" or "comprehend" something physical in the context.

The particle לֵאמֹר ("saying") is a signal that the reporting speaker makes less of a commitment to the truth of the speech act contents s/he is conveying, despite the appearance of *verbatim* transmission (Follingstad 2001:194). The reason for this explicit marking is some recontextualization or reinterpretation of the content of the speech act which has taken place.

---

[6] Sanders (1994) used Fauconnier's insights for the analysis of texts and some of her insights are used in biblical exegesis, too; see, among others, Van Wolde (1994; 1995), Chatelion Counet and Van Tilborg (2000).

[7] The particles וְהִנֵּה אֲשֶׁר כִּי, and לֵאמֹר, share two features: they all have a deictic function and are "complementizers." In grammar, a complement is an adjectival group or noun group that comes after a verb and which adds information about the subject or object of the verb; complementizers (be they a word, particle, clitic, or affix) have the function to identify an entity as a complement (cf. Noonan (1985:44) cited by Follingstad (2001:152)).

In other words, with respect to complement constructions אֲשֶׁר has an "indicative mood" flavor, due to the specification of the viewpoint in the narrator space. וְהִנֵּה has a "direct evidence" type of modality, due to the location of the viewpoint in the character space, implying a construal of the complement restricted to the character לֵאמֹר indicates that direct speech material is represented with less epistemic commitment than direct speech without it. Finally, כִּי indicates a shift to the complement itself, indicating that it is a propositional content about some state of affairs. Therefore, "these particles mark in specific ways the location of the viewpoint space and how the propositional content of utterances are to be accessed with respect to other spaces" (Follingstad 2001:162).

5. *Mental Spaces and Viewpoints in Gen 28:10–22*

The value of these cognitive linguistic insights for biblical exegesis can be considerable. So far, only few cognitive linguistic studies of biblical texts have been published (Van Hecke 1999, 2001, 2003; Kamp 2001, 2003, 2004a; Yri 1998; Van Wolde 2001, 2003a, 2003b, 2003c). In order to explain the contribution of cognitive linguistics for the study of the Hebrew bible, in the next section an analysis will be made of the mental spaces and viewpoint positions in the story of Jacob's ladder.

In the standard view on Gen 28:10–22, the story of Jacob's dream in Bethel is explained in the context of a covenant theology: in a nightly vision Yhwh promises Jacob, as he did before to Abraham and Isaac, the land and multiple offspring. This "dream theophany" functions in this text to support the sanctity (*hieros logos*) of Bethel, which explains the repetitive use of the word הַמָּקוֹם, the place, in Gen 28, viz., in vv. 11 (three times), 16, 17, and 19.[8] Other scholars stress the ancient Near Eastern background of the text, and explain its meaning in relation to ancient Egyptian or Babylonian texts and buildings, some of them interpreting the ladder as an object resembling a Babylonian *ziggurat* tower.[9] Problematic in all these stud-

---

[8] Gunkel (1910), Alt (1953), Westermann (1981), Sarna (1972), de Pury (1975), Houtman (1977).
[9] Parrot (1953), von Rad (1953), Speiser (1964), Griffiths (1966–67), Millard (1966–67), Lipton (1999), Oblath (2001).

ies, in both the Bethel and the Babylonian interpretations, is that hardly any attention is paid to the linguistic features of Gen 28. This is a great pity for, in my view, a linguistic study lays the foundation for a historical, comparative, theological, or literary reading of the text. In order to substantiate this thesis and to explain the advantages of a cognitive linguistic analysis, I will analyze some linguistic characteristics of Gen 28 and the consequence of such an analysis for a interpretation.

The story starts in Gen 28 with a narrator's text in vv. 10 and 11, which is the text's base (B) mental space.

10a Jacob left Beer-sheba
10b and set out for Haran.
11a He came upon a certain place
11b and stayed there for the night,
11c for the sun had set.
11d He took one of the stones of the place,
11e he put it under his head
11f and lay down in that place.

The information offered here is related to the deictic center of the narrator, that is, the personal forms, the spatial and temporal coordinates are related to the narrator, and, in vv. 10–11, the readers get access to the information through the narrator's mind. However, it is not as simple as it looks. Verse 11c, "for the sun had set," begins with the particle כִּי which is a space builder and, therefore, generates a new mental space. Follingstad (2001) demonstrated that this particle is a marker of a shift in viewpoint position: it profiles the complement or the propositional content as a thought of the character involved. Hence, כִּי indicates that the viewpoint is shifted from the narrator to the character Jacob and it expresses Jacob's thought and viewpoint. If v. 11c had had the relative particle אֲשֶׁר ("which, that"), i.e., a sort of indicative-like particle, then the complement ("the sun had set") would have been constructed from the narrator's viewpoint. The difference is clear: with the particle אֲשֶׁר, v. 11c would have been merely a description of a fact at the time; instead, the particle כִּי profiles the propositional content as a thought of the character Jacob. Thus, the thought attributed to Jacob is the point of access for the information in v. 11c.

12a He had a dream.
12b Behold, a ladder was set up towards the earth, the top of it reaching to heaven.

12c Behold, messengers of god were ascending and descending on it.
13a Behold, Yhwh was positioned over it.

In vv. 12b, 12c, and 13a, the particle וְהִנֵּה ("behold") indicates a viewpoint shift, too, but this time not to the propositional content space (as did כִּי in v. 11c) but to the character space: it locates the viewpoint in the character space itself. The attention marker וְהִנֵּה typically implies that the character can actually "see" or "comprehend" something physical in the context. This time, the reader is led to share Jacob's viewpoint, to look with him and see a ladder, messengers of god, and Yhwh. The difference between v. 11c on the one hand and vv. 12b, 12c, and 13a on the other is that, in the former, the viewpoint shifts via Jacob's thought to the proposition ("for the sun had set"), so that the reader gets access to the information *indirectly* via Jacob's mind, whereas in vv. 12b, 12c, and 13a, the viewpoint shifts to the character, so that the reader shares Jacob's viewpoint and perception and gets *direct* access to the information.

The next question is whether the three clauses with וְהִנֵּה in vv. 12b, 12c, and 13a give the very same access to Jacob's mental space.

In diagrams 3 and 4, the left-hand circles represent the narrator's mental space external to the embedded text, whereas the spaces on

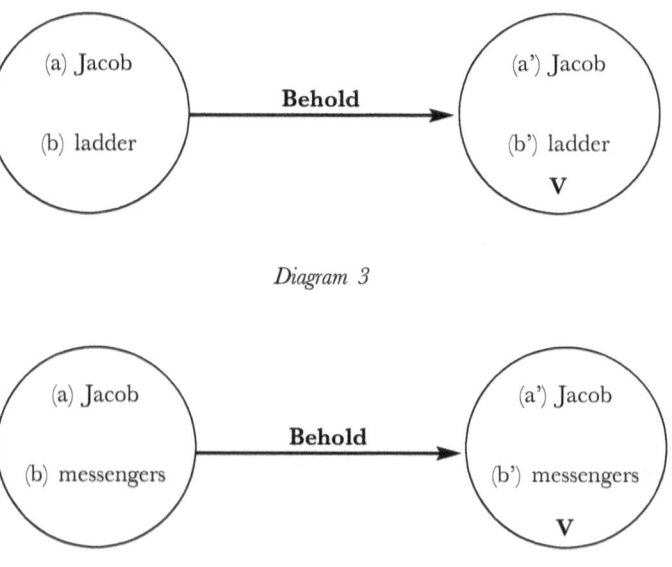

Diagram 3

Diagram 4

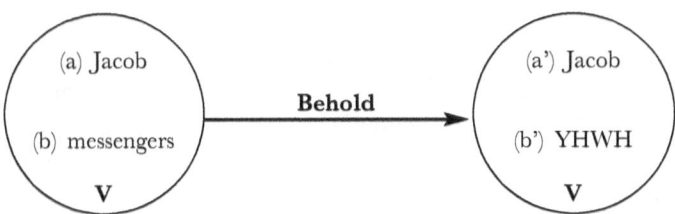

Diagram 5

the right represent Jacob's character mental space. In both v. 12b and v. 12c, the narrator describes Jacob's view and the viewpoint is restricted to Jacob in his mental space only: the viewpoint is placed in Jacob's mental space [**V** with Jacob].

Instead, in diagram 5, representing v. 13a, reference is made to Yhwh. The use of this name indicates that the viewpoint is that of the narrator who is describing Jacob's belief, which represents a different partitioning of information: [V with narrator], that is, it indicates that the mental path via which the reader gets access to the information is the narrator's. How do we know this? In the next verse, v. 13b, Yhwh introduces himself to Jacob, but before that moment, Jacob cannot have known that it was Yhwh who was standing there. Only after Yhwh had told who he was, could he have phrased it like this. It is as in the Ursula-Bond example: the term used to refer to an entity or person can reveal whose viewpoint is shared. Here, in v. 13a, reference is made to the character who will reveal his identity in v. 13, and the narrator anticipates this self-revelation. Thus, the access to this character is partitioned in the narrator's words, and the prepositions used in vv. 12b, 12c, and 13a confirm these differences in viewpoint.

In v. 12b, the noun "the land" (אֶרֶץ) contains a place marker (ה-locale), indicating the direction "towards the earth." The viewpoint shared is Jacob's: he sees the ladder (coming) downwards towards the earth. This is remarkable because the verb used, the *hophʻal* form of the root נצב ("to set up, erect"), meaning "was set up," denotes a vertical movement directed upwards. The same root returns in v. 13a in the *niphʻal*, meaning "to stand" or "to station," always used with the preposition עַל ("on," "over") and this collocation means "to stand over" and expresses implicitly a vertical orientation "upwards" ("Yhwh was stationed / positioned over"). In v. 12b, the ladder is, uncharacteristically, "set up downwards," in which the verb's upward orientation conflicts with the place marker's downward orientation. The reader gets access to this information through Jacob's mental space and shares his viewpoint position. Thus, the reader sees with Jacob the ladder directed downwards to the earth and looks with him from the basis of the ladder upwards to the top of it reaching to heaven.

In v. 12c, the same pattern occurs: "Behold, messengers of god were ascending and descending on it." The orientation of the first verb, עלה "to climb" or "to ascend," is vertically upwards, whereas the second verb, ירד, "to come down" or "to descend," expresses a downward movement. Here again, the reader shares Jacob's mental space and viewpoint position and sees with Jacob the messengers moving up and down the ladder. Again it is so indicated that the starting point is Jacob's, and the reader looks with him and upwards from his position.

However, v. 13a is different. The preposition "above" or "over" does not mark a direction or orientation related to a subject's viewpoint position, such as "downwards" and "upwards" in v. 12b or "climbing up" and "coming down" in v. 12c. The pronominal suffix "it" or "him" to the preposition עָלָיו has given rise to a lot of discussion. If this suffix is understood to relate to Jacob, then v. 13a states that Yhwh was positioned "over him," that is, on earth; if the suffix is understood to relate to the ladder, then v. 13a describes that Yhwh was positioned "by or above the ladder," that is, in heaven.[10] Three arguments support the second view. Firstly, from a syntactic point of view, the subject introduced in v. 12b is the ladder and the pronominal suffixes in v. 12c ("the messengers going up and down *on it*")

---

[10] The translators of the Septuagint and Vulgate understood עליו to relate to the ladder. Most commentators relate it to Jacob (so Houtman 1977:348, n. 42). Houtman (1977:348) prefers to understand עליו as "by him," because in other texts in the Hebrew bible, persons are positioned in relation to one another (Gen 18:2: the three men are standing, while Abraham is sitting down; Gen 24:13.43: Abraham's servant is standing near the well; Gen 40:1: the servants are standing, while Joseph, the prince, is sitting down; Ex 18:14: Moses is judging, seated). However, the situation in Gen 28 is different, because the involved parties are not all human. In itself, the preposition may relate to a thing or a person, as Houtman acknowledges, but he only selects the texts referring to human beings. More importantly, in every text, possessive or pronominal suffixes are related to persons or things in relation to the perspective from which something is viewed and in relation to the way access is given to the information and, therefore, occurrences elsewhere in the Hebrew bible cannot teach us about a specific occurrence which is characterized by its very own perspective.

refer back to the ladder. Further on in v. 13, Jacob is the subject and, in biblical grammar, v. 12c cannot place a personal pronoun ("him") before the noun to which it refers. Secondly, as mental space theory can easily explain, the suffixed preposition "above him" or "above it" does not mark a direction or orientation related to a subject's viewpoint position (as in v. 12b and v. 12c), עָלָיו; "above him/it" indicates a place *per se*. Thirdly, and, in my view, the most important contribution mental space theory can offer, is the way access is given to the information in these verses. In vv. 12b, 12c, and 13a, access is given to Jacob's mental space, as is marked by the particle "behold," and the suffix cannot but refer to the ladder, for Jacob himself is not present in the dream vision. In conclusion, the pronominal suffix relates to the ladder. Thus, the preposition confirms that the reader sees what Jacob sees in his dream, and the vision about Yhwh attributed to Jacob is accessed here through Jacob's mental space, although the viewpoint position and the mental path on which the reader is led to perceive are with the narrator.

13b   He said,
13c   I am Yhwh, the god of Abraham your father and the god of Isaac;
13d   the land
13e   on which you lie
13d   I will give it to you and to your offspring.
14a   It will happen that your offspring will be like the dust of the earth,
14b   that you will spread to the west and to the east and to the north and to the south;
14c   and that all the families of the earth will be blessed in you and in your offspring.
15a   Behold I am with you
15b   I will protect you
15c   wherever you go,
15d   and I will bring you back to this land.
15e   For I will not leave you
15f   until I have done
15g   what I am telling you.

The next clause in v. 13b is וַיֹּאמֶר, "he said." The content of this directly presented speech shows that Yhwh is the reported speaker: "I am Yhwh, the god of Abraham." This speech is introduced by the narrator in v. 13b, as the *wayyiqtol* form of וַיֹּאמֶר shows. In the other representations of dreams in the Hebrew bible, viz., Gen 37:6–7 (Joseph's dreams), Gen 41:1–7 (Pharao's dreams), Judg. 7:13

(Gideon's dream), and Isa 29:7–8 (the prophet's dream), the very same structure is detectable. The vision of the dream embedded in the character's mental space is always opened by the perception marker וְהִנֵּה and a nominal clause which describes the perceived situation (cf. Gen 28:12). When this vision is followed by a reported speech, this is embedded in the character space although access is given to this information by the reporting speaker or narrator marked with וַיֹּאמֶר ("he said"). In this way, the narrator gives a signal that he is committed to the truth of the speech he is conveying through *verbatim* transmission. In short, vv. 13b–15g belong to Jacob's mental space, and the readers share what Jacob hears in his dream, but the access point to the information is the narrator, who thus indicates a high degree of epistemic commitment to the reported direct speech material.

Yhwh's directly reported speech contains four embedded mental spaces. The first of these is visible in v. 13c–13d, in which Yhwh identifies himself in a nominal clause ("I am Yhwh, the god of Abraham your father and the god of Isaac") and he then concentrates on the land. The *casus pendens* construction with a fronted "the land" and repeated in the suffix "it" to the verb form "give" ("the land, on which you lie, I will give it to you and to your offspring") emphasizes the importance of the land. Then, in v. 14a, the verb form וְהָיָה marks the opening of a new mental space. The verb הָיָה is a copular verb ("to be") that does not take complements of sentential verbs (perception, cognition, speech) and therefore describes a situation from a detached viewpoint position. וְהָיָה usually continues a *yiqtol* or a *wᵉqataltí* verb form in a previous clause and marks a situation that is the consequence of this *yiqtol* or *wᵉqataltí* act. In v. 14a, וְהָיָה takes the previous act of Yhwh's land giving act (*yiqtol*) in v. 13d as its base and marks the future situation (the spreading of Jacob's seed over this land) as its logical consequence. Because וְהָיָה indicates that the information is accessed in a detached viewpoint position, the causal relationship between Yhwh's land giving and the spread over the land is validated as reliable information.

The next embedded mental space is opened in v. 15a–15d by the particle וְהִנֵּה which gives access to the information from the personal viewpoint of the subject Yhwh: "Behold, I am with you." Actually, it locates the viewpoint in the character space and makes visible a strong epistemic commitment of the character Yhwh to the information in the complement: "I am with you." Subsequently, two aspects of this nominal predication, of this "being with you," are focused upon: "I will protect you" and "I will bring you back."

In v. 15e–15g, the particle or complementizer כִּי marks a shift to the contents of the complement: it gives access to Yhwh's inner thoughts, so that the reader is enabled to know and feel what Yhwh feels and thinks. In addition to that, the content of this thought is defended with a reference to his own words, the words the reader is reading at this very moment: "for I will not leave you until I have done what I am telling you."

16a	Jacob woke from his sleep.
16b	He said,
16c	Surely Yhwh is in this place
16d	and I did not know it!
17a	He was afraid,
17b	and said,
17c	How awesome is this place!
17d	This is none other than a house of god,
17e	and this is the gate of heaven.

In vv. 16 and 17, Jacob's reaction is reported directly in two speech acts, which let the reader share his mental space and his viewpoint.

18a	Jacob rose early in the morning,
18b	took the stone,
18c	that he had put under his head,
18d	set it up for a pillar
18e	and poured oil on the top of it.
19a	He called that place Bethel;
19b	but the name of the city was Luz at the first.

In vv. 18 and 19, the reader returns to the base, that is, the narrator's mental space. Only v. 19b is special, because it functions directly on the communicative axis of writer and reader, that is, in the communicative situation external to the story.

20a	Jacob made a vow, saying,
20b	If god will be with me,
20c	and will protect me in this way
20d	that I go,
20e	and will give me bread to eat and clothing to wear,
20f	and I will come again to my father's house in peace,
21a	then it will happen that Yhwh will be my god,
22a	and this stone,
22b	which I have set up for a pillar,
22c	will be god's house;

22d   and of all that you give me
22e   I will surely give one tenth to you.

These last three verses, vv. 20–22, contain another speech by Jacob. However, this time it is not marked by וַיֹּאמֶר ("he said"), but by לֵאמֹר ("saying"). This complementizer can be understood as a signal that expresses information obtained through hearsay and may indicate a lesser degree of epistemic commitment to the reported *verbatim* direct speech material marked by וַיֹּאמֶר (Follingstad 2001). In vv. 20–22, Jacob formulates a condition, in which the protasis ("if" clause) consists of a couple of clauses and in which the apodosis ("then" clause) consists of a series of clauses, too. There is discussion on where the apodosis starts. Some argue that it starts in v. 22a ("then this stone will be god's house.").[11] Others are of the opinion that the apodosis starts in v. 21b ("then it will happen that Yhwh will be my god and this stone will be god's house."). In my opinion, grammar forces us to decide that the apodosis begins in v. 21b, because it is opened by וְהָיָה ("it will happen"), whereas the previous three clauses are *weqaltí* or *waw* consecutive forms ("god will be, will protect, will give, I will come home"). This וְהָיָה always "precedes a sentence or an adverbial phrase (often with a temporal connotation) that *introduces a new paragraph or sub-paragraph*" (Van der Merwe, Naudé, and Kroeze 1999:331, their italics).[12] The conclusion is that Jacob here presents a consequential relation between god's promises (protasis) in v. 20a and the future events envisaged (apodosis) in vv. 21–22.

---

[11] Lipton (1999:75) states that "the grammatical construction (in vv. 20–22) suggests that the shift from 'if' to 'then' should take place not half waythrough v. 21 (...), but rather at the beginning of v. 22. The initial אִם־יִהְיֶה אֱלֹהִים עִמָּדִי ("if God will be with me") is followed by four waw consecutives in which the verb precedes the noun. Verse 22, in contrast, opens with a noun, הָאֶבֶן הַזֹּאת (this stone), while the verb, יִהְיֶה (will be) is in the imperfect. This grammatical change may well mark the shift from protasis to apodosis." Note 23 shows that she bases herself on Rashi ("This is Rashi's assumption").

[12] Cf. also Kamp (2004:17), who provides a cognitive linguistic study of וְהָיָה in Job 1:1–5 and concludes that the clause with וְהָיָה indicates a modal proposition, i.e., a durative or iterative state of affairs which characterizes Job's attitude in general (Idem Clines 1989:11). Cf. also Stipp 1991 on the iterative meaning of וְהָיָה. In the most recently published linguistic study of Gen 28:20–22, Huwyler (2001), too, is in favor of v. 21b as the opening clause of the apodosis.

6. *Towards a Different Interpretation of the Story*

As I stated earlier, meaning does not reside solely in the inherent properties of what the text describes, but it crucially involves the ways in which the events or situations are mentally portrayed. Above, the way in which access is given to the information in Gen 28 is studied, and a reflection on these cognitive linguistic data yields the following results.

A first element is the way in which Jacob refers in vv. 16–17 to his dream. In Jacob's dream as described in vv. 12b–13a, a situation with three elements presented, viz., a ladder, messengers of אֱלֹהִים going up and down, and Yhwh. After he wakes up, Jacob gives his reaction in a directly reported speech. Thus, the reader gets direct access to Jacob's two mental spaces, to his dream and to his reaction, and both relate to one another. In Jacob's mental space and from his vantage point,

the ladder	*corresponds to*	the gate of heaven
the messengers of אֱלֹהִים	*corresponds to*	the house of אֱלֹהִים
Yhwh stationed over him	*corresponds to*	Yhwh is in this place

A second element arises when a comparison is made between Jacob's view in vv. 20–22 and the narrator's conclusion in vv. 18–19. The narrator suggests, in vv. 18–19, that Jacob calls the place Bethel, בֵּית־אֵל, house of God, and he uses the term אֵל, that is, the singular term "god," whereas Jacob uses the plural form אֱלֹהִים.

A third element is Jacob's reaction in vv. 20–22 to Yhwh's directly reported speech in v. 15. After his identification as "Yhwh, the God of Abraham your father and the God of Isaac," Yhwh describes the future situation as follows:

> I will be with you
> I will protect you
> I will bring you back to this land.

In his reaction in vv. 20–22 Jacob refers back to this promise (cf. Rose 2001:83), saying:

> If אֱלֹהִים will be with me,
> And will protect me in this way that I go,
> and will give me bread to eat and clothing to wear,
> and I will come again to my father's house in peace,
> then it will happen that Yhwh will be my god,

and this stone, which I have set up for a pillar,
will be the house of אֱלֹהִים;
and of all that you give me
I will surely give one tenth to you.

In other words,

If אֱלֹהִים will be with me,
then Yhwh will be my אֱלֹהִים.
If he (אֱלֹהִים) will protect me
then this stone/pillar will be the house of אֱלֹהִים.
If he (אֱלֹהִים) will give food and clothes and I will return safely,
of all that you give me, I will surely give one tenth to you.

These three groups of differences induce us to look again at the terms used with reference to the divine. When, in v. 12b and v. 12c, Jacob's viewpoint is shared, the messengers of the divine are called מַלְאֲכֵי אֱלֹהִים, messengers of god(s), whereas in v. 13a the narrator's viewpoint is shared and the term Yhwh is used to describe the divine. Subsequently, in vv. 13c–15g, Yhwh's mental space is presented through his viewpoint. Here, the general category of אֱלֹהִים is specified and Yhwh is described as the god of Jacob's ancestors, the god who gives him the land and offspring, and who enables the offspring to grow and to spread over the land and the other people on earth to be blessed through Jacob and his offspring. Therefore, this Yhwh is closely related to land, to the ancestors, and to the children. The *verbatim* transmission by the narrator confirms the reliability of this information, which differs from his more distanced presentation (marked by לֵאמֹר) of Jacob's final reaction in vv. 20–22, in which:

- Jacob is not talking about the land
- Jacob is not talking about his offspring
- Jacob is not talking about the spread of his offspring on the land
- Jacob is not talking about other people being or not being blessed
- Jacob is not talking about Yhwh as the god of his father or grandfather.

However,

- he is very much concerned with himself
- he will be concerned with Yhwh if he protects him
- he is active in setting up a stone to represent a בֵּית אֱלֹהִים
- he is willing to give back one tenth of what he will receive.

These cognitive linguistic data offer a meaningful and verifiable basis for the interpretation of Gen 28 and demonstrate that the text offers a series of mental spaces related alternately to the narrator, to the character of Jacob, and to the character of Yhwh, which present different and even conflicting images.

The first image is conveyed by the narrator and the character of Yhwh, showing a picture of the divine being who is closely related to the land, to Jacob's ancestors, and to his children. It represents the idea of one god, one land, and one family: Jacob with his ancestors and his children. The narrator wants to stress the unique position and quality of this god and relates this idea to the place called בֵּית־אֵל, house of god. This is the mental image the writer wants the reader to construe via the narrator's and Yhwh's mental spaces.

However, Jacob's mental space and viewpoint show another picture. Jacob sees a vertical ladder with messengers of אֱלֹהִים going up and down and calls it a gate of heaven. He gives this gate the name בֵּית אֱלֹהִים and he calls his pillar on the place of this gate בֵּית אֱלֹהִים. In the end, he is prepared to serve one god only, if this god will protect him. Nevertheless, Jacob shows no awareness of the relation of this god with the land he is about to leave, of the relation of this god with his ancestors or with his children. It is the narrator who wants to stress the unique position and the quality of this god; he, and he alone, uses the name בֵּית־אֵל. Jacob sticks to the formula of בֵּית אֱלֹהִים to the very end of the story. Whereas the narrator and the character Yhwh refer to the divine in the singular, Jacob starts and finishes with the reference to the divine in the plural, though he is prepared to choose Yhwh as his god from among other gods.

Knowledge of some aspects of cognitive religious domains in the ancient Near Eastern cultures at the time may help us to understand these conflicting images of god in Gen 28:10–22. Since the Bronze Age, the prevalent religious domain in the ancient Near East has been henotheistic (see, among others, Porter [2000] and Noll [2001:131–34, 207–15]). Although a certain number of divine beings or gods were generally accepted, usually only one god was acknowledged as the most powerful in a certain region. Traditionally, the god of the capital city became the main god. In ancient Babylonia, Marduk was the highest god with the king in Babylon as his representative. In Assyria, the god Assur was the highest god and the king his representative. Thus, people adhered to one god without denying the existence of other gods. In Gen 28, traces of this henotheism are visible, most clearly in v. 12c, where the divine messengers (מַלְאָךְ) are a kind of lower-gods or go-between figures between (higher) gods and humans (in the Christian traditions usually translated as "angels"). The cognitive linguistic analysis has demonstrated that this henotheistic view is also present elsewhere in this text, especially in relationship to Jacob, whose mental space and viewpoints the reader is enabled to share. Jacob testifies to a more henotheistic viewpoint. This is understandable, because this story of his dream in Bethel is situated at the beginning of the Jacob cycle, and the narrator is going to tell us about Jacob's spiritual development.

Summarizing, the standard theological explanation of Gen 28, which confines itself to the narrator's and Yhwh's mental space, neglects the mental picture built up in Jacob's mental space and viewpoint. The recent explanation of this story with reference to the Bethel tradition relies completely on the narrator's text in vv. 18–20 and, moreover, ignores Jacob's reference to בֵּית אֱלֹהִים. The cognitive linguistic study of some features of this text, however, does explain the existence of two mental images in this text, which enables its readers to construe a mental representation of Gen 28 in which the conflict between the two concepts of god obviously function in the henotheistic conceptual network of the ancient Near East.

Bibliography

Allwood, J., & Gärdenfors, P. (1999), *Cognitive Semantics. Meaning and Cognition* (Pragmatics & Beyond, New Series 55), Amsterdam/Philadelphia: John Benjamins.
Alt, A. (1953), "Der Gott der Väter," and "Die Wahlfahrt von Sichem nach Bethel," in A. Alt, *Kleine Schriften zur Geschichte des Volkes Israel* (3 Vols.) München: C.H. Beck, 48–50; 145–53.
Chatelion Counet, P., & Van Tilborg, Sj. (2000), *Jesus' Appearances and Disappearances in Luke 24* (Biblical Interpretation Series 45), Leiden: Brill.
Dirven, R., and Verspoor, M. (1998), *Cognitive Exploration of Language and Linguistics* (Cognitive Linguistics in Practice), Amsterdam/Philadelphia.
Fauconnier, G. (1985), *Mental Spaces*. Cambridge: Cambridge University Press, 1995².
—— (1997), *Mappings in Thought and Language*, Cambridge: Cambridge University Press.
Fauconnier, G., & Turner, M. (1998), "Conceptual Integration Networks," *Cognitive Science* 22.2, 133–87.
Follingstad, C.M. (2001), *Deictic Viewpoint in Biblical Hebrew Text. A Syntagmatic and Paradigmatic Analysis of the Particle* כִּי *(kî)*. Dallas (TX): SIL International.
Griffiths, G.J. (1966–67), "The Celestial Ladder and the Gate of Heaven in Egyptian Ritual," *Expository Times* 78, 54–55.
Gunkel, H. (1910), *Genesis übersetzt und erklärt*. Göttingen: Vandenhoeck & Ruprecht.
Hecke, P. Van (1999), "Are People Walking After or Before God? On the Metaphorical Use of הלך אחרי and הלך פני," *Orientalia Lovaniensia Periodica* 30, 37–71.
—— (2001), "Polysemy or Homonymy in the Root(s) r'h in Biblical Hebrew. A Cognitive-Linguistic Approach," *Zeitschrift für Althebraistik* 14, 50–67.
—— (2003), "Searching for and Exploring Wisdom. A Cognitive-Semantic Approach to the Hebrew Verb *haqar* in Job 28," in: E. van Wolde (ed.), *Job 28. Cognition in Context* (Biblical Interpretation Series 64), Leiden: Brill, 139–62.

Houtman, C. (1977), "What Did Jacob See in His Dream at Bethel? Some Remarks on Genesis xxviii 10–22," *Vetus Testamentum* 27, 337–51.
Huwyler, B. (2001), "'Wenn Gott mit mir ist...' (Gen 28, 20–22). Zum sprachlichen und theologischen Problem des hebräischen Konditionalsatzes," *Theologische Zeitschrift* 57, 10–25.
Kamp, A.H. (2001), *Innerlijke Werelden. Een Cognitief Taalkundige Benadering van het Bijbelboek Jona*. (Dissertation, Tilburg University), Hengelo: A.H. Kamp.
—— (2003), "World Building in Job 28: A Case of Conceptual Logic," in E. van Wolde (ed.), *Job 28. Cognition in Context* (Biblical Interpretation Series 64), Leiden: Brill, 307–20.
—— (2004a), *Inner Worlds. A Cognitive Linguistic Approach to the Book of Jonah* (Biblical Interpretation Series), Leiden: Brill (forthcoming).
—— (2004b), "Conceptualisation and Modality in Job i 1–5," *Vetus Testamentum* (forthcoming).
Langacker, R.W. (1987), *Foundations of Cognitive Grammar. Volume 1: Theoretical Prerequisites*. Stanford (CA): Stanford University Press.
—— (1988), "An Overview of Cognitive Grammar," in: B. Rudzka-Ostyn (ed.), *Topics in Cognitive Linguistics* (Amsterdam Studies in the Theory and History of Linguistic Science 50). Amsterdam/Philadelphia: John Benjamins, 3–48.
—— (1990), *Concept, Image, and Symbol. The Cognitive Basis of Grammar*. Berlin/New York: Mouton de Gruyter.
—— (1991), *Foundations of Cognitive Grammar. Volume 2: Descriptive Application*. Stanford (CA): Stanford University Press.
—— (1997), "The Contextual Basis of Cognitive Semantics," J. Nuyts & E. Pederson (eds.), *Language and Conceptualization*, Cambridge: Cambridge University Press, 229–52.
—— (2003), "Context, Cognition, and Semantics: A Unified Dynamic Approach," E. van Wolde, *Job 28. Cognition in Context* (Biblical Interpretation Series 64), Leiden Boston: E.J. Brill, 179–230.
Lipton, D. (1999), *Revisions of the Night. Politics and Promises in the Patriarchal Dreams of Genesis* (JSOTS 288), Sheffield: Sheffield Academic Press.
Loader, J.A. (2003), "Job and Cognition in Context—Impressions and Prospects from the Perspective of Exegesis," in E. van Wolde (ed.), *Job 28. Cognition in Context* (Biblical Interpretation Series 64), Leiden: Brill, 321–30.
Merwe, C.H.J. van der, Naudé, J.A., & Kroeze, J.H. (1999), *A Biblical Hebrew Reference Grammar* (Biblical Languages: Hebrew, 3), Sheffield: Sheffield University Press.
Millard, A.R. (1966–67), "The Celestial Ladder and the Gate of Heaven," *Expository Times* 78, 86–87.
Noll, K.L. (2001), *Canaan and Israel in Antiquity. An Introduction* (The Biblical Seminar 83). London: Sheffield Academic Press.
Parrot, A. (1953), *La Tour de Babel*. Neuchâtel 1953 (Eng. translation: *The Tower of Babel*. London: SCM Press, 1955).
Pirson, R. (1999), "What Is Joseph Supposed to Be? On the Interpretation of r[n in Genesis 37. 2," in A. Brenner and J.W. van Henten (eds.), *Recycling Biblical Figures: Papers Read at the NOSTER Colloquium in Amsterdam May 1997* (Studies in Theology and Religion 1) Leiden: Deo, 81–92.
—— (2003), *Lord of the Dreams. A Semantic and Literary Study of Gen. 37–50* (Journal for the Study of the Old Testament Supplement Series 355), Sheffield: Sheffield Academic Press.
Porter, B.N. (2000), *One God or Many? Concepts of Divinity in the Ancient World* (Transactions of the Casco Bay Assyriological Institute, 1), Bethesda: CDL Press.
Pury, A. (1975), *Promesse divine et légende cultuelle dans le cycle de Jacob* (2 Vols.). Paris: J. Gabalda.
Rad, G. von (1953), *Das erste Buch Mose, Genesis*. Göttingen: Vandenhoeck & Ruprecht. (Eng. translation: *Genesis*. London: SCM Press, 1987 [1961].)

Rose, M. (2001), "Genèse 28, 10–22: L'exégèse doit muer en herméneutique théologique," in: J.-D. Macchi, and T. Römer (eds.), *Jacob. Commentaire à plusieurs voix de Ein mehrstimmiger Kommentar zu A Plural Commentary of Gen. 25–36. Mélanges offerts à Albert de Pury* (Le Monde de la Bible 44). Genève: Labor et Fides, 77–85.

Rudzka-Ostyn, B. (ed.) (1988), *Topics in Cognitive Linguistics* (Amsterdam Studies in the Theory and History of Linguistic Science 50). Amsterdam/Philadelphia: John Benjamins.

Sanders, J. (1994), *Perspective in Narrative Discourse*. (Diss.) Tilburg: Tilburg University.

Sarna, N. (1972), *Understanding Genesis: The Heritage of Biblical Israel*. New York: Schocken Books 197.

Speiser, E.A. (1962), *Genesis* (The Anchor Bible). New York: Doubleday.

Sweetser, E., & Fauconnier, G. (1996) (eds.), *Spaces, Worlds, and Grammar*, Chicago: Chicago University Press.

Taylor, J.R. (1989), *Linguistic Categorization. Prototypes in Linguistic Theory*. Oxford: Clarendon Press.

―― (1995), "Introduction: On Construing the World," in J.R. Taylor & R.E. MacLaury (eds.), *Language and the Cognitive Construal of the World*, Berlin/New York: Mouton de Gruyter, 1–21.

Taylor, J.R., & MacLaury, R.E. (1995), *Language and the Cognitive Construal of the World*, Berlin/New York: Mouton de Gruyter.

Taylor, J.R. (2003), "Categories and Concepts," in E.J. van Wolde (ed.), *Job 28. Cognition in Context* (Biblical Interpretation Series, 64), Leiden: Brill, 163–78.

Tilborg, Sj. van (1995), *Imaginative Love in John* (Biblical Interpretation Series 2), Leiden: Brill.

Ungerer, F., & Schmid, H.-J. (1996), *An Introduction to Cognitive Linguistics* (Learning about Language), London/New York: Longman.

Westermann, C. (1981), *Genesis 12–36*. Neukirchen-Vluyn: Neukirchener Verlag.

Werth, P.N. (1997), "Remote Worlds: The Conceptual Representation of Linguistic *Would*," in J. Nuyts & E. Pederson (eds.), *Language and Conceptualization*, Cambridge: Cambridge University Press, 84–115.

Wolde, E.J. van, & Sanders, J. (1994), "Kijken met de ogen van anderen. Perspectief in bijbelteksten," *Tijdschrift voor Theologie* 3, 221–45.

―― (1995), "Who Guides Whom? Embeddedness and Perspective in Biblical Hebrew and in 1 Kgs. 3:16–28," *Journal for Biblical Literature* 114, 623–42.

―― (1997), "Texts in Dialogue with Texts: Intertextuality in the Ruth and Tamar Narratives," *Biblical Interpretation* 5, 1–28.

―― (2002a), "The Dinah Story: Rape or Worse?," *Old Testament Essays* 15, 225–39.

―― (2002b), "Does ʿinnâ Denote Rape? A Semantic Analysis of a Controversial Word," *Vetus Testamentum* 52, 528–44.

―― (ed.) (2003a), *Job 28. Cognition in Context* (Biblical Interpretation Series 64), Leiden: Brill.

―― (2003b), "Wisdom, Who Can Find It? A Non-Cognitive and Cognitive Study of Job 28:1–11," in E.J. van Wolde (ed.), *Job 28. Cognition in Context* (Biblical Interpretation Series, 64), Leiden: Brill, 1–36.

―― (2003c), "In Words and Pictures. The Sun in 2 Samuel 12:7–12," *Biblical Interpretation* 11, 259–78.

Yri, K.M. (1998), *My Father Taught Me How to Cry, but Now I Have Forgotten. The Semantics of Religious Concepts with an Emphasis on Meaning, Interpretation and Translatability* (Acta Humaniora 29), Oslo: Scandinavian University Press.

CHAPTER EIGHT

"HEARING VOICES WHILE READING": ISAIAH 40–55 AS A DRAMA

Annemarieke van der Woude
University of Nijmegen, the Netherlands

1. *Introduction*

"Hearing voices while reading."[1] This is how Sjef van Tilborg, in his inaugural address, described the activity of an exegete. It certainly applies to reading Isa 40–55, for these chapters contain many voices. Especially at the beginning (Isa 40:1–11), several unnamed voices follow one another in rapid succession. The powerful and expressive language of Isa 40–55 also stimulates the reader to hear, see, and imagine what he or she is reading. The question which will concern me in this paper is whether Isa 40–55 is a drama.[2] In recent Isaiah research, this question has received much attention.[3] To find an answer to it, I will use the concepts of "drama" and "dramatic text" as they are developed within literary theory. Paraphrasing the words of Sjef van Tilborg, my leading question will be: does the fact that Isa 40–55 is a text that stimulates the reader to hear different voices while reading it make it a drama?

2. *Overview of Literature on Isa 40–55 as a Drama*

In Old Testament research, Isa 40–55 has often been called a "drama."[4] Nevertheless, the history of interpretation of these chapters

---

[1] Sj. van Tilborg, *Al lezend stemmen horen*.
[2] This article is a slightly revised version and translation of the first chapter of my doctoral thesis.
[3] Cf., most recently, C. Conroy, "Reflections on Some Recent Studies of Second Isaiah"; J.G.F. Wilks, "The Prophet as Incompetent Dramatist."
[4] Cf., for instance, H. Utzschneider, *Michas Reise in die Zeit. Studien zum Drama als Genre der prophetischen Literatur des Alten Testaments*, 46–50.

shows that this term can mean different things. Roughly speaking, four drama approaches can be distinguished. Representatives of the first movement consider Isa 40–55 to be a liturgical drama. In their view, language and imagery are liturgical in nature; these scholars assume that a liturgical setting has been the origin of these chapters. A second movement considers Isa 40–55 to be a theological drama. In this view, the term "drama" is not so much applied to the genre of the texts as to the events it describes; it is the relationship between Yhwh and Israel that is called "dramatic." The third one raises the possibility that these chapters have been the script of a play that was meant for performance. Representatives of this movement point to similarities with Greek drama. They divide the texts in acts and scenes. This third movement resembles the first one, for both assume a kind of performance. The fourth movement derives its definition of "drama" and "dramatic" from literary theory. This movement means to specify the genre of the texts in Isa 40–55 as texts that reveal dramatic traits. Even though drama as a literary phenomenon originates from a liturgical setting, it is nevertheless important to distinguish a literary drama from a liturgical one. I will come back to this.

Generally spoken, studies that belong to one of these four drama approaches show more interest in the composition of Isa 40–55 than in the history of its redaction. In recent overviews of literature on Isa 40–55, representatives of divergent drama aproaches, be they theological, theatrical, or literary, are headed under the title "composition."[5] These studies all focus on the texts in their final form. Thus it is possible, as stated by Werlitz, "(. . .) die Endgestalt von Jes 40–55 nicht nur als Komposition, sondern gar als ein Drama zu beschreiben (. . .)."[6] There are nuances, however. Treating these chapters as a drama is regarded as a specification of treating them as a composition. Representatives of the liturgical drama movement do not focus on the compositional structure in exactly the same way. The question that fascinates these scholars is: what kind of liturgical setting has functioned as a design for structure and composition of Isa 40–55? Thus, underneath a concentration on composition lies a

---

[5] Cf. H.-J. Hermisson, "Neue Literatur zu Deuterojesaja (I)," 257–69; H.-J. Hermisson, "Neue Literatur zu Deuterojesaja (II)," 380–82, 387–94; H.-J. Hermisson, "Deuterojesaja," 685–86. See also J. Werlitz, *Redaktion und Komposition. Zur Rückfrage hinter die Endgestalt von Jesaja 40–55*, 1–8.

[6] Werlitz, *Redaktion und Komposition*, 4.

diachronic question. This is even truer for those who take the view that the so-called Servant Songs originally did not belong to these chapters. In what follows, the four drama movements will be discussed in detail, together with their most important representatives.

2.1. *Isa 40–55 as a Liturgical Drama*

In the history of interpretation, the notion of Isa 40–55 as a liturgical drama has always been connected to the so-called Scandinavian school.[7] The oral nature of the language challenges these scholars to point to the relationship of these texts and some liturgical practice. Nevertheless, opinions differ on the exact nature of this relationship. Most scholars believe that a liturgical practice functioned as a model for the language and composition of Isa 40–55.[8] Vincent, however, believes that this connection was even stronger: the liturgy not only functioned as a model for Isa 40–55, but these chapters themselves operated in a liturgical setting.[9] Isa 40–55 reports on a cultic ritual. According to Vincent, the prophetic figure that is responsible for these chapters is an orator more than a writer. Next to the oral nature of the language, representatives of the Scandinavian school also assume that Isa 40–55 take their images from a liturgical setting. They point to the relationship between these texts and psalms on the kingship of Yhwh (Ps 47, 93, 95, 96, 97, 98, and 99). They involve the call to sing and praise the Lord, to worship and bow down and clap the hands. On the basis of these liturgical elements scholars suppose that before the Exile a festival was held in Jerusalem every autumn. This New Year festival celebrated the renewal of the kingship of Yhwh and his victory against the hostile forces.[10] The psalms on the kingship of Yhwh may have originated against the background of this festival. And it is the same liturgical practice that functioned as

---

[7] Cf. H. Haag, *Der Gottesknecht bei Deuterojesaja*, 156–67. Haag designates a Scandinavian school of research regarding the Servant Songs in Isa 40–55.

[8] E.g., H. Ringgren, "Zur Komposition von Jesaja 49–55;" J.H. Eaton, *Festal Drama in Deutero-Isaiah*.

[9] J.M. Vincent, *Studien zur literarischen Eigenart und zur geistigen Heimat von Jesaja, Kap. 40–55*, 30–33, 252–58.

[10] For an elaborate description of elements relating to this annual festival based on data from the psalms, see Eaton, *Festal Drama*, 8–37. In what follows, Eaton points to the relationship between these liturgical elements and Isa 40–55 and Isa 60–62, cf. Eaton, *Festal Drama*, 38–91. See also S. Mowinckel, *He That Cometh*, 138–154; H. Ringgren, *Israelitische Religion*, 264–68.

a model for Isa 40–55. According to Mowinckel, Isa 40–55 has used and transformed this cultic framework: "(...) Deutero-Isaiah (...) lifts the whole conception of restoration up into a supra-terrestrial sphere, presenting it as a drama of cosmic dimensions."[11]

Among scholars that belong to the Scandinavian school, the position of the so-called Servant Songs within Isa 40–55 is another point of discussion. Is there any relationship between the servant in Isa 40–55 and the so-called *ebed*-Yhwh-psalms (Ps 78, 89, 132, and 143)?[12] Within these psalms, the servant exhibits royal traits.[13] Moreover, this servant suffers vicariously for his people, the same motive as in the fourth Servant Song (Ps 89 a.o. // Isa 52:13–53:12). In views that accept a relationship between the servant figures in Isa 40–55 and in the psalms, the servant passages in Isa 40–55 are modelled on the same liturgy as the one underlying the *ebed*-psalms: the celebration of the renewal of the kingship of Yhwh and of the royal figure that is his representative on earth. In this line of thought, the Servant Songs are a constitutive part of the composition of Isa 40–55.[14] The opposite meaning, that is to say, the Servant Songs originally do not belong to Isa 40–55, is defended as well. Representatives of this position do believe that there was an annual festival in autumn, and they consider the psalms that are rooted in this festival as a model for the composition of Isa 40–55, but they do not include the Servant Songs. They do not recognize royal traits in the servant of Isa 40–55.[15]

This overview shows that among representatives of the Scandinavian school there is consensus that language and images in Isa 40–55 are "liturgisch verankert."[16] Opinions differ on two topics: the exact relationship between these chapters and its liturgical setting and the position of the Servant Songs within Isa 40–55.

---

[11] Mowinckel, *He That Cometh*, 138–39.
[12] Cf. Eaton, *Festal Drama*, 1–7; P.R. Ackroyd, *Exile and Restoration: A Study of Hebrew Thought of the Sixth Century BC*, 126–28.
[13] See esp. Eaton, *Festal Drama*, 29–30.
[14] E.g., Ringgren, *Israelitische Religion*, 268–71; Ringgren, "Jes 49–55," 374–76. See also I. Engnell, "The 'Ebed Yahweh Songs and the Suffering Messiah in 'Deutero-Isaiah.'"
[15] E.g., Mowinckel, *He That Cometh*, 219–33. Cf. Mowinckel, *He That Cometh*, 187–219.
[16] Ringgren, "Jes 49–55," 374.

2.2. *Isa 40–55 as a Theological Drama*

To a smaller or a larger degree, scholars who consider Isa 40–55 to be a theological drama intend to typify the relationship between Yhwh and his people. This appears to echo a classical view on drama that considers the conflict to be its fundamental quality.[17] In his 1956 commentary, for instance, Muilenburg describes Isa 40–55 as an "eschatological drama."[18] Both the theology and form of these chapters are dramatic. Because the way in which the God of Israel is present in creation, history, and redemption is described in relation to, or sometimes even in opposition with, other participants in history, such as the nations, Cyrus, Jacob/Israel and the servant, Muilenburg describes this theology as "dramatic." The dramatic form of these chapters relates to their rhetorical nature. As one of the features, Muilenburg points to the frequent use of הנה or הן. However, although he characterizes several subunits as "miniature dramas,"[19] Muilenburg does not consider the whole of Isa 40–55 a drama. The chapters do possess the materials of a drama, but in their entirety they do not reveal a dramatic structure: "Yet nowhere do we have anything approximating a drama; all the materials are here except the architectonics of the drama itself."[20] In this description, Muilenburg appears to allude to a theatrical drama approach.

In the way she treats Isa 40–55, Heßler shows a combination of a theological and a literary drama approach. She takes a literary definition of drama from Kayser as her starting point: "Wir haben ein Drama vor uns, wenn auf einem besonderen Raum von Rollenträgern ein Geschehen agiert wird."[21] This definition brings her to the following questions: what is the main action in Isa 40–55, what is the stage of the action, and what characters are at issue? Isa 40–55 is about "der Weg zur Weltherrschaft Jahwes."[22] The earth is the stage of the action, which revolves around the relationship between Yhwh

---

[17] Cf. H. van Gorp, D. Delabastita, and R. Ghesquiere, *Lexicon van literaire termen*, 125–26.
[18] J. Muilenburg, *The Book of Isaiah. Chapters 40–66*, 384–419.
[19] Muilenburg, *Isa 40–66*, 398.
[20] Muilenburg, *Isa 40–66*, 388.
[21] W. Kayser, *Das sprachliche Kunstwerk. Eine Einführung in die Literaturwissenschaft*, 368. Cf. E. Heßler, *Das Heilsdrama: Der Weg zur Weltherrschaft Jahwes (Jes. 40–55)*, 31, 320.
[22] Heßler, *Heilsdrama*. It is the subtitle of her study on Isa 40–55. Cf. Hermisson, "Neue Literatur (I)," 263–66.

and his people.²³ The drama takes place in Babylon at the end of the Exile. Yhwh is the main character in this drama. These chapters are properly understood as a "Heilsdrama,"²⁴ according to Heßler. Yhwh's plan of salvation is realized in the way he speaks; it is a "wortgewirktes Geschehen."²⁵ The language of these chapters expresses the execution of his plan: "Das Buch ist durchgängig als *ergehende Rede* formuliert, als direkte Rede, Anrede, die dem Hörer nicht in der Distanz beläßt, ihn also nicht nur informiert, sondern seine Reaktion herausfordert."²⁶ More than a theoretical treatise, Yhwh's plan of salvation is "eine Abfolge von Aktionen und Ereignisse."²⁷ The actions and events fit into his plan, as the smaller parts of a mosaic into the larger composition.

With reference to Heßler, Paganini also mentions the dramatic nature of Isaiah.²⁸ Isa 55 reveals "eine dramatische dialogische Struktur."²⁹ Four characters appear: Zion, a group of people, Yhwh, and an unidentified commentator. In different combinations, they participate in the four dialogues in this chapter. These dialogues tell about the relationships among Yhwh, Zion, and Yhwh's people. Yhwh, main actor in Isaiah, guides history. He makes Zion the center of the world and makes everybody move towards her. He offers the poor and needy a salutary future. Yet, while Paganini stresses the dramatic nature of Isaiah, he emphatically distances himself from a liturgical or a theatrical drama approach.

Like Muilenburg, Heßler, and Paganini, Seitz uses the term "drama" primarily to describe the relationship between Yhwh and his people.³⁰ He entitles Isa 1–66 in its entirety as "The Drama of God and Zion."³¹ Yhwh and Zion are the main characters. The drama is all

---

[23] Heßler, *Heilsdrama*, 20–31, 319–22.
[24] Heßler, *Heilsdrama*. It is the title of her study on Isa 40–55.
[25] Heßler, *Heilsdrama*, 27.
[26] Heßler, *Heilsdrama*, 22.
[27] Heßler, *Heilsdrama*, 21.
[28] S. Paganini, *Der Weg zur Frau Zion, Ziel unserer Hoffnung. Aufbau, Kontext, Sprache, Kommunikationsstruktur und theologische Motive in Jes 55, 1–13*, 156–200.
[29] Paganini, *Frau Zion*, 158.
[30] C.R. Seitz, "Isaiah 1–66: Making Sense of the Whole"; C.R. Seitz, "On the Question of Divisions Internal to the Book of Isaiah."
[31] Seitz, "Isa 1–66," 122. Cf. C.R. Seitz, *Zion's Final Destiny. The Development of the Book of Isaiah. A Reassessment of Isaiah 36–39*. See also D.M. Carr, "What Can We Say about the Tradition History of Isaiah? A Response to Christopher Seitz's *Zion's Final Destiny*"; U. Becker, "Jesajaforschung (Jes 1–39)," 14–17.

about Zion's fate and about the way in which Yhwh is concerned about her fate. His care for her expresses his care for his creation. In addition, Seitz relates the term "drama" to the way in which time, "chronos,"[32] advances in Isa 1–66. These chapters do not stick to a linear progression of time. Already the beginning tells us what Yhwh has in mind for Zion: everybody shall go up to her and she will be the heart of the world (2:1–5). Nevertheless, Jerusalem is condemned and threatened, because Israel shows no obedience to God (1–39). At the same time, these chapters tell about Zion's salvation and redemption (34–35 and 36–39). The final chapters describe her new future (40–66). In the reversal of Zion's fortune, the servant plays an essential role. Due to this dramatic progression of time, Seitz argues, we as readers have prior knowledge of the development of the drama, compared to the characters that participate in this drama. Already from the beginning, we know about her happy end: "(...) we as readers are privileged to see the whole journey in a twinkling in the opening chapters."[33] As will become clear in the following pages, a literary drama approach considers the use of time to be one of the distinctive features of dramatic texts, in comparison to that in poetic or narrative texts. It is interesting to note that Seitz, by connecting the term "drama" not only to the relationship between Yhwh and Zion but also to the way in which time advances in these chapters, adds a literary aspect to his theological drama approach.

2.3. *Isa 40–55 as a Play*

Two recent commentaries on Isaiah, one written by Watts and the other one written by Baltzer, defend the thesis that Isaiah is in fact the script of a play. In their view, these texts were meant for actual performance. According to Watts, this thesis affects Isa 1–66 in its entirety, whereas Baltzer considers Isa 40–55 to be a play. The notion that these texts evoke a visual representation and that language and images in Isaiah seem to demand a performance, is not new. After all, the same observations have made scholars assume a liturgical setting as a model for the structure and composition of Isa 40–55. Texts in Isaiah have also been compared to a piece of music, an oratorio,

---

[32] Seitz, "Isa 1–66," 122.
[33] Seitz, "Isa 1–66," 122.

that asks for a performance more than once.³⁴ Yet, Watts and Baltzer go one step further. Not only do these texts *evoke* a representation, but they are actually composed as a play, with acts, scenes, actors, and a choir on stage.

According to Watts, Isa 1–66 is a written rendering of "oral, multi-voiced theater, in which one or more actors, a narrator, and a chorus spoke its measured lines, challenged old ideas, and suggested new ones in Jerusalem under the Persians."³⁵ To make plausible that these chapters are a kind of drama, Watts points to cultic drama in ancient Israel and to parallels with Greek drama. Nevertheless, Watts admits that it is difficult to determine whether these texts originally were intended for an oral presentation. He considers the possibility that the stage directions for an actual performance have been lost under Ezra's reformation. Watts divides Isa 1–66 into acts, scenes, and episodes, with different voices speaking. Yhwh is the main speaker, while it is often difficult to determine to whom the other voices belong. Isa 1–66 contains ten acts, a prologue, and an epilogue. It presents Yhwh's history with Israel, from the eighth until the middle of the fifth century B.C.E. Every act reports the experiences of one generation, while a choir comments on these events. There is a tension between God's plan with his people and Israel's stubbornness to rely on him and its inclination to strive for political power. The essence of the drama emerges from this tension. The drama is composed in such a way as to appeal its audience in Jerusalem in the middle of the fifth century to make a choice: to agree to the Persian rule and to accept that Jerusalem's role on earth is a different one. She will be a place of pilgrimage for all nations. Isa 1–66 describes well over three centuries of history between God and his people, Watts argues, but at the same time these chapters represent the vision of Isaiah. Because it is a drama, it demands a double stage setting. The events that take place on earth form one setting, but at the same time the vision requests "an implied *stage setting* from which Yahweh and his

---

[34] Cf. W. Brueggemann, *Isaiah 40–66*, 1–15. Cf. K. Baltzer, *Deutero-Jesaja*, 43: "Ich vermute, dass der Gesamteindruck einer Aufführung des Werkes Dtjes mehr der eines Oratoriums war."

[35] J.D.W. Watts, *Isaiah 1–33*, xxiii–lvii. Quote: xlviii. Cf. Becker, "Jesajaforschung (I)," 10–13. See also P.D. Miscall, *Isaiah*; P.D. Quinn-Miscall, *Reading Isaiah: Poetry and Vision*. In both studies, Miscall uses the terms "drama" and "dramatic." His drama approach rests on the commentary of James Watts, but Miscall does not intend to present a systematic drama approach of Isaiah.

aides can see and relate to mundane events in Jerusalem, in Babylon, and other places."[36]

Baltzer, just like Watts, recognizes the structure of a play divided into acts and scenes in the chapters of Isaiah.[37] To found his thesis, Baltzer also points to parallels with cultic drama and Greek drama. Isa 40–55 contains six acts, preceded by a prologue and complemented by an epilogue. Moreover, five out of six acts are closed by a hymnic passage (42:10–13, 44:21–23, 45:25, 49:13, and 52:9). Different from Watts, Baltzer is convinced that Isa 40–55 was actually performed. The texts make up the "libretto,"[38] the script, for performance. Every year in spring, these chapters were presented during the Passover-Mazzot festival, Baltzer argues. It took place in Jerusalem as well as in places in the Jewish Diaspora. The play appeals to the audience to go up to Jerusalem. Because the drama was performed during this festival, Baltzer also describes Isa 40–55 as "ein *Liturgisches Drama*."[39] The chapters came into being in Jerusalem during the second half of the fifth century B.C.E., during Nehemia's time. Not only was Isa 40–55 performed every year, but these texts are even dependent on a performance to be properly called a "drama": "Erst die Aufführung macht den Text zum *Drama*, zum lebendigen Wort."[40] Baltzer indicates several stage directions in these chapters. For instance, going away and gathering (49:17–18) are indications as to how the scene on the restoration of Zion needs to be performed.[41] Kings and queens who bring her children and bow down to Zion (49:22–23) point to a procession.[42] There are also indications for a choir acting. Speaking in Zion's ears, for instance (49:20), points to the choir's loud screaming.[43] A choir also performs the hymnic passages. The sounds of the Hebrew language show directions for the pitch of the musical performance. As an example, the i-sounds and the a-sounds (49:14) indicate the pitch of the women's voices.[44] Also

---

[36] Watts, *Isaiah 1–33*, xlix.
[37] Baltzer, *Deutero-Jesaja*, 24–76. Cf. Hermisson, "Neue Literatur (II)," 387–94; K. Baltzer & P. Machinist, eds., *Deutero-Isaiah: A Commentary on Isaiah 40–55*.
[38] Baltzer, *Deutero-Jesaja*, 38.
[39] Baltzer, *Deutero-Jesaja*, 29.
[40] Baltzer, *Deutero-Jesaja*, 38.
[41] Baltzer, *Deutero-Jesaja*, 409.
[42] Baltzer, *Deutero-Jesaja*, 405, 416–17.
[43] Baltzer, *Deutero-Jesaja*, 411.
[44] Baltzer, *Deutero-Jesaja*, 407, n. 8.

the many deictic signals in Isa 40–55, for instance, the particle הִנֵּה, Baltzer considers to be an indication for a visual representation.

Up until now, three drama approaches have been under discussion: a liturgical, a theological, and a theatrical one. The liturgical and the theatrical approach demonstrates a strong affinity. They have in common that they relate the expressive nature of Isaiah and the visual representation these texts evoke to a practice of performance. Representatives of the Scandinavian school point to a liturgical setting, while both Watts and Baltzer point to a stage setting. Nevertheless, even within one and the same drama approach, opinions differ on how close the connection is between these texts and an actual performance. Baltzer is convinced that that tie is very strong: in fact, these texts form the script of a play that shows up best during the performance. Vincent also argues that the connection is close: the texts of Isa 40–55 are spoken, sung, and represented within the setting of a cultic ritual. Other representatives of the Scandinavian school consider this tie to be looser: a cultic setting only functioned as a model for the composition of Isaiah. And although Watts fully appreciates the scenic nature of these chapters, he does not dare to say whether Isa 1–66 was ever meant for an oral presentation.

2.4. *Isa 40–55 as a Dramatic Text*

Scholars, who regard Isa 40–55 as a dramatic text, take their definition from literary theory, more or less explixicitly. With "drama" or "dramatic" they designate a literary genre. The terms explicate the nature of these texts and point to a difference with narrative or poetic texts. And not only Isaiah, but in fact all prophetic texts in the Old Testament are dramatic texts, Utzschneider argues: "Prophetische Texte des AT, so unsere These, sind literaturwissenschaftlich gesehen als dramatische Texte anzusehen. Sie weisen folgende wichtige Kennzeichen des Genres auf: Sprachlich und strukturell sind sie durch die Figurenrede bestimmt; sie evozieren notwendig einen szenisch-visuellen Hintergrund (Opsis) und sind durch sinnhafte Handlungsentwürfe (Plot) bestimmt."[45]

---

[45] Utzschneider, *Michas Reise*, 57. In this study Utzschneider presents a dramatic analysis of Mic 1,1–4,7. Cf. H. Utzschneider, "Situation und Szene. Überlegungen zum Verhältnis historischer und literarischer Deutung prophetischer Texte am Beispiel von Hos 5,8–6,6." In this article Utzschneider offers a dramatic analysis of Hos

According to Utzschneider, direct speech dominates in dramatic texts, while at the same time the number of speakers is limited.[46] In prophetic texts, Yhwh is at issue, a prophetic figure and also a third party, that is often presented as speaking and is addressed as a "you." Next to this, these texts are dramatic because they evoke a visual representation. Not only their powerful language, but the so-called "Wortkulisse"[47] also contributes to this visual representation. What is a "verbal side wing" about? Dramatic texts do not have theatrical means at their disposal to visualize the stage setting of a particular scene. This is in contrast with a theatrical performance, where attributes are used to illustrate the stage setting, or side wings to indicate a change of scenery. Dramatic texts compensate this lack of theatrical means by using the "verbal side wing": a verbal description of the scenery. Isa 52 contains an example of a verbal side wing: an unidentified speaker paints the setting within which the messenger is rushing and bringing good news (52:7). The "visuelle Leerstellen"[48] in dramatic texts stimulate the reader's imagination to visualize what these texts describe. Anyhow, according to Utzschneider, this appeal to a visual representation is not enough to point necessarily to an actual performance of these texts. In the last part of his thesis, Utzschneider points to the plot that dramatic texts contain: a coherent sequence of events that spans time and space.

Like Utzschneider, Leene explicitly takes his description of "dramatic" from literary theory.[49] Leene mentions three features of a dramatic text. In contrast with a narrative text, a dramatic text lacks a narrator. A dramatic text does not have a textual instance that mediates between the story that is presented by the text, and the reader. Thus, a dramatic text suggests that its story is immediately at hand. As a consequence of this suggestion, it is typical for a dramatic text that

---

5,8–6,6. His theoretical framework particularly rests on B. Asmuth, *Einführung in die Dramenanalyse*. See also P.R. House, *Zephaniah. A Prophetic Drama*. On the basis of literary theories on genres, House presents a dramatic analysis of Zephaniah.

[46] Utzschneider, *Michas Reise*, 11–58.

[47] Utzschneider, *Michas Reise*, 18. Cf. M. Pfister, *Das Drama. Theorie und Analyse*, 37–38, 351–53.

[48] Utzschneider, *Michas Reise*, 57.

[49] H. Leene, *De vroegere en de nieuwe dingen bij Deuterojesaja*, 30–37. His theoretical framework particularly rests on Pfister, *Das Drama*. Cf. H. Leene, "History and Eschatology in Deutero-Isaiah," 234–38; H. Leene, *Een nieuwe hemel en een nieuwe aarde, slotakkoord van het boek Jesaja*, 12–14. See also R. Abma, *Bonds of Love: Methodic Studies of Prophetic Texts with Marriage Imagery (Isaiah 50:1–3 and 54:1–10, Hosea 1–3, Jeremiah 2–3)*, 59–61; Hermisson, "Neue Literatur (I)," 258–63.

the time required for presenting the story ("drama time"), is about equal to the time that spans the presented story ("dramatized time"). In contrast, a narrative text has more opportunities to vary. In a narrative text, telling an event ("narration time") can take shorter or longer than the event itself ("narrative time"). A second feature of a dramatic text is the central position of the dialogue. A third feature, according to Leene, concerns the fact that in these kinds of texts speaking itself is a kind of action.[50] Dramatic texts are performative in nature. To sum up, a text that shows these three features—the impression of an immediate presence of the story, speaking as the common way of presenting the story, and its performative nature—is a dramatic text, Leene argues. Nevertheless, these characteristics are not enough to make a drama out of it. A drama proper is also synaesthetic. It shows "Plurimedialität."[51] A text that is a drama prescribes several means to evoke a presentation. During the performance not only language is used, but also other means, such as image and sound, taste, smell, or touch, depending on the kind of drama. If there is no appeal to several senses simultaneously, then the text is not a drama. It is Leene's thesis that Isa 40–55 is not a drama precisely because these chapters, except for the language, do not aim at the use of other means to evoke a presentation. On the other hand, Isa 40–55 definitively is a *dramatic text*, because it contains performative moments. Moreover, these moments can be set out on a chronological line. The subsequent literary units in Isa 40–55 show a "dramatic progression."[52] Leene also relates the term "dramatic" to the impression these texts create of a story that is immediately present: "The progression [of action] deserves the adjective "dramatic" where the reader feels himself involved in a scenario of successive actions."[53]

Beuken is another scholar who points to a dramatic progression within Isa 40–55.[54] Although Beuken, different from Leene, does not offer a systematic explanation of what he understands by "dramatic,"

---

[50] Cf. Asmuth, *Dramenanalyse*, 8: "Die neuere Sprachwissenschaft (...) versteht das Reden (...) ausdrücklich als Handeln. Im Drama ist es die beherrschende Art des Handelns (...)."
[51] Pfister, *Das Drama*, 24.
[52] Leene, *Vroegere en nieuwe dingen*, 30: "dramatische voortgang."
[53] H. Leene, "The Coming of Yhwh as King: The Complementary Character of Psalms 96 and 98," 218.
[54] W.A.M. Beuken, *Jesaja*. Cf. H.-J. Hermisson, "Deuterojesaja-Probleme. Ein kritischer Literaturbericht," 64–66; Hermisson, "Neue Literatur (II)," 380–82.

their approaches resemble each other to such a degree that they have been referred to as a Dutch school of research into Isa 40–55, comparable to the way one might speak about a Scandinavian school in relation to a liturgical approach of these chapters. Beuken is considered "als einem Exponenten der niederländischen Deuterojesaja-Schule,"[55] and in this context Leene is mentioned as well.[56] Typical of these representatives of the Dutch school is that they consider Isa 40–55 to be a dramatic composition.

Isa 40–55 is "dramatic," because these chapters reveal their own dynamics, Beuken argues. They unfold an action within which the reader gets involved; more than that they form a sequence of themes or a report of events. These dynamics determine the unity of Isa 40–55. They reflect the history of Yhwh with his people. The reader is invited to participate in this history, so as to experience the deliverance out of captivity himself. Yhwh's journey to Zion, the stubbornness of his people to follow him, the servant as an example in the way he devotes his life to Yhwh: all this can be read as a drama that is enclosed in the course of these chapters. According to Beuken, the smaller units in Isa 40–55 take their meaning from their position within this dramatic development. As a consequence, one and the same literary genre can function in different ways and obtain different meanings, dependent on its position in the course of Isa 40–55. The same goes for motifs. They derive their meaning, at least partially, from the context within which they occur in the dramatic progression of these chapters.

2.5. *Evaluation*

In the preceding sections, research on Isa 40–55 was classified in four drama movements. The most important representatives of these movements were described in more detail. Scholars belonging to the

---

[55] Werlitz, *Redaktion und Komposition*, 4.
[56] Werlitz, *Redaktion und Komposition*, 4, n. 25. Cf. Hermisson, "Neue Literatur (I)," 257–58. When Hermisson discusses several studies on Isa 40–55 as a dramatic composition, he remarks: "Die bedeutendsten und respektablen Beispiele für dieses Verfahren kommen aus den Niederlanden (...)." In this context, he mentions Beuken and Leene. See also Hermisson, "Deuterojesaja-Probleme," 60. In an earlier overview of literature on Isa 40–55 Hermisson talks about "eine ganze niederländische Deuterojesaja-Schule," referring to H.H. Grosheide *et al.*, eds., *De Knecht. Studies rondom Deutero-Jesaja door collega's en oud-leerlingen aangeboden aan prof. dr. J. L. Koole.*

so-called Scandinavian school were mentioned as defenders of a liturgical drama approach (Ringgren, Eaton, Vincent, and Mowinckel). Representatives of a theological drama approach sometimes deal with Isa 40–55 (Muilenburg, Heßler), sometimes even with just one chapter (Paganini), or with the book of Isaiah in its entirety (Seitz). The most important representatives of a theatrical drama approach have laid down their thesis in a commentary, be it on Isa 1–66 (Watts), or be it on Isa 40–55 (Baltzer). Finally, those who consider Isa 40–55 to be a dramatice text take their definitions from literary theory (Leene, Beuken).[57] Within this literary approach, it is also defended that all prophetic texts from the Old Testament are in fact dramatic texts (Utzschneider).

It is beyond doubt that this categorization does not do justice to the diversity of drama approaches to Isaiah. Indeed, several scholars show a combination of more than one approach. An example may clarify that some kind of classification is useful, nevertheless. At several instances, Isaiah is designated as a "prophetic drama." For instance, Eaton considers Isa 40–55 to belong to the "prophetic liturgical dramas."[58] Watts typifies Isa 1–66 as "prophetic drama."[59] Utzschneider takes all prophetic literature from the Old Testament as *"prophetische Dramen."*[60] And Kratz characterizes the way in which Beuken and Leene treat Isa 40–55 as "prophetic drama."[61] This enumeration shows that "prophetic drama" can point to a liturgical approach of Isa 40–55 (Eaton), to an approach of Isa 1–66 as a play (Watts), to a notion of Isa 40–55 as a dramatic text (Leene, Beuken), or can designate a genre of literature in the Hebrew Bible (Utzschneider).

---

[57] Cf. Hermisson, "Neue Literatur (II)," 387. The difference between a drama approach of Leene and Beuken on the one hand and Baltzer on the other, Hermisson formulates as follows: "(. . .) was bei Leene und bei W.A.M. Beuken eine literarische Eigenart des Buchaufbaus ist, wird bei B. konsequent bis in Einzelheiten der Aufführungspraxis fortgeführt und durchdacht." For an analysis and evaluation of the drama approaches of Baltzer and Leene, see also A. van der Woude, "What is New in Isaiah 41:14–20? On the Drama Theories of Klaus Baltzer and Henk Leene."
[58] Eaton, *Festal Drama*, 122.
[59] Watts, *Isaiah 1–33*, xlvii.
[60] Utzschneider, *Michas Reise*, 56. Cf. House, *Zephaniah*. The subtitle reveals that House considers Zephaniah to be a "prophetic drama." See also W.D. Stacey, *Prophetic Drama in the Old Testament*. In this study on prohetic acts and gestures in the Old Testament, Stacey talks about "prophetic drama."
[61] Kratz, Review of Klaus Baltzer, *Deutero-Isaiah*.

Apart from these differences, points of agreement between the divergent drama approaches to Isa 40–55 can be found as well. For instance, almost all scholars point to the oral nature of these chapters. More than a written text, these chapters seem to be a spoken text, with Yhwh as its main speaker. The impression these texts give of a story that is immediately present goes together with their oral character. Moreover, these chapters evoke a visual representation. These features cause the "liturgicals" to suppose a connection between these texts and a liturgical setting. Although it is plausible that Isa 40–55 in images and text draw from a liturgical tradition in Ancient Israel to which also psalms on the kingship of Yhwh and on the servanthood of the king belong, the designation "liturgical drama" does not fit well to describe Isa 40–55. Referring to a liturgical practice recognizes insufficiently that these chapters possess their own dynamics. It is on the basis of the oral nature of Isa 40–55 that the "theologians" characterize the relationship between Yhwh and the other speakers in these chapters as "dramatic." In my view, however, the notion of "dramatic" or "drama" in this respect is not specific enough to qualify the dialogical nature of these chapters. For the "dramaturgists," the visual presentation that these chapters evoke is decisive to judge them as a play. I formulate my doubts regarding this thesis as two questions. The first one is: is the request for visualization compelling enough to consider Isa 40–55 as a play? My second question relates to the first: does an appeal to visualization only suffice to consider these texts as a play? When the "literary theorists" define these texts as "dramatic," they intend to point to a literary genre. Both Utzschneider and Leene are counted as their representatives. Utzschneider equates the visual representation that these texts evoke with a plurimedial representation. He believes that all prophetic texts from the Old Testament prescribe, next to language, other means as well to elicit a representation. For that reason, he designates these texts as a "drama" or as "dramatic." But as representatives of a theatrical drama approach did not convince me that the appeal that Isa 40–55 makes to visualization is compelling, in a similar way I am not convinced that these texts aim at the use of several means simultaneously to call for a presentation. In this respect, I share Leene's reservation and I also adopt his use of terminology. We only have a "drama" whenever these texts, in addition to language, prescribe other means as well to elicit a presentation. Another difference of opinion between Utzschneider and Leene concerns the plot. Its presence characterizes a dramatic text, Utzschneider argues. On that point, I do not agree with Utzschneider either. In my view, the presence of a plot does not distinguish a dramatic text from a narrative or a poetic one. Good narratives are based on a plot. And even a poem can contain a plot.

The next section is about the characteristics of a dramatic text, in comparison to narrative and poetic texts. As a conclusion of this section, it is important to state that the point of departure of this article lies in a drama approach that seeks contact with literary theory.

3. *Drama and Dramatic Text in Literary Theory*

3.1. *Introduction*

Generally spoken, literary theory regards a text as either narrative, dramatic, or poetic. One of the criteria to rank a text under one of these three genres concerns the language situation.[62] Apart from all kinds of mixtures that concrete texts reveal, the following is the standard: the language situation in a dramatic text is dialogical in nature, in a narrative text it is non-dialogical, and in a poetic text it is monological. This means that in a dramatic text the speech of the actors dominates, whereas the structure of a narrative text is determined by the speech of the narrator; this narrator can give up speech to several actors. In a poetic text there is only one spokesman. Furthermore, dramatic and narrative texts contain a story. In a poetic text, this is optional. A poetic text can resemble a narrative when a story is told in it, but most poems do not contain a story. This section of the paper discusses the features of a dramatic text. These are compared with those of a narrative text.[63]

---

[62] Cf. J. van Luxemburg, M. Bal, and W.G. Weststeijn, *Inleiding in de literatuurwetenschap*, 118–27. For the use of other criteria, see F.C. Maatje, *Literatuurwetenschap. Grondslagen van een theorie van het literaire werk*, 129–42; van Gorp, Delabastita, and Ghesquiere, *Lexicon literaire termen*, 181–83.

[63] Cf. H. Utzschneider, "Text—Leser—Autor. Bestandsaufnahme und Prolegomena zu einer Theorie der Exegese," 232: "Am weitesten fortgeschritten sind die genrespezifischen literaturwissenschaftlichen Ansätze für die atl Erzähltexte. Das *lyrische* Genre wird im Bereich der Psalmeninterpretation behandelt. Mehr oder weniger in den Anfängen steckt die Frage, ob auch in der prophetischen Literatur des AT ein Genre aufweisbar ist—etwa das *dramatische*."

Whereas both narrative texts and dramatic texts present a story (*geschiedenis, Geschichte*),[64] a difference lies in the way they present this story.[65] In a narrative text, a narrator is responsible for the presentation of the story. He holds the position to mediate between story and reader. In a dramatic text, this mediating position remains open.[66] As a consequence, the presented story seems to force itself upon the reader directly. Another characteristic, related to this suggestion of immediate presence, is that in a dramatic text, the time required to present the story roughly coincides with the time that spans the story. In a dramatic text, drama time and dramatized time correspond.[67] In a narrative text this is different. In such a text, the time required to tell the story can last much longer than the story that is told, but can also last much shorter. Thus, the proportion between narration time and narrative time in a narrative text can vary in innumerable ways. We have already seen that the speech of the narrator dominates the language situation in a narrative text. The narrator tells the story or hands the floor to actors who participate in it. In a dramatic text, on the other hand, the dialogue is the usual way of presenting the story. A dialogue is composed of "speaking engagements": "A dialogue consists of at least two speaking engagements of at least two actors (...)."[68] There is another difference between a narrative and a dramatic text. In a narrative text, speaking is making an utterance while in a dramatic text, speaking is itself an action. In a dramatic text, speaking is performative in nature. As a consequence, the function of speaking in both types of texts is not the same.

---

[64] Cf. M. Bal, *De theorie van vertellen en verhalen. Inleiding in de narratologie*, 18, where she defines a story as a logically and chronologically connected sequence of events, caused or undergone by actors.

[65] Cf. S. Chatman, *Story and Discourse. Narrative Structure in Fiction and Film*, 19 on a narrative text: "(...) the story is the *what* in a narrative that is depicted, discourse the *how*." In terms of Chatman, a dramatic and a narrative text does not diverge on the level of the "*what*," the story, but on the level of the "*how*," the discourse.

[66] Cf. Pfister, *Das Drama*, 19–33, 169–71, 369–74; van Luxemburg, Bal, and Weststeijn, *Literatuurwetenschap*, 166–82; van Gorp, Delabastita, and Ghesquiere, *Lexicon literaire termen*, 125–26.

[67] Cf. Leene, *Vroegere en nieuwe dingen*, 31; Pfister, *Das Drama*, 418, n. 80. The notions "drama time" and "dramatized time" are chosen by analogy with the notions "narration time" (*verteltijd, Erzählzeit*) and "narrative time" (*vertelde tijd, erzählte Zeit*), applying to narrative texts. Cf. J.L. Ska, *"Our Fathers Have Told Us." Introduction to the Analysis of Hebrew Narratives*, 7–8. See also M. Sternberg, *Expositional Modes and Temporal Ordering in Fiction*, 14. He uses the terms "representational time" and "represented time."

[68] van Luxemburg, Bal, and Weststeijn, *Literatuurwetenschap*, 168: "Een dialoog bestaat uit minstens twee spreekbeurten van minstens twee acteurs (...)."

In a narrative text, the events are talked about, while in a dramatic text the speaking engagements themselves are events.[69] Ultimately, a criterion for designating a text as a drama proper is that such a text is oriented towards performance.[70] The text of a drama or, even more so, the script of a play prescribes other means for an actual performance, apart from the lines. The script of a play aims at a plurimedial presentation. During actual performance, a drama does not only make use of words to present the story, but also of light, sound, costumes, décor, and so on. An ideal reader of drama even manages to imagine, while reading, a plurimedial performance, completed with attributes and décor.[71]

3.2. *Is Isa 40–55 a Drama?*

I come to the central question of this paper: does Isa 40–55 show the above-mentioned features of a dramatic text and a drama? Is a narrator speaking in these chapters, or do they lack an instance that communicates between story and reader? Do these texts suggest that the story presented in it is immediately present? Is dialogue the dominant mode of presentation? Is speaking in Isa 40–55 performative? Do these chapters also ask for other means besides language to evoke a presentation?

All these questions relate to the way in which the story is presented in these chapters. The questions concern the *how* of the presentation. But *what* is in fact presented in Isa 40–55? What is its story, in the sense of an orderly sequence of events? The most important event in Isa 40–55 is Yhwh's coming to Zion. The beginning announces his coming (40:9–11) and in what follows, his return to Zion is reported (52:7–10). Nevertheless, after Yhwh has returned to Zion as king, the story is not over. It now depends on the people to endorse Yhwh's kingship by following him. But that is not in the least obvious. In this project, the servant plays a decisive role. In the course of these chapters, he has stepped into the limelight more and more. Now he functions as a model for the people by showing them how they can find their way back to the LORD (52:13–53:12).

---

[69] Cf. van Luxemburg, Bal, and Weststeijn, *Literatuurwetenschap*, 171.
[70] Cf. H.v.d. Bergh, *Teksten voor toeschouwers. Inleiding in de dramatheorie*, 23–24. Bergh uses the notion "*opvoeringsgerichtheid*" (23).
[71] Cf. F.C. Maatje, *Open plekken*, 16. He talks about an "*optimale dramalezer.*"

Through his religious trust, the servant also encourages Zion. Earlier, she has wondered in amazement whether it could really be true that Yhwh will not forget her. Full of disbelief, she has objected that she seriously doubted the return of her children (49:14–26), which turned out to come true all the same (54:1–17). In summary, this is what the story of Isa 40–55 is about: the revelation of the kingship of Yhwh and its recognition by his people, exemplified by the servant and reluctantly taken up by Zion.

Now I will turn to the matter of how the story of Isa 40–55 is presented. Is it like a narrative or is it like a drama? In Hebrew language, a narrative can be recognized by its *wayyiqtol*-forms. These verbal forms do not dominate in Isa 40–55. A narrator does not appear often in these chapters. The narrative mode does not seem to be the usual way of presenting the reader the story of Yhwh who is coming to Zion. In what way then do these texts inform the reader about the progression of the story in these chapters? Is there another way, except via the speech of the actors? The same question, posed differently, reads: how can these texts break through their own "Absolutheit"?[72]

One of the *wayyiqtol*-forms in Isa 40–55 is ותאמר ציון (49:14). It introduces Zion's complaint that Yhwh has forgotten her. Although the position is held here of an instance that mediates between the story and the reader, it is different from that of a narrator. The communicating instance does not give information about what has happened in the past, as is the normal case with *wayyiqtol*-forms in a narrative text. This instance gives a live commentary of what happens at that very moment: "But Zion says." More than as a narrator, this mediating instance here functions as a commentator.[73] In Isa 40–55, there are other places as well where an instance holds the position to communicate between story and reader. At these instances, he gives the floor to several speakers. The *yiqtol*-form יאמר: "says your God" (40:1) serves as an example. The commenting quality of this verbal form confirms that the way the story of Isa 40–55 is presented resembles a report more than a distant way of telling. The utterance קול קורא (40:3) serves as another example. Thus, the

---

[72] Pfister, *Das Drama*, 22.
[73] Cf. Paganini, *Frau Zion*, 54,185–88. In relation to Isa 55, Paganini talks about a "Kommentator" (55,5,13).

commentator explicates the course of the communication in this passage to his reader. By this word, "a voice" is introduced as the next speaker. The utterance functions as a kind of stage direction.[74] The same goes for נאם־יהוה: "says the Lord" (49:18). It is a stage direction as well.

In Isa 40–55, the position of an instance that communicates to its reader about the story presented here does not remain open, although a narrator does not occupy it. Rather, a commentator acts at several places. It typifies this commentator that he comments on the story of Isa 40–55 in an involved manner. In doing so, he presents Yhwh's return to Zion and the establishment of his kingship in a way that resembles that of a radio commentator who calls to life for his listeners the story by his lively report. Besides the vivid commentator reports in Isa 40–55, the speech of the actors themselves also attributes to the suggestion of an immediate presence of the story in these chapters. The many *qetol*-forms, eleven times at the beginning of these chapters (Isa 40:1–11), can serve as an example. For instance, the appeal that stems from Yhwh's call: "Comfort, O comfort my people" (40:1) leaves no doubt. *Qetol*-forms especially appear in "besprechende Kontexte."[75] In addition, the frequent use of first and second person grammatical forms, rather than third person forms, involves the reader in the story presented here. Isa 49:14–26, a passage that can be labelled as a conversation between an "I" and a "you"—between Yhwh and Zion—serves as an example. The presence of deictic particles, such as הנה, is yet another way in which the reader gets the impression of experiencing the story of Isa 40–55 at first hand. So, in the words אליכם: "Here is your God!" (40:9), words that Zion is supposed to say, it is as if the reader actually perceives Yhwh coming. In a comparable way, the קול: "Listen!" (52:8), draws the reader's attention.

In literary theory, the lack of a narrator, together with the suggestion of an immediate presence of the story, are mentioned as characteristics of a dramatic text. The above analysis has shown that these features also apply for Isa 40–55. What about the third char-

---

[74] In relation to Isa 40–55, Baltzer also uses the term "stage direction." Baltzer aims at directions in the text for an actual performance. In this article however, the term points to directions that clarify the communication structure in a specific passage.

[75] W. Schneider, *Grammatik des Biblischen Hebräisch. Völlig neue Bearbeitung der Hebräischen Grammatik für den akademischen Unterricht« von Oskar Grether*, 200.

acteristic of a dramatic text? Is dialogue as the common mode of presentation of the story demonstrable in Isa 40–55 as well? Yhwh is the main speaker in these chapters. He addresses Jacob/Israel, the servant, Zion, or a "you." Sometimes this "you" indicates the coastlands, or the nations, or the idolmakers, but more often its referent remains unidentified. Moreover, it is significant that these addressees seldom speak for themselves. Although we hear Zion complaining in the course of Isa 40–55 because she believes that Yhwh has forgotten her (49:14), and although the servant speaks about his life and work (49:1–6; 50:4–9), it is mainly through the words of Yhwh that the reader receives the development of the story in these chapters. Dialogues in the strict sense of the word, which after all obtain their structure from a change of speaking engagements between several actors, hardly occur. It is more accurate to say that Isa 40–55 is a monological text. Nevertheless, speaking, and not narration, is the way in which the story of these texts is presented. Thus, they possess a dramatic structure. The performative nature of speech is another characteristic of a dramatic text that is mentioned in literary theory. In Isa 40–55, there are performative moments. At these moments, the pronouncement of the utterance coincides with the performance of the action. "Now, I will make you a threshing sledge, sharp, new, and having teeth" (41:15), serves as an example of a performative utterance.[76] The transformation of Jacob/Israel into a threshing sledge occurs at the very same moment that Yhwh addresses him. Even an utterance without a verbal form can express a moment of simultaneity. The הן עבדי: "Here is my servant" (42:1) is an example.[77] Here, the servant takes shape through the word of Yhwh.

The characteristics of a dramatic text so far all turn out to be demonstrable in Isa 40–55. I now arrive at a decisive point in my argument, however. Do these texts also show an orientation towards performance? Do they aim at the use of other means, besides language, for an accurate presentation of the story, such as light or sound? These questions, which originate from literary theory on drama and dramatic texts, all point in one direction: does the evoked

---

[76] For the grammatical features of a performative utterance, see Schneider, *Grammatik*, §48.6.2. Cf. E. Talstra, "Text Grammar and Hebrew Bible. II: Syntax and Semantics," 26–30.

[77] Cf. Leene, *Vroegere en nieuwe dingen*, 95–103; Leene, "History and Eschatology," 234–35.

presentation appeal to several senses at the same time? To put it differently: is this presentation plurimedial? The question under discussion is not the same as the question whether Isa 40–55 has ever been actually performed. A text that prescribes the use of several means simultaneously to call up a presentation is a drama, even when it might be true that no actual performance has ever taken place. Conversely, a text that is not a drama could nevertheless be performed; a stage director can feel challenged to perform a text with dramatic traits in a plurimedial way, even though the text itself only prescribes language as a medium to evoke a presentation and for that reason is not a drama.

Isa 40–55 is *not* a drama. The texts do not prescribe other means, except language, to call up a presentation. These chapters do not contain directions that require the use of music, décor, or attributes. The presentation that is evoked here is not plurimedial. Even a passage on the makers and devotees of idols (44:9–20), a passage that is known for its expressive language—the reader almost imagines the carpenter manufacturing an idol—does not make Isa 40–55 a drama. It is only by language that this image is evoked. The use of other means, such as a tool as attribute, a workshop as décor, or sounds from a workshop, is not prescribed in this passage.

Even though Isa 40–55 is not a drama, these chapters do display the characteristics of a dramatic text. I have already shown that these texts cannot fully do without an instance that mediates at some places between the story and the reader. In Isa 40–55, this instance functions more as a commentator than as a narrator. Strictly speaking, it is not the dialogue that dominates these chapters, but the speech of Yhwh. Nonetheless, the reader mainly receives the course of the story coming from one of the actors and not from a narrator. Moreover, Yhwh's word is performative in nature. It brings about whatever he wants it to. The word of Yhwh supports the servant and makes him an instrument in his hand. His word comforts Zion. It is reliable and calls on all people who have lost their way to return to him. Because speaking dominates these chapters, they suggest that the story presented here is immediately at hand. Somehow, the reader gets involved in the development of this story. While reading, the progression of action in Isa 40–55 unfolds. In conclusion, then, Isa 40–55 is not a drama, but a "reading drama."[78] Reading

---

[78] Bergh, *Dramatheorie*, 135–38: "leesdrama" (135). Bergh mentions a reading drama

dramas are "drama texts that are not oriented towards performance and appear to be meant for readers."[79]

4. Conclusion

The above analysis has shown that Isa 40–55 does deserve the title "dramatic text," but that these chapters are not a drama proper. They certainly have the quality to stimulate the reader's imagination. Yhwh's glorious comeback to Zion; the transformation of the desert; the activities of the idolmakers; the servant who grows in self-confidence; Zion's doubts; her prosperous future whereas daughter Babylon is humiliated; the hesitant behavior of the people: all this, the reader experiences while reading. The voices and images are evoked through language. These texts do not prescribe other means, such as visual or acoustic ones, to call up a presentation. The fact that "Hearing voices while reading," the motto of Sjef van Tilborg, definitively applies to Isa 40–55 does not make these texts a drama. In fact, Isa 40–55 is a *reading drama*. It reveals the directness of a dramatic text, its suggestion of an immediate presence of the story, its spoken and performative nature, but these chapters lack an orientation towards performance. They are meant not so much to be performed as to be read.

Bibliography

Abma, R., *Bonds of Love: Methodic Studies of Prophetic Texts with Marriage Imagery (Isaiah 50:1–3 and 54:1–10, Hosea 1–3, Jeremiah 2–3)* (SSN), Assen, 1999.
Abrams, M.H., *A Glossary of Literary Terms*, 6 ed., Fort Worth, 1993.

---

as one of the transitional forms between a narrative text on the one hand and a drama that is meant for performance on the other. Cf. van Gorp, Delabastita, and Ghesquiere, *Lexicon literaire termen*, 249–50. The notion 'reading drama' is used for different kinds of texts. It may concern a text with dramatic traits, complete with stage directions, but that is never meant to be performed. Cf. M.H. Abrams, *A Glossary of Literary Terms*, 48; House, *Zephaniah*, 50, on *"closet drama."* "Reading drama" is also used for a dramatic text that is meant for performance but the performance never takes place, for instance because the text turns out to be unsuitable for that. In fact, this text is an incomplete drama. Cf. Asmuth, *Dramenanalyse*, 10, 183–85.

[79] Bergh, *Dramatheorie*, 136: "drameteksten die niet opvoeringsgericht zijn en voor lezers bestemd lijken."

Ackroyd, P.R., *Exile and Restoration: A Study of Hebrew Thought of the Sixth Century BC* (OTL), London, 1968.
Asmuth, B., *Einführung in die Dramenanalyse*, 5 ed. (Sammlung Metzler 188), Stuttgart, 1997.
Bal, M., *De theorie van vertellen en verhalen. Inleiding in de narratologie*, 5 ed., Muiderberg, 1990.
Baltzer, K., *Deutero-Jesaja* (KAT 10/2), Gütersloh, 1999.
Baltzer, K., and P. Machinist, ed., *Deutero-Isaiah: A Commentary on Isaiah 40–55*, Translated by M. Kohl, Hermeneia, Minneapolis, 2001.
Becker, U., "Jesajaforschung (Jes 1–39)." *TRu* 64 (1999), pp. 1–37.
Berges, U., "Review of Klaus Baltzer, Deutero-Jesaja." *TRev* 97, no. 1 (2001), pp. 40–42.
Bergh, H.v.d., *Teksten voor toeschouwers. Inleiding in de dramatheorie*, Muiderberg, 1979.
Beuken, W.A.M., *Jesaja*, 2 ed. (POuT 2A), Nijkerk, 1986.
——, *Jesaja* (POuT 2B), Nijkerk, 1983.
Brueggemann, W., *Isaiah 40–66* (*Westminster Bible Companion* 2), Louisville, 1998.
Carr, D.M., "What Can We Say about the Tradition History of Isaiah? A Response to Christopher Seitz's *Zion's Final Destiny*," in *Society of Biblical Literature 1992 Seminar Papers*, edited by J. Eugene H. Lovering, pp. 583–97, Atlanta, 1992.
Chatman, S., *Story and Discourse. Narrative Structure in Fiction and Film*, 6 ed., Ithaca, 1993.
Conroy, C., "Reflections on Some Recent Studies of Second Isaiah," in *Palabra, Prodigio, Poesia. In Memoriam P. Luis Alonso Schökel, S.J.*, edited by V.C. Bertomeu, pp. 145–60, Roma, 2003.
Eaton, J.H., *Festal Drama in Deutero-Isaiah*, London, 1979.
Engnell, I., "The 'Ebed Yahweh Songs and the Suffering Messiah in 'Deutero-Isaiah.'" *BJRL* 31 (1948), pp. 54–93.
Gorp, H. van, D. Delabastita, and R. Ghesquiere, *Lexicon van literaire termen*, 7 ed., Groningen, 1998.
Grosheide, H.H., C.J. den Heyer, W. van der Meer, J.C. de Moor, S.E. Scheepstra, & E. de Vries (eds.), *De Knecht. Studies rondom Deutero-Jesaja door collega's en oud-leerlingen aangeboden aan prof. dr. J. L. Koole*, Kampen, 1978.
Haag, H., *Der Gottesknecht bei Deuterojesaja* (EdF 233), Darmstadt, 1985.
Hermisson, H.-J., "Deuterojesaja," in *RGG*, edited by E. Jüngel, pp. 684–88, Tübingen, 1999.
——, "Deuterojesaja-Probleme. Ein kritischer Literaturbericht." *VF* 31, no. 1 (1986), pp. 53–84.
——, "Neue Literatur zu Deuterojesaja (I)." *TRu* 65, no. 3 (2000), pp. 237–84.
——, "Neue Literatur zu Deuterojesaja (II)." *TRu* 65, no. 4 (2000), pp. 379–430.
Heßler, E., *Das Heilsdrama: Der Weg zur Weltherrschaft Jahwes* (Jes. 40–55) (Religionswissenschaftliche Texte und Studien 2), Hildesheim, 1988.
House, P.R., *Zephaniah. A Prophetic Drama* (JSOTSup 69), Sheffield, 1988.
Kayser, W., *Das sprachliche Kunstwerk. Eine Einführung in die Literaturwissenschaft*, 2 ed., Bern, 1951.
Köckert, M., "Review of Klaus Baltzer, Deutero-Jesaja." *ZAW* 113 (2001), p. 122.
Kratz, R.G., "Review of Klaus Baltzer, Deutero-Isaiah: A Commentary on Isaiah 40–55." *RBL*, no. 5 (2003).
Labahn, A., "Review of Klaus Baltzer, Deutero-Jesaja." *TLZ* 125, no. 10 (2000), pp. 1004–07.
Leene, H., "The Coming of YHWH as King: The Complementary Character of Psalms 96 and 98," in *Unless some one guide me... Festschrift for Karel A. Deurloo*, edited by R. Zuurmond, pp. 211–28, Maastricht, 2001.
——, *De vroegere en de nieuwe dingen bij Deuterojesaja*, Amsterdam, 1987.
——, *Een nieuwe hemel en een nieuwe aarde, slotakkoord van het boek Jesaja*, Amsterdam, 2002.
——, "History and Eschatology in Deutero-Isaiah," in *Studies in the Book of Isaiah. Festschrift Willem A.M. Beuken*, edited by M. Vervenne, pp. 223–49, Leuven, 1997.

van Luxemburg, J., M. Bal, and W.G. Weststeijn, *Inleiding in de literatuurwetenschap*, Muiderberg, 1981.
Maatje, F.C., *Literatuurwetenschap. Grondslagen van een theorie van het literaire werk*, 4 ed., Utrecht, 1977.
——, *Open plekken*, Utrecht, 1981.
Miscall, P.D., *Isaiah Readings: A New Biblical Commentary*, Sheffield, 1993.
Mowinckel, S., *He That Cometh*, Translated by G.W. Anderson, 2 ed., Oxford, 1959.
Muilenburg, J., *The Book of Isaiah. Chapters 40–66* (IB 5), New York, 1956.
Paganini, S., *Der Weg zur Frau Zion, Ziel unserer Hoffnung. Aufbau, Kontext, Sprache, Kommunikationsstruktur und theologische Motive in Jes 55,1–13* (SBB 49), Stuttgart, 2002.
Pfister, M., *Das Drama. Theorie und Analyse*, 6 ed. (*UTB* 580), München, 1988.
Quinn-Miscall, P.D., *Reading Isaiah: Poetry and Vision*, Louisville, 2001.
Ringgren, H., *Israelitische Religion* (*Die Religionen der Menschheit* 26), Stuttgart, 1963.
——, "Zur Komposition von Jesaja 49–55," in *Beiträge zur Alttestamentlichen Theologie. Festschrift für Walther Zimmerli zum 70. Geburtstag*, edited by R. Smend, pp. 371–76, Göttingen, 1977.
Schneider, W., *Grammatik des Biblischen Hebräisch. Völlig neue Bearbeitung der »Hebräischen Grammatik für den akademischen Unterricht« von Oskar Grether*, 7 ed., München, 1989.
Seitz, C.R., "Isaiah 1–66: Making Sense of the Whole," in *Reading and Preaching the Book of Isaiah*, edited by C.R. Seitz, pp. 105–26, Philadelphia, 1988.
——, "On the Question of Divisions Internal to the Book of Isaiah," in *Society of Biblical Literature 1993 Seminar Papers*, edited by J. Eugene and H. Lovering, pp. 260–66, Atlanta, 1993.
——, *Zion's Final Destiny. The Development of the Book of Isaiah. A Reassessment of Isaiah 36–39*, Minneapolis, 1991.
Ska, J.L., *"Our Fathers Have Told Us." Introduction to the Analysis of Hebrew Narratives* (SubBi 13), Roma, 1990.
Sommer, B.D., "Review of Klaus Baltzer, Deutero-Isaiah: A Commentary on Isaiah 40–55." *RBL*, no. 2 (2003).
Stacey, W.D., *Prophetic Drama in the Old Testament*, London, 1990.
Sternberg, M., *Expositional Modes and Temporal Ordering in Fiction*, Baltimore, 1978.
Talstra, E., "Text Grammar and Hebrew Bible. II: Syntax and Semantics." *BO* 39, no. 1/2 (1982), pp. 26–38.
van Tilborg, Sj., *Al lezend stemmen horen*, Nijmegen, 1994.
Utzschneider, H., *Michas Reise in die Zeit. Studien zum Drama als Genre der prophetischen Literatur des Alten Testaments* (SBS 180), Stuttgart, 1999.
——, "Situation und Szene. Überlegungen zum Verhältnis historischer und literarischer Deutung prophetischer Texte am Beispiel von Hos 5,8–6,6." *ZAW* 114 (2002), pp. 80–105.
——, "Text—Leser—Autor. Bestandsaufnahme und Prolegomena zu einer Theorie der Exegese." *BZ* 43, no. 2 (1999), pp. 224–38.
Vincent, J.M., *Studien zur literarischen Eigenart und zur geistigen Heimat von Jesaja, Kap. 40–55* (BBET 5), Frankfurt am Main, 1977.
Watts, J.D.W., *Isaiah 1–33* (*WBC 24*), Waco, 1985.
Werlitz, J., *Redaktion und Komposition. Zur Rückfrage hinter die Endgestalt von Jesaja 40–55* (BBB 122), Berlin, 1999.
Wilks, J.G.F., "The Prophet as Incompetent Dramatist." *VT* 53, no. 4 (2003), pp. 530–43.
van der Woude, A., "What Is New In Isaiah 41:14–20? On the Drama Theories of Klaus Baltzer and Henk Leene," in *The New Things: Eschatology in Old Testament Prophecy. Festschrift for Henk Leene*, edited by E. Talstra, pp. 261–67, Maastricht, 2002.

PART 2

NEW TESTAMENT

CHAPTER NINE

RESOLVING COMMUNICATION DISTURBANCES IN LUKE 12:35–48 THROUGH NARRATOLOGY

Andries van Aarde
University of Pretoria (South Africa)

1. *Introduction*

It is basic to narrative exegesis that a text should be approached holistically. The Gospel of Luke and the Acts of the Apostles are presented as a narrative unity, although recorded as two travel narratives. A probable reason for this is their mutual relevance. While the journey in the Gospel of Luke ends in Jerusalem, the journey in Acts ends in Rome. The author indicates that his work should be read as a "narrative" (διήγησις) (Lk 1:1).[1] He presents his narrative as the "correct way" (ἀκριβῶς) to understand the life of Jesus, the "Savior, who is Christ the Lord" (ὅς ἐστιν χριστὸς κύριος) (Lk 2:11).[2] It is addressed to a specific person, Theophilus (Lk 1:3), but also to the believing community to which the author himself belongs[3]—hence the pronoun "us" (Lk 1:2),[4] especially in the so-called "we passages" in Acts.[5]

Luke 12:35–48 forms part of the narrative which concerns the journey to Jerusalem (Lk 9:51–19:44). In Luke 9:51–19:44 there are two opposing perspectives:[6] that of the leaders of Israel and that of Jesus. Peter's question (Lk 12:41) at the end of the parable of the watchful servants (Lk 12:35–40), which is followed by the parable of the responsible manager (Lk 12:42–48), relates intratextually with

---

[1] See P.F. Esler, *Community and Gospel* (1996) 224 note 2; J.B. Green, *The Gospel of Luke* (1997) 1–6.
[2] See F. Bovon, *Luke the Theologian* (1983) 125–26; E.P. Sanders and M. Davies, *Studying* (1996) 293; J.B. Green, *The Gospel of Luke* (1997) 134–35.
[3] See P.F. Esler, *Community* (1996) 24–45.
[4] J.A. Fitzmyer, *Luke the Theologian* (1989) 16–22.
[5] See M.P. Bonz, *Past as Legacy* (2000) 170–73.
[6] See J.L. Resseguie, *Point of View* (1982) 44.

Jesus' remark in Luke 8:10, before the account of the journey to Jerusalem starts in Luke 9:51. In Luke 12:41 Peter asks: "Lord, are you telling this parable for us or for all?" And Jesus answers by telling another parable about a faithful and wise steward in Luke 12:42–48.

Earlier in the narrative, in Luke 8:10, before the journey to Jerusalem begins, Jesus says that the disciples have been given knowledge of the secrets of the kingdom of God, but for others (τοῖς λοιποῖς) these secrets remain obscure (ἐν παραβολαῖς). The result is that they look without seeing and hear without understanding.

The moral of the two intercalated metaphoric stories in Luke 12:35–48 is that knowledge of the secrets of the kingdom of God entails responsibility.[7] This responsibility requires watchfulness and a willingness to minister the word despite hindrance. During the journey to Jerusalem the hesitance to associate with Samaritans is one example of such a hindrance. During the journey to Rome the hesitance to associate with Gentiles is a repetition of the same obstacle. Throughout Luke-Acts this barrier remains. However, over against Israel, both the Samaritans (cf. Lk 10:25–37) and the Gentiles (cf. Acts 28:2) set an example of positive listening. What did those whom Jesus summoned to be leaders do? They were supposed to be the leaders who set an example for how to do the will of God (βουλή τοῦ θεοῦ). Above all, they were the *eyewitnesses* of Jesus' example and the *ministers of the word* "from the beginning" (Lk 1:2).

Although unseen, God is the main character, the one who directs the action.[8] The other characters in the story either help or hinder God's purpose (βουλή τοῦ θεοῦ). Jesus and his followers who play the role of the protagonist are the ones who work *with* God's purpose, whereas the Israelite leaders and those who conform to their ideology play the role of the antagonists and work *against* God's purpose. God's purpose is to save humankind. This purpose is realized in two contexts: for *Israel* the long-awaited hope of salvation through God's Messiah has been fulfilled and the *Gentiles* are included in God's act of salvation. Luke begins with the realization of Israel's hope[9] and gradually turns his attention to the Gentiles. He begins with the known, namely, the hope of Israel, to which he adds the new idea that this salvation is also for others, in fact that it is meant for *all*. However,

---

[7] S.D. Moore, *Literary Criticism* (1986) 200–1.
[8] J. Knight, *Luke's Gospel* (1998) 58; cf. J.B. Green, *The Gospel of Luke* (1997) 50.
[9] Cf. D.L. Tiede, *Glory* (1988) 24–26.

the question remains: do the followers of Jesus see and perceive and hear and understand what God's plan of salvation involves?

Answering this question the narrator tells his implied readers/listeners what the *eyewitnesses* and the *ministers of the word* had done. This seems to be the reason why he tells the "narrative of the things which had been accomplished among his readers/listeners, just as they were delivered by those who were there from the beginning, so that his readers/listeners may have accurate knowledge of what the will of God instructs" (Lk 1:1–4).

It is a story about Peter (and the other apostles) and Paul—how they paused and were uncertain, but overcame all disturbances. At strategic places Luke narrates how they in private (κατ' ἰδίαν) (Lk 10:23–24) were reminded that they are blessed, more than the prophets and kings of old, to see and hear, and have the knowledge of the "mystery" of God's all-inclusive kingdom (Lk 8:9–10)—a knowledge which demands responsibility from their part. However, at the end of the double narrative the narrator resounds again people's hearing without understanding and seeing without perceiving (Acts 28:26, 28). Yet, Paul, whose eyes were opened on the road to Damascus (Acts 9:8), preached the kingdom of God and taught about the Lord Jesus Christ "openly and unhindered" (μετὰ πάσης παρρησίας ἀκωλύτως) (Acts 28:31).

In Luke 12:35–48 the narrator communicates this same message to Peter as the narratee of not only the two parables as microtexts in this passage, but also of the whole Lukan story of Jesus in the first travel narrative. Other apostles and servants of the word, such as Stephen and Paul, will receive from Peter their calling of responsibility to convey this knowledge during the second travel narrative from Jerusalem onwards. In this essay I will illustrate, on the basis of a narratological reading of especially the temporal aspects in Luke 12:35–48, why the *ideological point of view* of the narrator in Luke-Acts is thus interpreted.

I devote this research to my dear friend Sjef van Tilborg. The 1980s were the years of my exploration of what narratology can contribute methodologically to the exegesis of the New Testament. My proclivity to escape the positivistic web of structuralism leads to the appreciation that narrative exegesis need not disregard the historical situation within which a particular text communicates. A narrative involves a network of themes and ideas, which are intended to have meaning within a particular context. In 1986 Sjef van Tilborg wrote a book on "ideology" in the Sermon on the Mount in which he expressed similar ideas. I met Sjef in 1986 during the annual meeting of the Studiorum Novi Testamenti Societas in Atlanta, GA. We immediately connected and became close friends. In 1998 my Doktervater, the late Willem Vorster, and I invited Sjef to visit South Africa and who taught extensively at the University of Pretoria. In later years Sjef became a "research associate" in a research project on Hermeneutics and Biblical at the University of Pretoria, of which I am the project leader. With this essay I pay tribute to an admired friend and colleague and, by revisiting narrative criticism as an exegetical instrument, I thank God for letting me share such a wonderful friendship and for the privilege to learn so much from a dear friend.

2. *Narrative Criticism*

Analyzing a narrative comprises an investigation into literary fundamentals such as author, narrator, narratees, implied reader, real reader, characters, and time and space in their various relationships.[10] The plot (how events are structured) of a story can be simplex or complex. Characterization is essential to the plot, which is determined by the relationships between the characters. Intrigue is created by elements of surprise and tension. The *point of view* of the narrator is the way in which the story is presented. The point of view refers to the perspective of the narrator, in other words how the world is seen and presented to the reader. It also refers to the ideological perspective which determines how the narrator evaluates the story world presented in the narrative.[11]

Sj. van Tilborg (1986) sees in his book, *The Sermon on the Mount as an Ideological Intervention: A Reconstruction of Meaning*, "ideology" as a literary device.[12] Ideology is not in the Marxist sense a direct reflection of material reality such as economic circumstances. It represents rather an imagined distortion of reality. In the framework of literariness texts are imagined accounts of realities and, therefore, belong to the sphere of ideology.[13] From this perspective of literary theory,

---

[10] See S.D. Moore, *Literary Criticism* (1989) 41–55.
[11] See M. Sternberg, *Poetics* (1985) 129.
[12] Sj. van Tilborg, *Sermon on the Mount* (1986).
[13] Sj. van Tilborg, *Sermon on the Mount* (1986) 9.

since the work of *B. Uspenski*,¹⁴ the term "ideology" has been used in narratology as the narrator's point of view which "emerged as an ideological crux and force."¹⁵

Whatever characters are doing in reciprocal relations, the exegete can visualize at least five levels, namely, characterization on a psychological, phraseological, temporal, spatial, and ideological level.¹⁶ These five levels are inextricably linked to the position(s) that the narrator assumes in the narration. In this sense, in the Lukan double story of Jesus and the church, Peter becomes the narratee who is characterized to be the focalization of the narrator's point of view. This point of view is narrated through Jesus as both the protagonist in the story and the main vehicle of the narrator's ideology.

The double narration Luke-Acts is not pure fiction, but a literary product of a narrator who is, at the same time, a redactor. The work of the redactor is to gather material from traditions and rework them in a creative way. From this perspective, phraseology refers, among other aspects of diction, to the choices that the narrator made when editing the source material. For the exegete it pertains to questions such as what is included, left out, expanded, or reduced. Sometimes the narrator-redactor is not completely successful in harmonizing the source material with the new created story and then the source becomes more visible to the analyst. However, a narrative interpretation is not so much interested in the redactor as a historical figure or in the question who the historical readers of the story could be, but rather in the narratological techniques the author uses, including that with regard to the choices which the narrator in the story makes.¹⁷ These techniques reveal the ideological motives behind the redactional work.

The psychological narrative situation is about the narrator's choice whether to describe the character internally (describing the characters' innermost thoughts, feelings and observations) or externally (the acts of the character are described in an impersonal manner). Luke's story is a "third person narrative," although some "we passages" in Acts are related to a "first person narrative."

---

¹⁴ B. Uspenski, *Poetics of Composition* (1973).
¹⁵ M. Sternberg, *Poetics* (1985) 129.
¹⁶ See B. Uspenski, *Poetics of Composition* (1973); cf. N.R. Petersen, *Point of View* (1978).
¹⁷ Cf. S.D. Moore, *Literary Criticism* (1989) 38.

The choice of a "third person narrative" as narrative strategy means that the narrator's position is outside of the story (not as in a first person narrative where the narrator is a character in the story). A third person narrator chooses the strategy of either an *omniscient point of view*, or a *limited point of view*, creating, respectively distance or proximity between characters and narrator/narratee.[18] An investigation of this strategy can elucidate whether a character acts according to the ideological perspective of the narrator (and becomes a bearer of it),[19] or in opposition to it. By choosing either an omniscient or limited point of view from which a character is portrayed the narrator manipulates the implied reader to distance or associate with the viewpoint of the character. If a character, for instance, reveals some uncertainty regarding anything that happens with him/her or someone else in the narrative, because of the limited point of view from which the character is portrayed, the narrator could convey a message to the implied reader/listener to acquire the proper knowledge through this "disturbance in communication." Omniscience, on the other hand, reveals complete knowledge not only of the character thus portrayed, but also of the implied reader/listener whom the narrator associates with this all-knowing and omnipresent character.

An analysis of phraseology also reveals how characters are portrayed. There are two types of characters.[20] The simplex character presents only one ideological perspective throughout the story. The complex character, on the other hand, often acts in an unexpected way, is at times hesitant, uncertain, and full of doubts. This creates tension. Some characters merely play a "decorative" role and are not important to the development of the plot. They can fulfill the function of, for instance, creating the norms for judging the main character.

The ideological perspective of the narrator is revealed in the way in which the characters relate to one another and give each other names. Naming can be used by the narrator to express the characters' perspectives on their relationships.[21] The ideological perspective of the narrator can also be seen in the emotions, observations, insights, thoughts, and names that the author him- or herself ascribes to the characters.

---

[18] See B. Uspenski, *Poetics of Composition* (1973) 83.
[19] B. Uspenski, *Poetics of Composition* (1973) 97–98.
[20] See W. Kenney, *Analyze Fiction* (1966) 29–30.
[21] See B. Uspenski, *Poetics of Composition* (1973) 22, 25–27.

3. Narrative Theory

According to the narrative theory of G. Genette, a narrative consists of three parts: narrative discourse, story, and the situation of the narrator. The narrator's position can be described as the "narrating process."[22] The "narrative discourse" (*récit*) is directly available to the exegete, while the "story" (*histoire*) should be abstracted from the narrative discourse. The interaction between the situation of the narrator and the narrative discourse is usually described in terms of "point of view" or focalization."

Although interrelated, these two expressions do not refer to the same concept.[23] Focalization relates to the way in which the narrator focuses, such as from the viewpoint of a third person or a first person. This focus is often directed from the perspective of a specific character. Point of view therefore does not pertain only to this technical angle of vision, but also involves the perceptual dimension from which a narrative discourse is compiled.[24]

Point of views concerned more with who is narrating than with how observation takes place. It involves the relationship between the narrator who observes and observed objects such as characters interacting within a network of spaces related to time. Commenting on a character's behavior, emotions, observations, feelings, thoughts, insights, knowledge, and the like, a narrator evaluates the character's viewpoint(s) and provides reasons for the implied reader/listener why association or disassociation would be the proper response to this specific character.

The narrator and all those characters who see or speak in a narrative discourse feature as interpreters and their views and diction are the result of a process of evaluation.[25] Thus, the entire narrative unfolds as an interrelation between the internal discourse, external social context, and ideology as the imagined account of this social reality in fictive form.

A text is not a configuration of language symbols as such, but a text is rather a complex language symbol within a constellation of

---

[22] G. Genette, *Narrative Discourse* (1980) 26–27.
[23] Cf. J. Culler, *Foreword* (1980) 10; G. Genette, *Narrative Discourse* (1980) 186; M. Bal, *Theorie* (1977) 108–9; S. Rimmon-Kenan, *Narrative Fiction* (1983) 74–77.
[24] Cf. J.M. Lotman, *Point of View* (1975).
[25] M. Sternberg, *Poetics* (1985) 129.

texts.²⁶ Language is a product of sociological interaction. Social context can be seen as the mechanism that generates texts. Every text reflects the social context from which it is communicated. No text, however, accurately reflects a specific context in its entirety. D.K. Danow quotes a remark from the work of B. Uspenski and J.M. Lotman, which has important intertextual implications: "A text can only be understood if it is compared extensively with the culture, or more precisely with the behavior of the people contemporary with it; and their behavior can likewise only be made sense of if it is juxtaposed with a large number of texts."²⁷

Social context is an indirect, rather than direct, "mechanism" behind the generation of texts. It is people who are directly responsible for the production of texts. According to M. Sternberg, the narrative critic's dismantling of these three aspects, narrative discourse, social context, and ideology, "forms neither a luxury nor a technicality but the very condition of making sense."²⁸

This yields to, according to threefold classification of "story" by G. Genette, "narrative discourse," and "narration," that a narrative represents a network of "time art." The South African novelist and literary theorist A. Brink formulates this network as follows: "While a narrating process (which takes time) results in a narrative discourse (which, in time, is read and which also offers codes in particular groups of time), it above all gives substance to a story that can be construed from the discourse and in which something happens to someone in a certain position in time and space" (my paraphrase and translation).²⁹

The narrating process pertains thus also to the choice which the narrator makes concerning *time*: either "story time" (the chronological, linear reconstruction of events), that is *histoire*, or "plotted time," that is *recit*.³⁰ The latter involves the way in which the narrator manipulates time in order to emphasize certain events. There is a similar distinction concerning *space* in a narrative: whether it simply indicates location, or whether the spaces in the story have some functional significance.³¹

---

[26] See D.K. Danow, Lotman, and Uspenski (1987).
[27] D.K. Danow, Lotman, and Uspenski (1987) 352.
[28] M. Sternberg, *Poetics* (1985) 129.
[29] A. Brink, *Vertelkunde* (1987) 90.
[30] Cf. A. Brink, *Vertelkunde* (1987) 92; N.R. Petersen, *Point of View* (1978) 47–48.
[31] See H. Vandermoere, *Structure* (1982).

Plotted time (narrated time) relates to two periods. One covers the story from the first moment to the last. The other concerns the various departures from the course.³² Since an investigation into the narrative point of view on the temporal and spatial level comprises, firstly, the period covered by the story and, secondly, departures from the linear-chronological course of that period, it is necessary to abstract the story from the narrative discourse.³³

4. *Luke 12:35–48 as a Narrative Discourse*

4.1. *Resonance*

Luke's prologue (Lk 1–4) refers to his narrative as one of several existing stories regarding "the things which have been fulfilled among us" (περὶ τῶν πεπληροφορημένων ἐν ἡμῖν πραγμάτων). The narrator is not only aware of the existence of these documents, but also that he uses them as sources. Scholarship shows that they could include the Sayings Gospel Q, Mark, and other sources for the material found only in Luke. In Luke 12:35–49 the narrator creates a "new narrative discourse" by using material from Q that is also found in Matthew 25:1–13 and Matthew 24:43–44.45–51 (also creatively reworked) and in Mark 13:33–37.

The Lukan narrator is responsible for the creation of the inter-calculation of the two parables in Luke 12:35–48. The introduction of Peter as character in the metaphorical narrative of the journey that Jesus as Son of Man undertakes, while he expects from his disciples to watchfully await his return, is also a creation of the Lukan narrator. Through this creation the narrator resembles the double metaphorical story in Luke 12:35–48 with another episode on "watchfulness" (γρηγορεῖη) in Acts (20:26–30).³⁴ Seeking an answer from a narratological perspective why Peter is introduced in this metaphorical story, an investigation into the narrator's ideological point of view on especially the temporal level can be of help for the exegete.

The arrangement of events and sequences of events takes place, ac-cording to R. Jakobson,³⁵ in terms of the principle he calls

---

[32] A. Brink, *Vertelkunde* (1987) 92.
[33] Cf. P. Ricoeur, *Time* (1984) 56; P. Ricoeur, *Figuring* (1995) 189.
[34] Cf. R.C. Tannehill, *Narrative Unity* (1986) 250.
[35] See N.R. Petersen, *Literary Criticism* (1978) 116.

"equivalence," which consists of repetition and parallelism. R.C. Tannehill calls it "echo effect."[36] In the conversion of a "story" into a "narrative discourse," or the abstraction of the former from the latter, one should attempt to identify the "echo effect" in order to unravel the narrator's ideological point of view. The reason for this is that the "echo" between Peter in Luke 12:35–48 and Paul in Acts 20:26–30 concerns "resonance" which involves time. The aspect of "time" involved here is that which G. Genette calls "frequency" and which he describes as the investigation into the "relations between the repetitive capacities of the story and those of the narrative."[37] A very simple method of doing so is to identify the beginning, middle, and end of the story as well as the episodes comprising these three sections.

5. *The Story in Luke 12:35–48*

The story in Luke 12:35–48 tells of people (ἀνθρώποις) in a household (v. 36) who are waiting for the coming of the Son of Man (v. 40). The Son of Man appears to be presented metaphorically as the owner of the house (κύριος) who is attending a wedding (v. 36) and unexpectedly returns. The people in the household are the workers and they are portrayed as "slaves" (δοῦλοι) (v. 37), "household servants" (θεραπεία) (v. 42), and, typically according to a Lukan inclusive gender pattern,[38] as "men servants and women servants" (παίδας καὶ παιδίσκας) (v. 45). One of them is appointed as the "landlord" (οἰκοδεσπότης) (v. 39), also referred to as the "manager"/"foreman" (οἰκονόμος) (v. 42). The workers are expected to be prepared for the coming of the owner of the house (vv. 35, 40), and they will be rewarded accordingly.

By inference, this parable consists therein that the owner has appointed people in his household to perform specific household tasks and another to act as foreman. The foreman must feed the other workers at the right time (v. 42). The status of the foreman is that of *primus inter pares*, because he is also called a slave (δοῦλος) (v. 45). The owner of the house, however, delays his return and there is a

---

[36] R.C. Tannehill, *Composition* (1984).
[37] G. Genette, *Narrative Discourse* (1980) 35.
[38] See T.K. Seim, *Patterns* (1994); M.R. D'Angelo, *Women* (1990) 441–61; M.R. D'Angelo, *(Re)presentations* (1999) 181.

danger that the workers will cease to work ("gird their loins") and wait ("burn lamps") (v. 35). Instead of giving the workers their food, the foreman beats them and holds parties and gets drunk (v. 45). He does not prevent a thief from entering the house suddenly and unexpectedly (v. 39). The owner also arrives suddenly and unexpectedly. If the workers are still working the owner will reverse their status by becoming a slave himself and serving them as lords (v 37). The faithful and wise manager will be appointed over all the owner's possessions (v. 46). The manager, however, who knew what was expected of him but did not do it will share the fate of the unfaithful and be severely punished (v. 47). Had he not known, his punishment would be less severe (v. 48).

Western logical conditioning has accustomed us to logical, linear, chronological "story time." Departures from the chronology therefore draw our attention and strongly contribute to the identification and development of the tension in a story. According to G. Genette,[39] these departures can be studied in terms of temporal order, duration, and frequency.[40] As far as "temporal order" is concerned, a story may, for example, not be told linearly from the time of someone's birth to his death, but may begin with his death and end at some other phase of the person's life. Many such variations are possible.

The story in Luke 12:35–48 is considerably confusing to the narratees, that is, the disciples whom Jesus is addressing—as well as to the implied reader. This is because there is some uncertainty over the references to characters and places in the story. For example, is the coming of the Son of Man to be equated to the return from the wedding banquet of the owner of the house? The answer to this question will also clarify the following uncertainty: is the action of the owner, who will serve the servants like lords on his return, the last incident to which reference is made in the story? Or is the owner's giving of all his possessions to the wise and faithful foreman the last incident? The action of the workers and that of the foreman may not necessarily take place simultaneously, but sequentially. The same phenomenon of intercalculation occurs in other narrative discourses where, from the perspective of "plotted time," it is represented as though the incidents take place simultaneously while, from the

---

[39] G. Genette, *Narrative Discourse* (1980) 33–85, 86–112, 113–60.
[40] A. Brink, *Vertelkunde* (1987) 96–105.

perspective of "story time," they actually happen sequentially.⁴¹ The incidents in the story in Luke 12:35-48 can be summarized as follows on the basis of the first parable (vv. 35-40):

a. The owner of the house appoints people in his household.
b. He gives them orders: some as workers and one of them as foreman.
c. The owner of the house goes to a wedding.
d. His return is delayed because the wedding has not ended.
e. Some of the people stop working and waiting and others obey the call to be ready for the owner's return.
f. The owner returns after the wedding is over, becomes the servant of the watchful, and serves them as lords.
g. And the foreman? Is the watchful landlord (οἰκοδεσπότης), who prevents the unexpected thief from breaking into the house, similarly rewarded?

6. *"Pauses" and "Ellipses"*

The *beginning* of the abstracted "story" consists of incidents a, b, and c. The *middle* of incidents d and e. The *end* of incidents f and g. The "pause,"⁴² which poses Peter's question in Luke 12:41, lets the implied reader wonder if the story indeed ends at incident f (v. 38) and if the references to the action of the landlord and the coming of the Son of Man (v. 29) do not point to further incidents in the story. If this is so, incident g continues even after the narrating time has elapsed.

Incidents a and b indeed represent a clear "ellipsis"⁴³ within the temporal order of the story. They refer to moments in the story which are not part of the narrative discourse at all. The narrative strategies "pause" and "ellipsis" are aspects that G. Genette handles under the category of "duration" and are means of departing from the linear, chronological sequence in the course of the story.

As a result of the distorted sequence (*verkapte volgorde* in terms of

---

⁴¹ See G. Prince, *Narratology* (1982) 64-65; S. Rimmon-Kenan, *Narrative Fiction* (1983) 89-91.
⁴² See G. Genette, *Narrative Discourse* (1980) 99-106.
⁴³ See G. Genette, *Narrative Discourse* (1980) 106-9.

A. Brink)[44] in the "plotted time" of Luke 12:35–48, as well as the phenomenon "ellipsis" that some incidents are not at all included in the narrative discourse, the wider context of the double story Luke-Acts must be taken into account to obtain greater clarity on all the uncertainties in Luke 12:35–48. In this regard the second facet of G. Genette's focus on temporal order, namely, *flashbacks* ("analepses") and *previews* ("prolepses"),[45] is for the exegete of help. These aspects involve *past* and *future* references that may occur within the framework of the whole narrative—even in those untold incidents beyond the beginning or end of the narrative. They can leave deliberate gaps in the narrative to be filled in later. In this way a reference to the past and a preview are sooner or later a repetition of an incident or episode already narrated, and this enters the domain that G. Genette terms "frequency"[46] and J. Lyons[47] (in R.C. Tannehill)[48] "disturbance" by comparing it to resonance in music.

7. *Disturbances in Communication*

In this connection and with regard to Luke-Acts as a narrative unity, R.C. Tannehill expresses the following as a result of J. Lyons's insights (quotation from J. Lyons):[49]

> Information theorists note that every channel of communication is subject to "noise," i.e., "disturbances ... which interfere with the faithful transmission of signals," and "a certain degree of redundancy is essential ... in any communication system in order to counteract the disturbing effects of noise. In Luke-Acts one major source of "noise" is the length of the narrative, offering the reader a large opportunity to forget what has already happened. Redundancy combats the tendency to forget.

The disturbing effect of the length of Luke-Acts as a double travel narrative on the (implied or real) reader/listener may for many give rise to the question of why it is necessary to add the story of the journey to Rome to that of the journey to Jerusalem in Luke-Acts

---

[44] A. Brink, *Vertelkunde* (1987) 96.
[45] G. Genette, *Narrative Discourse* (1980) 47–70.
[46] G. Genette, *Narrative Discourse* (1980) 113–60.
[47] J. Lyons, *Language* (1981).
[48] R.C. Tannehill, *Composition* (1984) 238.
[49] R.C. Tannehill, *Composition* (1984) 238.

as one narrative discourse. Its length has the results that the link between the two travel stories is often not perceived during the narrating process of the smaller narrative discourses which form the building blocks of the whole narrative. This disturbing effect repeats itself in the discourse that is narrated in Luke 12:35–48. The disturbance is reflected in the interrogative nature of the abstracted incident g in the "story time": What about the leader of the workers? Does the owner of the house reward this watchful managing housekeeper (οἰκοδεσπότης), who prevents the unexpected thief from breaking into the house, in a similar way to the other watchful workers? In other words, when the wedding ends, is he also treated as a lord?

This disturbance in the story in Luke 12:35–48 is the uncertainty whether the servantlike behavior of the owner of the house toward his men servants and women servants forms indeed the last incident to which the story refers. Should this be so, can the manager of the serving men and maids expect the same treatment from the owner on his return from the wedding?

8. *Peter as Narratee in Luke 12:35–48*

The disturbance of the above-mentioned uncertainty is reinforced by two factors: the vagueness with regard to who the narratees are whom Jesus addresses throughout the whole narrative discourse, and Peter's doubt which he expresses in Luke 12:35–48.

It is remarkable how the narratees whom Jesus addresses on the journey to Jerusalem, and especially in the immediate literary context of Luke 12:35–48, change. In Luke 12:1–12 the disciples are addressed in general; in 12:13–21 Jesus speaks to someone in the crowd; in 12:22 the audience switches back to the disciples. As for the disciples, in the Gospel of Luke they are not an uncomplicated, uniform, separate group of characters as in Mark and Matthew.[50] Unlike in the other two synoptic gospels the disciples, Jesus' followers, are not depicted as a group separate from Israel.[51] What can be distinguished, however, are three types of characters: those among

---

[50] Cf. T.K. Seim, *Patterns* (1994) 21; J.P. Meier, *Circle* (1997) 638 note 8.
[51] Cf. J.D. Kingsbury, *Jesus Christ* (1981) 122–23.

the crowds of Israel who, while seeing, did not see and, while hearing, did not understand (Lk 8:10 and Acts 28:26); the leaders in Israel who were "fighters against God" (θεομάχοι)[52] following on Acts 5:38–39; and the leaders among the followers of Jesus who acted with "divine authority."

The uncertainty is particularly evident from Peter's explicit question in Luke 12:41: "Lord, is the story of the watchful workers meant for *us* (ἡμᾶς) or for *everyone* (πάντας)? This question highlights the disturbing effect in the story up to and including verse 40. To whom do the "us" and the "everyone" refer?

Strictly speaking, on account of Luke 8:10 it should not have been possible for those among the crowds of Israel who did not wish to recognize and follow their Messiah (see Lk 9:57–62) to participate in either Peter's ἡμᾶς or his πάντας—that is, if the reader/listener has not forgotten what Jesus has already said in Luke 8:10: "To you it has been given to know the secrets of the kingdom of God; but for others they are in parables, so that seeing they may not see, and hearing they may not understand." Nevertheless, the presence of this group in Israel is not irrelevant to the solution of the disturbance of which Peter's question bears witness.

It is precisely because Luke 8:10 previews the story in Luke 12:35–48 that the references in this story can be better understood. The men servants and the women servants probably refer to the disciples in general. Those among them that give up waiting for the wedding feast are like those who, seeing, do not see and, hearing, do not understand, although the feast was originally intended for their benefit (Lk 14:7–14.15–24; Acts 28:25–28). However, the status of those who joyously receive their Messiah (Lk 19:37–39) is paradoxically reversed since their Lord serves them like a slave until death. For Luke the servant motif relates to the crucifixion of Jesus.

By allowing the Jesus saying "But I am among you as one who serves" (Lk 22:27c) to resound in the words of the "unknown" man going to Emmaus, whom they recognize as the crucified and risen one when he serves them (Lk 24:30–31), at least one uncertainty in the story of Luke 12:35–48 is resolved. Because of the previews in Luke 12:35–48 regarding incidents beyond the end of this section, it becomes clear that the owner of the house serving as a slave is

---

[52] R.C. Tannehill, *Composition* (1984) 225.

not the last incident to which the story refers. There is another ending, and that is the coming of the Son of Man. The story's continuation after the paradoxical actions of the owner of the house is an indication of the point around which the narrator's ideological point of view in Luke 12:35–48 revolves. This point is Peter's question: What about us, the leaders of the disciples? Does the reference to the Lord's slavelike action concern us as well?

At least one episode further on in the Gospel of Luke deals with this question, that is, Luke 17:7–10. This passage makes it clear that the work of the leaders among the followers of Jesus, symbolized as slaves, to whom metaphorical reference is made in Luke 12:35–48, do not cease at the end of the journey to Jerusalem. Under pressure from the temple authorities it was, however, possible that the ministering of the word could be smothered in Jerusalem (Lk 19:39–40). For this reason it was necessary to tell a second story, one which would echo the first in many places.

But when the narrating time runs out and there are no more pages to read, the question, "And what about us, the foremen?" remains apparently, although ironically, unanswered for many. However, the story continues until the coming of the Son of Man. For the faithful and wise manager these words will apply: "Indeed, I tell you, the master will put that servant in charge of all his property" (Lk 12:44). So that no leader of the church can say that he or she does not know whether he or she is included among the implied readers of the Jesus narrative, much was entrusted to, among others, Peter and Paul, and much would be required of them. In Luke 12:41, Peter asks on behalf of all other leaders, and Luke lets Jesus answer by not only telling the second parable about watchful servants (Lk 12:42–48), but also narrates a second narrative in Luke-Acts where Paul demands, *like that in Luke 12:35–48*, watchfulness from the elders of Ephesus:

> So I solemnly declare to you this very day: if any of you should be lost I am not responsible. For I have not held back from announcing to you the whole purpose of God. So keep watch over yourselves and over all the flock which the Holy Spirit has placed in your care. Be shepherds of the church of God, which [God] made [God's] own through the death of [God's] Son. I know that after I leave, fierce wolves will come among you, and they will not spare the flock. The time will come when some men from your own group will tell lies to lead the believers away after them.
>
> (Paul, according to Acts 20:26–30; NEB)

9. The Narrator's Ideological Point of View

The study by J.L. Resseguie[53] on the narrative point of view in Luke 9:51–19:44 confirms the findings of my narratological reading of Luke 12:35–48. J.L. Resseguie[54] indicates that in the story of Jesus' journey to Jerusalem there are two opposing ideological points of view: that of Jesus and that of his opponents (from which perspective the Pharisees and the scribes are presented). The antagonists' ideological perspective is that of self-aggrandisement and arrogance. "It presents an exaltation-oriented point of view that is diametrically opposed to the humiliation-oriented viewpoint that Jesus commends."

The three parables in the travel narrative that focus consecutively and explicitly on the theme of the messianic banquet (Lk 14:7–11; 14:12–14; 14:15–24) strongly emphasize these opposing points of view, namely "humankind's way of thinking and acting" and "God's way of thinking and acting."[55] The former is reflected in the desire to get the best seats at the banquet, to expect to be rewarded for good deeds, and to regard earthly bonds more important than participation at the banquet.

In the framework of the social context of the author and his readers this "humankind thinking" yields to an exclusive community in which there was only room for "unpolluted" insiders and definitely not for impure outsiders.[56] The narrator's ideological point of view concentrates on the straightforward question: will his narratees (according to Luke 6:17, a "great crowd of his disciples and a great multitude of people from all Judea and Jerusalem and the seacoast of Tyre and Sidon") see and hear from the eyewitnesses, the "apostles" (Lk 6:13–16), Jesus' message of being "merciful, even as your Father is merciful" (Lk 6:36)—and will they "do likewise" (Lk 10:37)?

In terms of the social context of the intended readers/listeners backsliding among the early Christian leaders could mean that they adopt the view that was more characteristic of the antagonists in Luke's narrative discourse. The double narrative Luke-Acts displays this "humankind's way of thinking and acting" in distinctive ways

---

[53] J.L. Resseguie, *Point of View* (1982).
[54] J.L. Resseguie, *Point of View* (1982) 44.
[55] J.L. Resseguie, *Point of View* (1982) 46.
[56] J.H. Neyrey, *Social World* (1991).

in the narration of the journey to Jerusalem and that of the journey to Rome. The ideological purpose of narrating this double narrative is: "... in order that you might know the truth concerning the things about which you have been instructed" (ἵνα ἐπιγνῷς περὶ ὧν κατηχήθης λόγων τὴν ἀσφάλειαν) (Lk 1:4).

In other words, the narrator wants to "inform" (ἐπιγνώσκω) the implied readers'/listeners', "accurate knowledge" (ἀσφάλεια) about God's work in Jesus that has been "taught" (κατηχέω) to them by "apostles" (αὐτόπται), such as Peter, and "servants of the word" (ὑπηρέται τοῦ λόγου), such as Paul. The "apostle convent" (see especially Acts 15:6–12) serves the deliberate purpose to link Peter and Paul with each other. Because of "disturbance" in communication when the implied reader/listener loses sight of the tie between the worlds of these two actors, the narrator builds "pauses" and "ellipses" into the narrative. Peter's question in Luke 12:41 is one of these "pauses." Here the narrator clarifies how to resolve the "disturbance effect." According to the story in Luke 12:35–48, careful catechism furnishes knowledge (Lk 1:4). Knowledge brings responsibility and it makes one fully accountable.

Bibliography

Bal, M., *De Theorie van Vertellen en Verhalen: Inleiding in de Narratologie*, Muiderberg 1980.
Bonz, M.P., *The Past as Legacy: Luke-Acts and Ancient Epic*, Minneapolis 2000.
Bovon, F., *Luke the Theologian: Thirty-three Years of Research* (1950–1983), Allison Park, PA 1983.
Brink, A.P., *Vertelkunde: 'n Inleiding tot die Lees van Verhalende Tekste*, Pretoria 1987.
Culler, J., Foreword, in: G. Genette, *Narrative Discourse*, translated by J.E. Lewin, Oxford 1980, 1–13.
D'Angelo, M.R., "Women in Luke-Acts. A Redactional View": *JBL* 109 (1990) 441–61.
———, "(Re)presentations of Women in the Gospel of Matthew and Luke-Acts," in: R.S. Kraemer and M.R. D'Angelo (eds), *Women & Christian Origins*, New York 1999, 171–95.
Danow, D.K., Lotman and Uspenski, B., "A Perfusion of Models": *Semiotica* 64 (1987) 343–57.
Esler, P.F., *Community and Gospel in Luke-Acts. The Social and Political Motivations of Lucan Theology*, Cambridge, UK ²1996.
Fitzmyer, J.A., *Luke the Theologian: Aspects of His Teaching*, London 1989.
Genette, G., *Narrative Discourse*, translated by J.E. Lewin, Oxford 1980.
Green, J.B., *The Gospel of Luke*, Grand Rapids 1997.
Kenney, W., *How to Analyze Fiction*, New York 1966.
Kingsbury, J.D., *Jesus Christ in Matthew, Mark, and Luke* (Proclamation Commentaries), Philadelphia 1981.
Knight, J., *Luke's Gospel*, London 1998.

Lotman, J.M., "Point of View in a Text": *New Literary History* 6 (1975) 339–52.
Lyons, J., *Language, Meaning, and Context*, London ²1981.
Meier, J.P., "The Circle of the Twelve. Did It Exist during Jesus' Public Ministry?": *JBL* 116 (1997) 635–72.
Moore, S.D., *Literary Criticism and the Gospels. The Theoretical Challenge*, New Haven, MA 1989.
Neyrey, J.H. (ed.), *The Social World of Luke-Acts. Models for Interpretation*, Peabody, MA 1991.
Petersen, N.R., "'Point of view' in Mark's narrative": *Semeia* 12 (1978a) 97–121.
——, *Literary Criticism for New Testament Critics*, Philadelphia 1978b.
Prince, G., *Narratology. The Form and Function of Narrative*, Berlin 1982.
Resseguie, J.L., "Point of View in the Central Section of Luke (9:51–19:44)": *JETS* 25 (1982) 41–47.
Ricoeur, P., *Time and Narrative*, I, Chicago 1984.
——, *Figuring the Sacred: Religion, Narrative and Imagination*, translated by D. Pellauer, edited by M.I. Wallace, Minneapolis 1995.
Rimmon-Kenan, S., *Narrative Fiction. Contemporary Poetics*, London 1982.
Sanders, E.P., and Davies, M., *Studying the Synoptic Gospels*, London ⁵1996.
Seim, T.K., *Patterns in Gender in Luke-Acts*, Edinburgh 1994.
Sternberg, M., *The Poetics of Biblical Narrative. Ideological Literature and the Drama of Reading*, Bloomington, IN 1985.
Tannehill, R.C., "The Composition of Acts 3–5. A Narrative Development and Echo Effect," in: K.H. Richards (ed.), *Society of Biblical Literature 1984 Seminar Papers*, Chico, CA 1984, 217–40.
——, *The Narrative Unity of Luke-Acts*, Volume 1. The Gospel According to Luke, Philadelphia 1986.
Tiede, D.L., "Glory to Thy People, Israel. Luke-Acts and the Jews," in: J.B. Tyson (ed.), *Luke-Acts and the Jewish People*, Minneapolis 1988, 21–34.
Uspenski, B., *A Poetics of Composition. The Structure of the Artistic Text and Typology of a Compositional Form*, translated by V. Zavarin and S. Wittig, Berkeley, CA 1973.
Vandermoere, H., *The Structure of the Novel*, Leuven ²1982.
Van Tilborg, Sj., *The Sermon on the Mount as an Ideological Intervention. A Reconstruction of Meaning*, Assen 1986.

CHAPTER TEN

NO ANTI-JUDAISM IN THE FOURTH GOSPEL: A DECONSTRUCTION OF READINGS OF JOHN 8

Patrick Chatelion Counet
University of Nijmegen, the Netherlands

Deconstruction can be seen as the disjoining note in a harmonious consensus.[1] Sometimes, however, deconstruction is the mediation between opposites.[2] Against the latter, the transferring of the intra-Jewish discussion between Jesus and his fellow Jews from the narrative in the gospel of John to a "historical" discussion between Johannine Christians and Jews from the synagogues is a dangerous development in the debate on the supposed anti-Judaism of the Fourth Gospel. It creates an extra-textual conflict between Jews and Christians in post-Jesus times and destroys the Gospel of John as the story of Jesus and his people.

1. *Introduction*

1.1. *Theology or Narration?*

The hypothesis of an existing Johannine community is considered to be a fact by many scholars, and since J.L. Martyn's *History and Theology in the Fourth Gospel*,[3] it absorbed most of the studies on the

---

[1] In this sense, deconstruction is resistance to "logocentrism," resistance to the *logos* imagined as the truth, the present *primum cognitum*, the transcendental signified: *ens, unum, verum, bonum*; see J. Derrida, *De la Grammatologie*, p. 33. Derrida refers to a history of "métaphysique de présence" (p. 11) that needs to be deconstructed because of its semblance of truth.
[2] This mediation does not erase the opposition but turns it into an undecidable. Undecidables disrupt the oppositional logic and open the door to indeterminacy. Derrida speaks of a "supplément" that means both addition and replacement; see J. Derrida, "La Pharmacie de Platon," pp. 117–18 and 124.
[3] J.L. Martyn, *History and Theology in the Fourth Gospel*, New York 1968.

so-called anti-Judaism of John.⁴ The original two-level drama which Martyn describes, on the one hand, as the conflict of Jesus with the Jewish authorities and, on the other hand, the conflict of the Johannine community with the synagogue, is reduced to a one-dimensional theological conflict that—beyond the gospel narrative and apart from the story line—reflects the "Sitz im Leben" of an early Christian community. Even R.A. Culpepper, the godfather of the Johannine narratology, loses his religion by ignoring the narrative through a strict theological solution of the problem.⁵

Sjef van Tilborg contends that in order to take the narrative structure of the Fourth Gospel seriously, readers ought to translate "the Jews" in John: ". . . into 'the Jews, who, according to this story, are present at this narrative place and in this narrative time.'"⁶ In her article on the hermeneutics of John 8 J. Lieu remarks that to ignore the narrative character of the Fourth Gospel in favor of a thematic, conceptual, or "theological" reading is to do violence to the specificity of the text with its self-conscious "history-like" quality.⁷ This means that we should not reduce the problem to a discussion of the Johannine community and its antagonists on the level of christological concepts.

Lieu further states that John's rhetoric of calling someone "of the devil" reflects a *process of othering*.⁸ This implies the idea that John writes an "intra-familial" polemic "from within" the Jewish tradition.⁹

---

⁴ See the articles of J. McHugh, J. Dunn, and Chr. Rowland in James D.G. Dunn (ed.): *Jews and Christians. The Parting of the Ways A.D. 70 to 135*, Tübingen 1992; see also most of the (25) articles in R. Bieringer, D. Pollefeyt, and F. Vandecasteele-Vanneuville (ed.): *Anti-Judaism and the Fourth Gospel. Papers of the Leuven Colloquium, 2000*, Assen 2001; exceptions here are the articles of J. Lieu, R.F. Collins, and A. Reinhartz which either stress the necessity of more narrative approaches or criticize the self-evident consensus about the Johannine conflict with the Synagogue.

⁵ R.A. Culpepper, "Anti-Judaism in the Fourth Gospel as a Theological Problem for Christian Interpreters," pp. 68–91.

⁶ Sj. van Tilborg, "Jezus temidden van de Joden van het Loofhuttenfeest in Johannes 8," p. 66.

⁷ J. Lieu, "Anti-Judaism in the Fourth Gospel. Explanation and Hermeneutics," p. 136.

⁸ Lieu, "Anti-Judaism," p. 132.

⁹ Cf. Kl. Scholtissek, "Antijudaismus im Johannesevangelium?," who considers the polemic in John as "innerjüdisch" (p. 176); see against this Tomson who projects his distinction of *Yisrael* (as the internal designation of the People of the Covenant) and *Yehudim/Ioudaioi* (as used in interaction with non-Jews) to the Gospel of John; because of the hybrid character (John speaks of *Yisrael* and of *Ioudaioi*) he presupposes an older Jewish-Christian gospel which was left untouched during a non-Jewish editing; P. Tomson, "The Names Israel and Jew in Ancient Judaism and in the New Testament," esp. pp. 129 and 281; the same ideas we find in his book: *"If this be from heaven . . .,"* esp. pp. 110–11 and 328.

The process of othering compels us to define the notions of "self" and "other." Othering presupposes an original familiarity. The enemy outside your door is not susceptible to a process of other*ing*, he *is* already the other. In his deconstruction of John's anti-Judaism, Culpepper sets in opposition the anti-Jewish elements against the Jewish elements. His analysis presupposes a closed door and separate houses: the Jews are already the others because the process of othering has ended some time ago. Culpepper comments on the result of this process. Lieu's idea of othering, however, starts in the middle of the process and that is, I think, the way one should analyze the situation of John 8. In paragraph 4, I will deconstruct Culpepper's deconstruction using B. Johnson's reduction of a "difference between" opposite matters to a "difference within" one of the opposing elements.[10]

1.2. *Deconstruction*

Between the opposites and contradictions of John 8:31–59, there exists an area of "betwixt and between," a state of liminality, an ambiguous threshold.[11] The "Jews" in this text are, at one and the same time, believers and antagonists of Jesus; they are τοὺς πεπιστευκότας αὐτῷ Ἰουδαίους, believers (8:31), but also ἐκ τοῦ πατρὸς τοῦ διαβόλου ἐστὲ, children of the devil (8:44). What is the explanation for this? Most answers ignore the fact that in the first case, the narrator speaks (8:31) while in the second case, it is Jesus who speaks (8:44). They consider the two voices as one and the same and not distinct from the voice of the evangelist.[12] As a result, the problem is solved by historical, conceptual, c.q. theological solutions (i.e., the Johannine community and its ideology).

Using the deconstructive strategy of reading which Johnson developed in her book *The Critical Difference*, I believe that the difference *between* a supposed Johannine and a supposed Jewish identity in the Gospel of John can be reduced to a (partly unrecognized) difference *within* Jewish thinking as such. Jesus, and his Jewish followers, *and*

---

[10] B. Johnson, *The Critical Difference*, p. 4.
[11] Cf. E.R. Leach and D.A. Aycock, *Structuralist Interpretation of Biblical Myth*, pp. 15–16.
[12] Culpepper thinks that the author of John gives his opinions through the main character as well as through the narrator, *The Anatomy of the Fourth Gospel*, pp. 34 and 43; cf. also J. Zumstein, "Analyse narrative, critique rhétorique et exégèse johannique," p. 41 footnote 43.

his Jewish antagonists, share the same house and their discussion takes place on the threshold. They form a religious *communitas* associated with a state of liminality. The contradictions—a community of protagonists and antagonists, children of God and children of the devil—refer to the common and shared truth of the betwixt and between.

Of course, deconstruction is not just about reducing external opposites to internal opposites.[13] Culpepper, who tries to be a deconstructionist "without subscribing the school's view," defines deconstruction as a vision: "Deconstruction holds that texts do not yield to consistent, stable interpretations."[14] In order to deconstruct the anti-Jewishness of John's christology—note that anti-Jewishness is the starting point—he searches for elements in John that undermine the coherence of its anti-Jewishness; he tries to set in opposition the anti-Jewish elements against the Jewish elements. I do not think this is deconstruction. Deconstruction would be showing that John's supposed anti-Jewish elements are in fact Jewish.[15]

1.3. *The Three Levels of Communication in John 8*

One has to read John 8:31–59 on three levels: the level of the story, the level of the narration, and the level of enunciation. This corresponds to three levels of communication: communication between characters (paragraph 2), communication between the narrator and the narratee (paragraph 3), communication between the text of the Gospel and its reader (paragraph 4).

Most scholars tend to read the text only on the level of enunciation by explaining it as a kind of communication between the author and his (implied) reader. Some of them confound the idea of an implied reader with the notion of the narratee and by doing so they mix up the level of narration with that of enunciation. Mistaking

---

[13] On the question of what deconstruction implies, Jacques Derrida answers: "Ce que la déconstruction n'est pas? mais tout! Qu'est-ce que la déconstruction? mais rien!," J. Derrida: "Lettre à un ami japonais," p. 392; in my book, *John: a Postmodern Gospel*, I distinguish four categories in the collection of reading/writing advices for a deconstructive exegesis (pp. 154–71).
[14] Culpepper, "Anti-Judaism," p. 82.
[15] Derrida describes the "general strategy" of deconstruction as follows: "Celle-ci devrait éviter à la fois de *neutraliser* simplement les oppositions binaires de la métaphysique et de *résider* simplement, en le confirmant, dans le champ clos de ces oppositions," J. Derrida: *Positions*, p. 56.

their interpretation as the intention of the author, they commit an intentional fallacy.

The problem of the identity of "the Jews" in John 8 has to be divided in three categories. On the level of the story, the actorial communication of "Jesus" and the "Jews" takes place. On the level of narration, the narrative communication of the narrator and his narratee takes place, mostly understood as communication of "John" and the "Johannine community" on their relation with "Jews." On the level of enunciation, the implicit communication between the implied author and its implied reader takes place. The implied reader is not the narratee, i.e., not the "you" of pisteu‚jhte in John 20:31. The implied reader is the universal reader of all times, especially me and you. "Me" being a Western, white male of the 21th century of a postmodern, post-Shoah, and post-christian secularized culture, and "you" being the implied reader of this article. In other words, "I" am the only implied reader of John 8 and that is why "I" have to operate cautiously on this level of enunciation, trying not to confuse the ideas and notions of my interpretive community with the intention of the text. Every word that does not belong to the signifiers of the text is, more or less, a scholarly projection of the implied reader. The author never gives meaning to the text—even the famous Johannine intention of 20:31, "ταῦτα δὲ γέγραπται ἵνα" should be taken for what it is: communication of the narrator with his narratee—it is always the implied reader that gives meaning, for instance, by putting the narrator on a par with the (implied) author.

The projection follows a two-way direction. The implied reader projects ideas to the text but, conversely, the level of the story and the level of the narration also try to project meanings to the level of enunciation. One has to be mindful of an intentional fallacy if one takes words or norms of characters as the intention of the author. For instance, if one takes the words of a character like Nathanael in John 1:49 σὺ εἶ ὁ υἱὸς τοῦ θεοῦ as the theology of the narrator ("John") or, even more strongly, as "enunciation" instead of actorial communication, then one should treat words of other characters like the Pharisees in 9:24 in the same way: οὗτος ὁ ἄνθρωπος ἁμαρτωλός ἐστιν. Why should we jump from the actorial level to that of enunciation only in positive cases ("Jesus is the Son of God") and not in negative cases ("Jesus is a sinner")? While it is true that Nathanael speaks the words of the narrator (cf. 1:49 and 20:31), the enunciation of the text might produce completely different norms.

From a (other) Jewish perspective Jesus may be a sinner indeed. Implied readers belonging to a modern Jewish interpretive community could deduct anti-Christian norms from the Johannine text. They might agree with the Pharisees in chapter 9 and the "Jews" in chapter 5 and 8. In doing so they evaluate the discussion on the actorial level in favor of Jesus' antagonists. On the narrative level they might reject the evaluations of the narrator, e.g., his claim that Jesus is the Son of God (20:31) and that Judas is a betrayer. They even might say that this narrator is unreliable because he tells things which turn out to be untrue later on (cf. 3:22 and 4:2). Thus, in the end, there is no iron logic that forces all readers to jump to the same conclusions by identifying the first two levels of communication with the last one. It is quite possible that the text tells us different things on the level of enunciation than on the narrative (or actorial) level. By this I do not refer to the history within the story from which scholars deduce the biography of a Johannine community. Rather, I refer to the plurality of meanings, the disseminate fact that different readers read different ideas from one and the same signifier. The reason for this dissemination is that we are not able to produce criteria from a text to stipulate which notion or idea of the actorial or narrative level may be transferred to the level of enunciation. This is analogous to the poststructuralist idea that there is no such thing as a transcendental signified belonging to one signifier.

Nevertheless, many scholars on John 8 act as if these criteria exist. They jump from the actorial and the narrative level to the level of enunciation, declaring that the intention of the narrator is the intention of the evangelist, and declaring that the level of the story reflects the level of history. This might indeed be the case, but for the same reason, it is not. Besides, it is hermeneutically naive. The levels are distinguished to make analyses of each level separate, not to mix them up. Different from novels in which the fictive element prevails, the gospel genre is built up by all sorts of material such as oral and written traditions, historical sources, and fictive material. Different from novels, a gospel text tells stories and events that were not all invented by the author. Perhaps he selects them with a certain intention but this *intentio auctoris* should be distinguished from the *intentio operis*. Both these intentions have to be reconstructed by the (implied) reader; it would be a mistake to identify them in advance.

2. *The Level of the Story: Actorial Communication (Jesus and the Jews)*

Every story is told by a narrator, visible or invisible. Most of the time the narrator focalizes the events[16] but in the direct speech of John 8:31–59, he gives up the perspective several times. By reducing all the story elements and all the words of Jesus to the perspective of the narrator/evangelist (i.e., *the focalization of the narrator reflects the vision of the author towards late first century Jewish synagogue leaders*),[17] exegetes are submitted to a referential fallacy: the one-dimensionality of history and story. On the story level, however, Jesus presents the focalisation of several kinds of "Jews": Ἰουδαῖοι believing in him, Ἰουδαῖοι confronting him with distinctive theology, and Ἰουδαῖοι searching for a charge to sentence him to death. Christian anti-Judaism comes in sight only if one transfers this scene to the conflict of the Johannine community and the synagogue, a conflict that plays a role in the presupposed historical "Sitz im Leben" of a Christian writer and his Christian community. But in the special case of the gospel as a genre that mingles fiction and facts, we have to reckon with the possibility that the narrator tells events that really occurred in the told world. And in that world, a Jew is discussing a matter with other Jews. Originally, these Jews believe in him (see the conversion and confirmation in 8:30–31) but as the discussion goes along, they prove to be antagonists.

2.1. *John 8 Mirrors John 6*

John 8 repeats the apostasy of John 6. In the beginning, a great multitude (6:2) followed Jesus. This multitude is referred to in terms of the Exodus-story as the "people" of Moses: "Our fathers did eat manna in the desert" (6:31). Jesus confirms this association: "Moses gave you not that bread from heaven" (6:32). So if the story further on speaks from Ἰουδαῖοι, "the Jews," these Jews are the followers

---

[16] For definitions of narration and focalization see D.F. Tolmie, *Narratology and Biblical Narratives*; "... to analyze focalization in a narrative text, we should ask the question: Through whose eyes do we view the events that are being narrated to us?" (p. 32).

[17] R. Kysar, "Anti-Semitism and the Gospel of John" (p. 123), summarizes the case as follows: "... the opponents of Jesus in the narrative were only thinly disguised opponents of the writer's own contemporary Christian community"; see also Culpepper and Zumstein as referred to in note 12.

and disciples of Jesus. Moreover, these Jews, in discussion with Jesus at the lake of Galilee in the synagogue of Capernaum, are the disciples (οἱ μαθηταὶ) "who went back and walked no more with him" (6:66). Only the Twelve remain. In narrative terms, it is much too early to transfer this story of abandonment to the "Sitz im Leben" of the first Johannine Christians in the synagogues of Minor Asia. That would erase the idea that John tells the story of Jesus and his people. The Twelve are part of the people and part of the disciples described as Jews in John 6. On the story-level, the Jews as characters ask for a characterization in their role as first disciples, then deserters of Jesus and not as characters on the historical level of a writing evangelist and his environment.

This story of abandonment repeats itself in John 8. The Jews, Ἰουδαῖοι, in Galilee are not the same as the Ἰουδαῖοι mentioned in 7:1. At first, Jesus stays in Galilee "for he would not walk in Judea because the Ἰουδαῖοι sought to kill him." The reader knows now that he has to distinguish between Jews in Galilee of whom Jesus has nothing to fear and certain Jews in Judea who seek to kill Jesus. And then there is a third group of Jews ("the people") at the feast of Tabernacles in Jerusalem who discuss whether Jesus is a good man or a deceiver (7:12). John 8 thus mirrors John 6 on several levels:

- the Exodus background of John 6 (the manna of Ex 16:1–35) is continued in the Feast of Tabernacles of John 7–9 (the feast of remembrance of staying in the desert Ex 34:22);
- the Moses-argumentation of John 6 turns into the Abraham-argumentation of John 8;
- the narrative place Galilee turns into Jerusalem and likewise the narrative scene of the synagogue turns into the Temple;[18]
- the Jews of Galilee that are the people of John 6 who believe in Jesus become the Jews of Jerusalem in John 8 who are coming to believe (in both cases they are represented as disciples of Jesus);
- most of the Jewish disciples of Jesus abandon him "because of his hard sayings" in John 6 and the devilish discussion in John 8;
- the only unchanging element of John 5–6 and John 7–9 are the Jews who try to kill Jesus (5:18 and 7:1); they have to be distinguished from the Jews who are the disciples of Jesus.

---

[18] Cf. W. Meeks, "Galilee and Judea in the Fourth Gospel," 159–69.

Conclusion A: on the story-level one has to choose between five groups of Ἰουδαῖοι to identify the Jews:

1. Ἰουδαῖοι, Jews, of (a) Galilee and (b) Judea who believe in Jesus but after some discussion abandon him.
2. Jews of Judea who think Jesus is a deceiver. Since M. Lowe's article from 1976 exegetes refer to the Jews of these first two categories as "regional."[19]
3. Jews in the general sense of the people of Israel; this "national" sense shows itself in expressions as "the feast of the Jews," "the king of the Jews," and the like.
4. Jews who try to kill Jesus. Since the article of U. von Wahlde exegetes refer to these Jews as "Judean authorities."[20]
5. Jews who believe in Jesus and never leave him.

Conclusion B: in this part of the Gospel there are no non-Jews who take part in the story. This holds true, in fact, for the whole of the Gospel, with a small and rather disappointing exception in chapter 12 for some Greeks: they are not allowed to see Jesus (12:20–23).[21] So in the end John's story is absolutely not interested in Jesus' relation to the *gojïm*.[22]

Conclusion C: if the story is focalized from the perspective of a character, all the viewpoints are Jewish. On the story-level, there is no opportunity for anti-Judaism. The actorial communication is purely intra-Jewish. If Culpepper states that we find nowhere in the scrolls authors writing about "the Jews" as a people apart from themselves or referring to the Torah as "your law" (8:17) so that John's position "in relation to Judaism can no longer be regarded as an intra-Jewish debate,"[23] he confuses the voice of the author with that of Jesus 8:17 presents actorial communication: it is Jesus who speaks

---

[19] See M. Lowe, "Who were the IOUDAIOI?," 101–130.
[20] See U. von Wahlde, "The Johannine 'Jews.' A Critical Survey," 33–60.
[21] "... ihr Auftreten erscheint unwirklich und eigenartig anachronistisch," J. Frey: "Heiden-Griechen-Gotteskinder," p. 231.
[22] This applies to the story of the Gospel and the actorial level; on another level there can be a hidden theme for the readers to reveal. Frey presupposes that the mission to the gentiles is a hidden theme ("verdeckt ... thematisiert"); he considers the Greeks as a "Chiffre für die heidenchristlichen Adressaten des Evangeliums und für die kleinasiatischen Adressaten des Evangeliums;" J. Frey: "Heiden-Griechen-Gotteskinder," pp. 237 and 263; here, we enter the enunciative level of implied communication and, as a consequence, the free world of interpretations (the word "chiffre" makes the modest presence of Greeks in the Gospel rather big).
[23] Culpepper, "Anti-Judaism," pp. 70–71.

to the Ἰουδαῖοι about "your law"; it is not the evangelist speaking to Jews in a synagogue in Ephesos. In this narrative situation Jesus speaks the language of the prophets. Isaiah reprimanding Israel says: "Your iniquities have separated between you and your God" (Isa 59:2). Although Isaiah speaks about "your God" and not about "our God" (cf. Isa 59:13), it does not deprive the communication of Isaiah with his people of its intra-Jewish character.[24]

2.1. *John 8: The Temple as a Law-Court*

So how must the reader understand Jesus' discussion with the Ἰουδαῖοι in John 8? In the first place as a discussion with "his own," even if they might turn out to be authorities. In the second place as a discussion in the tradition of the Scriptures, both in content and in tone. In content it evokes the Jewish apostasy in times of Abraham, Moses, and the prophets. In tone it evokes the voices of Isaiah, Jeremiah, and other prophets who rebuke their people. Jesus' discussion-partners understand him at the right level: in denying that they were born "of fornication" (8:41) they refer to the unfaithfulness against God depicted in the Scriptures as adultery of the bride Israel (e.g., Ezek 16:28–29; Hos 1:2 and 2:4–5). And how about this calling each other "devils": "You are of your father the devil (διαβόλος)" (Jesus in 8:44); "You are a Samaritan and have a devil (δαιμόνιος)" (the Ἰουδαῖοι in 8:48)? In this narrative situation, one Jew talking to other Jews, we must again keep in mind the prophetic situation of counting the crimes and sins of the people of Israel, of the prophets rebuking Israel for searching evil and injustice (e.g., Amos 5:12; Mic 3:2), and of the many predictions of catastrophes (e.g., Jer 7:30–8:3). The history of Israel's sometimes-violent reaction to its prophets resounds in this conflict among Jews. And just as the murmuring of the Ἰουδαῖοι in John 6 (Ἐγόγγυζον) is reminiscent of the murmuring of the people in the desert of Exodus, so the attempt of the Ἰουδαῖοι to stone Jesus at the end of the discussion (8:59) reminds the reader that they interpret Jesus' words again at the right level:

---

[24] Of course there are many examples of this kind of prophetical speech; see, for instance, how in Jeremiah 42:1–43:2 the growing distance between Jeremiah and his Jewish opponents is expressed in the transition of "our God" to "your God" and "their God." The strongest case is made by the speeches of Moses who constantly refers to "your God" when he addresses Israel (cf. Deuteronomy *passim*).

it is a Jewish discussion on the nature of God at the edge—or as some Ἰουδαῖοι would say: over the edge—of blasphemy (cf. Lev 24:16 and John 10:33).

On the story-level, there is no anti-Judaism. The starting situation—Ἰουδαῖοι that believe[25] in Jesus—is changed immediately in Ἰουδαῖοι who try to kill Jesus. So there is a jump from the first category (1b) to the fourth. Jesus recognizes among the believing Jews Ἰουδαῖοι who try to kill him. The narrative situation prohibits saying that all the Jews are willing to kill Jesus because of blasphemy. It is only this small group of Jews—some Jews from Judea present at the treasury of the temple in Jerusalem—who respond in this way to the hard sayings of Jesus. In the perspective of the narrator (see the next paragraph) these Ἰουδαῖοι have to be identified as authorities. Are there indications on the story-level to transfer this perspective to that of Jesus? Jesus says: "ζητεῖτέ με ἀποκτεῖναι" (8:37). This cannot be a response to the inhabitants of Judea and Jerusalem who came to believe in him at the feast of Tabernacles. We must conclude that among the Ἰουδαῖοι meant in 8:30–31 there are some representatives of the authorities that were as such recognized by Jesus. His debate functions as a demasqué. The verb ζητεῖν has juridical sense and means "investigate" or "trying to make a case" in order to arrest or execute somebody (cf. ζητεῖν πιάσαι: 7:30; 10:39; ζητεῖν ἀποκτεῖναι: 5:18; 7:1.19.20.25; 8:37.40; ζητεῖν λιθάσαι: 11:8).[26] This juridical context is confirmed in Jesus, words in 8:50 where the verb is connected with κρίνειν, to judge.[27] It brings to mind the original context of the story: the law-session of the woman caught in adultery (8:2–11; synchronically this story gives chapter 8 its juridical isotopy)[28] and the proceeding discussion of Jesus with the scribes and the Pharisees (8:3.13) about right judgements, the law, true testimonies, and the testimony of the Father (8:12–19: κρίνειν; νόμος;

---

[25] Πεπιστευκότας of 8:31 is understood by some translators in the sense of a plusquamperfectum: "Jews who *had believed* in Jesus" (cf. G. Caron, *Qui sont les Juifs de l'évangile de Jean?* p. 203). However, the logic connection with 8:30 and the grammatical connection with πεπιστεύκαμεν in 6:69 suggest us to translate this word in the same way as in 6:69: "Jews who *came to believe* in Jesus."

[26] Cf. Liddell-Scott who gives examples of the judicial sense of ζητέω from Plato to Lucianus.

[27] Against Dunn, "The Question of Anti-semitism in the New Testament," who considers κρίσις as "the escalating process of separation and division" (p. 198).

[28] An isotopy is a group of expressions linked by a common "semantic denominator." It identifies one of the text's themes. For John 8 the theme is juridical.

μαρτυρεῖν). So the perspective of Jesus in talking to the specific Ἰουδαῖοι in 8:31–59 is a juridical one. The temple functions as a law-court, the discussion is still about true juridical testimonies (like that of the Father), the stones for the adulterous woman are still on hand to stone Jesus, and the Ἰουδαῖοι are in the eyes of Jesus authoritative persons, probably the scribes and Pharisees of 8:2 and 13. He exposes them as non-believers. Exposure is the main program of the phase of performance. The narrative program to formulate this conclusion about 8:31–59 is as follows:[29]

$$DS^{Jesus} => (S^{Ἰουδαῖοι} \lor O^{Belief}) (S^{Ἰουδαῖοι} \land O^{Belief})$$

Jesus is the dynamic subject (DS) that transforms (=>) the situation that subjects are connected (V) with the object belief to a situation that these subjects are disconnected (Λ) with that object.

Of course, one can ask whether the group of Ἰουδαῖοι in 8:31 is the same as the group exposed by Jesus. Greimas uses a square of veridiction to show how the positions in the story are related. If, for instance, the villain turns out to be the hero in the end, then the square shows another qualification of truth than when the villain is indeed a villain. Four positions are possible: (1) if a person or situation appears as it really is, the position is true; (2) if it is not as it appears, the position is a lie; (3) if it does not appear as it really is, the position concerns a secret; (4) if it is not as it does not appear, the position is false:

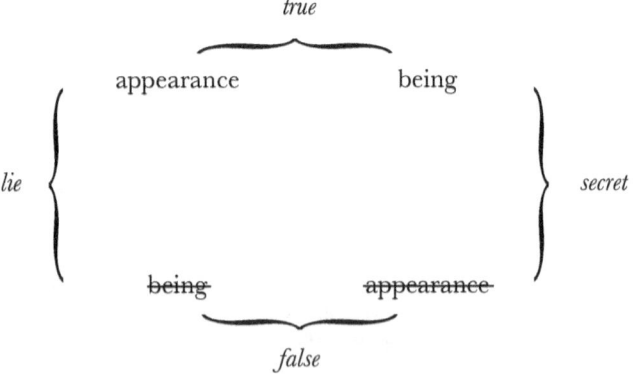

---

[29] Cf. A.J. Greimas and J. Courtès, *Sémiotique: dictionaire raisonné de la théorie du langage*, 1979/1986.

Greimas takes the term "appear" in the French sense of *apparaître*, "to make one's appearance," "to become visible as" (rather than the meaning "seems to be"). Transferred to the story of 8:31–59, the Ἰουδαῖοι who believe in Jesus appear to be Ἰουδαῖοι in a regional sense, the Judaic people present in the temple at the Feast of Tabernacles. In the discussion, however, they turn out—at least some of them and apparently their would-be spokesmen—to be representatives of the juridical authorities, if not of themselves (cf. 12:42). In the end, these authoritative persons claim to possess the right to execute anyone accused of blasphemy. Thus, there is an inclusion with the story of the adulterous woman because of the presence of authorities, on one hand; and because the stoning does not take place, on the other hand. The persons who have to start the stoning are not the judges but the witnesses, including the witnesses for the defense.[30] By taking the initiative, they show the collective character of the administration of justice. But just as in the case of the adulterous woman, the people of Israel are not willing to take the initiative and this is why Jesus is able to leave the temple unhurt. In the square of veridiction, the position of the belief of the Ἰουδαῖοι between 8:31 and 8:59 has to be placed at the left side:

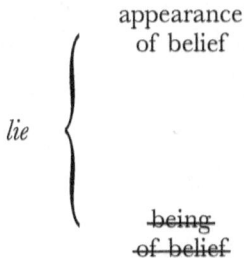

The belief of the Ἰουδαῖοι appears, at first sight, as a true belief (8:31), but changes into no belief at all (8:59). In the narratologic grammar of Greimas, this position is called a "lie." The explanation is found in the true composition of the Ἰουδαῖοι. Their position is found at the right side of the square:

---

[30] Cf. Deut 17:7; the collective character of the execution is stated in Deut 13:10; cf. I Kings 21:10.13; R. de Vaux, *Les Institutions de l'Ancien Testament* (part I, par. J, 9), thinks that the regulation of Deut 17:7 has to be read as *"all* the witnesses."

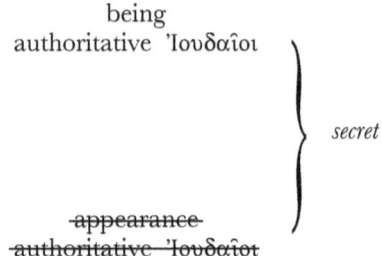

The Ἰουδαῖοι are juridical authorities but they do not appear as authorities. In the grammar of Greimas, this position is called a secret.

Once more, the conclusion is that on the story-level, there is no question of anti-Judaism. The isotopy of the story is juridical, the Ἰουδαῖοι are legal authorities, and the context is that of a law-court. The authorities in the temple are not the only Ἰουδαῖοι, and their response to kill Jesus is not the only one thinkable. Other responses are possible and were given: simply walk away (John 6:66) or stay with Jesus and believe in him (like many other Ἰουδαῖοι).

The art of analyzing the narrative situation and its actorial communication as an intra-Jewish debate first consists of entangling the level of the story with how the narrator situates it, and, secondly, in not entangling it with the way readers respond to the text. The first two levels are intra-textual while the third is extra-textual.

3. *The Level of Narration: Communication Between Narrator and Narratee ("John" and the Jews)*

In analysing the level of narration, one must avoid identifying the narrator with the (implied) author or evangelist. They are not the same. The author forms no part of the text and in this sense, Roland Barthes is right in stating that he is dead (although in fact he or she may be alive or even immortal). The narrator forms part of the text. In John, this narrator shows himself at the end of the Gospel first as a "we" (21:24; cf. 1:14) and then as an "I" (21:25). The narratee is the "you" of 19:35 and 20:31.

Certain deictic terms serve as indicators to distinguish the extra-diegetic Johannine narrator from the characters in the text. They are used in such a way that they do not refer to the narrated world,[31]

---

[31] Tolmie, *Narratology and Biblical Narratives*, pp. 13–25; also Shl. Rimmon-Kenan, *Narrative Fiction*, pp. 94–105.

like the commentary that the narrator gives on a situation or a person, i.e., when he explains what the word "Rabbi" means or the word "Messiah" (1:38.41). References to the Ἰουδαῖοι, however, are most of the time without deictic commentary. The Gospel uses the word Ἰουδαῖος 67 times in plural and 3 times in singular. On the level of narration, there are—apart from 9 more or less superficial references to practices and feasts of the Jews (which however show that the narrator communicates with an at least partly non-Jewish narratee)[32]—only 3 comments on "the Jews" that inform the narratee about their character. In 4:9, the narrator (if not the Samaritan woman) informs the narratee that Jews have no dealings with the Samaritans. In 9:22b the narrator explains to the narratee why the parents of the man born blind fear the Ἰουδαῖοι: because "the Ἰουδαῖοι had decided" (juridical term: συνετέθειντο) to put out of the synagogue anyone who confessed that "this man was Christ." The third commentary concerns the information on the identity of Caiaphas: "he which gave counsel to the Ἰουδαῖοι that it was expedient that one man should die for the people" (18:14 referring to 11:47–53). This is important because it shows that the Ἰουδαῖοι in 18:14 must be identified with the persons of 11:47–53 which took counsel together to put Jesus to death. These persons are "the chief priests and the Pharisees."[33] So here we have proof that *if* the term "Ἰουδαῖοι" is used within a juridical isotopy, Ἰουδαῖοι means "the Jewish authorities" and not the people of Israel (national sense) or the inhabitants of Judea or Jerusalem (regional sense).

This conclusion is in agreement with several other conclusions submitted by contemporary scholars about the "world" (cf. Von Wahlde; Ashton; Culpepper; Menken as just quoted), but there is a difference. I do not transfer this conclusion to an extra-textual (supposed historical) world. Ashton thinks that the reference of "Ἰουδαῖοι" indeed concerns the "Jewish authorities" but the sense of the term symbolizes "human obduracy and incomprehension when confronted with the revelation of Jesus."[34] He jumps from one level (the story) to

---

[32] Concerning πάσχα τῶν ... Ἰουδαίων (2:13; 5:1; 6:4; 11:55), σκηνοπηγία (7:2), παρασκευὴ (19:31.42), καθαρισμός (2:6), and ἐνταφιάζειν (19:40).

[33] Cf. M. Menken: "Jezus tegenover de Farizeeën in het vierde evangelie: Joh. 8,12–20"; Menken thinks that the evangelist relates the chief priests and Pharisees to the trial of Jesus; he considers this as a reminiscence to a factual, historical affair (p. 104).

[34] J. Ashton, *Understanding the Fourth Gospel*, p. 136.

another (history). In like manner, Von Wahlde thinks that the term was "intended to refer to the hostility of authoritative "Jewish" synagogue officials"; he says that it historically portrays "the confrontation between the Johannine group and the synagogue leaders."[35] J. Dunn is even more specific by identifying them as the "Yavnean rabbis."[36]

I think more restraint is called for here. First of all, the indications on the narrative level refer to how to understand the story. The reader must be aware of a referential fallacy taking the indications to a reality outside the text: the narration tells the story of its characters, not the history of its author. On the narrative level we can conclude only two things:

a. the narratees are non-Jewish persons—the narrator has to inform them about Jewish practices, feasts, and religious terms like Messiah and Rabbi;
b. two times the narrator informs the narratees directly about how to understand the term "'Ιουδαῖοι"; in 9:22b and 18:14 he suggests that if the term is used in a juridical context the term means "authorities."

With this information, we have to re-enter Martyn's so-called two-level drama. What does it mean on the story-level and on the level of history (see paragraph 4)? On the story-level, we may say that each time the term "'Ιουδαῖοι" occurs within a juridical isotopy, what is referred to are the official authorities and not the people of Israel. In chapter 11, for instance, "'Ιουδαῖοι" is at first meant in a regional sense and the meaning is very positive; the 'Ιουδαῖοι love the sisters of Lazarus and many of them come to believe in Jesus (11:45). After the council had juridically sentenced Jesus to death (11:53), the meaning turns negative. The narratee (and the reader), however, knows that the term 'Ιουδαῖοι is influenced by its juridical context and that it is not the people of Israel nor even the inhabitants of Judea who threaten Jesus. This mirrors the situation of the two groups of 'Ιουδαῖοι in John 8: believers and would-be executioners.

This argument is of utmost importance in the context of chapters 18:28–19:19 on Jesus' trial. The scene is dominated by Pilate's question: "What accusation (κατηγορία) do you bring against this man?"

---

[35] Von Wahlde, "The 'Jews' in the Gospel of John," esp. p. 54 and footnote 108.
[36] Dunn, "The Question of Anti-semitism," pp. 199–200.

(18:29). Here again the narratee and the reader know that the Ἰουδαῖοι in this juridical context (κατηγορία) are the authorities. This context is confirmed by Pilate's suggestion to the Ἰουδαῖοι to judge Jesus according to their law (νόμος) and their reply that they do not have this right (οὐκ ἔξεστιν; 18:31). The juridical isotopy is continued in Jesus' words where he speaks of his extradition: παραδοθῶ τοῖς Ἰουδαίιος. Of course Ἰουδαῖοι here are the authorities (18:36). The same counts for the Ἰουδαῖοι who have the right to decide which criminal is freed on Passover; the authorities—not the Jewish people—choose for Barabbas. The juridical debate between Pilate and the Jewish authorities—in 19:6 identified as the high priests and the officers—continues in 19:7 ("We have a law (νόμος) and according to this law...") and in 19:12 as these same Ἰουδαῖοι try to convince Pilate that in the case of Jesus the legal authority of Caesar is at stake.

The conclusion is that common people, i.e., common Jews, are excluded from Pilate's consultation of the authorities, i.e., the Ἰουδαῖοι, near his hall of judgement. There are no ordinary Jews involved in Jesus' trial, nor in the demand to put Barabbas free, nor in the outcry to crucify Jesus. The scene of 18:28–19:19 is a complete internal juridical affair between Pilate and the representatives of the legal authorities in Jerusalem.[37] The Ἰουδαῖοι as people in a regional sense only come in again in 19:20 "because the place were Jesus was crucified was near to the city."

What does the connection between juridical indications and the understanding of Ἰουδαῖοι in an authoritative sense mean for the interpretation of John 8:31–59? At first Ἰουδαῖοι is meant in a regional or perhaps even national sense: Jews in Jerusalem who came to believe in Jesus. But are the Ἰουδαῖοι who discuss with Jesus matters like slavery and freedom, lineal descent and birthright, bondage to sin and injustice, the same group? We have deconstructed this idea already on the story-level by using a scheme of veridiction. According to the words of Jesus he is talking to the Ἰουδαῖοι which try to kill him (8:37). As mentioned before, ζητέω has a juridical connotation and means "investigate" or "trying to make a case." The juridical isotopy is confirmed through the use of κρίνω. Thus,

---

[37] Cf. D. Granskou: "Anti-Judaism in the Passion Accounts of the Fourth Gospel," pp. 214–15.

the narratee has an indication that the Ἰουδαῖοι Jesus is talking to do not represent the believing Ἰουδαῖοι but the authorities in the temple. Then the act of stoning in 8:59 is not a form of summary justice by the people but by representatives of the official authorities who think they have "a case." Otherwise it would be impossible to understand that Jesus still has adherents among the Ἰουδαῖοι as the following chapters suggest.

The conclusion is that the level of narration confirms the interpretation of the story-level. There is no anti-Judaism. The Ἰουδαῖοι that are rejected by Jesus in John 8, the Ἰουδαῖοι that are involved in the verdict to execute Jesus, and the Ἰουδαῖοι that are in debate with Pilate and agree with the crucifixion are no ordinary Jews but are identified by the narrator as authorities, not in the "real" world of the (first) readers but in the narrated world of Jesus and his people.

4. *The Contextual Level: Communication of the Reader with the Text (The Reader and the Jews)*

The second level of Martyn's two-level drama overshadows the first. Most of the exegetes concentrate on the history of the Johannine school while neglecting the fact that John tries to tell a story about Jesus and his time. They identify the narrator, almost unproblematically, with the evangelist, the Ἰουδαῖοι with the leaders in the synagogues of Asia Minor, and the narratee with the Johannine community. But what if we do not comply with this hypothesis that first became consensus and then doctrine?

Analyzing the communication between narrator and narratee, the conclusion is that the narrator is well informed on Judaism but his narratee is not. The fact that he informs his narratee about Jewish practices like burials and purity, feasts like Passover and Tabernacles, special days like preparation, and religious terms like Messiah and rabbi means that if we are going to deduce an extra-textual context for the Gospel of John, we cannot think of Jewish Christians formerly connected to the synagogue. Martyn thinks of four groups of Jews as possible "referents" in the time the Gospel was written: (1) "Jews" within the synagogue that rejected the belief in Jesus; (2) "Christian Jews" within the synagogue that believed secretly in Jesus; (3) other "Jewish Christians" who had been expelled from the synagogue; (4) the Johannine community of "Jewish Christians."[38] Although there exists a huge consensus among post-Martynnian scholars to this idea,[39] on the basis of a narrative analysis this idea has to be called to question. The idea that the first readers of the Gospel were Christian Jews, expelled from the synagogue or rejecting the high christology of the Johannine group, is contrary to the notion of a non-Jewish narratee. If there were conflicts—ecclesiological or theological—they did not belong to the present or the recent past of the first Johannine readers.

The context of the Gospel of John is not given by the text. It is a reconstruction of the exegete, i.e., the reader, on the base of indications of the text. If ἀποσυνάγωγος refers to a historical situation post-Jesus—but that is not necessary—it might as well refer to the period before the destruction of the Temple. A. Reinhartz questions Martyn's two-level reading on narrative arguments and abandons the exclusion theory of Johannine Christians.[40] The Gospel tells its story to non-Jewish readers; intramural problems between Jews (Jewish Christians, Crypto-Christians, and Jews that reject Jesus) are of no concern for them. So if the Gospel reflects intramural conflicts they were really intramural; the narrator takes his non-Jewish audience back to the old times of conflicting Jews. The Johannine polemic parallels debates that existed among various competing religious groups within Judaism. C. Evans parallels its polemic with that of Qumran that surpasses John's in intensity and harshness; Qumran's opponents are the authorities of Jerusalem, the Pharisees, and the

---

[38] J.L. Martyn, "Glimpses into the History of the Johannine Community," pp. 149–75.

[39] R.E. Brown, *The Community of the Beloved Disciple* (pp. 76–78), identifies the "Jews" in John 8:31 as "Jewish Christians" that rejected the high christology of the Johannine Christians; this idea is elaborated by M. Rissi: "'Die Juden' im Johannesevangelium," who identifies the Jews as "Christian Jews" with a low christology (p. 2119); he calls their existence "das Problem der johanneischen Gemeinde" (p. 2127); see also J. McHugh, "'In Him was Light': John's Gospel and the Parting of the Ways," who states that 8:3–59 is "a polemic ... not against Jews but against Jewish converts ... unwilling to accept the full Johannine doctrine about Jesus Christ" (p. 143); see also, with some small changes, H.J. de Jonge, "'The Jews' in the Gospel of John," who thinks that the polemic was not aimed against non-Christian Jews but against non-Johannine Christians (p. 240).

[40] A. Reinhartz, "'Jews' and Jews in the Fourth Gospel," pp. 351–53; see also De Jonge, "'The Jews' in the Gospel of John," who claims that the excommunication is a literary invention of the evangelist (p. 257).

High Priest who is called the "Wicked Priest" and a "Preacher of Lies."[41] So it is not impossible to date the harsh polemic in John at the time of Jesus. And although Culpepper sticks to a date after the destruction of the Temple, he tries to prove that the debates reflect really Jewish ideas. He calls his analysis a deconstruction of the anti-Judaic character of John's theology.[42]

Most scholars, even the ones that reject the exclusion theory, think that the high christology of John is the obstacle between Christian Jews and the Johannine group. They understand Ἰουδαῖοι as Christian Jews with a low christology. This is probably not incorrect (and not incompatible with the idea that these low-christology Jews were contemporaries of Jesus). But how about these scholars' understanding of Jesus' part in the discussion as non-Jewish theology? How about the understanding of high christology as anti-Judaic? D. Hagner defines anti-Judaism—in contrast with anti-Semitism as racial hatred of the Jews—as "theological disagreement with Judaism."[43] How opposed are the theological ideas of the Johannine Jesus against Judaism? Culpepper states that the christology of the Fourth Gospel as well as its theology and ecclesiology are "thoroughly Jewish."[44] At the same time they are anti-Jewish, Culpepper says, because they leave no place for Judaism apart from Jesus. He thinks that this fulfillment-replacement motif renders Judaism invalid by Jesus' coming.[45] He is mistaken.

The idea that the coming of the Messiah fulfills Judaism is not an anti-Judaic idea. Even the claim (false or not) that the Messiah is identified in Jesus (which is the story of John) is not anti-Judaic, certainly not in Jesus' time. It is, perhaps not really an open but truly Judaic discussion. Culpepper's idea that the deconstructive elements in John must be found in bridging Jewish and anti-Jewish elements lies one bridge too far. The deconstruction of the anti-Jewish theology of John is not a matter of setting in opposition the anti-Jewish elements against the Jewish elements (as Culpepper does), but by showing that its supposed anti-Jewish elements are in fact Jewish.

---

[41] Evans, "Introduction," p. 8, in C. Evans and P.W. Flint (ed.), *Eschatology, Messianism, and the Dead Sea Scrolls*.
[42] Culpepper, "Anti-Judaism," p. 91.
[43] D.A. Hagner, "Paul's Quarrel with Judaism," p. 128.
[44] Culpepper, "Anti-Judaism," pp. 80, 85, and 87.
[45] Culpepper, "Anti-Judaism," p. 81.

Of course there is no clear-cut first century Jewish theology. There are many competing notions, not least concerning the concept of the messiah. Alleged anti-Judaic, in the sense of deviating newfangled theology and invalidating Jewish practices, are the following elements in the Fourth Gospel summed up by Culpepper:[46]

- replacement of the festivals by Jesus' person
- replacement of the Temple by Jesus' person (2:21; 4:23)
- the Scriptures testify on Jesus' behalf (5:39)
- Sabbath observance is superseded by worship on the first day of the week (21:19.26)
- the Torah is abolished: it is "your law" (8:17)
- the three principal covenants—the Abrahamic covenant of sonship, the Mosaic covenant of deliverance and fidelity, the Davidic covenant of kingship—are abolished by John's claim of salvation exclusively through Jesus
- the high christology of John supersedes the revelation of God in Israel
- the church has taken the place of Israel.

Contrary to Culpepper, I submit that the deconstructive elements have to be sought not (only) in John's affirmation of Jewish heritage—"Salvation is of the Jews" (4:22)—but in deconstructing the Christian interpretation of John. I agree with Culpepper that "texts do not yield to consistent, stable interpretations."[47] However, Culpepper himself reproduces some hardened interpretations. None of the summed up anti-Judaic elements of John are in the text of the Gospel. They all belong to Christian interpretations of nineteenth and twentieth century cultures where supersessionism—the superiority of Christianity over Judaism—was a (regretted and excused for) starting point for exegesis. But it is not in John; it is read into John.

The Christian interpretations of John are deconstructed if we can show that the difference between alleged anti-Judaic and Judaic elements in John could be brought back to a difference within Judaic discussions. For this deconstructive project, I can only give some indications:

1) The festivals are not replaced by Jesus. The context of John 8 is the Feast of Tabernacles and John does not abolish this feast. He

---

[46] Culpepper, "Anti-Judaism," pp. 81–87.
[47] Culpepper, "Anti-Judaism," p. 82.

uses Judaic festival elements such as Light and Water[48] to characterize the figure of the Messiah. The fact that Christians in later times do not celebrate this feast anymore influenced the interpretation that the Johannine Jesus replaced the festival; as such, it is not found in John. The same applies to the Passover; it is not replaced but undergoes interpretive (not anti-Judaic) work; the abolition of human sacrifices through Abraham is universalized; that is not a Christian replacement but a distinctive Judaic meaning.[49]

2) In the Gospel narrative, the Temple is not an invalid Judaic place but "the house of my Father," confirmed by a quotation from Psalm 69:10: "Zeal for thy house will consume me" (2:16–17).[50]

3) The Scriptures do not simply testify on Jesus' behalf, but on the Messiah's behalf. On the story-level, the identification of the Messiah is established at the outset, starting with the cross-examination of John the Baptist (1:19–23), which is an intra-Jewish affair. The questions about the Messiah, Elijah, and the Prophet (Deut 18:15–17), in this context, make clear that the Judaic debates are not only about the identification of the Messiah but also about the nature of his function. The person of Jesus does not tell the Jews what the function of the Messiah is, the Scriptures do. The Scriptures, as such, are not abolished by Jesus. That the fulfilment of the Scriptures should be an anti-Judaic element is nonsense in se. The fact that many Jews against many others saw the fulfillment in Jesus is another proof of the intra-Judaic debate; and, as pointed out in the analysis of the story-level, the Gospel shows no interest in the gojim.

4) The idea that the Sabbath is replaced by "worship on the first day of the week" (21:19.26) is either an example of eisegesis or a historical projection. It could be that later Christians read an installation of a new Sabbath in these verses, but there is no textual indication that John meant it that way.

5) The same applies to the alleged abolition of the Law. Culpepper and others read 8:17 as though some Christian had spoken those

---

[48] Cf. H. Ulfgard, *Feast and Future. Revelation 7:9–17 and the Feast of Tabernacles*, who sees John's interpretation of the water as a sign of the Spirit as a parallel to later rabbinic discussion (pp. 117–18).

[49] Cf. B. Chilton, *The Temple of Jesus*, who considers Jesus' teaching of purity culminated in the sacrifice of his body as a Jewish program (pp. 155–54).

[50] According to Chilton, Jesus' occupation of the Temple was a natural result of his teaching as a rabbi: "Jesus was a rabbi who developed a distinctive view of what purity was"; Chilton, *The Temple of Jesus*, p. 138.

words ("your Law") but, as mentioned above, it is the voice of a Jewish prophet reprimanding his people in a traditional prophetic way.

6) The abolition of the three principal covenants is also pure interpretation. Again, fulfillment is not anti-Judaic. It only sounds like that if one equals fulfillment with replacement. But this equalization is a late Christian thought and not a Johannine idea. We must learn to read John as a Jewish document again. The way the narrator introduces Judaic practices and inside information makes it possible to understand the implied author against a Judaic background, telling a Jewish story with intramural Judaic debates to a partly non-Jewish implied reader.

7) The idea that the high christology of the Gospel of John underwent a non-Jewish or non-Palestinian influence is incorrect.[51] The connection of the notions Son of God and Messiah turned out to be known in Qumran.[52] The deification of human beings in early Judaism is confirmed by many scholars as of the latest current in the Historical Jesus Research.[53] So-called typical Johannine ideas as the indwelling of God in human beings and the μένειν ἐν proved to be ideas from the MT and the LXX.[54] The idea of a pre-existent Messiah in early Judaism was rejected by Strack and Billerbeck,[55] but since then it has been many times confirmed, for instance, by Culpepper himself.[56]

---

[51] Charlesworth has listed fifteen examples of the term "Son of God" in the literature that has been preserved from Early Judaism; because of this he rejects the idea that "it cannot derive from the Jew, Jesus of Nazareth"; J. Charlesworth, *Jesus within Judaism*, pp. 149–52; see also J. McGrath, *John's Apologetic Christology*, pp. 52–67.

[52] 4Q246; cf. C. Evans, "Jesus and the Dead Sea Scrolls from Qumran Cave 4"; Evans thinks that the identification of the Messiah as the Son of God goes against the view that this language derives from non-Palestinian Hellenistic sources (p. 94).

[53] See the overview in C. Newman (et al.), *The Jewish Roots of Monotheism*, Leiden etc. 1999; see also W. Telford, "Major Trends and Interpretation Issues in the Study of Jesus," pp. 33–74; see more specific L. Hurtado, *One God, One Lord*, London 1988; and recently M.G. Abegg, Jr., "Who Ascended to Heaven? 4Q491, 4Q427, and the Teacher of Righteousness," esp. p. 63. An older study about the deification of human beings is W. Meeks, "Moses as God and King," pp. 354–71.

[54] Cf. E. Malatesta, *Interiority and Covenant*, pp. 42–77; see also Kl. Scholtissek, *In ihm sein und bleiben*, pp. 75–96.

[55] H. Strack and P. Billerbeck, *Das Evangelium nach Markus, Lukas und Johannes und die Apostelgeschichte erläutert aus Talmud und Midrasch*, pp. 333–52.

[56] Culpepper, "Anti-Judaism," pp. 85–86; on the pre-existence and hypostases of Wisdom and Tora not as teaching, salvation, or guidance but as a real person and

8) Finally, the suggestion that the church in John has taken the place of Israel is again pure interpretation, prompted by shame over the historical grown idea of supersessionism. John sticks to really Jewish ideas like the Good Shepherd and his Sheep (John 10:1–18; cf. Ezek 34:1–31; Num 27:16–17), the Vine and his Branches (John 15:1–8; cf. Ps 80:8–18; Isa 5:1–7), but also the idea of the chosen people and the twelve tribes of Israel (οὐκ ἐγὼ ὑμᾶς τοὺς δώδεκα ἐξελεξάμην; John 6:70; cf. Deut 7:6; Ps 89:3).[57] Again we have to be careful not to mix up fulfillment with replacement. Because of the absence of non-Jewish characters in the story and because of John's silence on the gojim and their entrance into the community of the Children of God, one has to conclude that in the end only Jewish people are followers of Jesus.[58] Every other context does not form part of the text and is brought in by readers.

5. *Conclusions*

This article has undertaken a threefold deconstruction (story, narration, and context) of two objects. These objects are at the one hand the interpretations of John's Gospel: Culpepper's deconstructive attempt as well as the many interpretations of anti-Judaism as a "historical" conflict; and on the other hand the text of the Gospel itself: the opposition between "Jesus" (or, according to many interpretations, "the Johannine community")[59] and the "Jews" can be deconstructed as an opposition between Jews. Deconstruction here is akin to the approach taken by B. Johnson who considers a situation, or a text, or an interpretation, to be deconstructed if the opposites between matters are reduced to an opposition within one of these matters.

"a calling I," see G. von Rad, *Theologie des Alten Testaments, Band I, Die Theologie der geschichtlichen Überlieferungen Israels*, pp. 458–61; for a more recent discussion see D. Boyarin: "The Gospel of the *Memra*: Jewish Binitarianism and the Prologue to John," pp. 243–84.

[57] Cf. Scholtissek, "Antijudaismus im Johannesevangelium?," who states that the Fourth Gospel elaborates the mission of Jesus to Israel as the people of God (p. 176).

[58] The broadening to non-Jewish people can only be read at one place in the Gospel: κἀγὼ ἀπέστειλα αὐτοὺς εἰς κόσμον (17:18).

[59] Tomson states that "Jesus is the editor's champion in his own community's conflict with 'The Jews' and 'their law'" (Tomson, "The Names Israel and Jew," p. 282).

On the story-level, the grammar and logic of John 8 clash with each other. The narrative logic forbids to identify the Ἰουδαῖοι who came to believe in Jesus (v. 31) with the persons who try to kill him (37 and 40). Although grammatically, verse 33 (and thus 37 and 40) refers to 31, it logically refers to persons who have the authority to execute death penalties, such as the ones who enter the scene in 8:3. I choose logic and narrative force above grammatical rigor: in verse 8:31 the Ἰουδαῖοι are believers out of the common people; in 8:33ff. (ἀπεκρίθησαν, "they answered") *they* refers to the authorities. The deconstruction of the idea that the Ἰουδαῖοι of 8:31 (believing Jews) are the same as the ones that try to kill him is illustrated by the scheme of veridiction. In the narrative grammar of Greimas, the identification of both categories is called a lie and (after the démasqué) a secret. The Ἰουδαῖοι are legal authorities and the context of John 8 is that of a law-court. The authorities in the temple are not the only Ἰουδαῖοι and their response to kill Jesus is not the only thinkable. Other responses are possible and were given: simply walk away (John 6:66) or stay with Jesus and believe in him (passim).

On the level of narration (the technique of telling the story), this deconstruction is confirmed by the juridical isotopy handled by the narrator. Every time juridical terms and situations appear, the narrator, and in his mind, the (implied) reader, knows that the Ἰουδαῖοι in this context have to be considered as authorities. John 8 is the preliminary state of the questioning in John 18–19, the authorities are preparing a case as if it was a pilot-process. The discussion of Law-interpretation, starting with the case of the adulterous woman, the debate on witnessing and testimonies, is embedded by the stones of verdict that threaten the woman in 8:5 and Jesus in 8:59. From this juridical isotopy, the narratee and the implied reader have to conclude that the Ἰουδαῖοι in John 8 are Jewish authorities. The juridical debate with the Pharisees and the scribes stressed in 8:5, 8:13–19, and 8:26 by words like νόμος, μαρτυρία, κρίνω, and κρίσις is continued in 8:33ff. The narrative situation forces us to distinguish between a situation of teaching the Jewish people (8:2 and 8:31) and a situation of discussing Law (passim in John 8). Jesus tries to continue in 8:31 his teachings of 8:2. But he is interrupted by the authorities in 8:33. The Jews that believe in Jesus (8:31) are not the same as the ones who seek to kill him (8:37.40)—which would be pure nonsense. Apart from the threatening death-sentence and the use of juridical terms the continuation of the juridical discussion is clearly shown in 8:46—τίς ἐξ ὑμῶν ἐλέγχει με περὶ ἁμαρτίας "which of you convicts me of sin?"—and by the statement that in the end God ("my Father") will judge (8:50; κρίνων).

Deconstruction on the third level, that is, the contextual level of the communication between the text and its (current) readers, consists of analyzing (current) interpretations as Christian interpretations. The reader is free to interpret the scene of John 8 on several historical levels. However, the interpretation that "the Jews" in John are taken rhetorically as non-Johannine Christians is anti-Semitic. For, in that case, one says that the Christian writer teaches erring Christians a lesson by telling them that they are as wrong as Jews in the times of Jesus, as if the evangelist sees Jews as a wrongful category.[60] This is not Johannine at all. John has an exclusive interest in Jews and a remarkable indifference towards the gojim. This observation is even more special considering the fact that the supposed narratees are non-Jewish persons. It indicates that the (Jewish informed) narrator wants them to see the mission of Jesus really and originally as a Jewish mission. Furthermore, it can be shown that none of the summed up anti-Judaic elements of John is in the text of the Gospel itself. They all belong to Christian interpretations of nineteenth and twentieth century cultures where supersessionism— the superiority of Christianity over Judaism—was a (regretted and excused for) starting point for exegesis. But again, it is not in John; it is read into John. The Christian interpretations of John can be considered as deconstructed if the difference *between* alleged anti-Judaic and Judaic elements in John are brought back to a difference *within* Judaic discussions.

In his paper for the Leuven Colloquium, R.A. Culpepper apologetically qualifies that his deconstruction of the Johannine anti-Judaism is only a first step, but—so he quotes an old Chinese proverb— "... even the longest journey begins with a single step."[61] By this modest quotation, Culpepper claims to be the first one ever to have deconstructed the anti-Judaism in John. Well, let's say that I have tried, not to take a second step, but to go back to the point of departure.

---

[60] Cf. M.C. de Boer, "The Depiction of 'the Jews' in John's Gospel: Matters of Behavior and Identity," who states that Johannine Jewish Christians came to abandon the term "the Jews" for themselves and generalized it to identify in an ironic (even sarcastic) way Jesus' opponents (p. 279).

[61] Culpepper, "Anti-Judaism," p. 91.

Some years ago I asked Sjef van Tilborg, who was a dedicated practitioner of Tai Chi for years, how long it took before he received his diploma. Ignoring the irony, he answered: "I hear that you are not acquainted with the old Taoist saying that 'life is just one step'; accomplishing this step would mean death, you fool." Sjef used to teach his students that wisdom and truth are seldom friends. Truth is given by scholars, wisdom by gurus. Truth can be deconstructed, wisdom lies beyond our grasp.

Bibliography

Abegg, M.G. Jr., "Who Ascended to Heaven? 4Q491, 4Q427, and the Teacher of Rigtheousness" (61–73) in C.A. Evans and P.W. Flint (editors), *Eschatology, Messianism, and the Dead Sea Scrolls*, Grand Rapids, Michigan-Cambridge, U.K. 1997.
Ashton, J., *Understanding the Fourth Gospel*, Oxford 1991.
Bieringer R., Pollefeyt D., and Vandecasteele-Vanneuville F. (ed.), *Anti-Judaism and the Fourth Gospel. Papers of the Leuven Colloquium, 2000*, Assen 2001.
Boer, M.C. de, "The Depiction of "the Jews" in John's Gospel: Matters of Behavior and Identity" (260–80) in R. Bieringer, D. Pollefeyt, and F. Vandecasteele-Vanneuville (ed.), *Anti-Judaism and the Fourth Gospel. Papers of the Leuven Colloquium, 2000*, Assen 2001.
Boyarin, D., "The Gospel of the *Memra*: Jewish Binitarianism and the Prologue to John," in *Harvard Theological Review*, 94 (2001) 243–84.
Brown, R.E., *The Community of the Beloved Disciple. The Life, Loves, and Hates of an Individual Church in New Testament Times*, New York-Mahwah 1979.
Caron, G., *Qui sont les Juifs de l'évangile de Jean?* Québec 1997.
Charlesworth, J., *Jesus within Judaism. New Light from Exciting Archaeological Discoveries*, London 1989.
Chatelion Counet, P., *John a Postmodern Gospel; Introduction to Deconstructive Exegesis Applied to the Fourth Gospel*, Leiden etc. 2000.
Chilton, B., *The Temple of Jesus. His Sacrificial Program Within a Cultural History of Sacrifice*, Pennsylvania 1992.
Culpepper, R.A., *The Anatomy of the Fourth Gospel: A Study in Literary Design*, Philadelphia 1983.
———, "Anti-Judaism in the Fourth Gospel as a Theological Problem for Christian Interpreters" (68–91) in R. Bieringer, D. Pollefeyt, and F. Vandecasteele-Vanneuville (ed.), *Anti-Judaism and the Fourth Gospel. Papers of the Leuven Colloquium, 2000*, Assen 2001.
Derrida, J., *De la grammatologie*, Paris 1967.
———, "La Pharmacie de Platon," in J. Derrida, *La dissémination*, Paris 1972.
———, *Positions. Entretiens avec Henri Rose, Julia Kristeva, Jean-Luis Houdebine, Guy Scarpetta*, Paris 1972.
———, "Lettre à un ami japonais" (387–93), in J. Derrida, *Psyché. Inventions de l'autre*, Paris 1987.
Dunn, J.D.G. (ed.), *Jews and Christians. The Parting of the Ways A.D. 70 to 135*, Tübingen 1992.
———, "The Question of Anti-semitism in the New Testament" (177–211) in J.D.G. Dunn (ed.), *Jews and Christians. The Parting of the Ways A.D. 70 to 135*, Tübingen 1992.

Evans, C.A., "Jesus and the Dead Sea Scrolls from Qumran Cave 4" (91–100) in C.A. Evans and P.W. Flint (editors), *Eschatology, Messianism, and the Dead Sea Scrolls*, Grand Rapids, Michigan-Cambridge, U.K. 1997.

Frey, J., "Heiden-Griechen-Gotteskinder. Zu Gestalt und Funktion der Rede von den Heiden im 4. Evangelium," in R. Feldmeier and U. Heckel (Hrsg.), *Die Heiden. Juden, Christen und das Problem des Fremden* (228–68), Tübingen 1994.

Granskou, D., "Anti-Judaism in the Passion Accounts of the Fourth Gospel" (201–16) in P. Richardson (ed.), *Anti-Judaism in Early Christianity. Vol. 1. Paul and the Gospels*, Waterloo, Ontario 1986.

Greimas, A.J., and J. Courtès, *Sémiotique: Dictionaire Raisonné de la Théorie du Langage* (Tome 1 et 2), Paris 1979/1986.

Hagner, D.A., "Paul's Quarrel with Judaism" (128–50) in C.A. Evans and P.W. Flint (ed.), *Eschatology, Messianism, and the Dead Sea Scrolls*, Grand Rapids, Michigan-Cambridge, U.K. 1997.

Hurtado, L., *One God, One Lord. Early Christian Devotion and Ancient Jewish Monotheism*, London 1988.

Johnson, B., *The Critical Difference. Essays in the Contemporary Rhetoric of Reading*, Baltimore-London 1980.

Jonge, H.J. de, "'The Jews' in the Gospel of John" (239–59) in R. Bieringer, D. Pollefeyt, and F. Vandecasteele-Vanneuville (ed.), *Anti-Judaism and the Fourth Gospel. Papers of the Leuven Colloquium, 2000*, Assen 2001.

Kysar, R., "Anti-Semitism and the Gospel of John (113–27) in C.A. Evans and P.W. Flint (ed.), *Eschatology, Messianism, and the Dead Sea Scrolls*, Grand Rapids, Michigan-Cambridge, U.K. 1997.

Leach, E.R. and D. Alan Aycock, *Structuralist Interpretation of Biblical Myth*, Cambridge 1983.

Lieu, J., "Anti-Judaism in the Fourth Gospel. Explanation and Hermeneutics" (126–43) in R. Bieringer, D. Pollefeyt, and F. Vandecasteele-Vanneuville (ed.), *Anti-Judaism and the Fourth Gospel. Papers of the Leuven Colloquium, 2000*, Assen 2001.

Lowe, M., "Who Were the IOUDAIOI?," in *Novum Testamentum*, 19 (1976), 101–30.

Malatesta, E., *Interiority and Covenant. A Study of ei=nai evn and me,nein evn in the First Letter of Saint John*, Rome 1978.

Martyn, J.L., *History and Theology in the Fourth Gospel*, New York 1968.

——, "Glimpses into the History of the Johannine Community" (149–75) in M. de Jonge, *L'Evangile de Jean: Sources, Rédaction, Théologie*, Gembloux 1977.

McGrath, J., *John's Apologetic Christology. Legitimation and Development in Johannine Christology*, Cambridge 2001.

McHugh, J., "'In Him Was Light': John's Gospel and the Parting of the Ways" (123–58) in J.D.G. Dunn (ed.), *Jews and Christians. The Parting of the Ways A.D. 70 to 135*, Tübingen 1992.

Meeks, W., "Galilee and Judea in the Fourth Gospel," *Journal of Biblical Literature*, 85 (1966), 159–69.

——, "Moses as God and King" (354–71) in J. Neusner (ed.), *Religions in Antiquity; Essays in Memory of E.R. Goodenough*, Leiden 1968.

Menken, M., "Jezus tegenover de Farizeeën in het vierde evangelie: Joh. 8,12–20" (103–18) in T. Baarda et al. (ed.), *Jodendom en vroeg christendom; continuïteit en discontinuïteit*, Kampen 1991.

Newman, C. (et al.), *The Jewish Roots of Monotheism: Papers from the St. Andrews Conference on the Historical Origins of the Worship of Jesus*, Leiden etc. 1999.

Rad, G. von, *Theologie des Alten Testaments, Band I, Die Theologie der geschichtlichen Überlieferungen Israels*, München 1969.

Reinhartz, A., "'Jews' and Jews in the Fourth Gospel" (341–69) in R. Bieringer, D. Pollefeyt, and F. Vandecasteele-Vanneuville (ed.), *Anti-Judaism and the Fourth Gospel. Papers of the Leuven Colloquium, 2000*, Assen 2001.

Rimmon-Kenan, S., *Narrative Fiction. Contemporary Poetics*, London and New York 1983.
Rissi, M., "'Die Juden' im Johannesevangelium" (2099–2141) in *Aufstieg und Niedergang der römischen Welt (Teil II: Principat; Band 26.3)*, Berlin-New York 1996.
Scholtissek, K., "Antijudaismus im Johannesevangelium? Ein Gesprächsbeitrag" (151–81) in R. Kampling (hrsg.), *"Nun steht aber diese Sache im Evangelium..." Zur Frage nach den Anfängen des christlichen Antijudaismus*, Paderborn 1999.
———, *In ihm sein und bleiben: die Sprache der Immanenz in den johanneischen Schriften*, Freiburg etc. 1999.
Strack, H., and P. Billerbeck, *Das Evangelium nach Markus, Lukas und Johannes und die Apostelgeschichte erläutert aus Talmud und Midrasch*, München 1924.
Telford, W., "Major Trends and Interpretation Issues in the Study of Jesus" (33–74) in Bruce Chilton and Craig Evans (ed.), *Studying the Historical Jesus: Evaluations of the State of Current Research*, Leiden 1994.
Tilborg, Sj. van, "Jezus temidden van de Joden van het Loofhuttenfeest in Johannes 8," in H.J.M. Schoot (ed.), *Theologie en Exegese—Jaarboek 2001 Thomas Instituut Utrecht*, 21 (2002) 53–66.
Tolmie, D.F., *Narratology and Biblical Narratives: A Practical Guide*, San Francisco etc. 1999.
Tomson, P., *"If this be from heaven..." Jesus and the New Testament Authors in Their Relationship to Judaism*, Sheffield 2001.
———, "The Names Israel and Jew in Ancient Judaism and in the New Testament," in *Bijdragen, tijdschrift voor filosofie en theologie*, 47 (1986) 120–40 and 266–89.
Ulfgard, H., *Feast and Future. Revelation 7:9–17 and the Feast of Tabernacles*, Stockholm 1989.
Vaux, R. de, *Les Institutions de l'Ancien Testament*, Paris 1958.
Wahlde, U. von, "The Johannine 'Jews.' A Critical Survey," in *New Testament Studies*, 28 (1982) 33–60.
———, "The 'Jews' in the Gospel of John. Fifteen years of research (1983–1998)," in *Ephemerides Theologicae Lovanienses* 79 (2000) 30–55.
Zumstein, J., "Analyse narrative, critique rhétorique et exégèse johannique," in P. Bühler and J.F. Habermacher (ed.), *La Narration: Quand le récit devient communication*, Genève 1988.

CHAPTER ELEVEN

WHAT ON EARTH (OR IN HEAVEN) IS A RESURRECTED BODY? THE OUTLINE OF A HISTORICAL-ANTHROPOLOGICAL ANSWER

Pieter F. Craffert
Department of New Testament
University of South Africa

In this essay, which is offered as a tribute to the memory of a friend, a great scholar, and an exceptional person, the outline of a historical-anthropological answer to the above question will be sketched. A few weeks before his untimely death, I received an e-mail from Sjef encouraging me to complete the research project on Jesus as historical figure from a historical-anthropological point of view. It is an approach which, in search of the "living reality" of others, goes a step further than the "content-oriented approach" which he supported. As far as I know, he never ventured into that terrain himself, but his encouragement and critical responses to my attempts are highly appreciated and will be missed in the future. This essay is offered in the spirit (not *pneuma*) in which he approached research: experimental, preliminary, and pushing against the boundaries.

1. *"With What Kind of Body Do They Come?"*

It is virtually impossible to read the New Testament and not be confronted with the question of what a resurrected body consisted in the conception of those authors. The gospels tell of Jesus' resurrected body which appeared and disappeared after his death and Paul talks about a *soma pneumatikon* which awaits believing followers of Jesus and which presumably befell Jesus. Therefore, the question what on earth did their conceptions of a resurrected body consist of follows naturally.

This question is matched by a similar question about the composition of the sun, asked at the beginning of the last century. In the early 1920's a young Harvard doctoral student, Cecelia Payne, looked at the evidence of the spectroscope lines of the sun and suggested that the sun was over 90 percent hydrogen with the rest being like helium. "Her thesis adviser declared her wrong, and then *his* old thesis adviser, the imperious Henry Norris Russell, declared her wrong, and against him there was very little recourse" (Bodanis 2000:181) because up to that point the evidence was interpreted that the sun was about 66 percent pure iron. They forced her to insert the following humiliating line in her published thesis: "The enormous abundance [of hydrogen] ... is almost certainly not real" (quoted in 181). Today there is not a single sun-as-iron theorist left (not even at Harvard University!) while it is accepted that almost 75% of this spectroscope, indeed, reflects hydrogen and another 24% helium.

There are several lessons to be learned from this incident. The first is that Harvard University (as all other prestigious universities in the world) presumably had a large annual budget for the sun-as-iron research. That theory constituted a set of assumptions about an aspect of the world which were taken as real and which governed scientists' reality-talk. Secondly, it would not cross our minds to call the sun-as-iron theory *mythological* or only *apparently real*. Thirdly, if Harvard professors at the beginning of the last century did not share the commonly accepted view of today's scientists about the sun, we should not think that ancient people had a remotely similar view of the sun or the planets. In fact, they did not, and that only reminds us that they also did not have remotely similar views on many other aspects of life, such as on the nature of the human body or being or the acquisition of knowledge about them.

Back to the question of what a resurrected body is, what is real, and what is not. This is no new question since in his first letter to the Corinthians (15:35) already Paul says that there are some people who ask: "How are the dead raised? With what kind of body do they come?" There is no easy answer to this question, as the variety of scholarly proposals demonstrates. It is patently clear that exegetes are aware that references to resurrected bodies (either that of Jesus shortly after his death or the future resurrection bodies which await believers) are odd and require some explanation or translation in a modern world-view.

Two ethnocentric and anachronistic strategies are followed in bridging the gap. Those which start with ancient concepts and translate them into quasi-modern equivalents short-circuit the cultural gap from the ancient side. At the one end of the spectrum are forms of pure mystification where the foreign cultural concepts are explained by using mystifying concepts which have no reality value in our world-view. For example, Wright (1999:120) describes Jesus' resurrected body as a body of *"transformed* physicality, with new properties and attributes but still concrete and physical." Quantum physics has sophisticated ways of explaining how mass, energy, and information are reverse sides of each other, but that is a long shot from something like *transformed physicality*. Is this something like *supernatural chemistry*?

At the other end of the same mystifying spectrum are those who explicitly rely on supernaturalism as an explanatory principle: "It seems that an omnipotent being would have it well within its power to make a human body materialize in a room" (Davis 1997:134). Is this something like *supernatural biology*? As will become clear below, both positions are the product of a Cartesian world-view where the *supernatural* category was created.

Another position claims that Jesus' resurrected body was a *material object* of some kind which took up space and occupied a certain location because it could be *seen*. As far as the argument goes, because it was *seen* it must have been a *material* body; "a glorified body (*soma*) is still a body—that is, still a material object that can be seen" (Davis 1997:140). The weaknesses of both the foregoing positions are discussed in detail in another study (see Craffert 2002c) where the ethnocentric view on *seeing* is discussed. Seeing, in this view, can only imply the seeing of a material object with physical eyes (but that was not the case, as will become clear below).

It is now time to turn to the issue of *materiality*. Craig (1995:157), for example, says that the transformation of the earthly body to a *soma pneumatikon* "does not rescue it from materiality, but from mortality." While some commentators do try to explain Paul's concept of a resurrected body as a nonmaterial or nonphysical body, this strategy correctly points out that for Paul it was, indeed, a material object since he could not conceive a "noncorporeal" or a "nonbody body" (Martin 1995:128). The problem with this strategy, however, is the assumption that *materiality* is a universal concept. It is one thing to admit that for Paul such a body was a material entity; it is quite a different cup of tea to assume that we can share his view of materiality.

Strategies in the other direction short-circuit the cultural gap from the side of a modern view of reality by declaring those ancient accounts "mythological" or not "really real." Whatever they were, they were not about *our reality*. For example, in a recent study with his Nijmegen colleague, Patrick Chatelion Counet, van Tilborg (see 2000:187) offers a double-barrelled analysis of Luke 24 in which he offers the following description of Luke's image of Jesus' resurrected body:

> When Jesus died his *pneuma* was taken up into the hands of his father; Jesus was then in Paradise ... his body remained a day or two in Hades but God did not leave it there. God allowed Jesus' body to come alive again and so Jesus entered his glory.... Jesus became visible to the disciples in Jerusalem a number of times immediately after his resurrection. Then he was taken up into heaven by God.

This is foreign to his own world for, van Tilborg (2000:229) says, such stories are "about quite different things in our (I think late 20th century) minds." Here, he says, mythology "runs rampant" (2000:6) and "Luke is not the only author who creates room for leaps of imagination when mythological language and images are the order of the day" (2000:187).

Van Tilborg (2000:231) observes that "modern exegesis is text-oriented, while the old exegesis was more content-oriented." Luke told his stories "in a culture in which stories about Greek heroes and heroines were a living reality" he says. *Content-oriented* exegesis clearly means that such stories were a "living reality" for ancient people in the sense of real and living stories in their world.

One of the most ethnocentric interpretations on this spectrum comes from Crossan (see 1998:37), who is well aware that the ancient world was filled with stories about gods, goddesses, spirits, immortals and the like which often assumed *bodily* forms. They had *bodies* but not flesh, and therefore he claims, those were "seeming-bodies, play-bodies, in-appearance-only bodies." The bodies with which these divine beings appeared were "like our special-effects movies today. Sometimes we see body but not flesh..." (1998:xxviii).

This strategy is to short-circuit the cross-cultural process by applying modern distinctions to ancient descriptions. In other words, he realizes that ancient people had different descriptions about human beings (and divine beings for that matter) but those are not treated as expressions of any cultural reality. They were "not *really* real... only *apparently* real" (1998:37). Their descriptions are immediately assumed into a modern view of reality and thus translated into modern jargon. This is a very special form of ethnocentrism where other people's descriptions of experienced bodies are incorporated in a modern distinction between real bodies and apparent (or special effects) bodies.

His explanation of Jesus' bodily resurrection thus finds expression within this strategy: it "has nothing to do with a resuscitated body coming out of its tomb.... Bodily resurrection means that the embodied life and death of the historical Jesus continues to be experienced, by believers, as powerfully efficacious and salvifically present in this world" (Crossan 1999:46). What exactly this last description means is not at all clear. This kind of mystification does not help a bit in unravelling the meaning of cultural realities which exist as lived and experienced realities for other people.

How do we bridge the cultural gap and arrive at an understanding of what ancient people were talking about when they spoke about resurrected bodies? From a historical-anthropological point of view, the fact is stressed that this very question is culturally stamped because resurrected bodies were related to ancient conceptions of human beings and bodies (as Paul's version of the question illustrates: the assumption was it was a *body*; the question was, what *kind of body*). Our questions are what did he mean by body and can we share his view on the many kinds of bodies?

The road to an answer is littered with several pitfalls. One is that of cross-cultural interpretation: how to go about conceptions of the body or human beings in one's own and a foreign culture and how to bridge the gap of cultural alienness that is encountered. Then there is the history of reflection about the body which has left us with the legacy of dualistic thinking, first ancient dualisms furthered by the Cartesian dualism. The question inevitably arises of whether it is at all possible to make sense of the ancient notion of a resurrected body and, if so, whether that can be translated to another cultural system.

2. A Historical-Anthropological Strategy

Ten years ago already Martin (1993:115) remarked that "most scholars engaged in social approaches to the New Testament claim to find sociology less and less helpful and anthropology and ethnography more and more interesting." Consequently, the so-called social-scientific interpretation developed into what I call "the anthropological turn in New Testament interpretation" (see Craffert 1995; 2002a).

It is an interdisciplinary venture which aims at reducing ethnocentrism and anachronism by way of consistent historical and descriptive holistic interpretations. That is to say, by acting as historical anthropologists, New Testament scholars address both the temporal and cultural gaps which separate them from the documents and they do so by making use of the insights and models from the social sciences, especially anthropology. The anthropological turn is the product of at least two related insights which forced themselves with great vigor onto the scene of New Testament studies. The first is the recognition of not only the historical but especially the cultural alienness of the New Testament documents. The second is the admission that language has meaning within a cultural system (see Malina 1991). The anthropological turn takes both these insights seriously and therefore converts New Testament interpretation into a cross-cultural endeavor—something it should have been all along for people living in a post-industrial, scientific world.

A historical-anthropological answer to the question of resurrected bodies therefore implies more than a contextual one because all the comparative stories from that environment are in the same predicament in belonging to the same cultural environment. It consists of at least three distinct tasks which are not necessarily performed in consecutive order: grasping the subjects' cultural system in the strongest possible light, paying attention to the interpreter's cultural system, and, by way of contrast, conducting cross-cultural comparisons. In other words, it acknowledges the cultural gap between modern readers and ancient texts and asserts that this gap cannot merely be short-circuited by jumping from those texts and meanings to present-day language or from simply judging them from a modern-day perspective.

3. Cultural Realities, Dualisms, and the Cycle of Meaning

An obvious fact, which is particularly important in this strategy, is that no New Testament author provides a well-worked-out anthropology or picture of the human being. They simply assumed an understanding of the human person together with the concepts prevalent in their time. Therefore, neither a word-study approach (see Green 1998:153) nor a content-oriented approach, listing all the comparative stories, will suffice in grasping their meaning. Instead, it is necessary to start with the cultural realities which determined the content and meaning of their concepts and stories.

3.1. *The Ancient Body-Soul Dualism and the Cartesian Mind-Body Dualism*

Most modern Western exegetes are heirs of the Cartesian mind-body dualistic ontology regarding the human person. To exaggerate a bit with Martin (1995:4),

> Descartes *invented* the category of "nature" as a closed, self-contained system, over against which he could oppose mind, soul, the spiritual, the psychological, and the divine.... In fact, Descartes quite self-consciously redefined "nature" to exclude those aspects of reality that he believed could not (and should not) be studied in terms of physical mechanism.

In his lifetime, this was a philosophical invention to save the world of consciousness (mind, soul) from the increasing power of a mechanistic, materialist, and reductionist world-view of the natural sciences (see Kriel 2000:86). In the words of Vorster (2000:105, 106):

> To remain loyal to his [Descartes] faith and create room for the existence of God, the essence of a human being is located in the consciousness, which can be substantially distinguished from the body. A hierarchic dichotomy is established between "mind" and "body." Both are seen as separate substances, with their unique essentialities, properties and modifications. However, it is consciousness, the mind, that determines the essence of personhood... the dichotomy mind versus body, not only joins a world of already existing dichotomies, such as essential versus peripheral, real versus illusionary, necessary versus contingent, but it also functions as catalyst in creating dichotomies such as rational versus emotional, reason versus passion.

The central feature of this ontology is the notion that body and mind (soul) represent two distinct substances which were part of two radically different realms of reality. In other words, the modern understanding of the category of the "supernatural" was created in this philosophical move (see also Saler 1977). What could be analyzed by means of the natural sciences was *natural*; the rest, such as consciousness (soul or spirit, if you like), was *supernatural*. Mind or soul was an immaterial entity which in no way depended for its existence on the existence or structure of any body (see Spurrett 2002:194). In so far as *pneuma*, usually translated as spirit, is allowed in opposition to the body (and not as one of the composing elements of all things), it is also usually seen as an immaterial thing—the body being material.

But Descartes's dichotomy has misled countless readers in their reading of ancient authors (see Martin 1995:6). The body-soul dualism found in numerous ancient (including biblical) texts should not be confused with the Cartesian dualism of matter versus nonmatter or physical versus spiritual (or natural versus supernatural) because, for them, the human being was a "commingling of substances" (1995:25 and see 1995:115) and the primary substances were body-stuff and soul-stuff. This logic was not one of ontological separate components but of a symbiotic unity of entities.

One should be clear about this. In both dualisms the "soul" was an entity which could be separated and often was divorced from the body but unlike the Cartesian soul, for the ancients, it was not of a different substance. The experience of the human self in antiquity was that of a separate entity of the same substance while for Descartes it was a separate entity of a different substance.

Modern exegetes' adoption of the Cartesian dualism together with its (mis)application to ancient texts has had far-reaching implications for modern thinking regarding the human being. As Brown (1998:99) indicates, a "frequent and historically dominant answer within Christian tradition has been that humans are endowed by a special act of creation with a separate entity which is the soul; that the soul has separate existence and perhaps even a separate realm of awareness and agency." The result of this position is that the human self-conscious experience is taken as indicating "an objectively existing self, or soul, or mind 'inside' the body" (Kriel 2000:85) but unlike the ancient dualisms (and similar to the Cartesian dualism), of a totally different composition (it is immaterial). At the same time, when thinking about the body, it must be a material object with physical properties—a viewpoint obviously adopted (quite wrongfully) when talking about resurrected bodies.

A body-soul dichotomy (ascribed to the ancients but filled in with a Cartesian dualism) still dominates most modern exegetical constructions of the human being. See, for example, how casually van Tilborg (in 2000:168) refers to "the soul-body dichotomy of which one becomes acutely aware each time a person dies...." Even in his rejection of dualism, Crossan (1999:39) remains locked into this discourse when insisting that we are "spiritual flesh or fleshly spirit" (whatever that might mean). Such mystifying language is not yet monism although rejecting dualism is, in my view, a step in the right direction. These are, however, not the only ways modern people talk about the human being.

3.2. *Monistic Views on the Human Being*

Since cross-cultural interpretation and comparison include the position of the interpreter, it is necessary to look at other modern constructions of the human being where such dichotomies no longer exist. It should already be clear that the concept "soul" is a complex concept with an intricate history. Modern *soul*-talk often takes place in two contexts: as a description of the human being ("human capacity and experience") or as that "part of the self that continues beyond death" (Brown 1998:100). The focus here will be only on the first part.

What our ancestors called "the *soul*" is today often called "the *self*" but that does not necessarily include talk about a part which continues beyond death. That is the case because although the history of soul- or self-talk is characterized by various forms of dualism, lately a "growing support for a monist, or physicalist, account of the human being" (Green 1998:149) has been recorded.

The cultural position which promotes a monistic position, Taylor (1991:304) ascribes to "radical reflexivity," while Spurrett (2002:192) says it was bought at the cost of divorcing prepositional and experiential claims from real and apparent ones. He explains it with the common notion of sunset-speech which we all ascribe to while knowing perfectly well that relative to the earth, the sun does not move; "sunrises are really earth-turnings" (the terms *real* and *really* are used in this paragraph in the same meaning). Things are not always as they seem to us or as we experience them and this applies both to sunsets and to self-speak or soul-talk. Radical reflexivity refers to that practice of not only having experiences but of scrutinizing them and subjecting them to reflexive thinking. Self-speak ("I said to myself...") and experiences of the self (like sunsets) will not go away and neither will the ability we have as language-using animals to make our bodies and our selves objects of description and reflection. In the words of Kriel (2002:143), "I can *be* my lived body or I can *observe* my body—step back (metaphorically speaking) and see (experience) my body as an object in the world. I can distinguish in language between myself as a lived body, and my objectified body. When I am my lived body, I do not have a consciousness, *I am my conscious body*" (italics his). But such experiences are no longer the sole source for constructing knowledge about the self.

Monism is the cultural position which realizes that the self (although it can be separated from the body in the experience of the self or in language) is embodied and connected to practices. The "self" is constituted in interaction with a specific environment and in conversation with others; it is an engendered and bodily self within a social environment. For a transplant of this self or consciousness (or soul, if you like) to any known or imaginable form would depend far more on the structure of the body and the world in which it lives than is often assumed: "If who we are depends a lot on the bodies we are, and the environments we are in, then being us in a new incarnation depends as much on information beyond the brain as it does on structures and content in the brain" (Spurrett 2002:216). From this point of view, the self or consciousness (or soul) is not "something inside the body. It is a manner of existence of certain highly complex animals, a manner of being-in-the-world of certain animal species.... Being conscious is related to material processes, but has a reality that cannot be ignored. Consciousness is a non-spatial aspect of biological reality" (Kriel 2000:93–94). Far from reducing reality to materiality, this position is based on a systems ontology which acknowledges that reality is not located in building blocks (material entities) only, but is "variegated and essentially organized as levels of complex systems" (2000:80).

The categories used to explore this monistic position are as diverse as the ancient dualist positions. They include the idea of a human self as constituted in conversation as a "dialogical self" (Taylor 1991:314), as a "distributed coalition of agents" (Spurrett 2002:216), or as *nonreductive physicalism* which asserts that the embodied soul is a "dimension of human experiences" which arises out of personal relatedness (Brown 1998:101). The self is a way of being: bodily, socially, and culturally, and is neither a component of nor equivalent to any of these.

If the experience of the self (soul/spirit) as distinct from the body is taken as the point of departure, four different cultural positions have been sketched here. Ancient people (like Paul and Luke) expressed their experience of the self in material-dualist terms: body and soul are separate entities (but different configurations) of similar substances. In the Cartesian dualism, body and mind are experienced and expressed as different entities composed of different substances. Most modern exegetes (while claiming to be truly biblical) are heirs of the Cartesian dualism (which is also wrongfully ascribed to the ancients) in which body and soul are seen as belonging to separate realities and thus are different kinds of entities. The cultural position of monism is based on the practice of radical reflexivity plus a systems ontology in which experience is not the only source of knowledge and reality is not equal to the existence of material entities only (because reality is seen as a systems phenomenon). Despite the ability to experience the self (or soul) as separate from the body, it is no separate entity (thing) but a non-material reality inscribed into (or the result of) a complex bodily and environmental system.

Transferring a Cartesian dualism to antiquity is not the only inaccurate element in modern exegetical practices. There is also little respect for the actual content and nature of the ancient concepts used to talk about the human being. Therefore the question, what was the content of ancient talk about a human being?

3.3. *Ancient Physiological Concepts and Conceptions*

Besides a body-soul dualism, which was sometimes expressed as a body-soul-spirit tripartite entity, there were some fixed elements or a range of possibilities in ancient constructions of the human nature. Four of these will briefly be mentioned.

The first is a brief glimpse at the basic building blocks of reality as perceived by ancient people. The human self (body and soul) was composed of the same elements as the rest of the universe, namely, air (pneuma), earth, water, and fire (Martin 1995:16). All things, including the variety of forms of life, were seen as various compounds of these basic elements and therefore materiality was a spectrum of more or less (or different configurations of these elements) and not to be seen in a dichotomy with nonmatter (see Wright 1995:100; Martin 1995:14). Therefore, to say something was incorporeal (like a soul or spirit) did not translate to being immaterial. As *3 Enoch* (44:7) illustrates, the "souls of the fathers of the world, Abraham, Isaac and Jacob" could be seen (translated by Alexander 1983:295). Reality was conceived as a hierarchy of beings and things consisting of various degrees of materiality, or of various configurations of material elements. Both soul and spirit were, therefore, like the body, composed of stuff and part of nature and neither would have been considered immaterial substances.

The stars, like all other things, were composed of the four basic elements: fire, air, earth, and water (see Wright 1995:98–101) while there was no consensus on whether they were composed of fire, ether, pneuma, or all four of the primary elements. The exact nature of the composition of heavenly bodies from these elements were debated for centuries and eventually it was generally accepted that the soul (or mind) was of celestial substance and that the heavenly bodies were living creatures composed entirely of soul (mind). Whatever substance comprises the stars also comprises the soul (see Martin 1995:118–20).

Secondly, a central feature about the body was that it was porous—its boundaries were penetrable from both inside and outside (see Vorster 2002b:13–15). The body contained or consisted of many *poroi* ("channels" or "passages") through which blood, spirit, and other perceptions could flow. Perceptions of smell, taste, and the like were possible when something fitted into the correct poroi. In the words of Martin (1995:17–18):

> *Poroi* are channels that enable external material to enter and pervade the body and constitute passageways within the body for psychic and nutritive (or destructive) matter.... The concept of poroi in medical theory is one expression of the ancient assumption that the human body is of a piece with the elements surrounding and pervading it and that the surface of the body is not a sealed boundary.

This principle is well expressed in the ancient art of physiognomics: the study of human character on the basis of how people looked and acted (see Malina and Neyrey 1996:108ff.). The surface of the body is an expression of the forces and movement inside the body, or a reflection of the soul and/or spirit as these "fill" the body (see also Martin 1995:18). It is probably this cultural notion about the body which can also be detected underneath metaphors of the body as a container as is, for example, found in the *Testament of Naphtali* (2:2): "For just as a potter knows the pot, how much it holds, and brings clay for it accordingly, so also the Lord forms the body in correspondence to the spirit, and instils the spirit corresponding to the power of the body" (translated by Kee 1983:811). Diverse spirits could fill the poroi of a fleshly body.

Thirdly, hierarchies were fundamental to the ancient world-view (see Martin 1995:29ff.; Vorster 2002a) and so was the relationship between body and soul/spirit which were all different configurations of the same four elements, hierarchically ordered. It is understandable that within the spectrum of ways in which the relationship between them was expressed somewhere there would be a denigration of one of them. This is the case in some of Plato's writings where he refers to the body merely as the prison of the soul and in later gnostic texts where the body was seen as intrinsically evil and the spirit as intrinsically good. However, as Aune (see 1994:293, 296–97) points out, already Plotinus has noted that Plato did not say the same thing about the soul everywhere and calls attention to the positive assessment of the soul-body dualism in some of his writings.

A fourth feature is the cultural practice in which a part of the body may function as a substitute for another part or for the body itself, known as synedochic relationships (see Vorster 2002a:287–88). This applies not only where, for example, the knee is used for the genitals, but also where any one body part or organ is thought to be acting on behalf of the whole (Russel 1964:141), such as the soul or spirit representing the person. An example from 1 Enoch (71:1–11) will suffice: "(Thus) it happened after this that my spirit passed out of sight and ascended into the heavens. . . . He carried off my spirit, and I Enoch, was in the heaven of heavens. There I saw . . . And my spirit saw a ring . . . I fell on my face, my whole body mollified and my spirit transformed . . ." (translated by Isaac 1983:49–50). Here bodily functions of seeing and hearing are not only associated with his spirit journey, but his experience of travelling in the spirit resulted in the experience of a bodily presence in heaven. In other words, a pneuma was one of the ways in which a person could be bodily present via experiences and synedochic representation.

3.4. *The Cycle of Meaning of Inherited Pattern, Experience, and Expression*

None of the constituting components (body, soul or spirit) nor any configuration of them in combination was fixed in ancient physiological conceptions—neither in any specific tradition nor in the writings of any particular author. It is, for example, no longer a secret that neither Plato nor Paul had a single coherent system when conceptualizing human nature. As Aune (see 1994:292) points out, today it is impossible to speak of *the* Pauline, *the* Platonic, or *the* Aristotelean conception of the human being (see also Martin 1995:6ff.). Also, there was no orthodoxy among the various views for even the nature of matter itself was under dispute. All authors operated with a variety of various body and soul (and/or spirit) configurations. Paul employed a variety of dualisms (body-spirit, flesh-spirit, mind-flesh, etc.) and only once in 1 Thessalonians 5:13 speaks of a body-spirit-soul tripartite (see Aune 1994:299 for references).

There are two interesting scholarly reactions to this. The one is typically to complain that "logic and consistency" are the least of the virtues of ancient authors (see, e.g., Russel 1964:375) or, more specifically, Luke can be accused of a "lack of precision in statements about the afterlife" (based on his conception of the human being) while it can be said that "Paul's language may not be consistent in all cases" (Green 1998:169, 172).

The second is an observation about the nature of scholarly attempts to put into words the strangeness of the ancient conceptions. The following well-argued construction of Martin, in which he struggles to put into words Paul's conceptions of the nature of the human being, is a case in point. He has to rely on several qualifications, or "rathers" and "to put it more accurately" in order to put across what he thinks Paul actually meant (Martin 1995:128):

> Flesh, blood and pneuma are all parts of the body—or rather, different forms of substance that together make up a body. When Paul says that the resurrected body will be a pneumatic body rather than simply a psychic body or a flesh-and-blood body, he is saying that the immortal and incorruptible part of the human body will be resurrected—or, to put it more accurately, that the body will be raised, constituted (due to divine transformation) only by its immortal or incorruptible aspects, without its corruptible or corrupting aspects such as sarx. No physical/spiritual dichotomy is involved here, much less a material/immaterial one. Rather, Paul has a hierarchy of essences, probably all assumed to be stuff, but of varying degrees of density or "stuffness."

Much of ethnographic literature amply demonstrates that people in most societies operate psychologically within the context of a cosmos composed of multiple realities since they accept alternate state of consciousness experiences (such as visions, dreams, and possession) as meaningful and normal human experiences for obtaining knowledge about the world (see, e.g., Bourguignon 1979:245; Craffert 2002b). Such people, Laughlin, McManus, and d'Aquili (1990:155) say, "experience *polyphasic consciousness*, and consequently their cognized view of self constitutes a polyphasic integration." Such realities in polyphasic consciousness "are frequently coded as experiential." This is opposed to most Western (North American and Western European) people which they typify as subject to *monophasic consciousness*: the only *real world* experiences are those unfolding in the sensorium during the normal *waking* phase. What they (Laughlin, McManus, and d'Aquili 1990:155) say further about Western science in general is equally true for New Testament research: "The failure of modern Western culture to prepare individuals for an easy, fearless exploration of alternate phases of consciousness has the unfortunate consequence for science of not equipping most ethnographers with the experiential and conceptual material required for sophisticated research into the religious practices of other cultures." This is nowhere more visible than in modern strategies to explain what ancient authors could have meant with the notion of either a resurrected body or an experienced soul.

It should be realized that such experiences in alternate consciousness are often more real for the participants than those experienced in "normal" waking consciousness. This is not only the case with people sharing such cultures, but as Nordland indicates (see 1967:173), Western subjects under such experimental conditions also experience such states as so real that they sometimes need psychiatric treatment afterwards. This is so because all human perceptions and experiences, whether the chair you sit on or the ancestor you encounter in a vision, exist in the brain merely as blips and flashes (see Newberg and d'Aquili 2000:66–67; Craffert 2002b:79–81). "Reality" is created in the brain and dis/confirmed by society. But "normal" or "ordinary" consciousness is not an ontological given but a specialized cultural construction. Strenuous effort is required of a Western scientist, Laughlin, McManus, and d'Aquili (1990:226) point out, "to realize that his [sic] concrete view of reality is merely a construct... and thus an impediment placed in the way of comprehending a unitary cosmos in which his cognized environment is only one of many alternative ways." Each culture teaches its members what is "normal" and "real" (see Tart 1980:245; Laughlin, McManus, and d'Aquili 1990:142) and therefore such alternate states of consciousness can have the same ontological or reality value as any other experience or perception.

It is necessary to pay attention to a second and related feature which characterizes their knowledge formation and cultural system, namely, what is called the *cycle of meaning* between experience, expression and inherited pattern. Laughlin, McManus, and d'Aquili (1990:227–29) show that there is a specific dynamics at work in the creation and maintenance of knowledge in traditional societies which is called a "cycle of meaning." There is a real interplay between mythology, living experiences, and cultural expressions of various aspects of reality. Cosmology gives rise to mythical expressions which, in turn, make sense and are predictable in terms of the cosmology and mythology which originally impelled the experiences.

Neither mythology (be it about cosmology or physiology) nor the cycle of meaning is ever static because the very dynamics of such a system presupposes that they can all be transformed. Change may be accomplished at any given point; for example, fresh visionary experiences may result in new interpretations that transform their cosmology or physiology. The transformative processes are particularly fluid in cases where the textual material is not written down (see Laughlin, McManus, and d'Aquili 1990:227–31).

Besides the dynamics of this system, it is important to note the implication with regard to the nature of their knowledge-categories. What is suggested here is that within the dynamics of the experience-expression spiral, none of their categories is purely analytical or reflective, they are experiential-reflective categories because they are caught up in this dynamic process. To oversimplify this dynamics: they believed what they experienced and they experienced what they believed and their expressed versions are a product of the process. In this regard, Hadot (2001:389) makes an important (and independent) remark regarding the nature of ancient philosophical texts:

> We think that ancient philosophers were above all theoreticians: they supposedly first put forward a theory of the world, and then, in addition, deduced some practical consequences from it, and thus proposed a morality, a way of living, that ensued from their theory. I believe that exactly the opposite was the case. In Antiquity, the choice of a

certain way of living everyday life did not come at the end of a process of philosophical activity ... but on the contrary at the very beginning ... there is a certain experience of the human condition and an existential choice that corresponds to it ... there is a reciprocal causality between theory and choice of life.

Segal (see 1980:1376) illustrates that exactly such an interplay was at work in the ascension myth in early Christian, Second Temple Jewish, and other Greco-Roman communities. They all inherited certain expectations about the ascension myth; some were confirmed and others disconfirmed by their experiences which consequently led to a reorganization of their expressions of it.

One should be clear about the difference in nature between such a process and the method of radical reflexivity employed by modern science. Modern science produces "a view of the world, a cognized environment, that is intentionally disconnected from the direct, everyday experience of people while profoundly affecting people's lives" (Laughlin, McManus, and d'Aquili 1990:233). For this reason, the resemblances, for example, between quantum physical cosmologies and traditional cosmological systems exist largely at a superficial textual level. Quantum mechanics is not involved in a cycle of meaning in the sense mentioned above. In traditional world-views and cosmologies, flying spirits, ancestors, and the like can be seen and are experienced (in visions or dreams) in a sense in which photons, electrons, and black holes are not and cannot be experienced and are not part of everyday reality. The same differences exist between experiences of a soul or self divorced from the body (in a cycle of meaning) and radical reflection about the self which fundamentally undermines the status of such an experience or the independence of such a divorced entity, called a soul or self.

3.5. *Summary Remarks*

It has been suggested that it is a fallacy to look at ancient texts with Cartesian lenses. Respect both for the specific dualism and the content of their terms is required for an accurate understanding of their conception of a human being. However, it is not only the content but also the nature of their concepts which needs to be respected. Body and soul concepts were experiential concepts which operated within a cycle of meaning and were not purely analytical descriptions of substance.

They lived in a cultural reality where things (such as souls) could be seen and their ontological status be accepted because of the seeing (or experiencing), even without reflecting about the *stuffness* thereof. In other words, the reality of something was not dependent on its materiality; it was rather the other way round that the *materiality* could be accepted because of the reality as experienced entity. The materiality of something in such a system is totally different from that presupposed in the Cartesian heritage which states that reality is composed of material things and entities (obviously besides souls, which have a different ontological existence).

4. Resurrected Bodies Within the Context of Experiential-Reflective Bodies

It should be clear that what the ancients thought about the human body and being is something different from what modern exegetes and monistic theorists think. They not only ascribed a unique content to it, but employed different kinds of concepts in doing that. It is from within the spectrum of bodily experiences that insight about these concepts is generated.

4.1. Transformed into a Travelling Body: Heavenly Journey Experiences

Bodies, or humans in *bodily* form, could fly to heaven, or could experience heavenly journeys. Whether 2 Corinthians 12 is a reference to Paul's own or someone else's experience, it confirms that Christians experienced bodily journeys to heaven. Whether "in the body or out of the body" (2 Cor 12:2, 3), that is, in bodily form or as a bodiless soul/spirit, this man travelled to the third heaven where he heard unutterable words.

In Hellenistic literature in general, heavenly journeys are depicted either as a journey of the soul where the body is left behind, or as a bodily ascension (see Baird 1985:654). Rowland (see 1982:383) points out that the dominant view in Israelite apocalyptic literature is that of corporeal journeys, but as the above examples show, both were known.

4.2. Transformed into Ancestral Bodies: Possession Experiences

Demon possessions are well known in New Testament research (see, e.g., Twelftree 1993; Davies 1995). These can be described as body *poroi* filled with hostile spirits. There is, however, another form of possession experience which most often goes unnoticed. In a number of texts, both Jesus and John the Baptist are questioned about their identity. In Mark (8:27–28par) Jesus asks his disciples: "Who do men say that I am?" and receives the following answer: "John the Baptist; and others say, Elijah; and others one of the prophets." The same phenomenon appears in the report about Jesus' discussion with his disciples after the transfiguration scene (Mt 17:9–13) in which it is suggested that the soul or spirit of Elijah the ancestor could occupy a living person's body, in this case John the Baptist. It is also apparent in the question to John the Baptist himself when the Levites from Jerusalem reportedly asked him: "Who are you? ... Are you Elijah?" (Jn 1:19–21). Herod's alleged response to the question of Jesus' identity suggests that they thought ancestors could be raised in the bodily outfit of another person: "But when Herod heard of it he said, 'John, whom I beheaded, has been raised'" (Mk 6:16). It is worth noting that in Matthew's account of Jesus' death, a number of saints emerged (in a vision?) from their tombs (27:52–53). Resurrection, as such, was neither unique nor exclusive.

The tacit assumption in all these accounts is that someone in Jesus' day could be possessed (or filled) by an ancestral spirit or soul and in that way assume the identity of that ancestor. In other words, experienced by others not to be him- or herself, but someone else because of a transformed identity (see Davies 1995:94). None of these is a possession experience itself, but I am suggesting that the cultural logic of possession is at work in them. A body could be filled with an alien or ancestral pneuma—a phenomenon probably not strange to people encult urated in ancient physiognomics.

4.3. Astral Bodies of the Immortals: Visionary Experiences

A host of ancient texts indicates that humans could be turned into angels or astral beings after death. These all belong to the same astronomical complex—that is, the physics and physiology of the day which insisted that the stars, souls, and angels were of the same substance. The best known figures in the Israelite tradition probably are Moses and Enoch. In some Israelite circles Moses was seen as a divine being (see Van der Horst 1983; Lang 2002:21) while 1 Enoch (104) assures the righteous that they will one day shine like the lights of heaven—an idea also expressed in Daniel 12 (see Collins 2000:335). As Martin (1995:119) says: "The physiological common sense of this entire system thus underwrites the notion that the human soul after death will ascend to its natural level of cosmic substance and will become either a star or something like a star." Immortals, as opposed to eternals, were deities who were originally mortals but at the end of their careers were transformed into eternals while being assumed into heaven (see Talbert 1975:420–21). Within the ancient framework of things, the immortals had bodies because they often appeared to humans.

The New Testament contains several stories about ancestors or immortals appearing to the living in one way or another. Such is the case with the transfiguration scene (Mk 9:2–20par), which can be described as a double vision experience (Pilch 1995). At least as far as the disciples go, they saw Jesus conversing with Moses and Elijah and as far as the story goes, deceased ancestors could appear in recognizable form.

4.4. *A Resurrected Body: Visionary Experiences*

The *nature of things* was decided on in a cycle of meaning with a circular feedback between experience, expression, and mythological pattern. Similar to travelling, astral and ancestor bodies, notions about resurrected bodies developed and existed within such a cycle of meaning. None of these bodies was real because the ancients cared or analyzed what they were made of.

With these insights, it is not at all surprising that there is no fixed tradition in the New Testament itself as to the exact nature of Jesus' resurrected body. All the references to resurrected bodies could be understood within the framework of this cycle of meaning where their conceptions about different kinds of bodies were interlocked with visionary experiences (see Pilch 1998).

It is clear that all the appearances of Jesus mentioned outside the gospels were of a visionary nature (see Hamilton 1965:416). Paul is explicit about it that Jesus appeared (in visions) to all the witnesses which he listed (1 Cor 15). In his view, Jesus' resurrected body is not a flesh-and-blood body (15:50). Martin (see 1995:126–28) shows that the opposition for Paul is between earthly bodies and heavenly bodies and besides other differences (immortal vs. mortal, powerful vs. weak, etc.), the one is spiritual and the other pneumatic. Paul's term *pneumatic* is not equivalent to the modern *spiritual* (which stands opposed to *physical*). As already indicated, a *soma pneumatikon* was both material (made of pneuma stuff) and natural (bodily).

Luke clearly differs from Paul in being the only New Testament author who explicitly refers to Jesus' "flesh and bones" (24:39, and cf. Ac 2:31). Even the strongest supporter of this viewpoint has to admit that this is different from earthly bodies because within the immediate context this flesh-and-bones body appears and disappears in ways impossible for an earthly body. Our choice of understanding is between a "supernatural body" (which Luke would not have understood) or to take it seriously that in all the instances in this chapter Jesus appeared (in visions) to people (and again just disappeared): to those on the road to Emmaus (24:15), to Peter (24:34), and to the disciples (24:36). In other words, the emphasis on the fleshness of Jesus' resurrected body itself appears within visionary experiences. If it is taken into account that elsewhere Luke (20:35) suggests that resurrected bodies (persons) are unlike earthly humans for they do not marry, it should be asked why they saw "flesh and bones" in the visions.

Matthew's resurrected Jesus only appears to the disciples in a vision on a mountaintop in Galilee (28:16-18). Earlier he had emerged from the tomb without the stone being removed—which was only done by a heavenly being (angel) when the women arrived. Here we have to accept that either they lived in a world where heavenly beings from time to time performed manual labor on earth (by moving stones) or that it was simply a mythical story. The third alternative is that this is a report about a cultural experience of a vision in which more than one event took place (which is perfectly in order for visionary events).

The Johannine account of the various appearances (20:19-29) stresses another element. While Thomas's skepticism is usually read as evidence that ancient people distinguished between real bodies and spirits, this account could also be seen within the logic of visionary experiences. In both the appearance to the disciples and then eight days later to Thomas, Jesus appeared from behind closed doors. In both cases the content of the visions included seeing Jesus' bodily features. Why should people who cultivated such experiences in their culture be expected to know the difference between a physical encounter and a visionary encounter? Why should touching a scar in a waking state be more real for ancient people than doing it in a visionary experience?

4.5. *There is More to Seeing Than Meets the Eyeball*

This spectrum of bodily experiences enlarges the scope of their cultural realities considerably: bodies or souls could travel, bodies could be invaded by ancestral souls/spirits, or souls/spirits could migrate after death and appear again in visible forms. It shows how various experiences contributed to the formation of their corpus of knowledge about the body-soul entity. It furthermore assists us in grasping what the nature and substance of a resurrected body was for ancient people: one possible experience of afterlife-bodies which together with astral, transformed, and ancestor bodies existed as a living reality for biblical people. It can also be said that a resurrected body was one shape of a soul after death.

None of them argued from the point of view of a materially analyzed object to the reality of a resurrected body. The reality of Jesus' resurrected body is asserted on the basis of visions and substance and features follow when needed or necessary. Due to their construction of reality based on experiences, bodies were not only of a different nature, they also contained different properties. It is not only resurrected bodies that could fly around, it could also happen to the living body or soul.

But from a historical-anthropological perspective, this is only part of the answer because unless we copy all of the cultural assumptions and realities into our world, it will remain a foreign theoretical construct. Accepting and affirming the reality of such bodily experiences for them is only part of the interpretive task. Unless it is assumed that physical, earthly bodies in antiquity could take on exceptional features like being able to fly, to transform in shape or identity (to become an ancestor or like the stars), we have to engage in the second part of the interpretive process. Instead of jumping from their world directly into a modern world with strategies such as transformed physicality or universal materiality (or simply declare those not really real), a historical-anthropological approach follows the route of radical reflexivity, which requires that we move beyond local experiences.

That can be done by employing models with cross-cultural currency to deal with the variety of human phenomena in different cultural systems. One such model is that of alternate states of consciousness (ASC's) which is proved to be a homoversal model (see Craffert 2002b for a discussion). All the experiences described above form part of a larger corpus of bodily potentials today studied as ASC's.

Such experiences are related to neurophysiological processes because they can be induced by various chemical, surgical, or mystical means (see Ludwig 1968:71–75; Van Lommel et al. 2001:2044). For example, human beings are perfectly capable of out-of-body experiences of different kinds and take those as extremely real events (see Van Lommel et al. 2001). Hundreds of stories about out-of-body experiences are available today—many of them related to so-called near-death experience (see Moody 2001) while anthropologists are well aware of various forms of shamanic journeys (see, e.g., Walsh 1989). Within such a framework, the bodily experiences described above makes sense in a modern world.

Seeing physical objects is a theory-laden undertaking, as Hanson (1961:7, 19), from whom the title of this section was borrowed, indicates. With cultural realities, it is even more so. The reality of ancestral presence, for example, did not depend on either a bodily substance or a recognizable picture since the recognition of ancestors did not take place by means of identification but through creation in a vision. They had no pictures or records against which recognition could take place and even if ancestors were to appear in resuscitated bodies, they would not necessarily be recognized. The seeing was simultaneously the recognition or identification of the ancestors—who were literally *created* in the process of seeing (see further Craffert 2002c). From such a point of view, resurrected bodies (as astral, ancestor, or transformed bodies) originated and existed particularly in the cycle of meaning of ancient people.

5. *Conclusion*

The exegetical spectrum of a body of transformed physicality, a special effects apparent body, a body of ancient materiality, and the bodies in ancient mythological accounts all share the same ethnocentric feature: no recognition of the cycle of meaning of ancient people. Modern exegetical strategies short-circuit the process in forcing modern translations onto an ancient concept. It would be like asking what type of metal hydrogen actually is or to describe the sun-as-iron research as a pseudo-gas or mythical theory. Neither the content nor the nature of ancient concepts is taken seriously in such strategies. Therefore, instead of the mythology of the souls, immortals, and resurrected bodies, a historical-anthropological approach speaks about the living reality of souls, immortals, and resurrected bodies in ancient people's lives.

However, within a cultural system, things are connected and hang together and the aim of a historical-anthropological strategy is to approach ancient texts and their phenomena within the framework of cultural wholes while acknowledging the embeddedness in one's own cultural system. It therefore does not simply offer a different answer to what a resurrected body is, but suggests a different route of answering the question. Instead of short-circuiting the process by ethnocentric strategies, we are bound to give a double answer to the question of what a resurrected body was. It was a real experience of afterlife possibilities for ancient people which hung together with other bodily experiences, both prior to and after death. However, understanding what a resurrected body in antiquity was and even translating it cross-culturally to visionary experiences does not solve everything. Without the cultural assumptions from which it grew, it does not offer a meaningful answer to either afterlife options today or the dilemma of death nor does it contribute to contemporary reflection about the self. Put differently, while visionary experiences can be acknowledged to be real bodily experiences (which is what resurrected bodies were about), they no longer function in modern discourse about the human self (they do not constitute modern human selves) or in talk about death.

It has been suggested that the Cartesian dualism is no longer applicable to monist reflections about the self and is useless as a lens for understanding ancient dualisms. But it turns out the ancient dualist talk about the human being was so deeply embedded in their experience-expression cycle that it is also not applicable to modern reflection about the human being. It is like Cecelia Payne and her Harvard professors who did not see the same thing when looking at the sun because there "is a difference between a physical state and a visual experience" (Hanson 1961:8). In this case, there is a difference between culture-bound experiences and radical reflexivity about human experiences. Sunset-talk does not form the basis of astrophysics or astronomy because radical reflexivity provided a different framework. Perhaps it shows that we have to find a contemporary way of talking about the self and death in meaningful ways which are no longer dominated by dualistic modes of thinking or dualist language—in other words, in a way which does justice to our modern "experience" of a monistic body.

Bibliography

Alexander, P. 1983, "3 (Hebrew Apocalypse of) Enoch: A New Translation and Introduction." In *The Old Testament Pseudepigrapha, Vol. 1: Apocalyptic Literature and Testaments*, ed. J.H. Charlesworth, 223–315. New York: Doubleday.
Aune, D.E. 1994, "Human Nature and Ethics in Hellenistic Philosophical Traditions and Paul: Some Issues and Problems." In *Paul in his Hellenistic context*, ed. T. Engberg-Pedersen, 291–312. Edinburgh: T & T Clark.
Baird, W. 1985, "Visions, Revelations, and Ministry: Reflections on 2 Cor. 12:1–5 and Gal. 1:11–17." *JBL* 104(1):651–62.
Bodanis, D. 2000, $E=mc^2$: *A Biography of the World's Most Famous Equation*. London: Macmillan.
Bourguignon, E. 1979, *Psychological Anthropology: An Introduction to Human Nature and Cultural Differences*. New York: Holt, Rinehart & Winston.
Brown, W.S. 1998, Cognitive Contributions to Soul. In *Whatever Happened to the Soul? Scientific and Theological Portraits of Human Nature*, eds. W.S. Brown, N. Murphy, and H.N. Malony, 99–125. Minneapolis: Fortress.
Collins, J.J. 2000, "Eschatologies of Late Antiquity." In *Dictionary of New Testament Background*, eds. C.A. Evans and S.E. Porter, 330–37. Downers Grove: Intervarsity.
Craffert, P.F. 1995, "The Anthropological Turn in New Testament Interpretation: Dialogue as Negotiation and Cultural Critique." *Neotestamentica* 29(2):167–82.
———. 2002a, "Historical-anthropological Jesus Research: The Status of Authentic Pictures Beyond Authentic Material." *HTS* 58(2):440–71.
———. 2002b, "Religious Experience and/as (alternate) States of Consciousness from a Biopsychosocial Perspective." In *Brain, Mind and Soul: Unifying the Human Self*, ed. C.W. Du Toit, 53–97. Pretoria: Unisa.
———. 2002c, "'Seeing' a Body into Being: Reflections on Scholarly Interpretations of the Nature and Reality of Jesus' Resurrected Body." *R&T* 9(1&2):89–107.
Craig, W.L. 1995, "Did Jesus Rise from the Dead?" In *Jesus under Fire*, eds. M.J. Wilkins and J.P. Moreland, 141–76. Grand Rapids: Zondervan.
Crossan, J.D. 1998, *The Birth of Christianity: Discovering What Happened in the Years Immediately after the Execution of Jesus*. San Francisco: HarperSanFrancisco.
———. 1999, "Historical Jesus as risen Lord." In *The Jesus Controversy: Perspectives in Conflict*. J.D. Crossan, L.T. Johnson, and W.H. Kelber, 1–47. Harrisburg: Trinity.
Davies, S.L. 1995, *Jesus the Healer: Possession, Trance, and the Origins of Christianity*. London: SCM.
Davis, S.T. 1997, "'Seeing' the Risen Jesus." In *The Resurrection: An Interdisciplinary Symposium on the Resurrection of Jesus*, eds. S.T. Davis, D. Kendall, and G. O'Collins, 126–47. Oxford: Oxford University Press.
Green, J.B. 1998, "'Bodies—that is, Human Lives': A Re-examination of Human Nature in the Bible." In *Whatever Happened to the Soul? Scientific and Theological Portraits of Human Nature*, eds. W.S. Brown, N. Murphy, and H.N. Malony, 149–73. Minneapolis: Fortress.

Hadot, P. 2001, "Shamanism and Greek Philosophy." In *The Concept of Shamanism: Uses and Abuses*, eds. H.-P. Francfort and R.N. Hamayon, 389–401. Busapest: Akadémiai Kiadó.

Hamilton, N.Q. 1965, "Resurrection Tradition and the Composition of Mark." *JBL* 84(4):415–21.

Hanson, N.R. 1961, *Patterns of Discovery*. Cambridge: Cambridge University Press.

Isaac, E. 1983, "1 (Ethiopic Apocalypse of) Enoch: A New Translation and Introduction." In *The Old Testament Pseudepigrapha, Vol. 1: Apocalyptic Literature and Testaments*, ed. J.H. Charlesworth, 5–89. New York: Doubleday.

Kee, H.C. 1983, "The Testament of Naphtali, the Eighth Son of Jacob and Bilhah." In *The Old Testament Pseudepigrapha, Vol. 1: Apocalyptic Literature and Testaments*, ed. J.H. Charlesworth, 810–14. New York: Doubleday.

Kriel, J.R. 2000, *Matter, Mind, and Medicine: Transforming the Clinical Method*. Amsterdam: Ropodi.

———. 2002, "And the Flesh Became Mind: Evolution, Complexity and the Unification of Animal Consciousness." In *Brain, Mind and Soul: Unifying the Human Self*, ed. C.W. Du Toit, 135–78. Pretoria: Unisa.

Lang, B. 2002, *The Hebrew God: Portrait of an Ancient Deity*. New Haven/London: Yale University Press.

Laughlin, C.D., J. McManus, and E.G. d'Aquili 1990, *Brain, Symbol and Experience: Towards a Neurophenomenology of Human Consciousness*. Boston: Shambhala.

Ludwig, A.M. 1968, "Altered States of Consciousness." In *Trance and Possession States*, ed. R. Prince, 69–95. Montreal: Burke Memorial Society.

Malina, B.J. 1991, "Reading Theory Perspectives: Reading Luke-Acts." In *The Social World of Luke-Acts: Models for Interpretation*, ed. J.H. Neyrey, 3–23. Peabody: Hendrickson.

Malina, B.J., & J.H. Neyrey. 1996, *Portraits of Paul: An Archaeology of Ancient Personality*. Louisville: Westminster John Knox.

Martin, D.B. 1993, "Social-scientific Criticism." In *To Each Its Own Meaning: An Introduction to Biblical Criticisms and their Application*, eds. S.R. Haynes and S.L. McKenzie, 103–19. Louisville: Westminster/John Knox.

———. 1995, *The Corinthian Body*. New Haven/London: Yale University Press.

Moody, R.A. 2001, *Life After Life: The Investigation of a Phenomenon—Survival of Bodily Death*. London/Sydney/Auckland/Johannesburg: Rider.

Newberg, A.B., and E.G. d'Aquili. 2000, "The Creative Brain/the Creative Mind." *Zygon* 35(1):53–68.

Nordland, O. 1967, "Shamanism as an Experiencing of 'the Unreal.'" In *Studies in Shamanism*, ed. C.-M. Edsman, 166–85. Stockholm: Almqvist & Wiksell.

Pilch, J.J. 1995, "The Transfiguration of Jesus: An Experience of Alternate Reality." In *Modelling early Christianity: Social-scientific Studies of the New Testament in its Context*, ed. P.F. Esler, 47–64. London: Routledge.

———. 1998, "Appearances of the Risen Jesus in Cultural Context: Experiences of Alternate Reality." *BTB* 28(2):52–60.

Rowland, C. 1982, *The Open Heaven: A Study of Apocalyptic in Judaism and early Christianity*. London: SPCK.

Russel, D.S. 1964, *The Method and Message of Jewish Apocalyptic*. London: SCM.

Saler, B. 1977, "Supernatural as a Western Category." *Ethos* 5, 31–53.

Segal, A.F. 1980, "Heavenly Ascent in Hellenistic Judaism, Early Christianity and their Environment." *ANRW* II.23.2:1333–94.

Spurrett, D. 2002, "The Human Self as a Coalition of Distributed Agencies." In *Brain, Mind and Soul: Unifying the Human Self*, ed. C.W. Du Toit, 191–223. Pretoria: Unisa.

Talbert, C.H. 1975, "The Concept of Immortals in Mediterranean Antiquity." *JBL* 94:419–36.

Tart, C.T. 1980, "A Systems Approach to Altered States of Consciousness." In *The Psychobiology of Consciousness*, eds. J.M. Davidson and R.J. Davidson, 243–69. New York: Plenum.
Taylor, C. 1991, "The Dialogical Self." In *The Interpretive Turn: Philosophy, Science, Culture*, eds. J.F. Bohman, D.R. Hiley, and R. Shusterman, 304–14. Ithaca: Cornell University Press.
Twelftree, G.H. 1993, *Jesus the Exorcist: A Contribution to the Study of the Historical Jesus*. Massachusetts: Hendrickson.
Van der Horst, P.W. 1983, "Moses' Throne Vision in Ezekiel the Dramatist." *JJS* 34:21–29.
Van Lommel, P., R. Van Wees, V. Meyers, and I. Elfferich 2001, "Near-death Experience in Survivors of Cardiac Arrest: A Prospective Study in the Netherlands." *The Lancet* 358:2039–45.
Van Tilborg, S., and P. Chatelion Counet 2000, *Jesus' Appearances and Disappearances in Luke 24*. Leiden: Brill.
Vorster, J.N. 2000, "(E)mpersonating the Bodies of Early Christianity," *Neotestamentica* 34(1):103–24.
———. 2002a, "Bodily Parts Vying for Power: Hierarchies and Bodies in Early Christianity." *Scriptura* 80:287–306.
———. 2002b, *Wat sê die Bybel regtig oor . . . seks?* Pretoria: C.B. Powell Bybelsentrum.
Walsh, R. 1989, "The Shamanic Journey: Experiences, Origins, and Analogues." *ReVision* 12(1):25–32.
Wright, M.R. 1995, *Cosmology in Antiquity*. London/New York: Routledge.
Wright, N.T. 1999, "The Transforming Reality of the Bodily Resurrection." In *The Meaning of Jesus: Two Visions*, eds. M.J. Borg and N.T. Wright, 111–27. San Francisco: HarperSanFrancisco.

CHAPTER TWELVE

ACTS 8:26–40: PHILIP BAPTIZES THE ETHIOPIAN: NARRATIVE AND PRAGMATIC-LINGUISTIC ASPECTS

Detlev Dormeyer
University of Dortmund

S1
26 Ἄγγελος δὲ κυρίου ἐλάλησεν πρὸς Φίλιππον λέγων,
Ἀνάστηθι καὶ πορεύου κατὰ μεσημβρίαν ἐπὶ τὸν ὁδὸν τὴν καταβαίνουσαν ἀπὸ Ἰερουσαλὴμ εἰς Γάζαν, αὕτη ἐστὶν ἔρημος.
27 καὶ ἀναστὰς
ἐπορεύθη·

S2
καὶ ἰδοὺ ἀνὴρ Αἰθίοψ εὐνοῦχος δυνάστης Κανδάκης βασιλίσσης Αἰθιόπων, ὃς ἦν ἐπὶ πάσης τῆς γάζης αὐτῆς, ὃς ἐληλύθει προσκυνήσων εἰς Ἰερουσαλήμ,
28 ἦν τε ὑποστρέφων
καὶ καθήμενος ἐπὶ τοῦ ἅρματος αὐτοῦ
καὶ ἀνεγίνωσκεν τὸν προφήτην Ἠσαΐαν.

S3
29 εἶπεν δὲ τὸ πνεῦμα τῷ Φιλίππῳ.
Πρόσελθε καὶ κολλήθητι τῷ ἅρματι τούτῳ.
30 προσδραμὼν δὲ ὁ Φίλιππος
ἤκουσεν αὐτοῦ ἀναγινώσκοντος Ἠσαΐαν τὸν προφήτην

S4
καὶ εἶπεν,
Ἆρά γε γινώσκεις ἃ ἀναγινώσκεις;
31 ὁ δὲ εἶπεν,
Πῶς γὰρ ἂν δυναίμην ἐὰν μή τις ὁδηγήσει με;
παρεκάλεσέν τε τὸν Φίλιππον
ἀναβάντα καθίσαι σὺν αὐτῷ.

S5
32 ἡ δὲ περιοχὴ τῆς γραφῆς ἣν ἀνεγίνωσκεν ἦν αὕτη·
Ὡς πρόβατον ἐπὶ σφαγὴν ἤχθη
καὶ ὡς ἀμνὸς ἐναντίον τοῦ κείραντος αὐτὸν ἄφωνος,
οὕτως οὐκ ἀνοίγει τὸ στόμα αὐτοῦ.
33 Ἐν τῇ ταπεινώσει ἡ κρίσις αὐτοῦ ἤρθη.
τὴν γενεὰν αὐτοῦ τίς διηγήσεται;
ὅτι αἴρεται ἀπὸ τῆς γῆς ἡ ζωὴ αὐτοῦ.

34 Ἀποκριθεὶς δὲ ὁ εὐνοῦχος τῷ Φιλίππῳ εἶπεν,
   Δέομαί σου, περὶ τίνος ὁ προφήτης λέγει τοῦτο;
   περὶ ἑαυτοῦ ἢ περὶ ἑτέρου τινός;
35 ἀνοίξας δὲ ὁ Φίλιππος τὸ στόμα αὐτοῦ καὶ ἀρξάμενος ἀπὸ τῆς
   γραφῆς ταύτης εὐηγγελίσατο αὐτῷ τὸν Ἰησοῦν.

S6
36 ὡς δὲ ἐπορεύοντο κατὰ τὴν ὁδόν,
   ἦλθον ἐπί τι ὕδωρ,
   καὶ φησιν ὁ εὐνοῦχος,
   Ἰδοὺ ὕδωρ· τί κωλύει με βαπτισθῆναι;

S7
38 καὶ ἐκέλευσεν
   στῆναι τὸ ἅρμα,
   καὶ κατέβησαν ἀμφότεροι εἰς τὸ ὕδωρ, ὅ τε Φίλιππος καὶ ὁ εὐνοῦχος,
   καὶ ἐβάπτισεν αὐτόν.

S8
39 ὅτε δὲ ἀνέβησαν ἐκ τοῦ ὕδατος,
   πνεῦμα κυρίου ἥρπασεν τὸν Φίλιππον
   καὶ οὐκ εἶδεν αὐτὸν οὐκέτι ὁ εὐνοῦχος, ἐπορεύετο γὰρ τὴν ὁδὸν
   αὐτοῦ χαίρων.
40 Φίλιππος δὲ εὑρέθη εἰς Ἄζωτον·
   καὶ διερχόμενος
   εὐηγγελίζετο τὰς πόλεις πάσας ἕως τοῦ ἐλθεῖν αὐτὸν εἰς Καισάρειαν.

1. *Steps of Interpretation*

In each text three elements have to be differentiated: the external text-form, the content, and the pragmatic intention.

1.1. *Formal Signals of the Text Strategy*

In this step the external form of the text is analyzed according to narrative text theory (s. 1.1–1.2).[1]

From a literary perspective, the book of Acts is a theological-biographical history work.[2] The framework of actions forms a nar-

---

[1] Grilli, M., Consideraciones en torno a la sintáctica, in: Paz, C.M., Grilli, M., and Dillmann, R., Lectura, 31–41; Dormeyer, D., "Das Markusevangelium als Idealbiographie von Jesus Christus, dem Nazarener" (*SBB* 43), Stuttgart 2/2002, 11–31.

[2] Plümacher, E., Lukas als hellenistischer Schriftsteller. Studien zur Apostelgeschichte (StUNT 9), Göttingen 1972, 225–27; Radl, W., Paulus und Jesus im lukanischen Doppelwerk (EHS 23,49), Bern/Frankfurt 1975, 352–55; Thornton, C.J., Der Zeuge

rative with a complete sense. Words and speeches are embedded within the narrative. The narrative framework consists of many narrative units. These units contain events and action-sequences. The tense preferred in the narrative is the past tense. Each narrative is organized by actors and by the factors of space and time. Space is the condition for narrative events. It makes it possible for the figures of the narrative to initiate and develop actions with each other.

Time is the second structural element. Time allows a chronological operational sequence. A narrated world develops. The beginning and ending of a narrative section are marked by the appearance and disappearance of persons as well as by local and chronological data. Some sections contain leitmotivs, which determine the topic, or are linked by references with other sections. The reader will be motivated to notice these signals, to compare, to differentiate, to collect, and to sketch a first interpretation.[3]

Each narrative contains several levels of communication. The first level is the direct address of the author to the reader. In the book of Acts this address forms the preface (Acts 1:1). The "omniscient" author addresses the Catechumen Theophilos who represents the implicit reader. Like him all other readers should read the story of the Apostles as witness in connection with the first book. The first book represents a gospel/biography of Jesus' acts and teachings.[4]

---

des Zeugen. Lukas als Historiker der Paulusreisen (WUNT 56), Tübingen 1991, 355–60.

[3] Fischer, G., Wege in die Bibel. Leitfaden zur Auslegung. Unter Mitarbeit von Repschinski, B. und Vonach, A., Stuttgart 2000, 6–24.

[4] Radl, W., Das Lukas-Evangelium (Erträge der Forschung 261), Darmstadt 1988, 49–53; Dormeyer, D., Evangelium als literarische und theologische Gattung (Erträge der Forschung 263), Darmstadt 1989; Dormeyer, D., Das Neue Testament im Rahmen der antiken Literaturgeschichte. Eine Einführung, Darmstadt 1993, 225–27; Theissen, G., Nachwort, in Bultmann, R., Die Geschichte der synoptischen Tradition, Göttingen 10/1995, 409–53; Frickenschmidt, D., Evangelium als Biographie. Die vier Evangelien im Rahmen antiker Erzählkunst (TANZ 22), Tübingen/Basel 1997, 478–98; Broer, I., Einleitung in das Neue Testament 1 (NEBE 2/1), Würzburg 1998, 35–38; Riesner, R., Das lukanische Doppelwerk und die antike Biographie, in: Dormeyer, D., Mölle, H., and Ruster, Th. (Hg.), Lebenswege und Religion, Münster 2000, 131–45; Schnelle, U., Einführung in die neutestamentliche Exegese, Göttingen 5/2000, 117–19; Söding, Th., "Ein Jesus-Vier Evangelien," *ThGl* 91 (2001) 409–43; Reiser, M., Sprache und literarische Formen des Neuen Testaments, Paderborn 2001, 104f.; zurückhaltend: Frankemölle, H., "Evangelium. Begriff und Gattung. Ein Forschungsbericht" (*SBB* 15), Stuttgart 2/1994, 180–85; Roloff, J., Einführung in das Neue Testament, Stuttgart 1995, 146–52; Dawson, A., Freedom as Liberating Power, Freiburg/Göttingen 2000, 104–8.

The second book sets forth the continuation of the gospel after Jesus' resurrection and the day of ascension in the form of a biographical history-work. The community of the first Christians is addressed in particular.

The narrative itself forms the second level. It is shaped by space and time as well as by the action of actors. This second level in the Acts introduces the work of the apostles. The individual persons in the narrative interact with one another. Here the storyteller does not remain any longer in direct contact with his listener, but the narrated figures affect each other and interpret the events by their words.[5] In the Acts the interaction is stimulated in particular by the words of the apostles.

In the words and speeches new figures arise, and a further narrative level develops. The narrative levels are marked in the text arrangement by appropriate insertions: First Level: author-reader: insertion left at the edge; Second Level: narrative: single insertion; Third Level: speech in the narrative: double insertion. The author comment stands thus directly at the edge; it forms the first level of the author-reader communication. The narrated action is inserted; it represents the second level of communication. In the narrated action speech is inserted; it represents the third level of communication. The narrative figures communicate, not the author.[6]

The speeches of the narrative figures can agree with the author's intention, but they can also contradict the author's intention. When opponents of the apostles and of the Christian witnesses speak, the reader should reject them as wrong (an exception is the advice of Gamaliels Acts 5:34–39).

In order to arrange a slow reading, narrative sequences are formed (abbreviation S). Attention is directed toward each action verb. The verb produces the action together with the actors. An event exists in three states or conditions. First state is one of possibility with the beginning of change of the state, Second state is one of action acti-

---

[5] Egger, W., Methodenlehre zum Neuen Testament. Einführung in linguistische und historische Methoden, Freiburg 1/1987, 119–33; Dillmann, R., and Mora-Paz C., Lukas-Evangelium, 11.

[6] Gülich, E., and Raible, W., Überlegungen zu einer makrostrukturellen Textanalyse, in: Gülich, E., Heger, K., and Raible, W., Linguistische Textanalyse, Überlegungen zur Gliederung von Texten, Hamburg 2/1979, 73–127; Dormeyer, D., Markusevangelium, 12–21; Tilborg, Sj. van and Chatelion Counet, P., Jesus' Appearances and Disappearances in Luke 24 (BIS 45), Leiden a.o. 2000, 1–23.

vation or action change, Third state is a new condition or state.[7] One example:

> Paul went inside to him and prayed with the laying on of hands and healed him (Acts 28:8).

The three actions *going in*, *praying*, and *healing* result in the event "miracle healing." What would happen if one small event or one small speech unit were missing? The apostles would remain witnesses, but in a different way, without sympathy, without prayer, without the power of miracle. In order to break a prejudice obtained by long education, each single state must be observed. As the kingdom of God begins small and inconspicuously, the meaning and effect of its witness-history are found by slow reading. The builder/carpenter Jesus of Nazareth and his apostles were exact observers, the evangelist and his community were likewise. With the help of the diagram with S (sequence) the present reader also has a chance to become an exact observer. The sequences are sequentially numbered as S1, S2, ...

Genres pick up on reader expectations and guide them.[8] Genres are independent units. They consist of several narrative sequences and create an up-to-date form.[9] The structure of a genre belongs therefore to the step "formation." The narrated speech- and reader-situations supply the key to the interpretation. An appearance presupposes faith, a miracle history confident faith presupposes.[10] Processes anticipate legal protection and preparation for persecution as well;

---

[7] Bremond, C., Die Erzählnachricht, in: Ihwe (Hg.), Literaturwissenschaft und Linguistik 2, Frankfurt 1972, 177–218; Dormeyer, D., "Der Sinn des Leidens Jesu. Historisch-kristische und textpragmatische Analysen zur Markuspassion" (*SBS* 96), Stuttgart 1979, 94–102; van Dijk, T.A., Textwissenschaft. Eine interdisziplinäre Einführung, München 1980; Lentzen-Deis, F., Passionsbericht als Handlungsmodell? Überlegungen zu Anstößen aus der "pragmatischen" Sprachwissenschaft für die exegetischen Methoden, in: Kertelge, K. (Hg.), Der Prozess gegen Jesus (QD 112), Freiburg u.a. 1988, 191–233; Dormeyer, Markusevangelium, 12f.

[8] Hempfer, K.W., Gattungstheorie (UTB 133), München 1973; Breuer, D., Einführung in die pragmatische Texttheorie (UTB 106), München 1974, 165–75; McKnight, E.V., Post-Modern Use of the Bible. The Emergence of Reader-Orientated Criticism, Nashville 1988, 242–44. Dormeyer, D., Testament, 67–243; Egger, W., Methodenlehre, 146–59; Söding, Th., Wege der Schriftauslegung. Methodenbuch zum Neuen Testament, Freiburg u.a. 1998, 155–73.

[9] Dormeyer, D., Sinn, 102–5; Davidsen, O., The Narrative Jesus. A Semiotic Reading of Mark's Gospel, Aarhus 1993, 25–57.

[10] Theissen, Nachwort, 409–53; Dormeyer, Testament 159–90; Theissen, G., and Merz, A., Der historische Jesus, Göttingen 1996, 256–86.

words and speeches prepare for argumentation. The effect of genres continues until today.

Speech-acts affect the reader. The speech-acts at that time indicate whether an imperative should be understood as an instruction or a warning and whether a promise is regarded as successful or unsuccessful under the appropriate basic conditions within the text.[11] Pronouncements of the first and second person speak directly to the listener within the speech and refer to the reader indirectly. In many speeches the you-address grows to the level of an urgent staccato.

For treatment of biblical genres Paul Ricoeurs' considerations are particularly helpful.[12] Ricoeur differentiates between first and second order genres.[13] First order genres permit the direct questing of real experiences. Records of direct experiences belong to them. Second order genres suspend this experience. They are fictional, autopoetic units. With Ricoeur the transition to the genre of second order can be tied at any time to the genre of first order. It can succeed with historiographic genres because of names and elements held in memory. It cannot succeed with purely fictional genres, e.g., with the genre apocalypticism and parables. Therefore the historical quest is possible with some biblical genres. This quest directs the reader expectation. With other biblical genres the historical quest is not possible. The readers in those cases do not seek such a quest.

1.2. *Perspectives*

The perspectives contained in the text serve to influence the actions of the readers. The perspectives are not procedural instructions. The reader is not forced to action. There is not a "moral of history." The text of the book of Acts is so arranged that certain actions suggest themselves. The text offers action models.

In narrative texts the reader can identify himself with the individual figures of the narration and can experience the event from the perspective of the individual figures. In this way the reader sees how the behavior of individual persons is affected and how situa-

---

[11] Austin, J.L., Zur Theorie der Sprechakte, Stuttgart 1972; Searle, J.R., Sprechakte, Frankfurt 1971.
[12] Dormeyer, Testament, 59–62.
[13] Ricoeur, P., Erzählung, Metapher und Interpretationstheorie, ZThK 84 (1987), 232–54, 236ff.

tions are changed. The reader can transfer this experience to his own concrete situation. If the reader wants to change something, he must act accordingly.

In the narrative genres, roles are conspicuous opportunities given the reader for identification,[14] while the roles in the genre argumentation form only the framework of the relationship between addresser and the addressed.

With the narrated text in the narrative stories and letters the omniscient or hidden author addresses the real reader via the implicit reader, that is the anticipation of the reader by the author.

Communication   real author   real reader

Text   implicit author   implicit reader[15]

The real reader creates the implicit author through the implicit reader, which consists of an interaction of text structure and reader experience.[16] The reader infers the real author from the implicit author. According to the sender model the communication between author and reader runs not directly but indirectly.

The real author offers identifications, which work positively or negatively through the implicit reader by the characterization of the roles. The real author can arrange a complex character or a typical ("flat") character and he can value the character as good or bad in order to cause the real reader to assume his intentions over those of the implicit reader.[17] This reader-influence does not run however monocausally. Rather the author strategy is varied by the different constructions of the implicit author by the real readers. Implicit author and implicit reader remain polysemantic.[18] Thus the narrative roles can be explained as part of the text structure. The role-experiences can be explained as part of the act structure between the real reader and the implicit reader.

---

[14] Iser, W., Der Akt des Lesens (UTB 636), München 1976, 204f.
[15] Lategan, B.C., "Coming to Grips with the Reader in Biblical Literature," in: *Semeia* 48 (1989), 3–21, 10; W. Iser, Akt (s. Anm. 10) 204ff.
[16] "Aktstruktur," Iser, Akt, 61.
[17] Rhoads, D., and Michie, D., Mark as Story, Philadelphia 1982 39ff.; 103f.; 117f.
[18] Barthes, S/Z, 20f.; Fumagalli, Gesù 26–37.

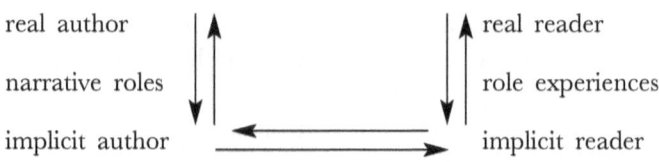

The implicit author creates and guides the narrative roles in an "omniscient" or in a more "hidden" fashion. The literary organization of the roles permits conclusions about the intentions of the real author. Does the real author want to represent the characters as good or as bad, complex or flat? On the other hand the real reader as implicit author examines how the real author linked the narrated roles with the experiences of the real reader. Is it a matter of a real or an unreal/fantastic history for the real reader,[19] is it a matter of a Christology that is far from the everyday experience or a Christology that is close to human experience? Through connotations, the identification with the narrative roles invests real life experience into the text and allows the text world to have an effect on real role-experiences.[20] The reader is able to confirm his life experience, expand and change, and "repent" (Acts 2:38).

In Redaction-Criticism the identification-figure of the gospels was not Jesus but the disciples.[21] Depth-psychological and text-pragmatic interpretations point out that the role of opponent calls for identification with the goal of the treatment.[22] Petersen gives attention to the fact that the author inevitably posits an identification with the Jesus as the main person.[23] The attraction of the biblical narrative texts lies

---

[19] Todorov, T., Einführung in die fantastische Literatur [frz. 1970], München 1975, 25ff.
[20] Ricoeur, P., "Erzählung, Metapher und Interpretationstheorie," in: *ZThK* 84 (1987) 232–54, 236ff.; McKnight, Use, 253–63.
[21] Egger, W., Nachfolge als Weg zum Leben. Chancen neuerer exegetischer Methoden (ÖBS 1), Klosterneuburg 1979, 208ff.; Breytenbach, C., Nachfolge und Zukunftserwartung nach Markus. Eine methodenkritische Studie (AThANT 71), Zürich 1984, 77ff.; Klauck, H.J., "Die erzählerische Rolle der Jünger im Markusevangelium," in: *NT* 24 (1982), 1–26, 2.
[22] Kassel, M., Biblische Urbilder. Tiefenpsychologische Auslegung nach C.G. Jung (Pfeiffer-Werkbücher 147), München 1980, 258ff.; Dormeyer, D., Die Passion Jesu als Verhaltensmodell. Literarische und theologische Analyse der Traditions- und Redaktionsgeschichte der Markuspassion (NTA 2 NF 11), Münster 1974, 283f.; ders., Sinn 109f.
[23] Petersen, N.R., "Die 'Perspektive' in der Erzählung des Markusevangeliums" [1978], in: Hahn, F. (Hrsg.), Der Erzähler des Evangeliums (SBS 118/119), Stuttgart 1985, 67–93, 69.

text-theoretically in the fact that the reader can fill up each role with his or her experience and can judge from the perspective of each role the relationships to the other roles within the action processes. The author perspective can be determined in distance from the narrative roles as meta-linguistic framing, because it grasps all subordinate genres in a hierarchical way. The author perspective oversees also the subordinated roles and can be examined independently of the narrated events.[24]

2. Interpretation

2.1. Text-Syntax

Nine narrative sequences form a large biographical apophthegm of Philip.[25]

Sequence 1 vv. 26–27a An angelophany is narrated briefly. The appearance of the angel is missing; only his message is reported.[26] The full form of the angelophany is well known from the first book (Lc 1–2; 24:1–12). The instructions demand a journey. Philip obeys by arising and seeking "at noon the road that leads down from Jerusalem to Gaza." A complex description of space is given.[27]

Sequence 2 vv. 27b–28 An Ethiopian God-fearer is returning from a pilgrimage to the temple of Jerusalem. He is sitting in his chariot reading from a scroll of the prophet Isaiah.

Sequence 3 vv. 29–30a The narrative changes again back to Philip. The holy Spirit no longer needs the angel, but speaks a message directly to Philip. Philip again obeys, running to the chariot of the Ethiopian. The hearing of the audible reading establishes a contact between the two persons. A meeting takes place.[28]

---

[24] Gülich, E., and Raible, W., Linguistische Textmodelle. Grundlagen und Möglichkeiten (UTB 130), Stuttgart 1973, 21ff.; Berger, K., Hermeneutik des Neuen Testaments, Gütersloh 1988, 232ff.

[25] Dormeyer, D., and Galindo, F., Die Apostelgeschichte. Ein Kommentar für die Praxis, Stuttgart 2003, 132–36.

[26] Roloff, J., Die Apostelgeschichte (NTD 5), Göttingen 1981, 139f.; Pesch, R., Die Apostelgeschichte, 2 Bde. (EKK 5,1–2), Zürich u.a. 1986–87, 280.

[27] Haenchen, E., Die Apostelgeschichte (KEKNT 3), Göttingen 7/1997, 299f.

[28] Haenchen, Apostelgeschichte, 304f. speaks correctly "vom dritten Ereignis, das die Handlung weitertreibt."

Sequence 4 vv. 30b–31 Philip continues to take the initiative. He is the first speaker. Because of his knowledge of the Holy Scripture he asks the Ethiopian about his understanding of the Scripture. The Ethiopian admits his ignorance. He implores Philip to sit with him and to explore the Scripture.

Sequence 5 vv. 32–35 Stands in the center. At first the author-commentary recites the passage for the reader. Then the action proceeds. The eunuch (called the second time by this depreciative term) reacts to the involvement of Philip. The eunuch asks about the application of the prophecy. Philip applies it to the gospel (*euangelizo*) of "Jesus." Jesus fulfils the Scripture.

Sequence 6 v. 36 They go forward and come to a body of water. The eunuch makes a request for water-baptism.

Sequence 7 v. 38 The eunuch halts the chariot. Both men climb down. Philip baptizes the eunuch.

Sequence 8 v. 39 They climb up into the chariot again. The Spirit intervenes for the third time.

Sequence 8 is connected to sequences 3 and 1 by means of the Spirit and creates a double closure. The Spirit sets Philip on another road. The eunuch does not see him any longer and goes his way with joy.

Sequence 9 v. 40 Philip is now in Ashdod, and he goes around proclaiming the gospel (euangelizo) in "all" the towns to Caesarea. Euangelizo connects the conclusion with the central sequence 5. The space-line runs from Samaria to the south-west—to Gaza in the direction of Egypt and Ethiopia—and returns from Gaza to the north—along the coast over Ashdod to Caesarea. The sharp angle of the old Philistine harbor-cities is fulfilled by the gospel. The old enemies of Judaea, the Philistines and Samaritans, first hear and believe the gospel.

2.2. *Explanation of the Text*

Verse 26 "Angel of the Lord" calls the reader's attention to the miracle of the opening of the door Acts 5:19 and to the many appearances of angels in the first book and in the Old Testament. The Spirit gives a message by an angel. Because the representation of the imagination is missing, the form of appearance is totally open. The evangelist could have replaced the angel with the Spirit, who is indeed represented later through speaking (v. 29) and taking Philip away (v. 39). The reader becomes aware that the angel is a form of appearance of the Spirit. The Spirit is able to act directly with and without the angel-figure.

The road from Jerusalem to Gaza leads at first through the Judaean highlands to the hilly southern Shephelah. This Shephelah has little water and is only sparsely inhabited then. Gaza is situated ca. 100 km southwest of Jerusalem on the coast. Gaza is the last "free" Hellenistic city (polis) on the trade route to Egypt. "Desert" prepares the reader for an undisturbed encounter.

Verse 27 "Walking" was the usual form of travel. From Samaria Philip needed at least one day to reach the branch road running from Jerusalem to Gaza. The main road went in the north-west direction to the Jewish harbour city of Joppa and connected to the coast-road in Lydda. Both towns are later named in connection with Peter (Acts 9:32–35.36–43). Philip becomes the missionary of south-west Judaea, the area of the old Philistine cities and the newly constructed (postexilic) Hellenistic cities of Gaza and Ashdod (v. 40) to the south of the main road to Joppa. "Ethiopia" is the Greek term for the Egyptian "Nubia." Nubia begins south of Aswan, located at the first cataract of the Nile. Nubia is included as part of Egypt in the list of nations in Acts 2:10. Nubia/Ethiopia was the southern end of the world known at that time. The king-mother had the title "Candace." She was the ruler. Their high officials were eunuchs.[29] "Eunuchos" (a castrated male person) describes exactly the situation. According to Dtn 23:2 a eunuch was not allowed to become a Jew. Therefore the "chief treasurer" could not be a proselyte.[30]

As "God-fearer" he traveled to the temple; there he was allowed to go only into the court of the gentiles. The *proskynesis* (worship) of the Ethiopian corresponds to the intention of the cleansing of the temple by Jesus. The court of the temple should become once more a house of prayer for all (Lc 19:46).

Verse 28 The mode of travel indicates a high government official. The Roman chariots were reserved only for the express post and

---

[29] Roloff, Apostelgeschichte, 140.

[30] von Dobbeler, A., Der Evangelist Philippus in der Geschichte des Urchristentums. Eine prosographische Skizze (TANZ 30), Tübingen/Basel 2000, 112f., against Pesch, Apostelgeschichte, 1, 288–91: probably not a eunuch and therefore a Proselyt; Haenchen, Apostelgeschichte, 300, and Kollmann, "Philippus der Evangelist und die Anfänge der Heidenmission," *Bibl* 81 (2000), 551–65, 557, anots Plutarch: "he (Lysimachos) was incensed that Demetrius considered him a eunuch (it was the general practise to have eunuchs for treasurers)" (Plut. Demetr. 25, transl. Perrin).

for high officials. Friendly states could get a permit to use a state-chariot or to travel with their own chariot. The audible reading of the book of Isaiah indicates the curiosity and education of the treasurer. He can read and he is reading aloud according to ancient custom.[31]

Verses 29–30 Philip needs the message of the Spirit to recognize the possibility of conversation with the high, foreign official. Philip "runs up" to the chariot and hears the audible reading. Isaiah was the most popular prophet. In the New Testament the book was the most quoted of all of the prophets. Every Jewish household should have a copy of the book (4 Macc 18:14). Philip takes the initiative to run alongside the chariot as if he were exercising. The question of "understanding" is central. In a similar way, the two disciples of Emmaus wonder about the "non-understanding" of the "stranger" (Lc 24:18).[32] Here the counterpart occurs. Philip who joins the chariot directly asks about the understanding, but Jesus asks about the content of the dialogue (Lc 24:17).

Verse 31 The treasurer immediately reveals his desire for instruction, but Jesus directs the attention of the disciples of Emmaus to their lack of understanding only after a long narrative (Lc 24:19–27). Both cases have a narrative of encounter with the goal of correct scripture-exegesis. Philip and the treasurer are in more direct contact with each other than the Emmaus-disciples and Jesus. The request of the Ethiopian shows the immediate acceptance of Philip as a competent exegete (*hodegeo*). Philip may go into the chariot and sit as an equal beside the high official. Philip is elevated.

Verses 32–33 The quotation of Isaiah 53:7–8 about the death of the suffering servant of God was cited in the Markan passion account (Mc 14:49.61). But the evangelist Luke had not taken over the scriptural reference of Scripture in those places. Now he cites the complete according to the LXX. Without resistance and speech the servant of God allows himself to be brought to execution. His shameful death becomes the turning point. "Judgement" is lifted; life is renewed by the "lifting up from the earth" to the heaven. With this theology of the suffering and elevated servant of God the early

---

[31] Haenchen, Apostelgeschichte, 300 cites Aug. Conf. 6,3; Plat. Phaidros could be added.
[32] von Dobbeler, Evangelist, 109–11.

Verses 34–35 The term "eunuch" emphasizes the suffering of the questioner. He asks the question not as a high official treasurer, but as a mutilated human being. He has experienced a destiny that is analogous to the fate of the servant of God.[33] Therefore the eunuch is interested in the controversial issue that continues to the present time. Does the prophet Second Isaiah (Jes 40–55) have in mind his own fate or the future fate of his nation? Philip finds a third solution. The prophet has in mind an individual future figure. The "gospel" of Jesus Christ fulfills this expectation. Jesus' fate is in line with the suffering prophet. The words and deeds of Jesus recounted in the first book proclaim salvation for those who are ill and mutilated. With the risen Christ they still experience healing and raising.[34] Therefore Philip "proclaims" to the eunuch the whole "gospel" of Jesus that forms the first book.

Verse 36 With his answer the eunuch allows time to elapse. He is reflecting. They come to "some water," maybe a cistern, or a pool fed by a spring, or a river. The water awakens the wish of the eunuch. He wants to be baptized. The quotation of Isaiah had spoken merely about death and raising, but the preaching of the gospel by Jesus began with water baptism. The water caused the eunuch to become aware that he could now participate in the forgiveness of sins and in the salvation of the coming kingdom of God.

With Verse 37 some manuscripts of the western tradition add a confession of faith. This addition is secondary and is missing in modern translations of the Bible.

Verse 38 The eunuch remains active. He commands the driver to stop. With Philip he climbs down from the chariot to the water and he humbly submits to baptism. Both are standing naked in the water according to the antique custom.

Verse 39 Both ascend out of the water. But there is no miraculous healing of the castration. Instead of this a miracle of a spatial shift

---

[33] von Dobbeler, Evangelist, 114 claims that the "model–reader" the quotation Jes 56,3–5 out of Third-Jesaja associates additional to Jes 53,7–8: "No eunuch should say 'Look, I am a dried-up tree'" (Js 53,3). This association is possible, but not hinted by the evangelist. The identification of the eunuch with the servant of God could be performed by the reader without this passage (so Haenchen, Apostelgeschichte, 300 Anm. 5).

[34] Roloff, Apostelgeschichte, 141f.

of Philip takes place.[35] The Spirit "snatched" Philip away just as the Spirit had come to Jesus (Lc 3:22) and led him in the desert (Lc 4:1). The eunuch cannot see Philip any longer. But he does not seek him. Full of joy he continues his way home. As in Emmaus the Jesus-proclaimer disappears (Lc 24:31). He is no longer needed. The baptism alone produces the joy. Bodily healings do not happen during the baptism. The encounter between the baptizer and the baptized remains brief. The incorporation in the community of the suffering and risen Jesus remains the more meaningful action. The eunuch also has a place in the restored Israel of Jesus.

Verse 40 Philip "is found" by others near the Hellenistic harbor city of Ashdod, 40 km. away. He travels around and proclaims the gospel in every town on the coast. To be sure, he spares the Jewish Joppa and Lydda (Acts 9:32–43). He later reaches the capital city of Caesarea. There he takes up residence with his four prophesying daughters (Acts 21:8–9). But first the mission in Caesarea is taken over by Peter (Acts 10).

2.3. *Impulses of Action*

Philip and the eunuch are identification figures. The story of the meeting with the eunuch is analogous to the model of the Greco-Roman novel of love. "Eros" brings friends and lovers together. Longus wrote the popular novel: "Daphnis and Chloe" (2nd C.E.). In the story, the two characters, shepherd and shepherdess, eventually come together permanently. At first, they are constantly separated, but at last they are allowed to marry.

Xenophon of Ephesus wrote the "Ephesiaka" (*The Ephesian Romance*) also in the 2nd century. The insulted "Eros" impels the young Habrocomes to love, disaster, and a happy ending.

The Spirit symbolizes holy restlessness. It drives the "evangelist" Philip (Act 21:8). Like Jesus Philip is moving about without permanent residence.[36] He is open for spontaneous meetings resulting in conversion. He overcomes social barriers. He recognizes the high official as a life-long mutilated suffering human being. Philip is able to grasp the religious question of that man. Bodily illness was taboo

---

[35] Roloff, Apostelgeschichte, 142.
[36] Roloff, Apostelgeschichte, 138f.; detailed von Dobbeler, Evangelist, 127–47, against Pesch, Apostelgeschichte, 1, 287–10: jerusalemer Gebietsmission.

in the ancient world. The eunuch was not allowed to become a Jew. In Hellenism, he was also not allowed to participate publically in sports. For only the totally healthy man was allowed to publically show his nakedness. The eunuch was separated from his sexuality, from his roles as husband and father, and from public attention.

The eunuch could find himself in the quotation concerning the suffering servant of God. The symbolism of water-baptism promises a new creation. The old stigmata are washed away; a new healthy human being climbs out of the water. Simultaneously the eschatological tension becomes visible. The exalted Ethiopian must continue to live as eunuch within the earthly conditions. Only when the completion of the kingdom of God comes will he receive bodily healing. This tension does not cloud the joy of the Ethiopian over his new Christian life.

But he has not yet received the Holy Spirit. The fact that the Spirit intervenes three times focuses upon the truth that to this point the Ethiopian sees only the effect of the Spirit. After his arrival in Nubia, the Ethiopian must make contact with the apostolic tradition in Jerusalem and Judaea. Then the Spirit will fall upon him completely. According to the evangelist, that time has not yet come. Therefore the Spirit does not bring to the Ethiopian an apostle who could lay his hands on the head of the Ethiopian. The evangelist has shaped a narrative of hope. The gospel will soon reach Ethiopia and will (according to the ancient geography) reach for the first time the "end of the world" (Act 1:8). The high official awaits the full yearning of love.

The cycle of Philip narratives ends with such a meeting-story. The verb *evangelizo* is used 15 times in the book of Acts. Four times the verb is used in reference to Philip (over one-fourth of the total number of uses). Only Philip gets the important title "evangelist" (Acts 21:8). Philip is the most important proclaimer of the gospel outside of the apostles (the twelve, Barnabas and Paul).[37] Beyond them,

---

[37] In oral tradition the conversion of the ethiopean God-fearing eunuch by Philippus has rivaled with the conversion-story of the pagan officer Cornelius by Peter in Acts 10: Haenchen, Apostelgeschichte, 305; Conzelmann, H., Die Apostelgeschichte (HNT 7), Tübingen 1963, 63; Schneider, G., Die Apostelgeschichte (HThK NT V 1–2), Freiburg 1980–82, 498; Roloff, Apostelgeschichte, 138f.; Weiser, A., Die Apostelgeschichte, 2 Bde., ÖTK 5,1–2, Gütersloh 1981–85, 211; Jervell, J., Die Apostelgeschichte (KEK 3), Göttingen 1998, 175; Avemarie, F., Die Tauferzählungen der Apostelgeschichte. Theologie und Geschichte (WUNT 139), Tübingen 2001, 288.

Jewish Hellenists proclaim the gospel in Antioch (Acts 11:20). The circle around Paul also proclaims the gospel (Acts 16:10). Like the apostles Philip is honored by the deeds of the Spirit and of the angel. Unique is the information concerning his family. In the first book there was information about the house of Simon Petrus and about his mother-in-law (Lc 4:38–39). In the second book there is no longer a word about the family of Peter or of the other members of the apostolic circle. Relatives of Barnabas and Paul, who are later called apostles (Acts 14:4.14), are indeed mentioned.

They make short guest appearances. One of them fails when tested (Acts 13:13; 15:36–41); the other stands the test (Acts 23:16–22). But the two are not selected to bear the Spirit. Only the four daughters of Philip have the special spiritual gift of prophecy (Acts 21:9).

With his four prophetic daughters, the evangelist "Philip" represents a charismatic group. They have done independent missionary work in Samaria and on the southern coast. They have had friendly contact with the movement of Simon. With ecstasy both have performed miracles and preached. Therefore the conversion of the travelling Ethiopian is historically probable.[38] The Philip-movement always acknowledged the priority of the apostolic tradition and did not demand equality with the apostolic circle of the twelve. Their high estimation of prophetic women continues the intention of Jesus. The gift of the Spirit and the apostolic tradition remains connected with the apostles.

2.4. *Mental Imagination*

Syntactic construction, production of semantic coherence, and the construction of models of action are works of cognitive linguistics. Sjef van Tilborg and Patrick Chatelion Counet show with Philostratus (*Imagines* 1:4, 23ff.) that evoking of images is a part of mental imagination. They conclude:

- Visual images are represented in a special spatial medium;
- the spatial medium has four essential properties: 1) it functions as a space of limited boundaries; it has a specified shape and

---

[38] Roloff, Apostelgeschichte, 139; Pesch, Apostelgeschichte, 1, 287; Jervell, Apostelgeschichte, 275; von Dobbeler, Evangelist, 125, 177–80; Avemarie, Apostelgeschichte, 289.

a capacity to depict spatial relationships; 2) its area of highest resolution is at its center; 3) the medium has a grain that obscures details on "small" images; 4) once the image is generated in the medium it begins to fade;
- a variety of processes use image files, prepositional files, and the spatial medium in order to generate, interpret, and transform images.[39]

On May 22, 2003, Sjef died. He had a weak heart. His death was anticipated, but his sudden death surprised and saddened all his friends.

Now I am looking at his picture, trying to imagine a dialogue with him. What would he say about my imaginative construction of the scene of Philip baptizing the eunuch? I think that he would encourage me to develop space more explicitly and the appearances and disappearances of the actors.

At the beginning of the narrative the space is not named. Only the main actor is announced. "An angel" appears unexpectedly and gives a command to Philip. The angel could be visualized by a small cupid (amor/putto). The command is full of local places. A "picture" develops. A classical master from Pompeii or a Dutch painter of landscapes might shape it precisely in this fashion: On the opposite edges of the painting are situated two skylines of cities. In between runs an isolated road beneath the mid-day sun. Now action begins to take place. Philip arises from his reclining position. He begins to realize externally the internal picture from a dream or a vision. He seeks to situate his picture in the correct geographical circumstances.

The narrator directs the view of the observer to a second person. The observer is not provided a name, but he is given a detailed description of character. For the character Philip the first name is enough, because Philip is well known to the reader. The second figure must be introduced by a laudatory description. The informations "man," "eunuch," "official," "queen," "treasurer" produce a brilliant figure; "Ethiopian" and "Candace" create an exotic color.

The city in the east, that is Jerusalem, is named again. "Pilgrimage" indicates a past scene in Jerusalem. The picture of Jerusalem includes the temple with its courts. In the court of the Gentiles, the God-fearing official makes a sign of homage, that is a *proskynese* (v. 27).

---

[39] van Tilborg and Chatelion Counet, *Jesus* 5.

The imagination moves to the present, but the new picture is situated on the same level of the canvas. The official is traveling on the road to Gaza and appears now in the middle of the canvas. He is sitting in the chariot, reading from a scroll of the prophet Isaiah. From the upper, northern frame Philip has reached the road during the chariot ride of the official. Philip now has the decision to let the chariot proceed or to join the action taking place on the "desert" road and to run beside the chariot. The Spirit (apart from the figure of an angel) inspires Philip a second time to join the chariot. The reader imagines a new internal process. The external realization of this imagination creates again a new picture: Philip running beside the chariot and talking with the Ethiopian.

Analysis of the syntax of the text allows the following interaction between Philip and the official.

Sequence 7 becomes the high point of the second part. The baptism is narrated. It realizes the Christian proclamation of Isaiah 53:7f. in the praxis of faith. Avemarie makes the following claim about this scene:

> The remaining details, the mutual going down into the water and the baptism ritual performed by the proclaimer, the description of the act of baptism, seem to be superfluous because the narrative has a strict limitation of themes. One suspects that Luke has preserved here an older tradition.[40]

The search for breaks and for old traditions leads Avemarie to a hasty devaluation of the baptism which is the high point of the second part. But Haenchen remarks briefly and correctly:

Baptizer and baptized go into the water.[41]

Indeed the goal of the narrative and imagination is situated here. The Spirit has brought together the God-seeking official and the Christ-proclaiming Philip. Philip has run; the treasurer has travelled with a chariot; they have sought each other; Philip has climbed up alongside the treasurer; they have conversed earnestly. They have found a solution.

Now it is usual in the ancient culture that after the labors the new friends and lovers take a bath together. A thermal bath is not

---

[40] Avemarie, Apostelgeschichte, 269.
[41] Haenchen, Apostelgeschichte, 302.

there. Such a bath would also not be the right place, for the everyday fun of bathing and relaxation is not intended, but the mystery-bath of the baptism. At the same time, it is necessary for the new friends to go together into the baptismal waters and become inseparable by this act. The healthy athletic evangelist touches the mutilated eunuch. Cultural and religious distances are effaced. The view of the narrator is narrowed to these two figures. The integration of the driver or other servants is not intended. The same concentration of view point is repeated during the baptism of Paul. Paul and not his companions are baptized (Acts 9:1–19). It is possible, but not necessary, that an early stage of the Christian mission is reflected in these baptisms involving only one person.[42] But the intention of the narrator is not directed to an old baptism-ritual, but to the meeting of two related souls. The later German classic romanticism dreamed of such an intensive meeting. Two friends go together out of the water. The mutual mystery = sacramental bath of baptism connects them for all time.

The picture is completed: The Spirit takes Philip away to his area of mission on the coast; the Spirit impels the official to continue his return to the southern end of the world. With joy they go in opposite directions. For as partners of dialogue and baptism they remain closely connected in all localities, nearby or at a distance. They can always imagine the personal presence of the other. Missionaries of the Holy Heart of Jesus (MSC, van Tilborg was a member) and all the other readers may find a fundamental basis in this meeting-narrative for their missionary work and their community—even according to the very heart of Sjef van Tilborg.

---

[42] von Dobbeler, Evangelist, 117–22.

CHAPTER THIRTEEN

THE RHETORICAL ANALYSIS OF GALATIANS: IS THERE ANOTHER WAY?

D. Francois Tolmie
University of the Free State
Bloemfontein, South Africa

To a large extent the rhetorical analysis of the Letter to the Galatians has reached an *impasse*. As is well known, H.D. Betz[1] carried out pioneering work on the rhetorical analysis of this Pauline letter. He proposed that it should be regarded as an example of the ancient "apologetic letter genre" and that it should therefore be analyzed by using Greco-Roman rhetoric and epistolography. Since then, scholars have spent much time in determining whether the letter should indeed be regarded as an apologetic letter or not. Whereas some scholars accept Betz's proposal in a qualified way,[2] others argue that the letter should be regarded as a mixture of two types of rhetoric,[3] whereas still other scholars believe that it should be regarded as an example of deliberative oratory.[4] In general it may be stated that many scholars still assume that one may use ancient rhetoric in some way or another to explain Paul's rhetorical strategy in the Letter to the Galatians. However, this view has recently been challenged by scholars such as Anderson and Kern. In his study on ancient rhetorical theory and Paul, R.D. Anderson reveals the weak foundations of many rhetorical analyses of Galatians (and of other Pauline letters).

---

[1] H.D. Betz, *Galatians* (1979).
[2] For example, B.H. Brinsmead, *Galatians* (1982), and H. Hübner, *Der Galaterbrief* (1993) 241–50.
[3] For example, D.E. Aune, *Review* (1981) 325–26 (a mixture of forensic and deliberative rhetoric) and J. Schoon-Janšen, *Apologien* (1991) 70–82, 112–13 (Galatians 1,10–2,14 can be classified as pure forensic oratory; Galatians 3,1–5,12 is a mixture of deliberative and forensic oratory; and Galatians 5,13–6,18 is pure deliberative oratory).
[4] For example, G.A. Kennedy, *New Testament Interpretation* (1984) 145–47, and J. Smit, *Deliberative Speech* (1989) 1–26.

For example, in his discussion of the available sources for ancient rhetorical theory, he points out several important aspects which New Testament scholars usually do not take into account when applying ancient rhetorical theory to New Testament texts. These include the fact that no uniform ancient rhetorical system existed; that there was a considerable difference between philosophical rhetoric (such as that of Aristotle) and the kind of rhetoric practiced in rhetorical schools; that actual rhetorical practice was more flexible than the seemingly endless distinctions and rules formulated in rhetorical schools appear to suggest; and that our knowledge of ancient rhetoric is incomplete owing to the fact that many the sources were lost.[5] This inevitably leads to the question: "Can we use ancient rhetorical criticism at all when studying Paul's letters?" Anderson's answer is that the only solution to this thorny issue would be to change one's approach. Instead of applying an ancient rhetorical model to one of Paul's letters, as if Paul had known and followed such a model closely, the question should be rephrased as follows: how would the ancient rhetorical theoretician have applied his theory to Paul's letter? However, as Anderson points out himself, this would inevitably tell us more of the ancient literary theoretician's views of Paul's literary ability than about what Paul himself might have thought.[6]

The study by P.H. Kern[7] should also be mentioned here, as he also challenges the notion that Galatians is either a sample of classical rhetoric or that it could be interpreted in the light of ancient rhetorical textbooks. To my mind, he refutes this hypothesis convincingly.

In the light of the criticism raised by Anderson and Kern in respect of the dominant approach to the rhetorical analysis of Galatians, I wish to suggest another alternative in this article: instead of choosing a specific ancient rhetorical model (or, for that matter, even a modern rhetorical model) and "applying" it to the text, why not work the other way around and instead use the letter itself as the starting-point in an attempt to reconstruct Paul's rhetorical strategy from the text itself? In other words, why not attempt to do a *text-centered descriptive analysis of the way in which Paul attempts to persuade the Galatians*? In the rest of the article I wish to demonstrate how such

---

[5] R.D. Anderson, *Ancient Rhetorical Theory* (1999) 35–97.
[6] R.D. Anderson, *Ancient Rhetorical Theory* (1999) 104–05.
[7] P.H. Kern, *Rhetoric and Galatians* (1998).

a study could be done. Owing to the limitations imposed by the required length of the article, I will demonstrate this by analyzing two brief sections in the letter, namely Gal 1:1–5 and 1:6–10.

Of course, one would need a basic guideline, a minimal theoretical framework, to guide such an analysis. I suggest the following: the first step in the analysis of a particular section could comprise the identification of what I wish to call the *dominant rhetorical strategy* in that particular section. In this regard I shall try to answer the following two questions, namely: "How can one describe Paul's primary rhetorical objective in the specific section?," and, secondly, "How does he attempt to achieve this objective?" Secondly, the identification of the dominant rhetorical strategy can then be followed by a detailed analysis of Paul's rhetorical strategy in the particular section. In this case I shall focus primarily on the *types of arguments* he uses and why they are effective. I use the expression "type of argument" in a very specific sense, namely to indicate the nature of the specific argument. Lastly, I will indicate what I wish to call "rhetorical techniques." This refers to the various ways in which Paul enhances the effectiveness of his communication. Most of the techniques that are identified are well known, for example, the use of metaphor, rhetorical questions, and chiasm.

1. *Galatians 1:1–5: Adapting the Salutation in Order to Emphasize the Divine Origin of his Apostleship*

In the opening salutation of his letters Paul usually follows a particular pattern: he employs the three traditional elements (sender, receiver, and greetings), but normally describes the sender and receiver elements in more precise terms.[8] He also changes the normal χαῖρειν to the fuller "grace to you and peace" and christianizes it. However, it is also true that he never uses a static pattern for the opening salutation of his letters, as he usually adapts the salutation to the particular occasion. This also happens in Galatians: he adapts the salutation of this letter to the specific situation in several ways. It is important to realize that he does this to persuade the Galatians to adopt his point of view. The dominant rhetorical strategy in this

---

[8] F. Schnider and W. Stenger, *Briefformular* (1987) 4–24.

section can thus be described as *adapting typical letter elements (in this case, the salutation) in order to persuade the Galatians*. Three aspects deserve attention, but, as will become clear, the first one is the most important.

1.1. *Emphasis on the Divine Origin of his Apostleship*

To the modern reader, the fact that Galatians is the first of Paul's extant letters in which he introduces himself as an apostle is important, but, of course, the Galatians would not have realized this. However, the way in which Paul immediately proceeds to qualify his apostleship could not have gone unnoticed: οὐκ ἀπ' ἀνθρώπων οὐδὲ δι' ἀνθρώπου ἀλλὰ διὰ Ἰησοῦ Χριστοῦ καὶ θεοῦ πατρὸς. The abruptness of these words is often noted in analyses of this passage. In a rhetorical study the important issue is to identify Paul's purpose in doing this. The most obvious answer is that he is defending his apostleship against accusations by his opponents in Galatia—as pointed out by most scholars. In this case the abrupt and unexpected use of these words implies that the issue of his apostleship was so important to him that he used the first opportunity in the letter to address it.

An examination of the contents of Paul's statement in Galatians 1:1 reveals that its primary purpose is to emphasize in a forceful way the notion that his apostleship is dependent on (and thus authorized by) God and not on (a) human being(s). The type of argument he uses may thus be identified as *an argument based on the notion of divine authorization*. It is based on the presupposition that, in order to be an apostle, one should have been called by God. In this case Paul claims that he is indeed an apostle, because he has been called by God. The importance of this argument from Paul's perspective is evident from the fact that he introduces it at the outset of the letter.

It should also be noted that the way in which Paul conveys this notion to the audience enhances its effect. Instead of merely mentioning the positive side of the argument, he begins with two denials before expressing the notion he wishes to convey. The rhetorical technique he uses in this instance may be called *antithetic presentation*. This antithetic οὐκ... οὐδὲ... ἀλλὰ structure is more persuasive than a mere positive statement. It thus serves an accentuating purpose.[9]

---

[9] Thus, correctly, C.J. Classen, *Rhetorical Criticism* (2000) 18.

Furthermore, it should be noted that this is the only argument that is emphasized in Galatians 1:1–5: his apostleship is not only mentioned in passing, but it is also forcefully highlighted by means of the antithetical way in which it is expressed. The other notions in Galatians 1:1–5 are not emphasized to a similar extent, but are merely mentioned (see the discussion below). It is thus clear that the issue of the divine origin of Paul's apostleship dominates the first five verses of the letter.

1.2. *The Reference to Co-senders*

As usual,[10] Paul also refers to co-senders in Galatians. Contrary to his usual procedure, he does not mention specific co-senders, such as Sosthenes (1 Corinthians 1:1) or Timothy (2 Corinthians 1:1) in Galatians, but rather indicates the co-senders as "all the brothers with me" (οἱ σὺν ἐμοὶ πάντες ἀδελφοί). The rhetorical function of these words is to convey the notion of a group of people standing behind him, endorsing and underscoring everything in the letter. It is also important to note that πάντες is used in an emphatic way in order to suggest solid support for his position. It must be noted, however, that Paul does not develop this issue to any extent. It is merely implied and can thus only be indicated as a supportive strategy.

1.3. *Appeal to Tradition*

The third significant feature in Paul's persuasive strategy in this section is his frequent reference to core ideas in the early Christian tradition—in particular, in Galatians 1:1 and 1:4:

1:1: . . . καὶ θεοῦ πατρὸς τοῦ ἐγείραντος αὐτὸν ἐκ νεκρῶν.

1:4: τοῦ δόντος ἑαυτὸν ὑπὲρ τῶν ἁμαρτιῶν ἡμῶν, ὅπως ἐξέληται ἡμᾶς ἐκ τοῦ αἰῶνος τοῦ ἐνεστῶτος πονηροῦ κατὰ τὸ θέλημα τοῦ θεοῦ καὶ πατρὸς ἡμῶν, ᾧ ἡ δόξα εἰς τοὺς αἰῶνας τῶν αἰώνων.

Both these statements refer to shared knowledge in early Christianity and it is almost certain that Paul is echoing well-known credal formulae of the time.[11] Three aspects should be noted.

---

[10] See the table in F. Schnider and W. Stenger, *Briefformular* (1987) 5–6.
[11] This is often noted in commentaries. See, for example, F. Mussner, *Galaterbrief* (1977) 46–50 and J.L. Martyn, *Galatians* (1998) 89.

First, a general remark should be made about the use of tradition when a person tries to persuade someone else. Tradition is an example of knowledge shared by both speaker and audience, and it may thus be used rhetorically in a highly effective manner, since its truth will not be disputed by the audience. In fact, the speaker can accept that the audience will believe it to be true. This shared knowledge may then be used as a common ground for the view advocated by the speaker. This is also true in this instance. The type of argument Paul uses in this case may be called an *argument based on Christian tradition*. This type of argument is highly effective. In this regard the research by A. Eriksson[12] should be cited, since Eriksson shows convincingly how effectively Paul uses Christian tradition as rhetorical proof in 1 Corinthians—not only on a logical level, but also in other ways.[13] This is also true of Paul's use of Christian tradition in the Letter to the Galatians.

Secondly, one should ask what Paul's purpose is in using tradition at this stage in his letter. If one considers what is quoted here, one will observe that it focuses on the inauguration of the eschatological age by Christ's resurrection,[14] and, in particular, in the case of verse 4, on the interpretation of Jesus' voluntary death as something that happened according to God's will in order to effect eschatological liberation.[15] Thus, one can summarize the notion which Paul wishes to convey as follows: (according to Christian tradition) Jesus Christ gave himself in order to liberate humankind from the present age of evil. This is extremely relevant to the issues debated in this letter and, in particular, to the notion of spiritual liberty which becomes so important in Paul's argument later. However, it should be noted that he does not use tradition as a basis for proving any-

---

[12] A. Eriksson, *Traditions* (1998).

[13] What Eriksson writes in this regard about Paul's use of tradition in 1 Corinthians, is certainly true of Galatians, too: "Looking at the traditions from a rhetorical point of view, we can assume that, besides their logos or theological content, the traditions would also have had strong ethos and pathos. The ethos would derive directly from the authority the traditions had as saving messages. The pathos comes from the use the traditions had in the Corinthian church. Included would have been all those memories, saturated with emotional significance, from various stages of their initiation in the Christian group (which would have included conversion and baptism) and from their joint worship (including celebrations of the Lord's Supper)." (A. Eriksson, *Traditions* [1998] 134.)

[14] See R.A. Bryant, *Christ in Galatians* (2001) 144–46, for a detailed discussion of this issue.

[15] Thus, correctly, L. de Saeger, *Sünden* (2001) 179.

thing at this stage. He merely mentions it. Thus, it seems fair to assume that his purpose in using tradition in this section is not so much polemical, but rather to "bind" the audience to him, and to achieve a common understanding as a potential ground for an agreement before proceeding to controversial issues later. This "binding effect" is further enhanced by the way in which he uses *inclusive language* as a rhetorical technique in this section: from "*Paul* and the brothers with *me*..." to "grace and peace to *you*" to "... from *our* Father...," "Christ who gave himself for *our* sins... rescue *us*." In fact, Paul only uses the inclusive "we" again in Galatians 3:14.

Thirdly, the fact that Paul does not use shared knowledge in a polemical way in this section is also important from another perspective. For example, one could speculate that it would have been fairly easy for him to slip in the crucial words "through belief (in Jesus Christ)," yet he refrains from doing so. The fact that he does not use the tradition in a polemic way in this instance highlights an important aspect of his rhetorical strategy. Apparently, from his perspective, the most decisive issue in this conflict was the issue of divine authorization: if this crucial point could be settled in his favor, his message would automatically be accepted. Thus, the fact that he immediately tackles the issue of divine authorization and avoids a polemical discussion of the contents of his gospel at this stage indicates that, from a strategic perspective, he thought that the best way to persuade the Galatians was not to begin with the contents of his gospel, but rather with the issue of divine authorization—formulated in this section in terms of the divine origin of his apostleship. The apparent logic behind this strategy is that it is futile to try to convince them of "his *gospel*" if they are not convinced that the "*he*" of "his gospel" has been authorized by God.

To conclude: in Galatians 1:1-5 Paul's dominant rhetorical strategy can be described as "adapting the salutation in order to emphasize the divine origin of his apostleship." Of the three ways in which he adapts the salutation, the most important is the way in which the sender element is adapted in order to convey the notion that he is an apostle, because he has been called by God (an argument based on the notion of divine authorization). This notion is conveyed effectively by means of a rhetorical technique, identified as antithetic presentation.

Two other ways in which Paul adapts the salutation were also pointed out, namely the reference to co-senders (1:2) and an appeal to shared tradition (1:4–5)—the latter being enhanced by the use of inclusive language. However, Paul does not develop these aspects, indicating that the emphasis does not fall on them, but on the divine origin of his apostleship.

2. *Galatians 1:6–10: Expressing Disgust at Events in the Galatian Churches in Order to Force Them to Reconsider Their Position*

Scholars who choose to apply categories from ancient rhetorical criticism to the Letter to the Galatians usually identify this section (or part thereof) as the *exordium*.[16] However, J.S. Vos[17] has indicated that this is rather pointless, as in that case the concept must be used in a way that does not correspond to its use in antiquity, since the primary function of the exordium was to prepare the listeners psychologically for the speaker and his statement of case. Accordingly, I shall refrain from categorizing this section in terms of ancient rhetorical distinctions, and, instead, will draw attention to Paul's persuasive strategy here. To my mind the dominant rhetorical strategy in this section can be summarized as *expressing his disgust at the events in Galatia*. His primary purpose therefore seems to be to convey his *emotional dissatisfaction* with circumstances in Galatian churches. The presence of such intense feelings in this section explains the use of several forceful rhetorical techniques, which are effective for conveying such feelings, namely rebuke, vilification, a twofold curse, and rhetorical questions. The sole purpose of these techniques is to persuade the Galatians to *reconsider* what they are about to do. I would like to draw attention to four strategies which Paul employs to achieve this.

2.1. *Rebuke*

One of the features noted most frequently by scholars in this section is the absence of an introductory thanksgiving. Paul probably

---

[16] For example, H.D. Betz, *Galatians* (1979) 44 (he adds verse 11); G.A. Kennedy, *New Testament Interpretation* (1984) 148; J. Becker, *Paulus* (1981) 291; and G. Ebeling, *Wahrheit* (1981) 55. R.G. Hall, *Rhetorical Outline* (1987) 285, identifies it as the *propositio*.

[17] J.S. Vos, *Die Kunst der Argumentation* (2002) 92. See also his critical discussion of Betz's reasons for classifying this section as an *exordium*.

intended its omission as a definite sign of rebuke to the audience. However, the audience would seemingly not have realized that something was missing here, as they were not aware that Paul made a habit of including a thanksgiving at this point in the letter,[18] and it was not customary in Greek letters to include a prayer of thanksgiving. Numerous contemporary papyrus letters contain another element, namely a report of the writer's prayer for the recipients at the beginning of the letter.[19] One may assume that his audience would have been familiar with this habit, and that its absence—if not taken as a direct rebuke—would, at least, have been strange to them.

Instead of a thanksgiving Paul uses θαυμάζω—an element found regularly in letters of his time.[20] He uses this *expression of perplexity* with great rhetorical effect in order to rebuke the Galatians:[21] Θαυμάζω ὅτι οὕτως ταχέως μετατίθεσθε ἀπὸ τοῦ καλέσαντος ὑμᾶς ἐν χάριτι [Χριστοῦ] εἰς ἕτερον εὐαγγέλιον. By using the word μετατίθεσθε he conveys his negative views on the Galatians' turning away very forcefully, as this word bears the negative overtones of desertion or betrayal.[22] The rebuke is indeed harsh: he finds it shocking that they are becoming "traitors" so soon. He also emphasizes the real nature of their action: they are deserting the "one who called them." This is phrased in an ambiguous way. As a rule, he uses this expression to refer to God,[23] but it could also refer to himself in this case, as there certainly is a close connection between Paul's gospel and God's calling. As Schlier[24] puts it: "Ruf Gottes und apostolisches Kerygma des Paulus sind fur die hörenden Galater identisch." Furthermore, it should be noted that Paul describes their behavior as moving away from grace. Once again he uses an ambiguous expression: ἐν χάριτι can refer either to the state into which they were called or to the means by which they were called. Perhaps one should rather assume that both are intended.[25]

---

[18] Thus, correctly, D. Kremendahl, *Botschaft* (2000) 99.
[19] See the study by P. Arzt, *Thanksgiving* (1994) 29–46—in particular 44–46. Note that his study indicates that there was no such thing as a customary "introductory thanksgiving" in the papyrus letters contemporaneous with the New Testament letters, but that a set report of prayer does occur frequently.
[20] D. Kremendahl, *Botschaft* (2000) 99–103, discusses this in detail.
[21] J.K. Roberts, *Perplexity* (1992) 351–58.
[22] See H.D. Betz, *Galatians* (1979) 48, and J.D.G. Dunn, *Galatians* (1993) 39–40.
[23] R.N. Longenecker, *Galatians* (1990) 15.
[24] H. Schlier, *Galater* (1971) 38.
[25] See A. Oepke, *Galater* (1973) 48.

To summarize: in verse 6 Paul uses rebuke to express his disgust at the behavior of the Galatians. In particular, he wishes to convey two notions to them: 1. that it is wrong to change sides so quickly, and 2. that they are actually turning against God.

2.2. *Vilification of the Opponents*

In verse 7 Paul shifts the focus from the Galatians to his opponents, and his argumentative strategy changes from rebuke to vilification of his opponents. Vilification was a widespread phenomenon in early Christian epistolography and in the Mediterranean world.[26] In this case Paul achieves this as follows:

The opponents' message is denied the status of gospel: εἰς ἕτερον εὐαγγέλιον, ὃ οὐκ ἔστιν ἄλλο. Although he refers to their message at first as "gospel," he immediately corrects himself, thus using a rhetorical technique that could be called *correction*.[27] The notion Paul wants to convey is that the opponents' message is a different gospel which is not similar to the real gospel. Thus, it is not to be considered as gospel at all!

- Instead of naming his opponents directly, he refers to them merely as τινές. This was common practice in antiquity.[28] In this case its intended effect is to create the impression that Paul's opponents are insignificant, that their names are not worth mentioning, and that they are few in number. This serves to vilify them.
- Paul uses words with very negative overtones. He accuses his opponents of "disturbing" the Galatians and of "changing" the gospel. The first word (ταράσσω) has the connotation of political agitation whereby turmoil and confusion are caused,[29] and the second (μεταστρέφω) suggests a change for the worse; a perversion of the gospel.[30] In this way Paul succeeds in portraying the actions of his opponents in a very negative light, thereby casting

---

[26] A.B. du Toit, *Vilification* (1994) 403–12, distinguishes nine trends in this regard.

[27] In ancient rhetoric this was called metabolh and was thought to cause the audience to be more favorably disposed towards one's case or to highlight the correction, thus impressing it upon the listeners. See R.D. Anderson, *Greek Rhetorical Terms* (2000) 71.

[28] H.D. Betz, *Galatians* (1979) 49; J.S. Vos, *Die Kunst der Argumentation* (2002) 91, calls it "die Depersonalisierung der Gegner."

[29] H.D. Betz, *Galatians* (1979) 49.

[30] F.F. Bruce, *Galatians* (1982) 82, and J.D.G. Dunn, *Galatians* (1993) 43.

doubts as to their intention and behavior. Thus, the notion he wishes to convey is that they are insincere people with evil motives.

2.3. *A Twofold Curse*

In verses 8–9 a shift in Paul's persuasive strategy occurs once again. Now he uses a twofold curse. Pronouncing a curse is one of the most effective rhetorical devices one can use. In ancient rhetoric, the effectiveness of using curses was often noted.[31] The twofold curse which Paul uses in verses 8 and 9 is structured very carefully. In the first curse he mentions two unlikely possibilities: that he or an angel would preach a different gospel to them. In the second curse he changes it to a more general curse which is "applied" to the situation in Galatia. Those who preach a gospel different from that which the Galatians received are now cursed.

In terms of its rhetorical function, Paul uses the twofold curse very effectively, thus achieving several objectives:

First, he continues the vilification of his opponents which he started in the previous verse. By pronouncing a curse on them he succeeds in portraying them in a very negative light: they are heading for God's judgement—and are to be avoided!

Secondly, by uttering such a curse Paul is claiming divine authority. In a sense, the use of the curse presupposes the argument that Paul used in the previous section, namely that he was called by God.[32]

Furthermore, the twofold curse also serves indirectly as a very strict warning to the Galatians. Although it is phrased in such a way that it is directed against those who proclaim a gospel that is no gospel, its force is wider: if the Galatians accept the "gospel" proclaimed by the opponents they will share in their doom. The curse therefore serves as a warning to them to return to Paul's gospel or to suffer the consequences.

---

[31] See H.D. Betz, *Galatians* (1979) 45–46.
[32] J.A. Morland, *Curse* (1995) 15, puts it as follows: "The double anathema challenges the Galatian audience to regard the opponents as cursed persons. Such a curse cannot be overlooked once it has been uttered. The primary pragmatic aspect of the curse is that it puts before the Galatian churches a very serious choice: Either to accept the double anathema as a carrier of divine authority, and thus to isolate the opponents, or to reject it as false, and thus to question the authority of Paul himself. The curse claims to carry divine authority, and therefore it demands to be accepted as such. The only alternative is to reject it as false. Thus the situation cannot be as it was before in Galatia: Once the curse has been uttered, the churches are forced to choose between the authority of Paul and his opponents."

Lastly, by including himself under the curse (although it is presented as being a very unlikely scenario) Paul succeeds in conveying the notion that no human being in him/herself can serve as a criterion for the truth of the gospel. In this way he conveys the message that the gospel is more important than any human being—even himself. It has its own existence and independence, as, in the last instance, it is based on divine authority.

2.4. *Refutation of Criticism*

In verse 10 the focus of Paul's rhetorical strategy shifts yet again. Before considering this aspect it is necessary to clarify the meaning of this verse—in particular, the first three rhetorical questions which can be interpreted in various ways. The sense of the first phrase (ἀνθρώπους πείθω) is negative: Paul rejects the idea that he is doing what some philosophers and orators are accused of, namely using skilful techniques in order to persuade people.[33] This is followed by a second phrase (ἢ τὸν θεόν;), to which the word πείθω must be added. This could be taken in either a positive or a negative sense. If it is interpreted in a positive sense Paul is saying: I am not attempting to persuade people, instead I am concerned only with what God wants.[34] If it is taken in a negative sense, it means: I am neither trying to persuade people, nor am I seeking to "persuade," i.e., manipulate God.[35] It is very difficult to choose between the two possibilities, since either would be feasible. Perhaps the fact that πείθω should be supplied from the previous phrase indicates that its negative force should also be carried to the second phrase. In the third phrase (ἢ ζητῶ ἀνθρώποις ἀρέσκειν;) the sense is once again negative. "Pleasing men" was seen as an unacceptable technique practiced by orators and philosophers who adapted their message to suit the listeners.[36] Instead, Paul claims that he does not follow such practices, as he would then no longer be a servant of Christ.

How should Paul's rhetorical strategy in verse 10 be described? This verse makes sense if one assumes that he is refuting criticism

---

[33] J.L. Martyn, *Galatians* (1998) 139.

[34] A. Oepke, *Galater* (1973) 53.

[35] See G. Ebeling, *Wahrheit* (1981) 63: "Gott überreden wollen, ihn geneigt machen wollen."

[36] H.D. Betz, *Galatians* (1979) 55.

lodged against him by his opponents. Apparently, they accused him of adapting the gospel to make it easier for the Galatians to become Christians; he was therefore accused of trying to please them. The allegation that he was trying to manipulate God probably means that his opponents accused him of trying to "persuade" God to accept the new Christians on easier terms than those prescribed by the law.[37] Paul denies these accusations and uses two rhetorical techniques to heighten the impact of his refutation, namely rhetorical questions and an example. The rhetorical questions he uses—probably to convey his emotion—highlight the criticism lodged against him. He then answers the last rhetorical question himself and refutes the criticism by referring to what he has just said in the previous verses (this is the force of ἄρτι) as an example proving the opposite. He points out that the fact that he is prepared to pronounce a twofold curse on people indicates that he does not try to please human beings, but that he is concerned about the gospel only. He is indeed a servant of Christ!

In the above analysis I have indicated the effective strategies Paul uses in this section: rebuke in verse 6 (achieved/enhanced by means of an expression of perplexity, skillful choice of words [μετατίθεσθε] and [possibly] the omission of the thanksgiving); vilification in verses 6c–7 (achieved/enhanced by correction and the skillful choice of words: τινές, ταράσσω, and μεταστρέφω); a twofold curse in verses 8–9; and refutation of criticism in verse 10 (achieved/enhanced by means of rhetorical questions and an example). If one focuses on content, it is possible to identify a large variety of notions which Paul seems to want to convey to the audience, namely that it is wrong to change sides so quickly (verse 6); that they are actually turning away from God (verse 6); that the opponents are proclaiming a false gospel (verse 6c); that the opponents are insincere and have evil motives (verse 7); that the opponents are heading for God's judgement (verses 8–9); that he himself was called by God (verses 8–9); that by accepting the "gospel" of the opponents the Galatians run the risk of sharing the fate of the opponents (verses 8–9); that the gospel is more important than any human being (verses 8–9); and that he is a servant of God (verse 10). Developed in more detail, most of these notions could serve as powerful arguments or proofs

---

[37] J.D.G. Dunn, *Galatians* (1993) 49–51.

in themselves; yet Paul merely mentions or suggests most of them. To my mind, the reason for this is that it is not his primary intention in this section to persuade the audience by means of individual rational arguments, but to combine all of these notions in order to convey his feelings to them. He wants them to realize his emotional dissatisfaction with the events in Galatia. It could therefore be stated that his primary aim throughout this section is to convey his negative feelings to them in such a way that they will reconsider what they are about to do.

3. Conclusion

Hopefully, I have succeeded in demonstrating how one could use the text of the Letter to the Galatians itself as a point of departure for reconstructing Paul's rhetorical strategy in the letter instead of forcing a particular rhetorical model on the letter. Although this article only considers two brief sections of the letter, I intend to work through the whole letter in a similar way with a view to publishing such an analysis of the letter as a whole at a later stage, thus presenting an alternative to existing rhetorical analyses of this fascinating Pauline letter.

This article is dedicated to the memory of Sjef van Tilborg. It was a privilege to know him. I will always remember him as someone who was constantly open to new theories and, furthermore, as a person for whom Christianity and theology were never an academic endeavor only.

Bibliography

Anderson, R.D., *Ancient Rhetorical Theory and Paul* (CBET 18), Leuven ^{rev}1999.
——, *Glossary of Greek Rhetorical Terms Connected to Methods of Argumentation, Figures and Tropes from Anaximenes to Quintilian* (CBET 24), Leuven 2000.
Arzt, P., "The 'Epistolary Introductory Thanksgiving' in the Papyri and in Paul": *NT* 36:1 (1994) 29–46.
Aune, D.E., Review of Betz, H.D., "Galatians. A Commentary on Paul's Letter to the Churches in Galatia" (Philadelphia: Fortress, 1979): *RStR* 7 (1981) 323–25.
Becker, J., *Der Brief an die Galater* (NTD 8), Göttingen ²1981.
Betz, H.D., *Galatians. A Commentary on Paul's Letter to the Churches in Galatia* (Hermeneia), Philadelphia 1979.
Brinsmead, B.H., *Galatians—Dialogical Response to Opponents* (SBL.DS 65), Chico 1982.

Bruce, F.F., *The Epistle to the Galatians. A Commentary on the Greek Text* (NIGNT), Grand Rapids 1982.
Bryant, R.A., *The Risen Crucified Christ in Galatians* (SBL.DS 185), Atlanta 2001.
Classen, C.J., *Rhetorical Criticism of the New Testament* (WUNT 128), Tübingen 2000.
De Saeger, L., "Für unsere Sünden." 1 Kor 15,3b und Gal 1,4a im exegetischen Vergleich": *EThL* 77:1 (2001) 169–91.
Dunn, J.D.G., *The Epistle to the Galatians* (BNTC), Peabody 1993.
Du Toit, A.B., "Vilification as a Pragmatic Device in Early Christian Epistolography": *Bib* 75:3 (1994) 403–12.
Ebeling, G., *Die Wahrheit des Evangeliums. Eine Lesehilfe zum Galaterbrief*, Tübingen 1981.
Eriksson, A., *Traditions as Rhetorical Proof. Pauline Argumentation in 1 Corinthians* (CB.NT 29), Stockholm 1998.
Hall, R.G., "The Rhetorical Outline for Galatians: A Reconsideration": *JBL* 106:2 (1987) 277–87.
Hübner, H., *Biblische Theologie des Neuen Testaments. Band 2: Die Theologie des Paulus und ihre neutestamentliche Wirkungsgeschichte*, Göttingen 1993.
Kennedy, G.A., *New Testament Interpretation through Rhetorical Criticism*, Chapel Hill 1984.
Kern, P.H., *Rhetoric and Galatians. Assessing an Approach to Paul's Epistle* (SNTS.MS 101), Cambridge 1998.
Kremendahl, D., *Die Botschaft der Form. Zum Verständnis von antiker Epistolografie und Rhetorik in Galaterbrief* (NTOA 46), Göttingen 2000.
Longenecker, R.N., *Galatians* (WBC 41), Dallas 1990.
Martyn, J.L., *Galatians. A New Translation with Introduction and Commentary* (AB 33A), New York 1998.
Mussner, F., *Der Galaterbrief* (HTKNT 9), Freiburg ³1977.
Oepke, A., *Der Brief des Paulus an die Galater* (ThHK 9), Berlin ⁴1973.
Roberts, J.K., "Paul's Expression of Perplexity in Galatians 1,6: The Force of Emotive Argumentation": *Neotest* 26:2 (1992) 351–58.
Schlier, H., *Der Brief an die Galater* (KEK 17), Berlin ⁵1971.
Schnider, F., and Stenger, W., *Studien zum neutestamentlichen Briefformular* (NTTS 12), Leiden 1987.
Schoon-Janßen, J., *Umstrittene "Apologien" in den Paulusbriefen. Studien zur rhetorischen Situation des 1. Thessalonicherbriefes, des Galaterbriefes und des Philipperbriefes* (GTA 45), Göttingen 1991.
Smit, J., "The Letter of Paul to the Galatians: A Deliberative Speech": *NTS* 35:1 (1989) 1–26.
Vos, J.S., *Die Kunst der Argumentation bei Paulus. Studien zur antiken Rhetorik* (WUNT 149), Tübingen 2002.

CHAPTER FOURTEEN

STYLE CRITICISM AND THE FOURTH GOSPEL

Gilbert Van Belle
University of Leuven, Belgium

1. *Introduction*

Everyone who had the privilege of knowing Professor Sjef van Tilborg will have been impressed by his engaged exegetical approach to Biblical texts. In his inaugural address on February 11, 1994, entitled *Al lezend stemmen horen*, he situated the exegetical endeavor at the crossroads between the literary sciences, communication theory, dogmatics, and psychiatry.[1] In his concise Dutch commentary on the Gospel of John published in 1988 and in an article published in 1989 Sj. van Tilborg was already aware of the fact that "a narrative text seeks to communicate with readers":[2]

> In his/her communication with the text the reader undergoes a complete metamorphosis: he/she is escorted into a different yet determined world. He/she is introduced to something new that may or may not find a point of contact with what he/she already knows. He/she becomes aware of tensions in the text and his/her efforts to resolve the questions they raise are more often than not without success. He/she is driven forward as the text continues, forward at the same time to a future that is yet to be fulfilled. Readers establish a bond with a text and react to it. This commentary on the gospel of John thus takes the reader's response as its point of departure. Its aim is to describe the communicative process that a reader enters into with a text that he/she finds interesting.[3]

The present contribution represents an appeal to incorporate this communicative aspect within style-critical research into the gospel of

---

[1] Sj. van Tilborg, Al lezend stemmen horen (1994). See P. Nissen, Sjef van Tilborg (2003); G. Van Belle, S. van Tilborg (2003).
[2] Sj. van Tilborg, Communicative Processes (1989) 20.
[3] Sj. van Tilborg, Johannes (1988) 5.

John to a greater extent than has hitherto been the case. Our work will consist of three sections: (i) a brief survey of style-critical research into the gospel of John; (ii) a study of the methodology of style criticism; (iii) an endeavor to formulate a new definition of style. It is our hope that what follows will serve as a grateful and fitting commemoration of the life and work of Sjef van Tilborg.

2. *Historical Survey*

In the first chapter of his 1991 study entitled "Johannine Style in Past Research,"[4] J.E. Botha stated that

> the whole question of the style of the Johannine Writings and specifically the style of the Gospel is a rather neglected field in both past and current research.[5]

While the situation has changed little since 1991, there has nevertheless been an, albeit limited, degree of progress in the field.

As early as the 16th century, scholars engaged themselves in the composition of lists of characteristic words, phrases, and grammatical constructions that were considered to be typical of John's gospel.[6]

---

[4] J.E. Botha, Samaritan Woman (1991) 1–40. For the history of style criticism, see also S. Schulz, Untersuchungen (1957) 51–59; U. Schnelle, Christologie (1987) 171–77; Id., Christology (1992) 154–60; H.-P. Heekerens, Die Zeichen-Quelle (1984) 27–32; G. Van Belle, Parenthèses (1985) passim; Id., Parenthèses johanniques (1992) 1917–32; Id., Signs Source (1994) passim; E. Ruckstuhl and P. Dschulnigg, Stilkritik (1991) 10–22, 23–43; W. Schmithals, Johannesevangelium (1992) 137–39; J. Frey, Eschatologie, I (1998) 429–45; R.E. Brown, Introduction (2003) 278–97. On "Johannine style" see also, for example, J.P. Louw, Style (1986); J. Grosjean, Le style (1989); J.E. Botha, Style (1990); F. Thielman, Style (1991).

[5] J.E. Botha, Samaritan Woman (1991) 2.

[6] The oldest list known to me is from M. Flacius, Clavis (1581) 301–3. It was taken up by S. Glassius, Philologiae Sacrae (1694) 153–55. The list of Flacius is referred to by K.A. Credner, Einleitung (1836) 222–35, who brings together the most important characteristics of the Fourth Gospel in 83 categories. Apart from the list of M. Flacius, K.A. Credner also relied on the work of C.W. Stronck, Specimen (1797); J.D. Schulze, Charakter (1803, ²1811); J.A.L. Wegscheider, Versuch (1806) 253–76, 276–314; T.A. Seyffarth, Beitrag (1810); M. Weber, Authentia (1823).—Other studies from the 18th and 19th century are worthy of mention: S.G. Lange, Johannesbriefe (1842); E. Luthardt, Evangelium (1852) 21–69; H.J. Holtzmann, Problem (1881, 1882); and D. Zeller, Uebersicht (1893) 477–99.—Credner's list was widely known and was taken over, either entirely or in part, in the Introductions to the New Testament by H.E.F. Guerike, Einleitung (1843) 210 n. 3; W.M.L. de Wette, Lehrbuch (⁵1848, ⁶1860) 213; S. Davidson, Introduction, II (1849) 341–46.

At the beginning of the 20th century, E.A. Abbott investigated the language and style of John's gospel[7] and J. Wellhausen likewise published an important survey.[8] Indeed, M. Goguel,[9] M.-J. Lagrange,[10] J.H. Bernard,[11] and many others made ample use of the works of E.A. Abbott to describe John's style. In the meantime, the language and style of John's gospel have also been the subject of investigation by scholars who are inclined either to defend or to reject its Aramaic origin.[12]

There can be little doubt that the high point of style criticism is to be found in the work of those scholars who defend the literary unity of John's gospel. E. Schweizer listed 33 unifying characteristics in this regard[13] while E. Ruckstuhl increased that number to 50[14] (borrowing a number of characteristics from J. Jeremias[15] and P.-H. Menoud).[16] Both E. Schweizer and E. Ruckstuhl investigated the style of John's gospel in view of their critique of source theories (Schweizer studied the hypotheses of H.H. Wendt, F. Spitta, and E. Hirsch;[17] E. Ruckstuhl studied the theory of R. Bultmann).[18] Both

---

[7] E.A. Abbott, Vocabulary (1905); Id., Grammar (1906).

[8] J. Wellhausen, Evangelium (1908) 133–45.

[9] M. Goguel, Introduction, II (1923) 242–61; compare, for example, E. Jacquier, Histoire, IV (^{3}1908) 261–73.

[10] M.-J. Lagrange, Jean (1925) ci–cxix.

[11] J.H. Bernard, John (1928) passim; for "Johannine style" see also A.E. Brooke, Epistles (1912) i–xxvii; R.H. Charles, Revelation (1928) xxix–xxxvii.

[12] On the "Aramaic question," see esp. C.F. Burney, Question (1922); M. Black, Approach (1946, ^{2}1950; ^{3}1967); J.H. Moulton and W.F. Howard, Grammar (1928) 411–85; N. Turner, Style (1976) 64–79. See further the survey of S. Brown, From Burney to Black (1964) 323–39. M. Casey has recently studied the "Aramaic question" and has concluded: "Though we cannot exclude use of Aramaic sources, the Gospel as we have it was written in Greek"; cf. M. Casey, Is John's Gospel True? (1996) 87–97, esp. 97.

[13] E. Schweizer, Ego Eimi (1939, ^{2}1965) 82–112; see the list of Johannine style characteristics on pp. 104–5. On Schweizer, see esp. E. Lorenzini, Problematicità (1981).

[14] E. Ruckstuhl, Einheit (1951) 180–219; see the list of Johannine style characteristics on pp. 203–5; (^{2}1987) 203–5; 291–303: "Anhang: Liste der johanneischen Stilmerkmale mit allen Belegstellen aus dem johanneischen Schrifttum." Ruckstuhl's list is printed in F.-M. Braun, Jean (1959) 401–2. Braun adds one characteristic: no. 51: "Alternance de deux synonymes," with reference to W.F. Howard, The Fourth Gospel (^{3}1945, ^{4}1955) 276–96, esp. 278–79.

[15] J. Jeremias, Literarkritik (1941) 35, 40–41; cf. J. Coppens, Analyse (1941) 181.

[16] P.-H. Menoud, Jean (1943, ^{2}1947) 14–16.

[17] H.H. Wendt, Johannesevangelium (1900); Id., Schichten (1911); F. Spitta, Johannes-Evangelium (1910); E. Hirsch, Studien (1936). On Hirsch see R. Bultmann, Auslegung (1937).

[18] R. Bultmann, Johannes (1941) passim; Id., John (1971). On Bultmann's use of

scholars deemed it impossible to reconstruct different sources or redactions because the same characteristic style is found in nearly every passage of the gospel. It is worthy of note that T. Bromboszcz (as early as 1927) opposed source theories for the same reason, namely, the unity evident in the language of John's gospel.[19]

For their reconstructions of the signs source, neither R.T. Fortna[20] nor W. Nicol[21] could neglect the stylistic studies of E. Schweizer and E. Ruckstuhl. As a matter of fact, both authors ultimately point out that Johannine characteristics hardly occur in this source. Note deserves to be made of the fact that W. Nicol adds 32 categories to E. Ruckstuhl's list of 50 Johannine characteristics (while at the same time rejecting some others). E. Ruckstuhl reacted against this method during the *Colloquium Biblicum Lovaniense* of 1975.[22] H.M. Teeple offers an even longer list of characteristics and is confident of our capacity to distinguish different styles in each of the sources and redactions in John's gospel (narrative source, discourse source, passion source, the evangelist, the redactor).[23]

In their commentary on the gospel of John, M.-É. Boismard and A. Lamouille devote two appendixes to the style characteristics of the Fourth Gospel.[24] The list of Johannine characteristics in this commentary, containing 416 categories, broadly exceeds the available lists of Johannine characteristics. The literary style of the Fourth Evangelist is also given careful attention by E. Haenchen.[25] In the course of the last decade, research in this field has been stimulated by the publication of a monograph on the topic by E. Ruckstuhl and P. Dschulnigg[26] and the stylistic study of W. Schenk.[27] Moreover,

---

style see E. Hirsch, Stilkritik (1950–51); E. Ruckstuhl, Einheit (1951) 20–179; B. Noack, Tradition (1954) 9–17, 18–42; G. Van Belle, Parenthèses (1985) 35–42; Id., Signs Source (1994) 26–28.

[19] T. Bromboszcz, Einheit (1927) 76–106. See also W. Bauer, Johannesevangelium (1929) 138.

[20] R.T. Fortna, Signs (1970) 201–18; Id., Predecessor (1988) 218–20.

[21] W. Nicol, Sèmeia (1972) 16–27.

[22] E. Ruckstuhl, Language and Style (1977) 125–47; Id., Sprache und Stil (1987) 304–31.

[23] H.M. Teeple, Origin (1974) 253–60.

[24] M.-É. Boismard and A. Lamouille, Jean (1977) 491–514, 515–31; see F. Neirynck et al., L'évangile de Jean (1977) 400–29; Id., Jean et les Synoptiques (1979) 41–70. On the "Lucan" style of John see M.-É. Boismard, Luc (2001) 103–4.

[25] E. Haenchen, Johannesevangelium (1980) 57–74; Id., John, 1 (1984) 52–66.

[26] E. Ruckstuhl and P. Dschulnigg, Stilkritik (1991).

[27] W. Schenk, Lexikon (1993).

style criticism has come to play an important role in rhetorical and narratological investigation,[28] in studies that consider John's gospel as the result of a *relecture* or of a *réécriture*,[29] and in studies dealing with the "Johannine school."[30] It should be noted in this context that scholars such as H. Thyen and H.-P. Heekerens[31] reject E. Ruckstuhl's list of characteristics as check list results of literary criticism. They are convinced that one cannot make a distinction between "ideolect" and "sociolect."[32] Note, moreover, that several studies published in this same period pay special attention to particular characteristics, stylistic particularities, and literary devices.[33]

Style criticism played a central role in source and redaction criticism of the Fourth Gospel and in the study of its literary unity. The present author's research into the "parentheses" or "asides" in John led to the publication of a monograph on the topic in 1985.[34] John employs such "asides" to translate foreign words, explain Jewish customs, offer more precise information about certain people or about the time and place of a scene, comment on words and deeds of Jesus (or of others), and elucidate the intention of the evangelist in elaborate reflections, both in the stories and the discourses in his gospel. Our research has thus far allowed us to draw the following conclusions: (1) The language and style of the "parentheses" are

---

[28] See the literature mentioned by J.E. Botha, Samaritan Woman (1991) 31–39. See his comment on p. 54: "As indicated in the previous chapter, relatively little has been done in the field of Johannine studies that can be classified as 'style studies' in the *modern* sense. There have been rapid advances and progression in modern literary theory and stylistic and linguistic study in general since the 1950s, but unfortunately Johannine studies have not really been influenced by modern approaches, with the exception of the work of Culpepper (1983) on narratology, Staley (1986) on reception theory, and the literature quoted in Chapter I. A few other titles dealing with inter alia irony (Duke 1984) and O'Day (1986), literary devices (Wead 1970) and a few other studies which deal with aspects of literary criticism, stylistic features and linguistics on a smaller scale..., are perhaps the only studies incorporating modern literary and linguistic theory in Johannine studies." On narratology see, for example, M. Gourgues, Recherche (1995) 269–76.

[29] On the notion of "relecture" and "réécriture" see K. Scholtissek, Relecture (2000).

[30] See, e.g., U. Schnelle, Christologie (1987) 53–75, 171–77; Id., Christologie (1992) 41–70, 154–60. See also Id., Johannes (1998) 1–2, 8–10.

[31] See below, note 60.

[32] See the reaction of E. Ruckstuhl, Idiolekt-Soziolekt (1987).

[33] See the survey of J.E. Botha, Samaritan Woman (1991) 31–39.

[34] G. Van Belle, Parenthèses (1985) 206–10. For reactions on my 1985 monograph see Id., Parenthèses johanniques (1992) 1917–32.

identical with the language and style of the stories and discourses.[35] (2) This linguistic homogeneity does not allow us to explain the "asides" as secondary insertions (explanations of the source by the evangelist or comments from an ecclesiastical redactor or from an even later glossator, inserted after the completion of the gospel). (3) These parentheses are to be ascribed rather to the hand of the evangelist himself, explaining and commenting on his own gospel story for his readers. (4) The "parentheses" directly reflect the point of view of the evangelist: they form the key to the interpretation of the gospel. (5) The use of "parentheses" or "asides" is only one of the many literary devices used by the evangelist to help his readers understand his story. Indeed other literary devices, such as repetition, are abundantly evident.[36]

In line with J.E. Botha we might be inclined to conclude that "very little *specific* research has been done on the style of John's Gospel" because "the style of John was invariably studied not for the sole purpose of determining its style and the function of the features in the Gospel, but for subsidiary reasons such as to prove or disprove authorship, sources, redaction and so forth."[37] Nevertheless, one might be equally inclined to wonder whether such a statement is not something of an exaggeration.[38] A survey of the use of style criticism by a select but representative group of twentieth century authors should serve to clarify the matter. In what follows we will examine the work of those who adhere to source and redaction theories together with those who are convinced of the literary unity of the fourth gospel. We will begin, however, with a definition of style and style criticism.

---

[35] In my studies on the semeia hypothesis and on the asides, I always added an updated list of the Johannine style characteristics: Semeia-bron (1975) 149–53; Parenthèses (1985) 124–55; Signs Source (1994) 405–17.

[36] G. Van Belle, Parenthèses (1985) 207: "En outre, le recours fréquent aux parenthèses n'est pas un phénomène isolé dans le quatrième évangile, mais relève d'une manière d'écrire qui comporte d'autres aspects analogues. Nous pensons surtout aux différents genres de répétition et de variation, soit sous forme de parallélisme ou d'antithèse, soit sous forme de chiasme ou d'inclusion. Ce seraient autant de moyens par lesquels l'évangéliste guide ses lecteurs à bien comprendre son écrit"; compare Id., Prolepsis (2001) 346–47. On the communicative character of the asides see also J. Frey, Eschatologie, I (1997) 442–45, esp. 443; Sj. van Tilborg, Communicative Processes (1989). On asides see also, for example, C.J. Bjerkelund, Tauta Egeneto (1987); B. Olsson, Structure (1974) 259–74.

[37] J.E. Botha, Samaritan Woman (1991) 2.

[38] Note that A.-J. Festugière, Observations (1974) studied John's style "for the sole purpose of determining its style and the function of the features in the Gospel."

3. The Methodology of Johannine Style Criticism

3.1. Style Criticism as Literary Method

The expression "Style Criticism"[39] is employed in the exegesis of John's gospel by E. Hirsch, J. Jeremias, and E. Ruckstuhl[40] among others. E. Ruckstuhl and P. Dschulnigg,[41] in particular, make frequent reference to "Stilkritik" and "stilkritische Untersuchungen," taking H. Bussmann's definition of style as their point of departure: "style is based on the selection of linguistic elements from a larger repertory and on the repetition of the chosen elements. The choice of elements and the repetition thereof are determined thereby by the communicative function of the text."[42] In line with P.-G. Müller,[43] "Style criticism" can be defined as a linguistic and exegetical discipline that draws attention to the specific style features and linguistic characteristics of various texts and text types or with the style of a particular author or a particular period in time. As an analytical and descriptive discipline, it studies and describes the rules governing the choice and combination of linguistic resources in order to determine, among other things, the intention, function, origin, age, and addressees of a text with a view to ascribing the said text to a particular text type.

It would be appropriate at the present juncture to endeavor to determine the concrete features of style criticism in practice and to ascertain the rules to which its proponents adhered.[44] We will begin, therefore, with the representatives of literary criticism, focusing in

---

[39] S. Schulz, Untersuchungen (1957) 51–52 n. 7 prefers "Stilstatistik" to "Style Criticism." See also H. Blauert, Bedeutung (1953) 7. For "Stilstatistik" see R. Morgenthaler, Statistik (1958) 181–85: "Statistische Listen von Vorzügwörtern" (for John, see p. 182).

[40] E. Hirsch, Stilkritik (1950–51); J. Jeremias, Literarkritik (1941) 39; E. Ruckstuhl, Einheit (1951), 180, 220, etc.; see also B. Noack, Tradition (1954) 9, 18, 172. We do not discuss "stylometry" at this juncture; on this method see, for example, T. Felton and T. Thatcher, Stylometry (2001) 208–19.

[41] See the title of their study: E. Ruckstuhl and P. Dschulnigg, Stilkritik (1991).

[42] H. Bussmann, Lexikon (1983) 505. Cf. E. Ruckstuhl and P. Dschulnigg, Stilkritik (1991) 19–20.

[43] P.-G. Müller, Lexikon (1985) 231–32.

[44] See especially H.-P. Heekerens, Zeichen-Quelle (1984) 27–32; U. Schnelle, Christologie (1987) 171–77; Id., Christology (1992) 154–60; J. Frey, Eschatologie I (1998) 429–45.

particular on the use of style criticism among the defenders of the σημεῖα hypothesis.[45]

3.2. *Style Criticism and Literary Criticism*

1. According to literary critics, the style of a source or redactional layer must be clearly distinguishable from another source or another redactional layer and from the evangelist's work. Older source critics were thus inclined to note the distinctive vocabulary and style in the parts they attributed respectively to the evangelist and the interpolator (e.g., A. Schweizer),[46] in narrative portions and discourses (e.g., H.H. Wendt),[47] or in Jn 1–12 (and 20:30–31) and Jn 13–21 (M.M. Thompson,[48] A. Faure).[49] R. Bultmann also made mention of such characteristics each time he ascribed a pericope to the "σημεῖα-Quelle."[50] Its style is clearly distinguishable from the language of both the Evangelist and the "Redenquelle" as well as from the miracle stories of the Synoptic tradition. The source's characteristic use of Semitisms, for example, led R. Bultmann to suggest that it was written in Greek by a Greek speaking Semite.[51] This in fact has become a commonly held opinion (see, for example, W. Hartke, S. Schulz, H. Koester, H.-P. Heekerens).[52] Moreover, U.C. von Wahlde[53] has argued that "linguistic differences" should serve as the

---

[45] G. Van Belle, Signs Source (1994) *passim* (see the "Index of subjects" under "Style of the source" and "Stylistic unity of the Gospel").

[46] A. Schweizer, Johannes (1841) 73–74, 79, 94. See G. Van Belle, Signs Source (1994) 3.

[47] H.H. Wendt, Johannesevangelium (1900) 54–61; Id., Schichten (1911) 35–42. See G. Van Belle, Signs Source (1994) 3.

[48] J.M. Thompson, Disarrangements (1915) 424, 433; Id., John XXI (1915) 145–146; Id., Structure (1915) 525–26; Id., Composition (1916) 46. Cf. G. Van Belle, Signs Source (1994) 15–17.

[49] A. Faure, Zitate (1922) 105–8. Cf. G. Van Belle, Signs Source (1994) 19.

[50] R. Bultmann, Johannes (1941) passim. Cf. G. Van Belle, Signs Source (1994) 26–28; Id., Parenthèses (1985) 38–42. Bultmann's first criterion for source criticism is undoubtedly that of style. In 1927 he wrote that the collection of style characteristics is the only way to a more objective source criticism. Cf. R. Bultmann, Forschung (1927) 503.

[51] R. Bultmann, Johannes (1941) 68 n. 7, 131 n. 5, 155 n. 5, 177 n. 4, 250 n. 1, 301 n. 2; Id., John (1971) 98 n. 7, 180 n. 2, 211 n. 1, 238 n. 1, 329 n. 2, 395 n. 2.

[52] W. Hartke, Parteien, I (1961) 132, 190; W. Nicol, Sèmeia (1972) 67; S. Schulz, Johannes (1972) 40; H. Koester, Überlieferung (1982) 1510; H.-P. Heekerens, Zeichen-Quelle (1984) 115–16.

[53] U.C. von Wahlde, Version (1989) 30–43.

basis upon which the literary analysis of the Fourth Gospel must be founded, considering them to be more objective than those used previously in the literary analysis of the Fourth Gospel.

2. Since E. Schweizer's and E. Ruckstuhl's attacks on Johannine source criticism, most signs source defenders have acknowledged that the stylistic unity of the Fourth Gospel makes it difficult to reconstruct sources and that the style-critical argument must converge with other evidence. J. Becker even gave up the use of style criticism altogether as a decisive means of source analysis.[54] Authors such as G. Ziener, S. Temple, R. Schnackenburg, and H. Conzelmann,[55] on the other hand, consider the complete or near complete absence of Johannine characteristics in some passages to be an indication of the signs source.

3. R.T. Fortna, W. Nicol, and H.H. Teeple[56] have attempted, each in his own way, to demonstrate that style criticism can even confirm the use of a signs source in the Gospel of John. Moreover, R.T. Fortna[57] has endeavored to indicate the stylistic unity between signs source (SQ) and passion source (PQ).

Proponents of the literary criticism, moreover, remain fully aware of the following rules or principles:

1. The homogeneous style of the gospel does not represent a priori evidence in support of the literary unity thereof: (a) The evangelist (or a redactor) may have entirely reworked the source (or the work of his predecessor) in his own style. It is also possible that the evangelist adopted the source as it was and proceeded to imitate its style in his own material.[58] (b) While a document may have come into existence in the same environment, it may also have done so in different phases; in such an instance it will be difficult to recognize the language and style of the various

---

[54] J. Becker, Wunder (1969–70) 131–35.
[55] G. Ziener, Passafeier (1958) 271–72; S. Temple, Two Signs (1962) 171; R. Schnackenburg, Johannesevangelium (1960) 1103; Id., Traditionsgeschichte (1964) 63–64; Id., Johannesevangelium, I, 50, 51, 329, 501; II, 30; Id., John, I, 62, 64, 324, 470; II, 22; H. Conzelmann, Arbeitsbuch (1975) 283; (⁴1979) 283; (⁹1988) 309. Cf. G. Van Belle, Signs Source, 58, 75–76 n. 24, 89, 94, 95, 99.
[56] See above, notes 21, 22, 24.
[57] R.T. Fortna, Predecessor (1988) 208–14.
[58] E. Hirsch, Stilkritik (1950–51) 135; R. Bultmann, Johannes (1941) 175 n. 5; E. Haenchen, Literatur (1955) 308; M.-É. Boismard and A. Lamouille, Jean (1977) 15; M.-É. Boismard, Vie (1980) 26; R.T. Fortna, Predecessor (1988) 210 n. 509; J. Wagner, Auferstehung (1988); J. Frey, Eschatologie, I (1998) 433, 434–35.

authors ("ideolect"), since they may have developed a common group language ("sociolect") within the said environment (in John's case "the Johannine school").[59] (c) One must also account for the possibility that one and the same author may have published his own work anew.[60]

2. Non-Johannine terminology need not necessarily signal the use of a source or a reworking of the gospel by an editor: (a) An expression that appears unusual in Johannine usage or would appear to signify a contrast to the latter should not be considered noteworthy if it only represents an isolated instance. When such an expression occurs in the plural in the same passage, however, this may represent evidence of a source or an editorial intervention.[61] (b) Non-Johannine terminology can also be ascribed to the influence of texts from the Old Testament or texts from the New Testament (the Synoptic Gospels, the Book of Acts, the Letters of Paul).[62] (c) One must also account for the fact that an author, rewriting his work after several years, will have evolved in his use of language.[63]

3. The conclusive force of style criticism depends essentially upon the text exegetes ascribe to a postulated source. Style criticism is more conclusive when the text of the source is more extensive.[64]

Counter to E. Schweizer and E. Ruckstuhl, furthermore, literary critics remark that: (a) it is impossible to characterize an author's style in contrast to other authors. Words, expressions, and constructions can also be considered Johannine if they appear in other books of the New Testament;[65] (b) many characteristics, which scholars maintain to be unique to the gospel of John because they occur with relative frequency in the latter when compared to other New Testament documents, are actually language characteristic of non-literary Koine:

---

[59] H. Thyen, Literatur (1974) 299; (1977) 214–15; H.-P. Heekerens, Zeichenquelle (1984) 29–30; M.-É. Boismard and A. Lamouille, Jean (1977) 15; E. Ruckstuhl, Idiolekt-Soziolekt (1987) passim; U. Schnelle, Christologie (1987) 172–73; Id., Christology (1992) 155; J. Frey, Eschatologie, I (1998) 433, 439–41.

[60] M.-É. Boismard and A. Lamouille, Jean (1977) 15; M.-É. Boismard, Vie (1980) 26–27.

[61] M.-É. Boismard and A. Lamouille, Jean (1977) 15; M.-É. Boismard, Vie (1980) 27.

[62] M.-É. Boismard and A. Lamouille, Jean (1977) 15; M.-É. Boismard, Vie (1980) 28.

[63] M.-É. Boismard and A. Lamouille, Jean (1977) 15–16; M.-É. Boismard, Vie (1980) 26.

[64] U. Schnelle, Christologie (1987) 173; Id., Christology (1992) 155.

[65] U. Schnelle, Christologie (1987) 172; Id., Christology (1992) 155.

"a phenomenon of Koine in general is misunderstood as the preference of an individual author. The weaknesses of the attempt to introduce "objective" characteristics of the language of the Gospel of John as arguments against partition into sources thereby become especially evident."[66] Thus, as U. Schnelle remarked, it is insufficient to compare the style of the Gospel of John with the New Testament alone. Many "Johannine" style characteristics also appear in the Koine. By extending the comparable texts, the number of Johannine characteristics will be reduced.[67]

4. *The Use of Style Criticism by the Defenders of the Literary Unity of the Gospel*

1. Those that defend the literary unity of John's gospel tend in the first instance to collect together the characteristics that are peculiar to the latter, basing themselves on the comparative frequency of use in John and in the rest of the New Testament.[68] Researchers speak of a "positive" style feature when the said characteristic occurs exclusively or at least for the most part in John and a "negative" style feature when the said characteristic never or almost never occurs.[69] The style characteristics, together with indications of frequency, are brought together in lists with a view to creating a convenient arrangement and thereby facilitating their use in research. It is argued that approaching John from the perspective of style statistic should make it possible to reveal whether another author has reworked or added to a particular text.[70]

2. It goes without saying, of course, that any method based on style statistics cannot expect to achieve objectively certifiable results but can only aspire to determine probability statements.[71] The only objective details such an approach can provide are in fact the numerical frequencies of particular style features. The evaluation of such

---

[66] E. Haenchen, Johannes (1980) 73–74; Id., John, I (1984) 66. See also E. Hirsch, Stilkritik (1950–51) 135; J. Frey, Eschatologie, I (1998) 433, 435–38.
[67] U. Schnelle, Christologie (1987) 172; Id., Christology (1992) 155.
[68] S. Schulz, Untersuchungen (1957) 54.
[69] E. Ruckstuhl, Einheit (1951) 205.
[70] J. Frey, Eschatologie I (1998) 434.
[71] In the words of C. Demke, Logoshymnus (1967) 48: "Ergebnisse der sogenannten Stilkritik sind für literarkritische Fragen ... allerhöchstens Prüfungs-, nie aber Entscheidungsinstanz"; compare H.-P. Heekerens, Zeichen-Quelle (1984) 28.

information, however, and the conclusions to which it gives rise stand open for discussion.[72]

3. E. Schweizer, E. Ruckstuhl, and P. Dschulnigg have established their criteria on the basis of painstaking study: they opt not only for particular word preferences or striking syntactical association but also for the, from time to time, inconspicuous words, constructions, and formulations that mean virtually nothing in terms of content and theology.[73]

4. Furthermore, they pay particular attention to the distribution and the "Vernetzung" of the style characteristics, in other words to the interconnected network of style characteristic throughout the Fourth Gospel as a whole.[74]

5. Taking the lists of style characteristics as their point of departure, some scholars have formulated a number of objections to the way in which style criticism is used within the context of literary criticism: (a) The stylistic criteria for isolating sources are the weakest. Most critics, even those who distinguish sources and redactional elaboration in the Fourth Gospel, have accepted its unity of language and style: it seems to be a "seamless robe" out of which different literary layers can scarcely be separated.[75] (b) E. Schweizer, J. Jeremias, P.-H. Menoud, E. Ruckstuhl (and P. Dschulnigg), and U. Schnelle have argued in contradiction to the literary theories of R. Bultmann and R.T. Fortna that Johannine characteristics are more or less evenly distributed throughout the Gospel and that they offer no evidence for source reconstructions.[76] (c) R.T. Fortna's endeavor to support the literary unity of the *Gospel of Signs* is undermined by an error of logic: he uses Johannine style characteristics to distinguish the Johannine material and to uncover the Gospel of Signs; in his assessment of the presence of Johannine characteristics in the source, however, he then comes to the conclusion that his source is free of such characteristics. Johannine style criticism would

---

[72] J. Frey, Eschatologie I (1998) 434.
[73] J. Frey, Eschatologie I (1998) 434.
[74] E. Schweizer, Ego Eimi (1939) 100–2; E. Ruckstuhl, Einheit (1951) 183–85, 205–7; E. Ruckstuhl and P. Dschulnigg, Stilkritik (1991) 35–38; J. Frey, Eschatologie I (1998) 434.
[75] The image "seamless robe" comes from D.F. Strauss, Vorrede (^{3}1890) 556 (original edition: 1860, p. xliv), cited by W.F. Howard, Fourth Gospel (^{4}1955) 297; see also M. Hengel, Question (1989) 1, 136 n. 1; Id., Frage (1993) 9 and n. 1.
[76] G. Van Belle, Signs Source (1994) 373. See also S. Schulz, Untersuchungen (1957) 55, 58–59.

thus appear to be constantly in danger of engaging in circular argumentation.[77] (d) In addition, the absence of Johannine characteristics in some narrative parts of the Fourth Gospel (miracle stories and the passion narrative) does not prove that these passages belong to a source, and even less, as Fortna claims, to *one* source. It can represent no more than an indication that John may possibly have used traditional material.[78] U. Schnelle agrees with W. Nicol's observation, however, that five miracle stories (2:1–12; 4:46–47.50–54; 5:1–9; 6:16–21; 9:1–2.6–7) contain only a few Johannine characteristics and that the said stories can thus be ascribed to John's tradition. He adds, nevertheless, that this does not mean that John employed a continuous source. (e) In most cases, the absence of Johannine characteristics is meaningless, because the characteristics do not appear in any narrative material in John. (f) U. Schnelle rightly remarks: "Extensive literary-critical or tradition-historical theories based on stylistic criticism cannot rest simply on words that occur once, twice, or three times in the whole of the Gospel."[79] (g) Finally, R.T. Fortna's description of the source's own style is not sufficient to prove the existence of a source or to support the hypothesis that the Signs Gospel represents a pre-Johannine combination of the signs source and the Passion narrative.[80]

6. The literary features used by E.D. Freed and R.B. Hunt[81] in support of Fortna's Gospel of Signs are open to question and cannot be used to assess the narrative segments. (a) If one tests the purity of R.T. Fortna's Gospel of Signs with characteristics that are typically Johannine—and variation is indeed such a characteristic—it appears that the source contains no such variations.[82] (b) Given the fact that they are bound to the particular circumstances at hand, the high number of *hapax legomena* cannot be considered a characteristic of the source and cannot be usefully employed, therefore, for testing it.[83] (c) It is obvious that the stylistic, verbal, and theological

---

[77] U. Schnelle, Christologie (1987) 173; Id., Christology (1992) 155.
[78] U. Schnelle, Christologie (1987) 173; Id., Christology (1992) 156. Compare S. Schulz, Untersuchungen (1957) 56.
[79] U. Schnelle, Christologie (1987) 172; Id., Christology (1992) 156.
[80] G. Van Belle, Signs Source (1994) 172–74, 264 n. 78.
[81] E.D. Freed and R.B. Hunt, Signs-Source (1975). Cf. G. Van Belle, Signs Source (1994) 198–200.
[82] D.A. Carson, Source Criticism (1978) 425.
[83] D.A. Carson, Source Criticism (1978) 425.

parallels between the Fourth Gospel and 1 Jn involve characteristics found in the Johannine material but not in the Gospel of Signs since they occur for the most part in the discourses.[84]

7. R.T. Fortna and other source critics assign the asides, remarks, comments, or parentheses to both the source and the evangelist. In the present author's study *Les parenthèses dans l'évangile de Jean*, I was able to conclude that parenthesis is a mark of the evangelist's work and that it provides no support for theories of composite origin or (post-evangelist) redaction.[85] I came to this conclusion by considering grammar and style together with the gospel's narrative art. Also the distribution of the historic present (J.J. O'Rourke),[86] the principal conjunctions (V.S. Poythress),[87] the phenomenon of parallelism (P.F. Ellis),[88] and the double meaning expressions (E. Richard)[89] in John's Gospel do not confirm R.T. Fortna's Gospel of Signs or any other source theory. In addition, the occurrence of the "repetitive resumptive," "framing repetition," or "Wiederaufnahme,"[90] also mentioned by R.T. Fortna, is not necessarily an indication that the evangelist is working with primitive sources.

8. J. Frey[91] has rightly pointed out that one would be incorrect to argue in line with E. Haenchen that Johannine style characteristics are in fact characteristics of Koine Greek.[92] (a) E. Haenchen's work alludes in particular to that of E.C. Colwell,[93] the latter offering his reaction to C.F. Burney's hypothesis. While C.F. Burney[94] argued that the gospel of John was originally written in Aramaic, E.C. Colwell responded by pointing out that the so-called Aramaisms also occurred in Koine. His arguments are based on Epictetus' "Dissertationes" and a collection of roughly 200 non-literary papyri from the Roman period. In light of the fact that E.C. Colwell's hypotheses

---

[84] D.A. Carson, Source Criticism (1978) 427.
[85] See above, note 35.
[86] J.J. O'Rourke, Historic Present (1974).
[87] V.S. Poythress, Testing (1984); Id., Use (1984).
[88] P.F. Ellis, Genius (1984); Id., Inclusion (1999).
[89] E. Richard, Expressions (1985).
[90] M.-É. Boismard, Wiederaufnahme (1977); F. Neirynck, Epanalepsis (1980); see also U.C. von Wahlde, Technique (1976); Id., Wiederaufnahme (1983); R.F. Person Jr., Reassessment (1999).
[91] J. Frey, Eschatologie, I (1998) 435–38.
[92] See above, note 26.
[93] E.C. Colwell, Greek (1931).
[94] F.C. Burney, Origin (1922).

are clearly founded on a relatively small textual basis, it thus becomes evident that the substantiation if the individual character of Johannine language usage or of the literary unity of the gospel was absolutely not his intention. (b) It goes without saying that the various style characteristics proposed by E. Schweizer and E. Ruckstuhl ought to be subject to critical discussion. A few such characteristics, criticized by E. Haenchen, have been scrapped from the recent list where the criticism was considered justified by E. Ruckstuhl and P. Dschulnigg.[95] E. Haenchen would appear to be unaware of the fact that a construction's occurrence in Koine Greek need not necessarily imply that the said construction cannot thereby be considered characteristic of a particular author. It is not the absolute uniqueness of a phenomenon that points to typical Johannine language usage, but rather the exceptional frequency of the characteristic and the network of interconnections it establishes. (c) E. Ruckstuhl and P. Dschulnigg devoted much of their study to the extent to which Johannine style characteristics occur in the works of 32 Hellenistic authors who wrote between 100 B.C.E. and 150 C.E.[96] Their endeavor to authenticate Johannine style characteristics thus extends far beyond the New Testament context. Rooted in the latter and employing more incisive criteria, the old list of style characteristics has been completely reworked. The new list consists of 153 characteristics subdivided into three categories and presented in descending order of frequency. While a few characteristics found in the earlier list compiled by E. Ruckstuhl have been omitted,[97] the majority have nevertheless survived the broader comparison. It is thus not only within the New Testament but also within the broader framework of the literature of the time that we find evidence of the remarkable homogeneity and striking independence of the style of the Fourth Gospel and the Johannine Letters, which is clearly to be distinguished from that of the Apocalypse.[98]

---

[95] E. Ruckstuhl and P. Dschulnigg, Stilkritik (1991), have not retained the following nine characteristics of the earlier list: 3, 10, 21, 27, 28, 35, 36, 37, and 38.
[96] E. Ruckstuhl and P. Dschulnigg, Stilkritik (1991).
[97] See above, note 96.
[98] Cf. J. Frey, Erwägungen (1993).

5. *Towards a New Definition of Style in Johannine Research*

It is probably fair to say that style criticism in the exegesis of the Fourth Gospel has not always been exercised as an independent discipline. Indeed, scholars have tended to employ it for the most part within classical literary criticism in order to distinguish source from redaction or to support the literary unity of the gospel of John. Given the rules and principles maintained by its proponents and outlined above, however, it would clearly be a mistake to argue that style criticism has not been methodical in its approach. It should be noted, nevertheless, that the style characteristics that are included in the lists generally tend to relate primarily to word usage and the use of certain expressions and grammatical constructions and only rarely to rhetorical figures and style procedures. It is for this reason that J.E. Botha's critique of Johannine style criticism (and of that relating to the New Testament in general) is justified: "The study of style and stylistics in New Testament research is to a great extent static and inadequate, and ... the scope of these studies is very limited."[99]

B. Kowalski[100] and A. Denaux[101] arrive at the same conclusion with respect to style criticism in New Testament exegesis (in particular with respect to Luke) and argue in favor of a broader definition of style. B. Kowalski refers,[102] for example, to E. Ruckstuhl and P. Dschulnigg, who are themselves forced to admit that while the definition of style they employ (taken from H. Bussmann)[103] may be extremely broad it has only allowed them to study a limited portion of Johannine style. Their definition nevertheless provides the opportunity to involve the author, the text, and the reader in the process of style research.

Every definition of style takes its point of departure from a well-determined textual theory. While New Testament scholars frequently employed the expression "the language and style" of the author, the terms in question are often not further defined. According to A. Denaux, it would be incorrect to understand "language and style"

---

[99] J.E. Botha, Style, Stylistics (1990) 173.
[100] B. Kowalski, Stil (2003).
[101] A. Denaux, Style (2003).
[102] B. Kowalski, Stil (2003) 107.
[103] See above, note 43.

as a hendiadys.[104] Such a distinction has its roots in the linguistic theory of F. de Saussure,[105] who insisted on the difference between "langage" ("language in its entirety"), "langue" ("language as a structured system"), and "speech" ("parole"). The latter two terms serve in particular to explain the customary use of the expression "language and style": (1) *Language* ("langue" or linguistic system) is a means of communication, a system of "signes," intended to convey thoughts, and thus its origin is psychic and social. Language consists of a given linguistic system, with, on the one hand, words in their semantic, grammatical, and morphological dimensions, and, on the other hand, more complex elements, such as word groups, sentences, juxtaposition, and contraction, as described in syntax. The lexical-semantic aspect of words (the "unmarked" meaning) is described in lexica; linguistic systems are described in grammars. (2) Within this linguistic system the individual language user is free to develop a particular *style* ("parole") which makes his linguistic expression individually recognizable. Both A. Denaux and B. Kowalski argue in favor of a communicative text theory with respect to biblical texts, since the latter contain the Word of God addressed to human persons.[106] They find just such a theory in the work of H. Utzchneider[107] who draws our attention to three essential aspects of the biblical text: 1. The relative autonomy of the text; 2. The orientation towards the reader; and 3. no reduction of the text to its auctorial original situation. A. Denaux and B. Kowalski[108] both insist that an adequate

---

[104] A. Denaux, Style (2003) 1–2. On the expression "language and style," see below, note 113.

[105] F. de Saussure, Course (1916); Id., Course (1983) 10.

[106] B. Kowalski, Stil (2003) 122; A. Denaux, Style (2003) 2–3.

[107] U. Utzschneider, Text (1999) 227. See also the definition of style in J.E. Botha, Samaritan Woman (1991) 53: "Style has to do with the *choices* available to users of language, and since these choices are determined by specific needs and circumstances, style is a *contextually determined* phenomenon. Because of this, style in effect deals with *the successful communication* of texts in context. Every aspect of language which facilitates this process of communication, therefore, has to do with the style of the text. This, however, does not mean that a general description of all the innumerable linguistic and literary features in a text, will amount to a description of the style of a text. Far from it. Only those features which facilitate the specific communication in that specific circumstance can be considered of stylistic value in this paradigm. The features in a text which facilitate this process should not be limited, and can vary according to the specific needs of a specific text or context."

[108] B. Kowalski, Stil (2003) 121–28; A. Denaux, Style (2003) 4–9, 15–16.

definition of style must account for these three levels of communication: the author, the text, and the reader. Taken together, these three elements constitute the fundamental basis of both diachronic and synchronic interpretation of the bible and correspond to the three intentions necessary, according to U. Eco,[109] for the interpretation of every text: "intentio auctoris," "intentio operis," and "intentio lectoris." The interpretation of the text ("intentio operis") can be described at three different levels: 1. linguistic-literary form or surface structure; 2. thematic content or depth structure; and 3. pragmatic-communicative content.

Based on the aforementioned text theory, A. Denaux and B. Kowalski offer the following description of "style," which accounts for the three aspects of the "intentio operis":[110]

1. Style is the option for and variation of (repetition, omission, alteration) linguistic possibilities at every level (words, sentences, text structure, or discourse) within the boundaries of the existing grammar of the language, the development of the language, and the literary genre.
2. Style manifests itself at various different levels: (a) *word level*: characteristic words, word forms, and word combinations that are not only defined by content or literary genre; the richness of vocabulary compared to the text length; (b) *sentence level*: syntactical structures; (c) *rhetorical-narrative level*: style figures, rhetorical-structural features constructing the text; (d) *socio-rhetorical level*: communication between author, text, and recipient in their sociological dimension.
3. A distinction must be made between the style of the author, of one of his documents, and of the language community to which he and his documents belong.
4. The possibility of "style-switching" on the part of the author or within a particular work should also be accounted for.[111]

The above definition provides us with sufficient space to collect together everything formerly classified under "Style and Language," "Lexicography," and "Literary Forms and Devices"[112] under the single

---

[109] U. Eco, Grenzen (1992) 35.
[110] B. Kowalski, Stil (2003) 124–25; A. Denaux, Style (2003) 15–16.
[111] See I.H. Henderson, Style-Switching (1995).
[112] See G. Van Belle, Johannine Bibliography (1988) 53–56, 56–103, 120–28.

title "style" and thereby to extend style research to include its rhetorical-narrative and socio-rhetorical aspects. The following literary techniques thus take their place as style characteristics:[113] chiasm (in a sentence, in a pericope, in a section), concentric structure, spiral structure, double meaning, dramatic techniques (change of scenes, alternating scenes, double-stage action, law of stage duality, technique of seven scenes, of diptych), "epanalepsis," explanatory notes or asides, hook-words, inclusions, irony, misunderstanding, narrative art in John, numerical patterns, parables, parallelism (synonymous, antithetic, synthetic), repetitions and variations, riddle, symbolic language. More particularly, the present author is especially interested in repetitions and variations. These literary devices "have received limited attention in Johannine scholarship."[114] Only some of the lists of Johannine characteristics mention that "remarkable repetitions are typical of John." This is the case in the lists of M. Flacius, S. Glassius, K.A. Credner,[115] and, more recently, W. Nicol.[116] E. Schweizer was nevertheless inclined to exclude repetition from his list because he found the technique difficult to describe.[117] The recent study of T. Popp[118] has clearly confronted the difficult issue of repetition in John and dared to provide an exhaustive study thereof. His detailed analysis of existing literature is intelligently integrated into his description of the "Grammar of the Spirit," which manifests itself primarily in the literary techniques of repetition, variation, and amplification. By employing the paradigm of "réécriture," his study of these techniques is elaborated within the framework of the literary art of the author rather than in critical reaction to source-critical and redaction-critical analysis. In so doing, Popp has provided a comprehensive study of one of the aspects of literary technique that serve to help the reader understand the text.

---

[113] For this enumeration see G. Mlakuzhyil, Structure (1987) 87–135; G. Van Belle, Johannine Bibliography (1988) 120–28; J.E. Botha, Samaritan Woman (1991) 31–39.

[114] J.E. Botha, Samaritan Woman (1991) 36.

[115] M. Flacius, Clavis, II (1581), 502 (no. 4); S. Glassius, Philologiae Sacrae (1694) 154 (no. 3); K.A. Credner, Einleitung (1836) 226 (no. 29).

[116] W. Nicol, The Sèmeia (1972) 24 (no. 76).

[117] E. Schweizer, Ego Eimi (1939) 99.

[118] T. Popp, Grammatik (2001). See G. Van Belle, Repetition (2003). On repetitions and variations in John, see also T.F. Glasson, Repetitions (1945–46); E.D. Freed, Variations (1964); P; L. Morris, Studies (1969) 293–319; S.-C. Chang, Repetitions and Variations (1975); J. Gerhard, Unity (1975); N.G. Timmins, Variation (1994); J.A. du Rand, Repetitions (1996).

6. Conclusion

The aforementioned study by T. Popp conforms to the description of style that we have proposed in the latter part of the present contribution. He studies the style of the evangelist and, in particular his preference for repetitions, variations, and amplifications, not only at the "word level" and "sentence level" but also at the "rhetorical-narrative level" and "socio-rhetorical level." In other words, he not only integrates the study of rhetorical figures into style criticism but also examines how the technique of repetition represents the evangelist's primary technique for entering into communication with his readers. Such concern for the reader is similarly reflected in the work of Professor Sj. van Tilborg.

Bibliography

Abbott, E.A., *Johannine Vocabulary* (Diatessarica 5), London 1905; repr. Farnborough 1968.

——, *Johannine Grammar: A Comparison of the Words of the Fourth Gospel with Those of the Three* (Diatessarica 6), London 1906; repr. Farnborough 1968.

Ball, D., "Some Recent Literature on John: A Review Article," in: *Themelios* 19 (1993–94) n. 1, 13–18.

Bauer, W., "Johannesevangelium und Johannesbriefe," in: *TR* 1 (1929) 135–60.

Becker, J., "Wunder und Christologie. Zum literarkritischen und christologischen Problem der Wunder im Johannesevangelium," in: *NTS* 16 (1969–70) 130–48; = A. Suhl (ed.), Der Wunderbegriff im Neuen Testament (WdF 245), Darmstadt 1980, 435–63.

Bernard, J.H., *A Critical and Exegetical Commentary on the Gospel According to St. John* (ICC), 2 vols., Edinburgh 1928.

Bjerkelund, C.J., "Tauta Egeneto. Die Präzisierungssätze im Johannesevangelium" (*WUNT* 40), Tübingen 1987.

Black, M., *An Aramaic Approach to the Gospels and Acts*, Oxford 1946, ^{2}1950, ^{3}1967 (with an Appendix on *The Son of Man*, by G. Vermes). German translation: *Die Muttersprache Jesus. Das Aramäische der Evangelien und der Apostelgeschichte*, trans. G. Schwarz (BWANT 115; 6/15), Stuttgart 1982.

Blauert, H., *Die Bedeutung der Zeit in der johanneischen Theologie. Eine Untersuchung an Hand von Joh 1–17 unter besonderer Berücksichtigung des literarkritischen Problems*, diss. Tübingen 1953.

Boismard, M.-É., "Un procédé rédactionnel dans le quatrième évangile: la Wiederaufnahme," in: M. de Jonge (ed.), L'évangile de Jean: Source, rédaction, théologie (*BETL* 44), Leuven 1977 (^{2}1987), 235–41.

——, "Comment Luc a remanié l'évangile de Jean" (*Cahiers de la Revue Biblique* 51), Paris 2001.

Boismard, M.-É., and Lamouille, A., *La vie des évangiles. Initiation à la critique des textes (Initiations)*, Paris 1980; German transl. *Aus der Werkstatt der Evangelisten. Einführung in die Literarkritik*, trans. M.-T. Wacker, München 1980.

Boismard, M.-É., and Lamouille, A., in collaboration with G. Rochais, "L'évangile de Jean. Commentaire" (*Synopse des quatre évangiles en français* 3), Paris 1977.
Botha, J.E., "Style, Stylistics and the Study of the New Testament," in: *Neotestamentica* 24 (1990) 173–84.
———, "Jesus and the Samaritan Woman: A Speech Act Reading of John 4:1–42" (*SupplNT* 65), Leiden 1991.
Braun, F.-M., *Jean le théologien et son évangile dans l'Église ancienne* (ÉtB), Paris 1959.
Bromboszcz, T., *Die Einheit des Johannes-Evangeliums*, Katowice 1927.
Brooke, A.E., *A Critical and Exegetical Commentary on the Johannine Epistles* (ICC), Edinburgh 1912.
Brown, R.E., *An Introduction to the Gospel of John. Edited, updated, introduced, and concluded by F.J. Moloney* (The Anchor Bible Reference Library), New York-London 2003.
Brown, S., "From Burney to Black: The Fourth Gospel and the Aramaic Question," in: *CBQ* 26 (1964) 323–39.
Bultmann, R., "Das Johannesevangelium in der neuesten Forschung," in: *CW* 41 (1927) 502–11.
———, "Hirsch's Auslegung des Johannes-Evangeliums," in: *EvT* 4 (1937) 115–42.
———, *Das Evangelium des Johannes* (*KEK* 2), Göttingen 1941. English translation: The *Gospel of John: A Commentary*, trans. G.R. Beasley-Murray, Oxford 1971.
Burney, C.F., *The Aramaic Origin of the Fourth Gospel*, Oxford 1922.
Bussmann, H., *Lexikon der Sprachwissenschaft* (*KTA* 452), Stuttgart 1983.
Carson, D.A., "Current Source Criticism of the Fourth Gospel: Some Methodological Questions," in: *JBL* 97 (1978) 411–29.
Casey, M., *Is John's Gospel True?*, London-New York 1996.
Chang, P.S.-C., *Repetitions and Variations in the Gospel of John*, diss. Strasbourg 1975.
Charles, R.H., *A Critical and Exegetical Commentary on the Revelation of St. John* (ICC), 2 vols., Edinburgh 1928.
Colwell, E.C., *The Greek of the Fourth Gospel: A Study of Its Aramaisms in the Light of Hellenistic Greek*, Chicago, IL 1931.
Conzelmann, H., and Lindemann, A., *Arbeitsbuch zum Neuen Testament* (*UTB* 52), Tübingen 1975, ²1976, ³1977, ⁴1979, ⁵1980, ⁶1982, ⁷1983, ⁸1985, ⁹1988.
Coppens, J., "L'analyse critique du IVᵉ évangile," in: *ETL* 18 (1941) 180–82.
Credner, K.A., *Einleitung in das Neue Testament. Erster Theil. Erste Abteilung*, Halle 1836.
Culpepper, R.A., *Anatomy of the Fourth Gospel* (Foundations and Facets: New Testament), Philadelphia, PA 1983.
Davidson, S., *An Introduction to the New Testament: Containing an Examination of the Most Important Questions Relating to the Authority, Interpretation and Integrity of the Canonical Books, with Reference to the Latest Inquiries*. Vol. II: *The Acts of the Apostles to the Second Epistle to the Thessalonians*, London 1849.
Davies, M., *Rhetoric and Reference in the Fourth Gospel* (*JSNT SS* 69), Sheffield 1992.
Denaux, A., *Style and Stylistics of Luke-Acts*. Unpublished Seminar Paper Presented at the 58th Meeting of the SNTS in Bonn (2003).
de Saussure, F., *Cours de linguistique générale*, Paris 1916. English translation: *Course in General Linguistics*. Translated and Annotated by R. Harris, London, 1983.
de Wette, W.M.L., *Lehrbuch der historisch-kritischen Einleitung in die kanonischen Bücher des Neuen Testaments* (Lehrbuch der historisch-kritischen Einleitung in die Bibel Alten und *Neuen Testaments* 2), Berlin ⁵1848, ⁶1860 (ed. H. Messner-G. Lünemann).
Duke, P.D., *Irony in the Fourth Gospel*, Atlanta, GA 1985.
Du Rand, J.A., "Repetitions and Variations: Experiencing the Power of the Gospel of John as Literary Symphony," in: *Neotestamentica* 30 (1996) 59–70.
Eco, U., *Die Grenzen der Interpretation*, München 1992.
Ellis, P.F., *The Genius of John: A Composition-Critical Commentary on the Fourth Gospel*, Collegeville, MN 1984.

——, "Inclusion, Chiasm, and the Division of the Fourth Gospel," in: *St. Vladimir's Theological Quarterly* 43 (1999) 269–338.

Faure, A., "Die alttestamentlichen Zitate im 4. Evangelium und die Quellenscheidungshypothese," in: *ZNW* 21 (1922) 99–121.

Felton, T., and Thatcher, T., "Stylometry and the Signs Source," in: R.T. Fortna & T. Thatcher (eds.), *Jesus in Johannine Tradition*, Louisville 2001, 208–19.

Festugière, A.-J., *Observations stylistiques sur l'évangile de S. Jean* (*Études et commentaires* 74), Paris 1974.

Flacius, M., *Clavis Scripturae S. seu De Sermone Sacrarum Literarum*, 2 vols., Basel 1580–81.

Fortna, R.T., *The Gospel of Signs: A Reconstruction of the Narrative Source Underlying the Fourth Gospel* (*SNTS MS* 11), Cambridge 1970.

——, *The Fourth Gospel and Its Predecessor: From Narrative Source to Present Gospel*, Philadelphia, PA 1988.

Freed, E.D., "Variations in the Language and Thought of John," in: *ZNW* 55 (1964) 167–97.

Freed, E.D., and Hunt, R.B., "Fortna's Signs-Source in John," in: *JBL* 94 (1975) 563–79.

Frey, J., "Erwägungen zum Verhältnis der Johannesapokalypse zu den übrigen Schriften des Corpus Johanneum," in: M. Hengel (ed.), *Die johanneische Frage. Ein Lösungsversuch* (*WUNT* 67), Tübingen 1993, 326–429.

——, *Die johanneische Eschatologie. Band I: Ihre Probleme im Spiegel der Forschung seit Reimarus* (*WUNT* 96), Tübingen 1998.

——, "Das vierte Evangelium in neuer Perspektive," in *Theol. Beiträge* 31 (2000) 38–44.

Gerhard, J., *The Literary Unity and the Compositional Methods of the Gospel of John*, diss. Washington, DC, The Catholic University of America 1975.

Glassius, S., *Philologiae Sacrae, qua totius Sacrosanctae, Veteris et Novi Testamenti, Scripturae*, Amsterdam [1623–1636], 1694.

Glasson, T.F., "Inaccurate Repetitions in the Fourth Gospel," in: *ExpT* 57 (1945–46) 111–12.

Goguel, M., *Introduction au Nouveau Testament*. II. Le quatrième évangile, Paris 1923.

——, "Cinquante ans de recherche johannique. De Bultmann à la narratologie": in Id. and L. Laberge (eds.), "De Bien des manières": La recherche biblique aux abords du XXIe siècle (*LD* 63), Paris 1995, 229–306.

Grosjean, J., "Le style johannique," in D. Bourg, C. Coulot, and A. Lion (eds.), *Variations johanniques* (*Parole présente*), Paris 1989, 127–36.

Guerike, H.E.F., *Historisch-kritische Einleitung in das Neue Testament*, Leipzig 1843.

Haenchen, E., *Das Johannesevangelium. Ein Kommentar aus den nachgelassenen Manuskripten*, ed. U. Busse, Tübingen, 1980 (Preface by J.M. Robinson). English translation: *John 1/2. A Commentary on the Gospel of John*, trans. R.W. Funk, ed. R.W. Funk and U. Busse (Hermeneia), 2 vols., Philadelphia, PA 1984.

Haldimann, K., and Weder, H., "Aus der Literatur zum Johannesevangelium 1985–1994," in: *TR* 67 (2002) 328–48, 424–56.

Hartke, W., *Vier urchristliche Parteien und ihre Vereinigung zur apostolischen Kirche* (*SSA* 24), 2 vols., Berlin 1961.

Heekerens, H.-P., *Die Zeichen-Quelle der johanneischen Redaktion. Ein Beitrag zur Entstehungsgeschichte des vierten Evangeliums* (*SBS* 113), Stuttgart 1984.

Henderson, I.H., "Style-Switching in the Didache: Fingerprint or Argument," in: C.N. Jefford (ed.), *The Didache in Context: Essays on Its Text, History and Transmission* (*SupplNT* 77), Leiden 1995, 177–209.

Hengel, M., *The Johannine Question*, trans. J. Bowden, London-Philadelphia, PA 1989. German translation: *Die johanneische Frage. Ein Lösungsversuch* (*WUNT* 67), Tübingen 1993.

Hirsch, E., *Studien zum vierten Evangelium.* (Text/Literarkritik/Entstehungsgeschichte) (Beiträge zur historischen Theologie, 11), Tübingen 1936.
———, "Stilkritik und Literaranalyse im vierten Evangelium," in: *ZNW* 43 (1950–51) 128–43.
Holtzmann, H.J.," Über das Problem des ersten johanneischen Briefes in seinem Verhältnis zum Evangelium," in: *Jahrbücher für prot. Theol.* 7 (1881) 690–712; 8 (1882) 128–52, 316–42, 460–85.
Howard, W.F., *The Fourth Gospel in Recent Criticism and Interpretation*, London 1931, [4]1955 (ed. C.K. Barrett).
Jacquier, E., *Histoire des livres du Nouveau Testament.* IV. Les écrits johanniques, Paris [3]1908.
Jeremias, J., "Johanneische Literarkritik," in: *Theologische Blätter* 20 (1941) 33–46.
Kaiser, T.P.C., *De speciali Joannis apostoli grammatica culpa neglegentiae liberanda*, Erlangen 1842.
Koester, H., "Überlieferung und Geschichte der frühchristlichen Evangelienliteratur," in: *ANRW* II, 25/2 (1984) 1463–1542.
Kowalski, B., "Stil in der neutestamentlichen Exegese. Definition, Methodik und Konkretisierung am Beispiel des Lukasevangeliums," in: *Prokolle zur Bibel* 12 (2003) 105–28.
Lagrange, M.-J., *L'évangile de Jean* (ÉB), Paris 1925.
Lange, S.G., *Die drey Johannesbriefe nebst drey Abhandlungen über Johannis Charakter, Schreibart und Theologie*, Weimar 1797.
Léon-Dufour, X., "L'évangile de Jean," in: *RSR* 79 (1991) 291–315; 82 (1994) 227–50.
Lorenzini, E., "La problematicità dell'unità linguistica giovannea secondo il metodo dello Schweizer," in: *Vetera Christianorum* 18 (1981) 453–69.
Louw, J.P., "On Johannine Style," in: *Neotestamentica* 20 (1986) 5–12.
Luthardt, E., *Das johanneische Evangelium nach seiner Eigentümlichkeit geschildert und erklärt*, vol. I, Nürnberg 1852.
Maynard, H., *The Function of Apparent Synonyms and Ambiguous Words in the Fourth Gospel*, Diss. University of Southern California 1950.
Menoud, P.-H., "Le problème johannique," in: *RTP* 29 (1941) 236–56; 30 (1942) 155–75; 31 (1943) 80–101; = Id., "L'évangile de Jean d'après les recherches récentes" (*CTAP* 3), Neuchâtel-Paris 1943, [2]1947.
Mlakuzhyil, G., *The Christocentric Literary Structure of the Fourth Gospel* (AnBib 117), Rome 1987.
Moloney, F.J., "Where Does One Look? Reflections on Some Recent Johannine Scholarship," in: *Salesianum* 62 (2000) 223–51.
Morgen, M., "La littérature johannique," in: *RSR* 86 (1998) 291–320.
———, "Bulletin johannique," in: *RSR* 88 (2000) 561–91.
Morgenthaler, R., *Statistik des neutestamentlichen Wortschatzes*, Zürich-Frankfurt am Main 1958.
Morris, L., *Studies in the Fourth Gospel*, Grand Rapids, MI 1969.
Moulton, J.H., and Howard, W.F., *A Grammar of New Testament Greek.* Vol. II: Accidence and Word-Formation. With an Appendix on Semitisms in the New Testament, Edinburgh 1928.
Müller, P.-G., *Lexikon exegetischer Fachbegriffe* (Biblische Basis Bücher 1), Stuttgart-Kevelaer 1985.
Neirynck, F., in collaboration with J. Delobel, T. Snoy, G. Van Belle, and F. Van Segbroeck, "L'évangile de Jean. Examen critique du commentaire de M.-É. Boismard et A. Lamouille," in: *ETL* 53 (1977) 363–478.
———, *Jean et les Synoptiques. Examen critique de l'exégèse de M.-É. Boismard* (*BETL* 49), Leuven 1979.

Neirynck, F., "L'epanalepsis et la critique littéraire. À propos de l'évangile de Jean," in: *ETL* 56 (1980) 303–38; = Id., Evangelica. Gospel Studies—Études d'évangiles. Collected Essays, ed. F. Van Segbroeck (*BETL* 60), Leuven 1982, 143–78.

Nicol, W., *The Sèmeia in the Fourth Gospel. Tradition and Redaction* (*SupplNT*, 32), Leiden 1972.

Nielsen, H.K., "Johannine Research," in: J. Nissen and S. Pedersen (eds.), New Readings in John: Literary and Theological Perspectives (*JSNT SS* 182), Sheffield 1999, 11–30.

Nissen, P., "In Memoriam Prof. Dr. Sjef van Tilborg," in: *Intern Bulletin Faculteit der Theologie KUN* 41 (2003, 4 juni) 1–3.

Noack, B., *Zur johanneischen Tradition. Beiträge zur Kritik an der literarkritischen Analyse des vierten Evangeliums* (*LSSK T* 3), København 1954.

O'Day, G.R., *Irony and the Johannine Theology of Revelation: An Investigation of John 4*, diss. Graduate School of Emory University 1983.

Olsson, B., "Structure and Meaning in the Fourth Gospel: A Text-Linguistic Analysis of John 2:1–11 and 4:1–42" (*ConBibNT* 6), Lund 1974.

O'Rourke, J.J., "The Historic Present in the Gospel of John," in: *JBL* 93 (1974) 585–90.

Person, R.F. Jr., "A Reassessment of Wiederaufnahme from the Perspective of Conversation Analysis," in: *BZ* 43 (1999) 239–48.

Popp, T., *Grammatik des Geistes. Literarische Kunst und theologische Konzeption in Johannes 3 und 6* (Arbeiten zur Bibel und ihrer Geschichte 3), Leipzig 2001.

Poythress, V.S., "Testing for Johannine Authorship by Examining the Use of Conjunctions," in: *WestTJ* 46 (1984) 350–69.

——, "The Use of the Intersentence Conjunctions *De, Oun, Kai*, and Asyndeton in the Gospel of John," in: *NT* 26 (1984) 312–40.

Rakotoharintsifa, A., "Chronique johannique," in: *ÉTR* 75 (2000) 81–102.

Richard, E., "Expressions of Double Meaning and Their Function in the Gospel of John," in: *NTS* 31 (1985) 96–112.

Riesner, R., "Rückfrage nach Jesus. Teil 2: Neue Literatur zum Thomas- und Johannesevangelium," in: *Theol. Beiträge* 31 (2000) 152–62.

Ruckstuhl, E., *Die literarische Einheit des Johannesevangeliums*. Der gegenwärtige Stand der einschlägigen Forschungen (SF, NF 3), Freiburg/Schw., 1951. Second edition: Mit einem Vorwort von M. Hengel. Im Anhang: Liste der johanneischen Stilmerkmale mit allen Belegstellen aus dem johanneischen Schrifttum.—Sprache und Stil im johanneischen Schrifttum. Die Frage ihrer Einheit und Einheitlichkeit (*NTOA* 5), Freiburg/Schw.-Göttingen 1987.

——, "Johannine Language and Style: The Question of Their Unity," in: M. de Jonge (ed.), L'évangile de Jean: Source, rédaction, théologie (*BETL* 44), Leuven 1977 (²1987), 125–47. German translation: "Sprache und Stil im johanneischen Schrifttum. Die Frage ihrer Einheit und Einheitlichkeit," in: E. Ruckstuhl, *Die literarische Einheit* (²1987) 304–31.

——, "Zur Antithese Idiolekt-Soziolekt im johanneischen Schrifttum," in: *SNTU* 12 (1987) 141–81; = E. Ruckstuhl, "Jesus im Horizont der Evangelien" (*SBA* 3), Stuttgart 1988, 219–64.

Ruckstuhl, E., and Dschulnigg P., *Stilkritik und Verfasserfrage im Johannesevangelium. Die johanneischen Sprachmerkmale auf dem Hintergrund des Neuen Testaments und des zeitgenössischen hellenistischen Schrifttums* (*NTOA* 17), Freiburg/Schw.-Göttingen 1991.

Schenk, W., *Kommentiertes Lexikon zum vierten Evangelium: Seine Textkonstituenten in ihren Syntagmen und Wortfeldern* (Text-Theoretical Studies of the New Testament 1), Lewiston NY-Queenston (Ont.)-Lampeter 1993.

Schmithals, W., *Johannesevangelium und Johannesbriefe. Forschungsgeschichte und Analyse* (*BZNW* 64), Berlin-New York 1992.

Schnackenburg, R., "Johannesevangelium," in: *LTK*² 5 (1960) 1101–5.

———, "Zur Traditionsgeschichte von Joh 4,56–54," in: *BZ* 8 (1964) 58–88.
———, *Das Johannesevangelium* (HTKNT 4/1–4), 4 vols., Freiburg-Basel-Wien 1965, 1971, 1975, 1984; English translation: *The Gospel According to St. John* (HTCNT), 3 vols., New York 1968, 1980, 1982.
Schnelle U., *Antidoketische Christologie im Johannesevangelium. Eine Untersuchung zur Stellung des vierten Evangeliums in der johanneischen Schule* (FRLANT 144), Göttingen 1987. English translation: *Antidocetic Christology in the Gospel of John: An Investigation of the Place of the Fourth Gospel in the Johannine School*, trans. L.M. Maloney, Minneapolis, MN 1992.
———, *Das Evangelium nach Johannes* (Theologischer Handkommentar zum Neuen Testament 4). Leipzig, Evangelische Verlagsanstalt, 1998.
———, "Ein neuer Blick. Tendenzen gegenwärtiger Johannesforschung," in: *Berliner Theol. Zeitschrift* 16 (1999) 21–40.
———, "Recent Views of John's Gospel," in: *Word & World* 21 (2001) 352–59.
Scholtissek K., "Johannine Studies: A Survey of Recent Research with Special Regard to German Contributions," in: *CR:BS* 6 (1998) 227–59; 9 (2001) 277–305.
———, "Neue Wege der Johannesauslegung. Ein Forschungsbericht I–II," in: *Theol. und Glaube* 89 (1999) 263–95; 91 (2001) 109–33.
———, "Johannes auslegen I. Forschungsgeschichtliche und methodische Reflexionen. II. Methodische, hermeneutische und einleitungswissenschaftliche Reflexionen," in: *SNTU/A* 24 (1999) 35–84; 25 (2000) 98–140.
———, "Relecture und réécriture: Neue Paradigmen zum Methode und Inhalt der Johannesauslegung aufgewiesen am Prolog 1,1–18 und der ersten Abschiedsrede 13,31–41,31," in: *ThPh* 75 (2000) 1–29.
———, "Eine Renaissance des Evangeliums nach Johannes: Aktuelle Perspektiven der exegetischen Forschung," in: *TRev* 97 (2001) 267–88.
Schulz S., *Das Evangelium nach Johannes übersetzt und erklärt* (NTD 4), Göttingen 1972, ³1978.
Schulze J.D., *Der schriftstellerische Charakter und Werth des Johannes, zum Behuf der Specialhermeneutik seiner Schriften untersucht und bestimmt*. Voran ein Nachtrag über die Quellen der Briefe von Petrus, Jakobus und Judas, und über das Verhältniss dieser Briefe zu andern neutestamentlichen Schriften, Weissenfels-Leipzig 1803 (²1811).
Schweizer A., *Das Evangelium Johannes nach seinem innern Werthe und seiner Bedeutung für das Leben Jesu kritisch untersucht*, Leipzig 1841.
———, *Ego Eimi. Die religionsgeschichtliche Herkunft und theologische Bedeutung der johanneischen Bildreden, zugleich ein Beitrag zur Quellenfrage des vierten Evangeliums* (FRLANT NF 38), Göttingen 1939, ²1965.
Seyffarth T.A., *Ein Beitrag zur Specialcharakteristik des johanneischen Schriften besonders des johanneischen Evangeliums*, Leipzig 1810.
Smalley S.S., "The Johannine Literature: A Sample of Recent Studies in English," in: *Theology* 103 (2000) 13–28.
Spitta F., *Das Johannes-Evangelium als Quelle der Geschichte Jesu*, Göttingen 1910.
Staley J.L., *The Print's First Kiss: A Rhetorical Investigation of the Implied Reader in the Fourth Gospel* (SBL DS 82), Atlanta, GA 1988.
Strauss D.F., "Vorrede zu den Gesprächen von Ulrich von Hutten," in: Id., *Gesammelte Schriften*, vol. VII, ³1877 (original ed.: 1860).
Stronck C.W., *Specimen hermeneutico-theologicum, De doctrina et dictione Johannis apostoli ad Jesu magistri doctrinam dictionemque exacte composita*, Utrecht 1797.
Tarelli C.C., "Johannine Synonyms," in: *JTS* 47 (1946) 175–77.
Teeple H.M., *The Literary Origin of the Gospel of John*, Evanston, IL 1974.
Temple S., "The Two Signs in the Fourth Gospel," in: *JBL* 81 (1962) 169–74.
Thielman F., "The Style of the Fourth Gospel and Ancient Literary Critical Concepts of Religious Discourse," in: D.F. Watson (ed.), *Persuasive Artistry: Studies in New Testament Rhetoric in Honor of George A. Kennedy* (JSTN SS 50), Sheffield 1991, 169–83.

Thompson, J.M., "Accidental Disarrangements in the Fourth Gospel," in: *Expositor* 8th ser. 9 (1915) 421–37.
——, "Is John XXI an Appendix?," in: *Expositor* 8th ser. 10 (1915) 139–47.
——, "The Structure of the Fourth Gospel," in: *Expositor* 8th ser. 10 (1915) 512–26.
——, "The Composition of the Fourth Gospel," in: *Expositor* 8th ser. 11 (1916) 34–46.
Thyen, H., "Aus der Literatur zum Johannesevangelium," in: *TR* 39 (1974) 1–69, 222–52, 289–329; 42 (1977) 211–70; 43 (1978) 328–59; 44 (1979) 97–134.
Timmins, N.G., "Variation in Style in the Johannine Literature," in: *JSNT* 53 (1994) 47–64.
Turner, N., *Style* (J.H. Moulton, *A Grammar of New Testament Greek*, Vol. IV), Edinburgh 1976.
Untergassmair, F.G., "Das Johannesevangelium: Ein Bericht über neuere Literatur aus der Johannesforschung," in *TRev* 90 (1994) 91–108.
Utzschneider, U., "Text—Leser—Autor. Bestandaufnahme und Prolegomena zu einer Theorie der Exegese," in: *BZ NF* 43 (1999) 224–38.
Van Belle, G., *De Sèmeia-bron in het vierde evangelie. Ontstaan en groei van een hypothese* (*SNTA* 10), Leuven 1975.
——, *Les parenthèses dans l'évangile de Jean. Aperçu historique et classification. Texte grec de Jean* (*SNTA* 11), Leuven 1985.
——, *Johannine Bibliography 1966–1985: A Cumulative Bibliography on the Fourth Gospel* (*CoBRA* 1), Brussel 1988; = (*BETL* 82), Leuven 1988.
——, "Les parenthèses johanniques. Un premier bilan," in: F. Van Segbroeck, C.M. Tuckett, G. Van Belle, and J. Verheyden (eds.), *The Four Gospels 1992: FS Frans Neirynck* (*BETL* 100), Leuven, 1992, vol. III, 1901–33.
——, *The Signs Source in the Fourth Gospel: Historical Survey and Critical Evaluation of the Semeia Hypothesis* (*BETL* 116), Leuven 1994.
——, "Prolepsis in the Gospel of John," in: *NT* 63 (2001) 334–47.
——, "Repetition, Variation and Amplification: Thomas Popp's Recent Contribution on Johannine Style," in: *ETL* 79 (2003) 166–78.
——, "In Memoriam S. van Tilborg," in: *ETL* 79 (2003) 527–28.
van Tilborg Sj., "The Gospel of John: Communicative Processes in a Narrative Text," in: *Neotestamentica* 23 (1989) 19–31.
——, *Al lezend stemmen horen*. Inaugurele rede, Nijmegen 1994.
von Wahlde U.C., "A Redactional Technique in the Fourth Gospel," in: *CBQ* 38 (1976) 520–33.
——, "Wiederaufnahme as a Marker of Redaction in Jn 6,51–58," in: *Bib* 64 (1983) 542–49.
——, *The Earliest Version of John's Gospel: Recovering the Gospel of Signs*, Wilmington, DE 1989.
Wead, D.W., *The Literary Devices in John's Gospel* (*TDiss* 4), Basel 1970.
Weber, M., *Authentia capitis ultimi evangelii Johannei, hujusque evangelii totius, argumentorum internorum usu, vindicata*, Halle 1823.
Wegscheider, J.A.L., *Versuch einer vollständigen Einleitung in das Evangelium des Johannes*, Göttingen 1806.
Wellhausen, J., *Das Evangelium Johannis*, Berlin 1908; reprint: Id., *Evangelienkommentare*. Mit einer Einleitung von M. Hengel, Berlin-New York 1987, 601–746.
Wendt, H.H., *Das Johannesevangelium. Eine Untesuchung seiner Entstehung und seines geschichtlichen Wertes*, Göttingen 1900. English translation: *The Gospel According to St. John*, Edinburgh 1902.
——, *Die Schichten im vierten Evangelium*, Göttingen 1911.
Zeller, D., "Vergleichende Uebersicht über den Wörtervorrath der sämmtlichen neutestamentlichen Schriftsteller," in: *Theologische Jahrbücher* 2 (1893) 443–543.
Ziener, G., "Johannesevangelium und urchristliche Passafeier," in: *BZ* 2 (1958) 263–74.

CHAPTER FIFTEEN

INTERTEXTUALITY: TRACES OF MYSTICISM

Huub Welzen
University of Nijmegen, the Netherlands

Introduction

Wim Reedijk's recent thesis[1] ends with a remarkable conclusion on the truth of the interpretation of biblical texts. In his study Reedijk relates the *lectio divina* of the Egyptian desert fathers, more specifically the *Collatio XIV* of John Cassian, to modern biblical research and biblical hermeneutics. He concludes that reader-oriented study is most amenable to Cassian's aims. But Cassian also laid down conditions, more so than modern scholars do. To him the problem of discovering meaning lay with the readers rather than with the texts. Readers have to subordinate themselves entirely to the text. They are not above it but below it. In Reedijk's view this is a serious criticism of present-day biblical scholarship.

Yet there are also parallels between modern exegesis and *lectio divina*. Thus they use the same criteria of public exposure and objective testing of new-found insights. Discovering truth is not a purely subjective exercise. In Cassian's work such public exposure and testing assume two forms. In the dialogue with those who guide the readers—the teachers—one recognizes the public nature and testing found in present-day dialogue in the scholarly community. Accordingly Reedijk calls Bible reading a communitarian process. The second point is the most remarkable: "The truth of an interpretation is recognised by what it does to people. An interpretation that becomes visual is proof of its truth."[2] Reedijk explains in what respect this kind of discovery of truth goes beyond that of present-day science:

---

[1] W. Reedijk, *Zuiver Lezen. De* lectio divina *van Johannes Cassianus en de bijbelse hermeneutiek*. Delft 2003.
[2] W. Reedijk, op. cit. 252 (our translation).

"Such intersubjective observation is more comprehensive than that of scientific tests, which remain equally intersubjective but are conceptual and detached. In Cassian's work the truth of an interpretation always includes ethics."[3] More than that: "The truth that a reader discovers in a text stands or falls by the authenticity of the reader's life, by who the reader is."[4]

The life and works of Sjef van Tilborg definitely incorporate the ethical dimension of interpretation. From the period of what is known as materialistic exegesis we have a number of publications attesting to the ethical and social relevance of biblical texts. His monumental study of the Sermon on the Mount demonstrates a similar awareness.[5] Some of his less exegetically oriented publications likewise indicate awareness of this social and ethical impact.[6] And from the period when Sjef resided in Nijmegen we should mention his involvement with the Titus Brandsma community center in the Nijmegen district of Bottendaal and his concern about marginalized youths, whom he received hospitably in his home.

But that is not all. In addition to an ethical dimension the interpretation of biblical texts has a spiritual dimension. In Reedijk's study of Cassian's *lectio divina* this topic is broached when he deals with the silence of those who make the study of scriptural texts their life's work. Their silence has three dimensions.[7] The first dimension is that one should first put Scripture into practice before instructing others in it. This dimension of silence may be seen as a product of the ethical dimension of truth that the reader has discovered in the text. Cassian insisted on the importance of the reader's purity and he considered it impossible for impure readers to acquire spiritual knowledge of a text, however doggedly they pore over it. The second dimension of silence concerns the known experience that important insights have a way of obtruding themselves in the silence of the night. Silence is essential for penetrating deeply into a text. Such deep penetration into the secret of a text also has to do with the fact that it gives the text a chance to obtain a firm foothold in the

---

[3] Ibid. (our translation).
[4] Ibid. (our translation).
[5] Sj. van Tilborg, *The Sermon on the Mount as an Ideological Intervention. A Reconstruction of Meaning*. Assen 1986.
[6] Here we may mention Sj. van Tilborg, *Geloven tussen utopie en werkelijkheid*. Hilversum 1980; and Sj. van Tilborg, *Misschien dat God het ons vergeeft: uit de praktijk van een pastor voor vreemdelingen*. Baarn 1976.
[7] See W. Reedijk, op. cit. especially pp. 109–11.

reader's mind. In this we recognize the spiritual process that may be triggered by prolonged, profound contact with biblical and mystical texts. The third dimension of silence is didactic. It pertains to the silence that makes someone a good teacher. The knowledge and wisdom a good teacher has to offer are earned through assiduous effort and hard work. When dealing with people who want to come by such knowledge and wisdom easily, silence is the most apposite response. Caution and reticence are second nature to a good teacher.

Sjef had less to say about the spiritual dimension of the reading process, the contact with the mystery of Scripture, than about its ethical effect. I can recall only two sentences from an address on a festive occasion in the *"Bijbelatelier."*[8] Then, albeit hesitantly, Sjef linked the reading and study of biblical texts with commitment to God. To my mind he was touching on one of the most profound intuitions of Judaic and Christian Bible reading, namely that it is a process that engages readers in their innermost being, that transforms them and inducts them into the mystery that the text is about. That is the spirit in which I dedicate this article on mysticism and intertextuality to Sjef.

A number of biblical texts, as well as some texts from the Christian tradition, show that contact with the mystery these texts refer to is not where it ends. The reading process itself is a starting point for new text formation. Being touched by the mystery of a text itself triggers text production. Sometimes it triggers a creative process in which new texts are shaped. Both the text that was read and the reader's experience of it are verbalized in a new text, which carries within its newly created distinctiveness the echoes of the original text and the experience gained from it. This creative process may shed light on some forms of intertextuality, which in the methodological pluralism of our day is very much in the limelight.

The rest of this article is devoted to the following topics: 1. mysticism and language; 2. Bible reading as an event in the relationship between God and human beings; 3. intertextuality as linguistic re-creation; and 4. hidden intertextuality in the prologue to *Liber Scivias*.

---

[8] The designations *"Bijbelatelier" "Atelier Exegese"* and, formerly, *"Atelier Nieuwe Testament"* refer to periodic gatherings of lecturers and students of exegesis attached to the Faculty of Theology at Nijmegen. These workshops were held from the latter half of the 1970s onwards. Topics of discussion were new developments in exegesis and (first) results of one's own research.

1. *Mysticism and Language*

The complexity of the relation between mysticism and language stems from the very character of mystical experience, which is primarily an experience of breakthrough.[9] The word "breakthrough" cannot be taken literally enough. A radically new experience of reality breaks through so fundamentally that no existing frameworks are adequate to contain it. They collapse. Names and words fail. The reality that presents itself is ultimate and is experienced by the mystic as absolute. It eludes every humanly designed order. Yet this ultimate reality directly and profoundly affects the person, often so profoundly as to amount to an identity change. The impact has two facets. First there is direct contact, indicated by such terms as union, merging, fusion, oneness, communion. Secondly, there is the breakdown and bankruptcy of existing frameworks, indicated by such terms as "absence," "night," "wilderness," "solitude," "annihilation." The two facets of mystical experience have implications for the mystic's manner of knowing. On the one hand it is infinite not-knowing; on the other it derives from the God-human relationship as such, a knowing surpassing all objective knowledge. Ruusbroec comments thus:[10]

> And still, our reason stands open-eyed in the dark, that is in unfathomable unknowing. And in this darkness the unfathomable brightness remains covered and hidden from us, for its overwhelming unfathomableness blinds our reason, but it enfolds us in simplicity and transforms us with its own selfness. And so we are unwrought from ourselves and wrought by God until we are immersed in love where we possess bliss and are one with God. When we are united with God in that way, there remains a living knowledge and an active loving in us, for without our knowledge we cannot possess God and without our practise of loving we cannot be united with God, nor remain united with him.

It is noteworthy that Ruusbroec speaks of both unfathomable unknowing and living awareness or knowledge. Unknowing refers to knowl-

---

[9] The structural elements of mystical experience are described in O. Steggink and K. Waaijman, *Spiritualiteit en mystiek I. Inleiding*. Nijmegen 1985, pp. 100–8. Also see: K. Waaijman, Mystieke ervaring en mystieke weg, In: J. Baers, G. Brinkman, A. Jelsma, and O. Steggink (eds.), *Encyclopedie van de mystiek. Fundamenten, tradities, perspectieven*. Kampen, Tielt 2003, 57–79.

[10] Jan van Ruusbroec, *Opera Omnia X* (ed. G. De Baere). Corpus Christianorum Continuatio Mediaevalis CX Tielt-Turnhout 1991, 154.

edge gained by means of reason and the intellect. Such knowledge is of no use in mystical experience. Its unfathomableness blinds the intellect. But there is also living knowledge brought about by God's activity. This activity is twofold: we are both annihilated by God and created anew. In such annihilation and re-creation unfathomable unknowing is transformed into living knowledge that can be qualified more precisely as active loving. This qualification shows that we are no longer dealing with the objective and objectifiable knowledge proper to reason but with the relational knowledge peculiar to love relationships.

Mystical experience demands "expression" and seeks to express itself. The mystic's aporia, however, is that there are no longer any adequate means of expression, because mystical experience has broken them down. Neither are there any new means of expression as yet. The new experience of ultimate reality has put an end to existing means of expression, but new possibilities have yet to dawn. This aporia of a desire for self-expression when existing means of expression are inadequate is the matrix of mystical language. Its distinctiveness lies in its paradoxical character. Negation follows affirmation. Possible and impossible comparisons are made. Parables are applied in ways that readers and listeners do not expect. Proverbs and aphorisms provide food for thought. Throughout there is the driving force of the experience that creates new language where existing language cannot articulate the ineffable.

But the aporia of mystical experience in regard to linguistic expression goes beyond the mere inadequacy of existing language. Ineffability applies to all language. No language is capable of articulating the mystic's experience, yet it insists on articulation. Mystical language expresses an essential contradiction: compulsion, yet inability. Not only is existing language inadequate; the new language born of the aporia is equally so. The ineffable continually demands to be spoken, and so language is continually being generated, only to prove inadequate yet again.

A beautiful example of both the fundamental impossibility of mystical language and its paradoxical nature is the hymn of Gregory of Nazianzus, ῏Ω πάντων ἐπέκεινα (Oh Thou beyond everything).[11]

---

[11] The Greek text is from J.P. Migne, *Patrologiae cursus completus, Series Graeca.* Vol. 37, 507–8 (our translation).

Ὦ πάντων ἐπέκεινα· τί γὰρ θέμις ἄλλο σε μέλπειν;
Πῶς λόγος ὑμνήσει σε; σὺ γὰρ λόγῳ οὐδενὶ ῥητόν.
Πῶς νόος ἀθρήσει σε; σὺ γὰρ νόῳ οὐδενὶ ληπτός.
Μοῦνος ἐὼν ἄφραστος· ἐπεὶ τέκες ὅσσα λαλεῖται.
Μοῦνος ἐὼν ἄγνωστος· ἐπεὶ τέκες ὅσσα νοεῖται.
Πάντα σε καὶ λαλέοντα, καὶ οὐ λαλέοντα λιγαίνει.
Πάντα σε καὶ νοέοντα καὶ οὐ νοέοντα γεραίρει.
Ξυνοὶ γάρ τε πόθοι, ξυναὶ δ' ὠδῖνες ἁπάντων
Ἀμφὶ σέ· σοὶ δὲ τὰ πάντα προσεύχεται· εἰς σὲ δὲ πάντα
Σύνθεμα σὸν νοεόντα λαλεῖ σιγώμενον ὕμνον.
Σοὶ ἑνὶ πάντα μένει· σοὶ δ' ἀθρόα πάντα θοάζει.
Καὶ πάντων τέλος ἐσσι, καὶ εἷς, καὶ πάντα, καὶ οὐδεὶς,
Οὐχ ἕν ἐών, οὐ πάντα· πανώνυμε, πῶς σε καλέσσω,
Τὸν μόνον ἀκλήϊστον; Ὑπερνεφέας δὲ καλύπτρας
Τίς νόος οὐρανίδης εἰσδύσεται; Ἵλαος εἴης,
Ὦ πάντων ἐπέκεινα· τί γὰρ θέμις ἄλλο σε μέλπειν;

Oh Thou beyond everything,
How else to name Thee?

How can words praise Thee:
Thou who cannot be spoken by any word.
How can thoughts reach thee:
Thou who cannot be grasped by any thought.

Thou, Unique, Ineffable,
all that is said derives from Thee.
Thou, Unique, Unknowable,
all that is known derives from Thee.

All that speak and all that do not speak
praise Thee.
All that think and all that do not think
honour Thee.

Yearning everywhere, travail everywhere
all hanker for Thee, all pray to Thee,
while all who fathom Thy mystery
sing a song of silence.

Only with Thee everything is preserved,
on Thee all hopes are fixed,
Thou art the goal of everything.
Thou art one.
Thou art all.
Thou art nobody.
Thou art not one.
Thou art not all.

Thou that beareth all names,
How shall I name thee?

Thou the Only, the Unnameable,
what heavenly spirit penetrates to Thee
above the cloud cover?

Have mercy on me!
O Thou, beyond everything.
How else to sing you?

The essential aporia of articulating the essence of mystical experience is expressed mainly at the beginning of the hymn. God is beyond everything. Words and thoughts cannot reach him. No word can speak him, no thought can grasp him. He is ineffable and unknowable. Yet all that is spoken and known derives from him. That God is beyond everything is reiterated in the final lines, in the same words. The paradoxical character of mystical language is particularly evident in the second half of the hymn. In exquisite poetry it tells the effect of fathoming God's mystery: "... while all that fathom Thy mystery sing a song of silence" (λαλεῖ σιγώμενον ὕμνον). Lower down the text contains logical contradictions: "Thou art one. Thou art all. Thou art nobody. Thou art not one. Thou art not all." The paradoxes and contradictions, so to speak, make language and logic burst apart. In the resultant fissures and impossibilities comes the reference to the Mystery, whose mysteriousness and unknowability are maintained.

But there is more to mystical language than just its essential aporia. For while this language cannot encompass the Mystery, it conducts us into it. For centuries reading and meditating on biblical and mystical texts have put people into contact with the ineffable and inconceivable Mystery that is God. These texts need to be read with a spiritual attitude that is sensitive to the situation in which they originated. When that happens a mystical movement may be started in the process of reading the texts. "More precisely: mystical texts seek to induce an experience in the reader that the very reading generates love. Hence reading is not something that happens to a mystical text—taken from a dusty bookshelf for that purpose—after the event: the book (or the text) itself only reaches completion in the loving *practice of reading*. Clearly this demands a great deal both from the literary structure of the text and from the reading process. Everything should be focussed on achieving *an effect of love and attachment* in the reader. While reading the person is swept along into the unfathomable depth of God's loving power, which touches and transforms the very core of that person's nature. As a result he receives the ability to "grasp" from the inside what the text is saying. This in turn makes it possible for him—touched by God's love—to take another step on the steep road of love. In so doing the text can open itself up further and become active in the reader."[12]

In the next section we describe one of the methods used in the Christian tradition for spiritual reading of biblical texts. It is known as *lectio divina*. The reason we discuss this method of reading is that it rests on the belief that biblical texts have the potential to induct readers into the divine mystery they speak of. *Lectio divina* comes to grips with the mystagogic character of Scripture.

2. *Bible Reading as an Event in the Relationship Between God and Human Beings*

Reading Scripture means entering into a relational event between God and human beings. This intuition is found in the Bible itself. On every page of the New Testament one reads that the new religious experience—deriving from the passion, death, and resurrection of Jesus the Messiah—is deepened by relating it to what Scripture offers, while it also imbues old texts with new meaning. Until the advent of modern academic exegesis the methods and techniques of Bible reading always served the purposes of spiritual life. A particularly useful method is the model of *lectio divina* devised by Guigo II, the Carthusian, in the 12th century.

Guigo was the ninth prior of Grande Chartreuse from roughly 1173 to 1180. Little is known about his life. For a long time his two works, the *Scala claustralium* or *Scala paradisi* and a collection of *Meditationes*, were attributed to Bernard of Clairvaux.[13] His model, albeit in many variations, is used to this day.[14] In his *Scala claustra-*

---

[12] H. Blommestijn and F. Maas: Mystiek en taal. In: J. Baers, G. Brinkman, A. Jelsma, and O. Steggink (eds.), *Encyclopedie van de mystiek. Fundamenten, tradities, perspectieven*. Kampen, Tielt 2003 290–301. The quotation appears on pp. 294–95. The article was first published as "Mystieke taal voert naar haar bron." In: *Speling* 40 (1988) 3 90–98.

[13] P.A. Nissen, art. Guigo II. In: J. Baers, G. Brinkman, A. Jelsma, and O. Steggink (eds.), *Encyclopedie van de mystiek. Fundamenten, tradities, perspectieven*. Kampen, Tielt 2003, 975.

[14] E. Bianchi, *Pregare la parole: introduzione alla "lectio divina."* 12th rev. and amplified edition, Turin. C. Mesters, *Lectio Divina*. Middle Park Victoria 1996. "Lectio Divina et lecture spirituelle," in *Dictionnaire de Spiritualité* Tome 9 470–510. To Kees Waaijman

lium[15] he describes how the contemplative life correlates with the four steps of spiritual reading:

> One day when I was busy working with my hands I began to think about our spiritual work, and all at once four stages in spiritual exercise came into my mind: reading (lectio), meditation (meditatio), prayer (oratio) and contemplation (contemplatio). These make a ladder for monks by which they are lifted up from earth to heaven. It has few rungs, yet its length is immense and wonderful, for its lower end rests upon the earth, but its top pierces the clouds and touches heavenly secrets.[16]

The interrelationship of the four steps or rungs is vividly depicted in the following text fragment:

> Reading is the careful study of the Scriptures, concentrating all one's powers on it. Meditation is the busy application of the mind to seek with the help of one's own reason for knowledge of hidden truth. Prayer is the heart's devoted turning to God to drive away evil and obtain what is good. Contemplation is when the mind is in some sort lifted up to God and held above itself, so that it tastes the joys of everlasting sweetness.[17]

To describe the reading process Guigo uses a classical image: that of the digestive system of ruminants. In the reading process the text is first swallowed whole, then it is chewed morsel by morsel before it can be tasted and assimilated by the body so as to build it. The reading process probes ever deeper inwards:

> Reading seeks for the sweetness of a blessed life, meditation perceives it, prayer asks for it, contemplation tastes it. Reading, as it were, puts food whole into the mouth, meditation chews it and breaks it up, prayer extracts its flavor, contemplation is the sweetness itself which gladdens and refreshes. Reading works on the outside, meditation on the pith: prayer asks for what we long for, contemplation gives us delight in the sweetness which we have found.[18]

Guigo's model provides crucial support for his design of a spiritual hermeneutics. See K. Waaijman, *Spirituality. Forms, Foundations, Methods*. Louvain, Paris, Dudley 2002 689–773. We owe our description of *lectio divina* to this design.

[15] Guigo II, *Epistola de vita contemplativa/ Scala claustralium*. In: *Sources Chrétiennes*. Collection dirigée de Henri de Lubac et al., Paris 1941–... 163, 81–123. The English versions of the quotations are taken from: Guigo II, *The Ladder of Monks. A Letter on the Contemplative Life and Twelve Meditations*. Translated, with an introduction by E. Colledge O.S.A. and J. Walsh S.J. London and Oxford 1978.

[16] Guigo II, op. cit. 67–68.
[17] Guigo II, op. cit. 68.
[18] Guigo II, op. cit. 68–69.

The phases of reading (*lectio*) and meditation (*meditatio*) correspond to common reading and critical analysis of a text. Common reading includes all the activities involved in perusing of a text: recognizing the ink marks on the page as meaningful signals, combining letters into words, words into sentences, and sentences into larger textual entities. Decoding according to the code in which the meaningful signals are couched also forms part of the activity of common reading. In addition the passage has to be related to what was read previously and to anticipations of what still has to be read. Finally the act of common reading includes assigning meaning to the text. The meaning readers assign to a text is not arbitrary. In their interpretation they are again directed by the signals contained in the text. The act of common reading is a circular, interactive, hermeneutic process, entailing both direction of the reader by the text and the reader's interpretive activity in relation to the text.

Critical reading differs from common reading.[19] The critic stands back from the text so as to adopt a critical stance. The critic's attitude is objectifying. This differs from common reading, in which the distance between reader and text is minimal. A text permits the common reader to identify with it. Readers in a sense lose themselves in the text. The critic, by contrast, stands over against the text. The critic also forms judgments of the text and substantiates these. Common readers don't do this, because they do not approach the text as an object. To common readers the text is not an objective entity, which it is to the critic. The transition from *lectio* to *meditatio* entails crossing from the subjectifying pole of common reading to the objectifying pole of critical analysis. By critically and analytically inquiring into the composition, development, literary genre, intratextual relations, intertextual relations, and the like the critic discovers the inner truth and deep structure of the text. In the course of this critical and analytical chewing and rumination the text yields up its secrets. The manner in which texts are analyzed in scholarly exegesis is analogous to what happens in the meditative phase of *lectio divina*, but also differs from it. Exegetical techniques and procedures all focus on the text yielding up its meaning. To this end the exegete employs scientific methods and techniques. The questions asked in *meditatio*

---

[19] Cf. R. Fowler, *Let the Reader Understand. Reader-Response Criticism and the Gospel of Mark*. Minneapolis 1991, 27–31.

are fundamentally the same as those of scholarly exegesis, except they are not founded in scientific methodology.

In the orative and contemplative phases of the reading process commitment to God enters into it. Compared with *meditatio*, *oratio* entails a major transition. The focal issue is not extracting the meaning of the text but relating to its contents. Guigo characterizes this relationship as longing. He calls the basic movement of prayerful reading *desiderium* (longing). This longing is grounded in meditation. Prayer is kindled by meditation. The longing is explicitly directed to God: "... and all the while in my meditation the fire of longing, the desire to know you more fully, has increased."[20] Guigo explains this with reference to Jesus' conversation with the Samaritan woman, who asked him to give her living water to drink: "You can see that it was because she had heard the Lord's words and then had meditated on them that she was moved to prayer. How could she have pressed her petition, had she not first been fired by meditation?"[21]

For our purpose it is particularly pertinent to explore the contemplative phase. Firstly it is important to realize that what happens in *contemplatio* is not an automatic outcome of completing the successive phases of *lectio divina*. There is an initiative "from the other side." While this initiative relates to the longing that marks the orative phase and is a response to it, it does not depend on it. In a manner of speaking, God breaks in on the prayer. Guigo writes as follows:

> But the Lord, whose eyes are upon the just and whose ears can catch not only the words, but the very meaning of their prayers, does not wait until the longing soul has said all its say, but breaks in upon the middle of its prayer, runs to meet it in all haste.[22]

A second point to be noted is the paradoxical nature of what happens. Guigo speaks of the soul dying to itself and at the same time coming to life miraculously. He refers to the Lord intoxicating the soul and at the same time bringing it to its senses. It is in this context that he mentions the figure of speech known as antiphrasis. Antiphrasis is a stylistic device in which words are used in a different, often an opposite, sense to their usual meaning. Through the "interpenetration

---

[20] Guigo II, op. cit. 73.
[21] Guigo II, op. cit. 81.
[22] Guigo II, op. cit. 73–74.

of two opposing movements,"[23] the hallmark of mysticism in Guigo's view, everything acquires a different meaning:

> Can it be that the heralds and witnesses of this consolation and joy are sighs and tears? If it is so, then the word consolation is used in a completely new sense, the reverse of its ordinary connotation. What has consolation in common with sighs, joy with tears, if indeed these are to be called tears and not rather an abundance of spiritual dew, poured out from above and overflowing, an outward purification as a sign of inward cleansing.[24]

Changing normal meaning into something different indicates both the similarity and difference between *oratio* and *contemplatio*.

3. Intertextuality as Linguistic Recreation

The experience resulting from intensive reading of biblical texts, as outlined in the previous section, seeks expression. Often the experience affects people's behavior. Their dealings with people and society change, they become alert to the plight of the socially marginalized, conscience cannot disregard perceived and experienced injustice. People rearrange the hierarchy of values by which they live and become critical of the generally accepted hierarchy of values in their environment.

Sometimes the experience seeks expression in artistic creation. Artworks like sculptures, paintings, icons, and pictures can be products of intensive reading that culminated in experience of the Mystery. The experience can also express itself in language, in the creation of biblically inspired stories, poems, and the like. These are texts inspired by the reading of biblical texts, which in their turn may cause others to engage in mystical reading.

This is where the processes described above touch, or rather could touch, on intertextuality, a widely studied phenomenon in biblical exegesis. Our insistence on the modality "could touch" is deliberate. We don't want to reduce all intertextuality to mystical reading. We can readily imagine forms of intertextuality that have nothing to do with mystical experience but merely seek to clarify, substantiate, impart authority, or simply indicate a relation between two texts.

---

[23] K. Waaijman, *Spirituality* 723.
[24] Guigo II, op. cit. 74–75.

But we can also imagine that the reading of biblical texts evokes experiences that want to be expressed in terms of the text that gave rise to them. Readers express their experience in terms of the text they have read and meditated upon. They express what they experience while reading the text in the language in which Scripture addresses them. The Bible proffers the language to verbalize the new experience. But the new texts are rarely identical to the archetexts. They are re-creations, recomposed poems, and re-narrations with a distinctive texture. The late-Judaic anthological style of psalm writing produced texts with an exceptionally high intertextual quality, which can nonetheless be read and interpreted as independent entities. We also do the Lukan psalms (e.g., Mary's hymn of praise in Lk 1:46–55 and that of Zechariah in Lk 1:68–79) an injustice if we regard them merely as biblical anthologies. In the context of Luke's Gospel they are hymnal commentaries on the story of liberation that Luke is telling, with an expressive power and poetic structure of their own, as a result of which they have had a profound impact outside the Lukan context as well.

There are also less anthological instances. In many cases one can identify a specific archetext for a specific phenotext. Classical examples include the biblical Song of Songs, which in mystical tradition has often served as a starting point for new improvisations and re-creations, and Psalms, which has greatly influenced the prayer culture of the Christian tradition. We cite an example of each: the impact of the biblical Song of Songs on the *Cántico Espiritual* of John of the Cross, and a reading of his *Romance que va por "Super flumina Babylonis"* against the background of Psalm 137.

W.G. Tillmans devoted an extensive study to the presence of the biblical Song of Songs in the *Cántico Espiritual* of John of the Cross.[25] He specifies exactly which texts he used in his study, which is confined to the first version of the *Cántico Espiritual*, known as redaction A. For comparison with the biblical text he uses the Vulgate version, the Sixto Clementine text in the edition by J. Aubert.[26]

A first scrutiny shows that there is little homogeneity in the material that the two texts have in common. Some passages appear to

---

[25] W.G. Tillmans, *De aanwezigheid van het bijbels hooglied in het "Cantico Espiritual" van San Juan de la Cruz*. Mededelingen van de Koninklijke Vlaamse Academie voor wetenschappen, letteren en schone kunsten van België. Klasse der Letteren. Jaargang XXIX. Nr. 1. Brussel 1967.
[26] W.G. Tillmans, op. cit. 8–9.

be quoted entirely from the biblical Song of Songs, others seem wholly original when compared to the atmosphere and images of the biblical book. In between the two extremes Tillmans cites several stanzas which, while containing few verbal parallels with the biblical text, nonetheless permit associations with the events in Song of Songs because of their analogous atmosphere and imagery.[27] In a minute analysis of the text of the *Cántico* he shows where it appears to be inspired by the Song of Songs and where it is original. From this the first elements of its structure emerge: "This shows that the *Cántico* poem comprises two elements: a continuous narrative, constantly interrupted by contemplation or explanatory effusions, which were implicit in the narrative all along."[28]

Tillmans's next step is interesting from a methodological point of view. He wants to demonstrate the interrelationship of the stanzas as clearly as possible in a coherent interpretation, so as to discover the value of the biblical inspirational material for the poet. But before doing so he first examines the structure of the biblical Song of Songs to find out whether the associative power of this structure could have determined the composition of the poem.[29] The exegetical part of the study consists in a categorization, comparison, and critical evaluation of the dominant exegetical positions on Song of Songs at that time.[30] This is followed by a study of the *Cántico*.[31] In his conclusion he finds that the influence of the biblical Song of Songs on the *Cántico Espirtual* extends far beyond the purely verbal level. The movement discernible in the biblical text has become the movement of the *Cántico*. "From all this it is clear that John of the Cross definitely interpreted *Song of Songs* dramatically and respected the context of the "quoted" verses. At the very least the context of *Song of Songs* inspired a similar development in his poem . . . Consciously or unconsciously his structure of the *Cántico* was guided by the interrelationships in *Song of Songs*, the principal ones being: the bridegroom's call—the bride's longing and quest—the encounter with its confusion—the union."[32]

---

[27] W.G. Tillmans, op. cit. 23.
[28] W.G. Tillmans, op. cit. 27 (our translation).
[29] W.G. Tillmans, op. cit. 27–28.
[30] W.G. Tillmans, op. cit. 28–36.
[31] W.G. Tillmans, op. cit. 36–48.
[32] W.G. Tillmans, op. cit. 49 (our translation).

The parallelism between the two texts is then represented graphically in a scheme, indicating the function of the material common to both texts.[33] The conclusion of the comparative study is reiterated in the same words and in different phraseology. In an epilogue he looks into the phenomenon in both texts that the focus is primarily on the bride's movements, but that it is diverted fairly regularly from her to the bridegroom. The explanation is that the bride's longing rather than the groom's serves as a criterion of progress and satisfaction.[34]

The study ends with a brief discussion of two further questions: the nature of the original stanzas in the *Cántico*, and the attachment to nature in the poem. Only the first question concerns us. Tillmans feels that the "original" parts are important, because they deal with a theme that is not found in Song of Songs but which is close to the author's heart. Stanzas 6 to 10 contain hardly any references to Song of Songs. They are characterized by emphatic rejection of any mediation between bride and bridegroom. "In the mystical ascent to union in spiritual marriage no intrusive presence of third parties is permitted."[35] The same applies to stanzas 19 to 20 and stanza 34. "The struggle for union affects only the bride and her growing attachment to the beloved. She has to fight it out on her own by denying herself all outside 'assistance.'"[36] Tillmans explains this peculiarity of the "original" stanzas as adherence to the monastic tradition and the introverted mysticism of the north. The interiorization of the Christian's struggle takes the form of inner purification and continual liberation from all values that compete with the celestial bridegroom.[37]

What concerns us here is not the accuracy of Tillmans's exegesis of either the biblical Song of Songs or the *Cántico Espiritual*. Our point is that his study shows that the influence of the biblical Song of Songs was so profound that it affected the form of the *Cántico Espiritual*, not only at a verbal level but also its literary composition and dramatic progression. At the same time Tillmans acknowledges the originality of the *Cántico* and the experience underlying it. This originality is such that it cracks open the language and form of Song

---

[33] W.G. Tillmans, op. cit. 49–51.
[34] W.G. Tillmans, op. cit. 53–55.
[35] W.G. Tillmans, op. cit. 55 (our translation).
[36] Ibid. (our translation).
[37] Ibid.

of Songs in a way that allows John of the Cross's own distinctive mystical experience to fit into the resultant fissures in the biblical text.

Our second example shows even more clearly than the first that the mystic's personal experience cracks open the archetext, thus creating space for the articulation of that experience, albeit an articulation which, in view of the peculiar nature of mystical language, is always inadequate and demanding rearticulation. Since the two texts involved are relatively short, we can juxtapose them in two columns. They are Psalm 137 and the re-creation of this psalm by John of the Cross in his poem, *Romance que va por "Super flumina Babylonis."*[38]

Ballad on the Psalm *"By the streams of Babylon"*	*Psalm 137*
By the *streams* I found in *Babylon*— there I *sat* down *weeping*; there I sprinkled the land, *remembering* you, O *Zion* which I loved. Sweet was the memory of you: you made me weep even more. I took off my festive clothing and put on my work clothes; in the *green willows* I hung the music I carried with me; I hid it in hope for that which I hoped for in you. There Love wounded me— and took away my heart. I asked it to kill me, for it wounded me so. I threw myself in its fire, knowing that it consumed me, excusing the young bird that would die in the fire.	By the *streams* of *Babylon*— there we *sat down* and *wept*, remembering *Zion*. On the *willows* in her midst we *hung up* our *harp*.

---

[38] For the juxtaposition we used the article by K. Waaijman, "There Love Wounded Me," in: H. Blommestijn, J. Huls, and K. Waaijman, *The Footprints of Love. John of the Cross as Guide in the Wilderness.* Louvain 2000, 191–211. The italicised words indicate points of contact between the two texts. Errors in the layout have been corrected. The translation of Psalm 137 was also taken from this article. Other biblical quotations are from the *New Revised Standard Version*.

I was dying in myself
and breathed again only in you.
I died within myself for you
and for you I rose again,
for the memory of you
gave life and took it away.
I died in order to die
and my life killed me,
for it dragged on
and kept me from seeing you.

The strangers among whom   Yes: there our *captors* asked us
I was *captive* were *delighted*.   for expressive *songs*,
I noticed they did not see   our tormentors for *mirth*:
that the *mirth* deluded them.   "*Sing* us one of the *Zion* songs!"
They *asked* me for *songs*   How *could* we *sing* the *songs of Be-er*
about what I sang in *Zion*:   *in a foreign land!*
sing us a song about *Zion*,
let us see how it sounded!
Tell me *how, in a strange land*
where I wept over Zion,
I could sing about the happiness
that I left behind in Zion?
I would be tossing it into oblivion
if I rejoiced in a strange land.

May the tongue I speak with   *If I forgot you,* O Jerusalem,
stick to the roof of my mouth   *let my right hand forget me!*
if I forgot you   *Let* my *tongue stick*
in the land where I am staying!   *to the roof of my mouth*
Zion—by the green branches   *if I would not remember you*
which Babylon gave me!—   if I did lift up
may my right hand forget me   Jerusalem to be
(the land I loved most   the highest source
when I was at home in you)   of my *delight!*
if I would not remember you
in what *delighted* me most,
and if I celebrated,
feasted without you!

O *daughter of Babylon*,   Remember, O Be-er, against the
you *miserable* failure.   sons of Edom
Happiness came over   the day of Jerusalem['s fall],
the one in whom I trusted,   how they said:
who will punish you   "Strip her, strip her naked,
with the punishment   down to her foundations!"
I received from your hand,   O *daughter Babylon*,

and who will gather his *little ones*	O *wretched* one!
and me—for I wept in you—	*Happy* those who pay you back
on the *rock* that was Christ,	what you have done to us,
for whom I left you!	happy those who grab your *little ones*
	and dash them against the *rock*.

In his study of the *Romance* of John of the Cross Kees Waaijman, too, traces the similarities and differences from the biblical text.[39] He maintains that support can be found in the text of the psalm for every stanza of the ballad, even if some of them are transformations. The sole exception is the second stanza. Only one word in this stanza concurs with the biblical text: "there." Earlier in the article Kees Waaijman identified this stanza as the mystical core of the poem. It is about love blossoming in the midst of loss. He expounds this further. It is a love that is purely love and nothing but love. "To that end it is imperative that all points of support exterior to love—love as itself *the* point of support—be removed. Hence the idea is not that everything surrounding love should disappear—become bare and empty—but that all points of *support* exterior to love should disappear. Now then, the lack, the foreign land, the separatedness, the time spent outside of the narcissistic context, for all the pain and sorrow they bring about, make it possible for love to blossom from within its own core, that is to say, become genuine love, all love, and nothing other than love. Under these conditions I am truly outside myself: *with the other as genuinely other*. Then I am no longer imprisoned in my own pleasure, however valuable that pleasure may perhaps be as such, but it is nothing by comparison with the Love on which the mystic has put all his or her hope."[40]

The fact that this mystical core is linked to the biblical text of Psalm 137 only by the solitary word "there" thus acquires special meaning: "It is precisely *there* where the mystic lost his bearings [that] the poet completely relaxes his grip on the psalm. Where Love wounded the mystic there is in the poem an open space where the heart was torn away in memory and hope, where death—as in the bird Phoenix—was consumed. Where the mystic completely lost his familiar context—except that of Love itself—there the poem leaves the framework of the psalm behind. There the intimate uniqueness of the poem speaks its own language: the language of love."[41]

---

[39] K. Waaijman, op. cit. 202–8.
[40] K. Waaijman, op. cit. 201.
[41] K. Waaijman, op. cit. 207–8.

By abandoning the framework of the archetext the phenotext opens up so as to articulate the mystic's own experience, which is accompanied by the collapse of all frameworks.

4. *Hidden Intertextuality in the Prologue to* Liber Scivias

In the preceding sections we saw that mystical experience seeks to be expressed in language, but that language is fundamentally inadequate to do justice to it. This paradox is a kind of principle that continually generates language. We also saw that language in its turn can generate mystical experience. Biblical texts and classical mystical texts have a mystagogic character. The reading method of lectio divina respects that character. It focusses on revealing Mystery, which does not depend on any activity by the reader but does have a place in that activity. The effect of this reading process, together with the urge of mystical experience to express itself, could explain the intertextual quality of some texts, while the fundamentally paradoxical nature of mystical experience could explain why archetexts are cracked open, thus creating space for more and more phenotexts.

In this final section we put that proposition to the test. We explore the intertextual character of a mystical text which, viewed superficially, displays few intertextual features. On this basis we try to demonstrate the generative and creative nature of mystical experience. As our example we choose the prologue to *Liber Scivias* by Hildegard of Bingen. First we reproduce the Latin version and an English rendering of it.[42]

Incipit Liber Scivias Simplicis
Hominis
INCIPIT PRIMA PARS LIBRI SCIVIAS

PROTESTIFICATIO VERACIVM VISIONVM A DEO FLVENTIVM	THESE ARE TRUE VISIONS FLOWING FROM GOD
Et ecce quadragesimo tertio temporalis cursus mei anno, cum caelesti	And behold! In the forty-third year of my earthly course, as I was gazing

---

[42] The Latin text appears in *Hildegardis Scivias*, edidit Adelgundis Führkotter O.S.B. collaborante Angela Carlevaris O.S.B. Corpus Christianorum Continuatio Mediaevalis XLIII. Turnhout 1978. The English translation is taken from Hildegard of Bingen, *Scivias*. Translated by C. Hart and J. Bishop; introduced by B.J. Newman. Preface by C.W. Bynum. New York 1990.

uisioni magno timore et tremula intentione inhaererem, uidi maximum splendorem, in quo facta est uox de ceaelo ad me dicens:

"O homo fragilis, et cinis cineris, et putredo putredinis, dic et scribe quae uides et audis. Sed quia timida es ad loquendum et simplex ad exponendum et indocta ad scribendum ea, dic et scribe illa non secundum os hominis nec secundum intellectum humanae adinuentionis nec secundum uolentatem humanae compositionis, sed secundum id quod ea in caelestibus desuper in mirabilibus Dei uides et audis, ea sic edisserendo proferens, quemadmodum et auditor uerba praeceptoris sui percipiens, ea secundum tenorem locutionis illius, ipso uolente, ostendente et praecipiente propalat. Sic ergo et tu, o homo, dic ea quae uides et audis; et scribe ea non secundum te nec secundum alium hominem, sed secundum uoluntatem scientis, uidentis et disponentis omnia in secretis mysteriorum suorum."

Et iterum audiui uocem de caelo mihi dicentem:
"Dic ergo mirabilia haec et scribe ea hoc modo edocta et dic."

Factum est in millesimo centesimo quadragesimo primo Filii Dei Iesu Christi incarnationis anno, cum quadraginta duorum annorum septemque mensium essem, maximae coruscationis igneum lumen aperto caelo ueniens totum cerebrum meum transfudit et totum cor totumque pectus meum uelut flamma non tamen ardens sed calens ita inflammauit, ut sol rem aliquam calefacit super quam radios suos ponit. Et repenta intellectum expositionis librorum, uidelicet psalterii, euangelii et aliorum catho-

with great fear and trembling attention at a heavenly vision, I saw a great splendor in which resounded a voice from Heaven, saying to me:

"O fragile human, ashes of ashes, and filth of filth! Say and write what you see and hear. But since you are timid in speaking, and simple in expounding, and untaught in writing, speak and write these things not by a human mouth, and not by the understanding of human invention, and not by the requirements of human composition, but as you see and hear them on high in the heavenly places in the wonders of God. Explain these things in such a way that the hearer, receiving the words of his instructor, may expound them in those words, according to that will, vision and instruction. Thus therefore, O human, speak these things that you see and hear. And write them not by yourself or any other human being, but by the will of Him Who knows, sees and disposes all things in the secrets of His mysteries."

And again I heard the voice from Heaven saying to me:
"Speak therefore of these wonders, and, being so taught, write them and speak."

It happened that, in the eleven hundred and forty-first year of the Incarnation of the Son of God, Jesus Christ, when I was forty-two years and seven months old, Heaven was opened and a fiery light of exceeding brilliance came and permeated my whole brain, and inflamed my whole heart and my whole breast, not like a burning but like a warming flame, as the sun warms anything its rays touch. And immediately I knew the meaning of the exposition of the Scriptures, namely the Psalter,

licorum tam ueteris quam noui Testamenti uoluminum sapiebam, non autem interpretationem uerborum textus eorum nec diuisionem syllabarum nec cognitionem casuum aut temporum habebam. Virtutem autem et mysterium secretarum et admirandarum uisionum a puellari aetate, scilicet a tempore illo cum quinquennis essem usque ad praesens tempus mirabili modo in me senseram sicut et adhuc; quod tamen nulli hominum exceptis quibusdam paucis et religiosis qui in eadem conuersatione uiuebant, qua et ego eram, manifestaui; sed interim usque ad id temporis cum illud Deus sua gratia manifestari uoluit, sub quieto silentio depressi. Visiones uero quas uidi, non eas in somnis, nec dormiens, nec in phrenesi, nec corporeis oculis aut auribus exterioris hominis, nec in abditis locis percepi, sed eas uigilans et circumspecta in pura mente, oculis et auribus interioris hominis, in apertis locis, secundum uoluntatem Dei accepi. Quod quomodo sit, carnali homini perquirere difficile est.

Sed puellari meta transacta, cum ad praefatam aetatem perfectae fortitudinis peruenissem, audiui uocem de caelo dicentem:

"Ego lux uiuens et obscura illuminans hominem quem uolui et quem mirabiliter secundum quod mihi placuit excussi in magnis mirabilibus trans metam antiquorum hominum, qui in me multa secreta uiderunt, posui; sed in terram straui illum, quod se non erigeret in ulla elatione mentis suae. Mundus quoque non habuit in eo gaudium nec lasciuiam nec exercitationem in rebus illis quae ad mundum pertinent, quia eum de pertinaci audacia abstraxi, timorem habentem et in laboribus suis pauentem. Ipse enim in medullis et in uenis

the Gospel and the other catholic volumes of both the Old and the New Testaments, though I did not have the interpretation of the words of their texts or the division of the syllables or the knowledges of cases or tenses. But I had sensed in myself wonderfully the power and mystery of secret and admirable visions from my childhood—that is, from the age of five—up to that time, as I do now. This, however, I showed to no one except a few religious persons who were living in the same manner as I; but meanwhile, until the time when God by his grace wished it to be manifested, I concealed it in quiet silence. But the visions I saw I did not perceive in dreams, or sleep, or delirium, or by the eyes of the body, or by the ears of the outer self, or in hidden places; but I received them while awake and seeing with a pure mind and the eyes and ears of the inner self, in open places, as God willed it. How this might be is hard for mortal flesh to understand.

But when I had passed out of childhood and had reached the age of full maturity mentioned above, I heard a voice from Heaven saying:

"I am the Living Light, Who illuminates the darkness. The person [Hildegard] whom I have chosen and whom I have miraculously stricken as I willed, I have placed among great wonders, beyond the measure of the ancient people who saw in Me many secrets; but I have laid her low on the earth, that she might not set herself up in arrogance of mind. The world has had in her no joy or lewdness or use in worldly things, for I have withdrawn her from impudent boldness, and she feels fear and is timid in her works. For she suffers

carnis suae doluit, constrictum animum et sensum habens atque multam passionem corporis sustinens, ita quod in eo diuersa securitas non latuit, sed in omnibus sausis suis se culpabilem aestimauit. Nam rimas cordis eius circumsaepsi, ne mens ipsius per superbiam aut per gloriam se elaueret, sed ut magis in omnibus his timorem et dolorem quam gaudium aut quam petulantiam haberet. Vnde in amore meo scrutatus est in animo suo, ubi illum inueniret, qui uiam salutis curreret. Et quendam inuenit et eum amauit, agnoscens quod fidelis homo esset et simulis sibi in aliqua parte laboris illius qui ad me tendit. Tenensque eum simul cum illo in omnibus his per supernum studium contendit, ut absconsa miracula mea reuelarentur. Et idem homo super semetipsum se non posuit, sed ad illum in ascensione humilitatis et in intentione bonae uoluntatis, quem inuenit, se in multis suspiriis inclinauit. Tu ergo, o homo, qui haec non in inquietudine deceptionis, sed in puritate simplicitatis accipis ad manifestationem absconditorum directa, scribe quae uides et audis."

Sed ego, quamuis haec uiderem et audirem, tamen propter dubietatem et malam opinionem et propter diuersitatem uerborum hominum, tamdiu non in pertinacia, sed in humilitatis officio scribere recusaui, quousque in lectum aegritudinis flagello Dei depressa caderem; ita quod tandem multis infirmitatibus compulsa, testimonio cuiusdam nobilis et bonorum morum puellae et hominis illius, quem occulte, ut praefatum est, quaesiram et inueneram, manus ad scribendum apposui. Quod dum facerem, altam

in her inmost being and in the veins of her flesh; she is distressed in mind and sense and endures great pain of body, because no security has dwelt in her, but in all her undertakings she has judged herself guilty. For I have closed up the cracks in her heart that her mind may not exalt itself in pride or vainglory, but may feel fear and grief rather than joy and wantonness. Hence in My love she searched in her mind as to where she could find someone who would run in the path of salvation. And she found such a one and loved him,[43] knowing that he was a faithful man, working like herself on another part of the work that leads to Me. And, holding fast to him, she worked with him in great zeal so that My hidden miracles might be revealed. And she did not seek to exalt herself above herself but with many sighs bowed to him whom she found in the ascent of humility and the intention of good will. O human, who receives these things meant to manifest what is hidden not in the disquiet of deception but in the purity of simplicity, write, therefore, the things you see and hear."

But I, though I saw and heard these things, refused to write for a long time through doubt and bad opinion and the diversity of human words, not with stubbornness but in the exercise of humility, until, laid low by the scourge of God, I fell upon a bed of sickness; then, compelled at last by many illnesses, and by the witness of a certain noble maiden of good conduct [the nun Richardis of Stade] and of that man whom I secretly sought and found, as mentioned above, I set my hand to the

---

[43] The monk Volmar of Disibodenberg.

profunditatum expositionis librorum, ut praedixi, sentiens, uiribusque receptis de aegritudine me erigens, uix opus istud decem annis consummans ad finem perduxi.	writing. While I was doing, I sensed, as I mentioned before, the deep profundity of scriptural exposition; and raising myself from illness by the strength I received, I brought this work to a close—though just barely—in ten years.
In diebus Heinrici moguntini archiepiscopi et Conradi Romanorum Regis et Cunonis abbatis in monte beati Disibodi pontificis, sub papa Eugenio, hae uisones et uerba facta sunt.	These visions took place and these words were written in the days of Henry, Archbishop of Mainz, and of Conrad, King of the Romans, and of Cuno, Abbot of Disibodenberg, under Pope Eugenius.
Et dixi et scripsi haec non secundum adinuentionem cordis mei aut ullius hominis, sed ut in caelestibus uidi, audiui et percepi per secreta mysteria Dei.	And I spoke and wrote these things not by the invention of my heart or that of any other person, but as by the secret mysteries of God I heard and received them in the heavenly places.
Et iterum uadivi uocem de ceaelo mihi dicentem: "Clama ergo et scribe sic."	And again I heard a voice from Heaven saying to me, "Cry out therefore, and write thus."

Before we turn to the intertextual quality of the text a few observations are called for. The vision described in the prologue to *Liber Scivias* was the start of a lengthy writing process. The date of the vision is given as 1141. The work was not completed until ten years later. A major stimulus was that pope Eugenius III read a passage from the completed section at the synod of Trier in 1147–1148 and expressed his approval in a letter. *Liber Scivias* is divided into three volumes, respectively dealing with creation, salvation, and sanctification. The first volume contains six visions, the second seven, and the third thirteen. The prologue, too, is a vision. It starts with a summons to look: "Et ecce" (And behold!). Hildegard then tells what she saw in the vision: "as I was gazing with great fear and trembling attention at a heavenly vision, I saw a great splendor in which resounded a voice from Heaven." The prologue contains four time indicators:

1. At the outset the vision is dated to the 43rd year of Hildegard's life: "In the forty-third year of my earthly course...."
2. A second indicator situates the vision in both the Christian era and Hildegard's biography: "It happened that, in the eleven hundred and forty-first year of the Incarnation of the Son of

God, Jesus Christ, when I was forty-two years and seven months old...."
3. The third is a more general reference to Hildegard's age: "But when I had passed out of childhood and had reached the age of full maturity mentioned above...." This time indicator establishes a contrast between the visions mentioned in the previous context, which Hildegard had had since her fifth year, and the present vision.
4. The fourth reference to time locates not just the vision but also the process of writing *Liber Scivias*. It appears at the end of the prologue: "These visions took place and these words were written in the days of Henry, Archbishop of Mainz, and of Conrad, King of the Romans, and of Cuno, Abbot of Disibodenberg, under Pope Eugenius."

In the vision Hildegard sees a great light. The voice from heaven also speaks about a great light: "I am the Living Light, Who illuminates the darkness." Hildegard hears the voice speak four times. The first and the second time it is clearly addressing Hildegard. The salutation is striking: "*O homo fragilis*." The Latin word "*homo*" indicates a human being and not refer to the person's gender, hence the English version has the term "human." The word "*homo*" features again later on. The third time the voice sounds from heaven it speaks about Hildegard. Only the last sentence is addressed to her: "O human, who receives these things meant to manifest what is hidden not in the disquiet of deception but in the purity of simplicity, write, therefore, the things you see and hear." This sequence has the odd effect that in the preceding section Hildegard hears the voice speaking to her about herself in the third person. The fourth time the voice speaks is at the end of the prologue. The instruction is brief and simple: "Cry out therefore, and write thus."

Every time the voice speaks there is an instruction to write. This raises the question whether we are dealing with four separate events or four accounts of the same event. To my mind there are grounds for the view that Hildegard recounts the same event in four different ways. A first argument is the frequent repetition of the imperative: say and write what you see and hear; speak and write these things, speak these things that you see and hear; write them; speak therefore, write them and speak; write therefore the things you see and hear; cry out therefore, and write thus. A second argument concerns the structure of the visions in *Liber Scivias*. Hildegard starts each of these with a simple, usually concise description of what she saw. This is followed by an interpretation introduced by the formula: "And I heard a voice from heaven, saying...."[44] This formula, or variations of it, appears four times in the prologue as a preamble to the direct speech of the voice from heaven. It indicates that the voice is providing the interpretation of what Hildegard sees. A third argument is that in her text Hildegard refers back. She uses expressions like "as mentioned above" (*praefatum*) and "as mentioned before" (*ut praedixi*). There are also several repetitions, albeit not always verbatim. Again it indicates that the text in fact describes just one event, even though we are told four times that the voice speaks. This event is the experience of the vision. A voice from heaven commands Hildegard to write down what she hears and sees. For a long time she refuses. The reasons for her refusal are "doubt and bad opinion and the diversity of human words." Then she falls ill. Because of the illness she feels compelled to write. She receives help from Volmar of Disibodenberg[45] and Richardis of Stade.[46] The result is the *Liber Scivias*, the writing of which took some ten years.

With a view to our analysis of the intertextual quality of the text it is important to realize that Hildegard does not speak and write on her own behalf. That is explicitly indicated: "write these things not by a human mouth, and not by the understanding of human invention, and not by the requirements of human composition, but as you see and hear them on high in the heavenly places in the wonders of God. Explain these things in such a way that the hearer, receiving the words of his instructor, may expound them in those words, according to that will, vision, and instruction. Thus therefore, O human, speak these things that you see and hear. And write them not by yourself or any other human being, but by the will of Him Who knows, sees and disposes all things in the secrets of His mysteries." Hildegard assures us that she speaks and writes as the voice from heaven willed her to do: "And I spoke and wrote these things

---

[44] See Hildegard of Bingen, op. cit. 22.
[45] Volmar of Disibodenberg was Hildegard's teacher, confidant, and secretary for a large part of her life.
[46] Richardis of Stade was one of the sisters with whom Hildegard collaborated closely. After the establishment of the convent on Rupertsberg she left the convent, against Hildegard's wishes, to become abbess of Birsim.

not by the invention of my heart or that of any other person, but as by the secret mysteries of God I heard and received them in the heavenly places." It concerned the disclosure of secrets. There are several allusions to this in the text of the prologue. What Hildegard sees and hears is "on high in the heavenly places in the wonders of God." What she writes is the will of him who "disposes all things in the secrets of His mysteries." She feels in herself "the power and mystery of secret and admirable visions." God has placed Hildegard "among great wonders, beyond the measure of the ancient people who saw in Me many secrets." The purpose of Volmar of Disibodenberg's help is that God's "hidden miracles might be revealed." The revelations to Hildegard are intended "to manifest what is hidden." She speaks and writes "as by the secret mysteries of God I heard and received them in the heavenly places." As a result Hildegard has extraordinary knowledge of the meaning of Scripture: "And immediately I knew the meaning of the exposition of the Scriptures, namely the Psalter, the Gospel and the other catholic volumes of both the Old and the New Testaments, though I did not have the interpretation of the words of their texts or the division of the syllables or the knowledges of cases or tenses." Although not a learned biblical scholar, she knows the meaning of biblical texts. At the end of the prologue she again tells what happened while she was writing the *Liber Scivias*: "While I was doing, I sensed, as I mentioned before, the deep profundity of scriptural exposition."

Many introductions and commentaries refer to Hildegard as a prophetess. During the Middle Ages she was already described as "*prophetissa teutonica*," the German prophetess.[47] The vision in 1141, which prompted the writing of *Liber Scivias*, was called a prophetic calling.[48] Speaking about Hildegard in terms of prophecy makes good sense. Prophets do not speak on their own behalf. Their words are legitimized by their calling to prophecy, which often occurred in a vision. Because of this legitimizing function some elements in prophetic vocation stories are important. One is the exact date of the calling. On exactly that date the prophet was addressed by a divine reality and instructed to do or say something. Many accounts of prophetic callings mention the words the prophet has to proclaim. Sometimes

---

[47] Hildegard von Bingen, *Gott sehen*. Herausgegeben und eingeleitet von H. Schipperges. München, Zürich 1982² 21.
[48] Hildegard of Bingen, op. cit. 12.

the prophet refuses to obey the instruction or raises objections. An example is the story of the calling of the prophet Isaiah in Isaiah 6:1–13.

It has been observed that two kinds of vocation stories feature in the background to Isaiah 6.[49] The key characteristic of the first type is that everything is subordinate to the proclamation of God's word. The hesitancy and resistance of the called person form part of this scheme. Both are removed by a reassurance and the giving of a sign. Zimmerli calls Isaiah 6 one of the most impressive examples of the second type.[50] Here the accent is predominantly on the vision. The prophet sees God as a king in his royal court who passes a decree on the prophet. The prophet is prepared to implement God's decree on earth.

In our view elements of both types of prophetic vocation stories may be found in Isaiah 6:1–13. The events are dated exactly. The death of king Uzziah took place in 740–739 B.C. The vision is of God on a throne holding court in the temple. There is some deliberation on the question of whom to send. Isaiah offers himself: "Here am I; send me!" But there is also an episode telling of the prophet's fear: "Woe is me! I am lost, for I am a man of unclean lips and I live among a people of unclean lips, yet my eyes have seen the King, the Lord of hosts!" In this response one recognizes, apart from the fear that accompanies a theophany, an objection and resistance to the prophetic calling: "I am a man of unclean lips and I live among a people of unclean lips." The reason for the objection is removed by one of the seraphim, who touches the prophet's lips with a glowing coal from the altar, saying: "Now that this has touched your lips, your guilt has departed and your sin is blotted out." The words Isaiah has to proclaim and the things he has to do are enumerated in verses 9–10: "Go and say to this people: 'Keep listening, but do not comprehend; keep looking, but do not understand.' Make the mind of this people dull, and stop their ears, and shut their eyes, so that they may not look with their eyes, and listen with their ears, and comprehend with their minds, and turn and be healed."

---

[49] H. Wildberger. *Jesaja 1. Teilband Jesaja 1–12*. Neukirchen-Vluyn 1980² 235–37. For a more detailed description of the two types, see W. Zimmerli, *Ezechiel. 1. Teilband. Ezechiel 1–24*. Neukirchen-Vluyn 1979² 16–21.

[50] W. Zimmerli, op. cit. 18.

The prologue to *Liber Scivias* shows a number of similarities to prophetic vocation visions. We cite the following:

- The character of a visionary apparition is unmistakable. At the outset the apparition is described as a vision and in the vision Hildegard sees a great light.
- The event is dated exactly. We have noted that the prologue gives four indications of the time of the vision. Three of these are exact. The last mentions the names of the rulers of that time, just as king Uzziah is mentioned in Isaiah's vision.
- The voice from heaven addresses Hildegard as "*O homo fragilis.*" The use of the term "*homo*" is reminiscent of the voice addressing the prophet in Ezekiel as "Son of man." Here the Vulgate has "*fili hominis.*"
- Both the prologue to *Liber Scivias* and the prophetic vocation vision contain an injunction to proclaim what has been seen and heard. The prologue does not give the contents of what Hildegard is to say or write. One would imagine that it would be the contents of the three volumes of *Liber Scivias*.
- Hildegard's initial refusal to write corresponds to the hesitancy and refusal of the prophets to heed their call.
- Hildegard's illness that drives her to write and the assistance of Richardis of Stade and Volmar of Disibodenberg may be seen as the removal of the called person's objections and as the sign that finally persuades her to heed the call.
- As noted already, the prologue explicitly states that what Hildegard has to record is not of human origin. She does not speak on her own behalf but is a mouthpiece and a scribe conveying what she hears and sees.

Some scholars see a connection between Hildegard's vision and the last book of the Bible. Revelation 1:3 qualifies the contents of the book as "prophecy." Hildegard's position in relation to her visions is comparable with John's on the island of Patmos: "I was in the spirit on the Lord's day, and I heard behind me a loud voice like a trumpet saying: 'Write in a book what you see and send it to the seven churches, to Ephesus, to Smyrna, to Pergamum, to Thyatira, to Sardis, to Philadelphia, and Laodicea'" (Rev. 1:10–11). Like Hildegard, John acts as a mediator between the visions that are shown to him and the readers of the book he is to write.

In 2 Peter 1:20-21 one finds another pertinent text: "First of all you must understand this, that no prophecy of scripture is a matter of one's own interpretation, because no prophecy ever came by human will, but men and women moved by the Holy Spirit spoke from God." That is precisely how Hildegard sees herself as a prophetess. The first time the voice speaks from heaven it tells her to disregard all human interpretation ("... speak and write these things not by a human mouth, and not by the understanding of human invention, and not by the requirements of human composition ..."). Hildegard must speak and write what she hears and sees ("... but as you see and hear them on high in the heavenly places in the wonders of God"). Once again the voice says: "And write them not by yourself or any other human being, but by the will of Him Who knows, sees and disposes all things in the secrets of His mysteries." Hildegard is instructed by the visions she sees. And at the end of the prologue she assures us: "And I spoke and wrote these things not by the invention of my heart or that of any other person, but as by the secret mysteries of God I heard and received them in the heavenly places."

Hildegard's manner of telling about the knowledge acquired from her visions likewise reveals a biblical background. The secrets disclosed to her give her knowledge of the meaning of Scripture, but she makes it clear that this is not knowledge acquired by means of ordinary exegesis: "And immediately I knew the meaning of the exposition of the Scriptures, namely the Psalter, the Gospel and the other catholic volumes of both the Old and the New Testaments, though I did not have the interpretation of the words of their texts or the division of the syllables or the knowledges of cases or tenses. But I had sensed in myself wonderfully the power and mystery of secret and admirable visions from my childhood—that is, from the age of five—up to that time, as I do now." At the same time the prologue stresses that Hildegard is neither eloquent nor literate: "But since you are timid in speaking, and simple in expounding and untaught in writing...." Her status is lowly, she is not esteemed and is insecure: "but I have laid her low on the earth, that she might not set herself up in arrogance of mind. The world has had in her no joy or lewdness or use in worldly things, for I have withdrawn her from impudent boldness, and she feels fear and is timid in her works. For she suffers in her inmost being and in the veins of her flesh; she is distressed in mind and sense and endures great pain of body, because no security has dwelt in her, but in all her undertakings she has judged herself guilty. For I have closed up the cracks in her heart that her mind may not exalt itself in pride or vainglory, but may feel fear and grief rather than joy and wantonness."

The quotations remind us of Paul's contrast in the first chapters of the first letter to the Corinthians between the wisdom of the world and the folly of God, which is wiser than human wisdom. The secret, hidden wisdom of God has remained concealed from the rulers of this world. This wisdom can only be fathomed by the Spirit, which is from God (1 Cor 2:1–12).

Finally, another place where one discerns biblical echoes is the dating at the end of the prologue: "These visions took place and these words were written in the days of Henry, Archbishop of Mainz, and of Conrad, King of the Romans, and of Cuno, Abbot of Disibodenberg, under Pope Eugenius." This is reminiscent of Luke 3:1–2: "In the fifteenth year of the reign of Emperor Tiberius, when Pontius Pilate was governor of Judea, and Herod was ruler of Galilee, and his brother Philip ruler of the region of Ituraea and Trachonitis, and Lysanias ruler of Abilene, during the high priesthood of Annas and Caiaphas, the word of God came to John son of Zechariah in the wilderness." In both texts human history, symbolized by naming leaders and potentates, is related to God's initiative, symbolized by visions and the word. Yet there is a difference. In the prologue the visions are mentioned first, and then comes the reference to the leaders. In Luke's text it is the other way round. What the two texts have in common is that both make it possible for humans to participate in divine reality by correlating human history with divine initiative.

We are reaching our conclusion. The text of the prologue to *Liber Scivias* is a distinctive entity and looks like an original text. On closer scrutiny, however, one discovers a surprising amount of biblical data. One concludes that the spirituality in the prologue to *Liber Scivias* is biblical. It is another instance of the influence of biblical texts, an expression of living with these texts and being mystically moved by such living. Again one finds that biblical texts are constitutive for Christian spirituality; they, the archetexts, are contained in subsequent phenotexts; and as sources of experience they have served as an orientation for subsequent spiritual and mystical experiences and the expression of these experiences in written texts. The situation in the prologue of *Liber Scivias* differs from those in the two texts of John of the Cross discussed in the previous section. The intertextuality of the *Cántico Espiritual* and the romance of *Super Flumina* are immediately recognizable. To readers familiar with biblical texts the mystic's experience is clearly shaped by biblical tradition. The distinctive character of the experience is verbalized in these texts when the biblical archetexts are cracked open and make room for new, original expression. Deviation from the archetext has its own meaning, best displayed in the poem *Super Flumina*. In the prologue to *Liber Scivias* the situation seems to be reversed. The text serves primarily to express a personal, original experience. Only when one probes more deeply one discovers how profoundly this experience is shaped by constant association with biblical data.

PART 3

BIOGRAPHY AND BIBLIOGRAPHY

SJEF VAN TILBORG: A SHORT BIOGRAPHY

Ulrich Berges and Patrick Chatelion Counet

On May 22, 2003, our friend and colleague Prof. Dr. Josephus Henricus Adriaan van Tilborg, professor of New Testament exegesis at the University of Nijmegen, passed away.

Sjef—his name is short for Josephus—was born on April 10, 1939, in Tilburg, as the second child of five, the only boy. The family hadn't exactly made it. The father worked as a weaver, while the mother was the one who resourcefully kept creditors at bay. Even though Sjef was highly gifted, he was not allowed to attend the school of the upper middle class. He was confined to a working man's education and attended St. John's school, run by the friars. This utterly undistinguished school, of all places, turned out to be a blessing to him, and with the friars' support he was able to enter the mission house of the Missionaries of the Sacred Heart (msc).

His whole life, he has remained proud, in a playful way, of these three things: his place of birth ("Van Tilborg from Tilburg"), his descent from a poor family, and his life in the congregation of the Missionaries of the Sacred Heart. This congregation was founded in 1854 by Jules Chevalier, the son of a poor cobbler from Issoudun (near Bourges, France), out of great social and pastoral concern. In his own way, Sjef van Tilborg has lived to the full the founder's ideal and spirituality: making visible God's love for this world. He was a missionary of the Sacred Heart down to the bone.

Sjef completed his *gymnasium* studies effortlessly at the minor seminary on the Bredaseweg in Tilburg, inconspicuously tutoring classmates in the mean time, without making much of it; a practice he would continue throughout his further studies.

After his primary education at the *philosophicum* in Brummen and the *theologicum* in Stein, where he was ordained a priest on September 1, 1963, Sjef, who was a sometimes difficult and headstrong, but above all gifted and perseverant student, was sent to Rome by the congregation for further studies. There he obtained the licentiate in Theology at the Gregorian University (1965) and the licentiate in

Biblical Studies at the Biblical Institute. During his years in Rome, he deliberately left the safe shelter of the International Scholasticate, got into direct contact with the Italian people, and did pastoral work in various places. In doing so, he uprooted quite a few sacred truths and conventions.

After his return to the Netherlands, Sjef passed his Master's exam at the theological faculty of the University of Nijmegen. At the time, the faculty was experiencing a rapid growth because of the closure of the seminaries—the 1968–69 term saw a record number of 474 students—and the young exegete was recruited immediately. In September 1968, at the age of 29, Sjef was employed by the theological faculty as a part-time associate professor. In the following year, this part-time position grew, and from the year after that, 1970, Sjef held a full-time position at the faculty, some of which he spent as a supervisor in the department of pastoral theology for a number of years.

As an academic, Sjef has always been involved in pastoral ministry as well. Next to his university work, he worked as a pastor in the Italian community in the city of Arnhem. In 1976 he wrote a touching booklet on his experiences: *Misschien dat God het ons vergeeft: uit de praktijk van een pastor voor vreemdelingen* ("Perhaps God will forgive us: from the practice of a pastor for sojourners"). In the preface, he writes: "This is a collection of stories from a practice. The author calls himself a pastor. He who knows what that is, should not read this book. It would confuse him." Sjef was like that. Provocative and stimulating, but also insecure, vulnerable, defenseless, even helpless at times.

Through his pastoral work Sjef ran into politics. As the consistent man he was, he made a clear choice, a political statement, which left no room for doubt: he became an active member of the CPN, the Dutch communist party. These were the turbulent Seventies and Eighties, in which he marched in demonstrations against nuclear power, and collected signatures door to door for a petition against cruise missiles. All of these are great learning experiences for an academic, he used to say.

On May 18, 1972, Sjef received his doctoral degree at the theological faculty for his thesis *The Jewish Leaders in Matthew*; Willem Grossouw and Bas van Iersel had been his supervisors. Of the almost thirty-five years he would work at the theological faculty of the University of Nijmegen, the last ten years, from 1993 on, Sjef held the position of professor of New Testament exegesis, formerly held by his supervisors Grossouw and van Iersel. His appointment had not been an easy one. Sjef himself described his inaugural address in 1994 as "the final stage of an appointment history in which the ruthlessness of a bureaucracy with no eye for human emotions has played a role up to the very end."

Apart from bureaucracy, which he detested, another factor behind the duration of the procedures will undoubtedly have been Sjef's characteristic approach to his profession. As a biblical scholar, he did not excel on the public stage, nor in managing commitees and boards, but at his own desk, at home, or, first and foremost, at the faculty. There Sjef worked diligently; there he was immersed in his literature, his feet on the table as the case might be; there he would shuffle down the corridor in his slippers to retrieve the results of his work from the printer.

This diligent labor resulted in a steady flow of English monographs, which were published in renowned international series, and which had always been the result of the undeviating pursuit of a research project over a number of years. His production figures would bring any research director in a lyrical mood. In 1986, it was as if Sjef renewed his international début in his study *The Sermon on the Mount as an Ideological Intervention: A Reconstruction of Meaning*. In 1993 he wrote *Imaginative Love in John*; in 1996 *Reading John in Ephesus*; in 2000, in cooperation with Patrick Chatelion Counet, he wrote *Jesus' Appearances and Disappearances in Luke 24*. Previous to these international works, Sjef had also written two comprehensible Biblical commentaries for Dutch readers: one on the letters of John (Romen: 1974) and the other on the Gospel of John (Katholieke Bijbelstichting: 1988). And Sjef had more plans. He envisioned devoting the time after his retirement to the last book of the Bible, the Apocalypse of John.

Just like the present volume turns out to be a collection of quite diverse exegetical methods, so Sjef was a man of a broad methodological approach—which has also earned him a fair bit of negative criticism, especially within the Netherlands. During the Seventies, Sjef became known as an advocate of Structuralism and Materialist Exegesis. In the Eighties, he incorporated recent approaches from literary theory into his exegetical work. In his inaugural address on February 11, 1994, he situated the discipline of exegesis at the intersection of general literary theory, theory of communication, dogmatics, and, perhaps, psychiatry as well. Sjef included the latter because he maintained that reading texts involves hearing an intertextual web of voices inside one's head; reading Biblical texts is no exception to this. Exegesis means: to read and let read, and, in relation to this: to speak and to listen. In reading, Sjef developed a growing consciousness of the voices that the first readers of the texts must have heard. In his engaging study *Reading John in Ephesus*, he gives shape to this consciousness. On the basis of a large corpus of epigraphic material from the First Century city of Ephesus, he investigates which voices the readers of the Gospel of John must have heard. The scholarly term he has coined for these voices is "interferences." A groundbreaking application of this concept is found in *Imaginative Love in John*, in which Sjef demonstrates how John uses the Graeco-Roman institute of *paidestria* as a literary framework for the relationship between Jesus and his beloved disciple in order to let his text interfere with images and ideas from the Hellenistic world.

Listening to voices from the past that resonate in reading is also what Sjef has done concerning the theme of the death threats in the Apocalypse of John. In his last article he reconstructs the historico-sociological reality to which parts of the Apocalypse refer in a language that is similar to the language of the "munera," the gladiatorial games at the end of the First Century. The article was published posthumously in *Biblica* (Rome), as "The Danger at Midday: Death Threats in the Apocalypse."

As is apparent from the summary of his inaugural address, Sjef has always resisted, within the university as well as outside, any ruthlessness with no eye for human emotions. He was radical in that respect, but this was because he would always side with those put down by the powers that be, forced into the straitjackets of excessive regulations, authoritarianism, and pragmatic policy realized at the expense of people. In his last years he thoroughly enjoyed teaching for the Nijmegen Graduate School of Theology. Its students would come from Africa, Asia, and Eastern Europe and did not hesitate to address him as "Father." He would take this, with a smile.

From 1986 onward, Sjef could express his compassion for those who have been hurt, and his commitment to them, in the *Chesed* group, which he had founded together with Fons Meijers, a fellow member of his congregation. The *Chesed* group, situated in a Nijmegen neighborhood of relatively low standing, extends its hospitality to people who, for some reason or other, have run into a tight spot in their lives. For Sjef, this has always meant actually sharing these people's lives, and bearing "the heat of the day" with them. He called this "training an attitude of *chesed*," or "keeping up compassion as an act of faith."

His way of life, and the neighborhood in which he lived, indicated where he believed religious men and women belonged. Sjef assumed an active role in the community center, and taught Dutch to non-natives, which has won him lasting friendships in Kurdish and Moroccan communities. Up to the time of his death he chaired the community center's board of management. Practicing the Biblical concept of *chesed* meant extending hospitality to people at the fringes of society. Initially, many of these were youths that had fallen into some kind of crisis; later on, refugees found a home at the *Chesed* group, traumatized people, declared illegal, left out on the street without any means of existence. For Sjef, all this involved the loss of much of his privacy and a continuous struggle with questions like: Is what we do really beneficial to the other person? Where do our personal limits lie, and how do we handle them?

Sjef studied Buddhism extensively, and practiced Zen meditation and Tai Chi. To him, Zen was the way of freeing oneself from any attachments; meditation to him was the training ground that makes us free to encounter life's mystery. Sjef would have been the last to claim that he had realized this freedom to the full. In one of his meditations, he wrote: "We are on the way, and each of us, in his better moments, will have an inkling of what it will be like, or a longing, or an experience so much like it that it becomes unforgettable."

Sjef developed a serious heart condition and had to undergo surgery, from which he would only partially recover. He knew that the danger to his life had not passed. He loved life and could enjoy it like a bon vivant. After yet another fit of breathlessness, panic could strike relentlessly, as well as unease, anger, rebelliousness, or silent grief. In his last years, however, a serenity came over him, a calm, as if he had become reconciled with his course, and he could say, intensely peaceful: "My friends, I will not get old. I do not have a long time left to live!"

The profound way in which Sjef could experience the mystery of human life transpires from these words of his: "He who places his tears into the ocean of the world's grief, who compensates the shortcomings of the living beings, who takes the suffering of others to heart, gains for himself an unforeseeable space."

BIBLIOGRAPHY OF SJEF VAN TILBORG

Patrick Chatelion Counet

Monographs

The Jewish Leaders in Matthew, Brill-Leiden 1972.
De brieven van Johannes, vertaald en toegelicht (Het Nieuwe Testament), Romen-Bussum, 1974.
Misschien dat God het ons vergeeft. Uit de praktijk van een pastor voor vreemdelingen, Ten Have-Baarn 1976.
Geloven tussen utopie en werkelijkheid, Gooi & Sticht-Hilversum 1980.
The Sermon on the Mount as an Ideological Intervention. A Reconstruction of Meaning, Van Gorcum-Assen etc. 1986.
Johannes (Belichting van het bijbelboek), Katholieke Bijbelstichting etc.—Boxtel etc. 1988.
Imaginative Love in John, Brill-Leiden etc. 1993.
Al lezend stemmen horen, Universitair Publikatiebureau-Nijmegen 1994.
Reading John in Ephesus, Brill-Leiden etc. 1996.
De geliefde leerling: een toegang tot God? Villa Lila-Nijmegen 1998.
Jesus' Appearances and Disappearances in Luke 24 (with P. Chatelion Counet), Brill-Leiden etc. 2000.

Contributions to Books

"Een exegeet buigt zich over het Onze Vader," in Jan Peters (red.): *Bidden nu. Een realiseerbare opgave* (83–90), Romen-Roermond 1971.
"Exegetische Bemerkungen zu den wichtigsten Ehetexten aus dem Neuen Testament," in: P.J.M. Huizing (Hrsg.): *Für eine neue kirchliche Eheordnung. Ein Alternativentwurf* (9–25), Düsseldorf 1975.
"Tussen lezen en luisteren," in B.M.F. van Iersel, M. De Jonge, and J. Nelis (red.): *Van taal tot taal. Opstellen over het vertalen van de Schriften, aangeboden aan Prof. W.K. Grossouw* (91–100), Ambo-Baarn 1977.
"A Form-Criticism of the Lord's Prayer," in Vincent L. Tollers and John R. Maier (ed.): *The Bible in its Literary Milieu. Contemporary Essays* (334–43), Grand Rapids, Michigan 1979.
"De koningszoon geeft het volk in overvloed te eten: een politieke lezing van Lucas 9:10–17," in: *Dossier Bijbel en Katechese* (135–40), Hoger Katechetisch Instituut-Nijmegen 1985.
"De psyche als exegetische werkelijkheid: man-vrouw en man-man relaties in Johannes," in J.A. van Belzen and J.M. van der Lans (red.): *Rond godsdienst en psychoanalyse. Essays voor A. Uleyn* (174–87), Kok-Kampen (ca.) 1986.
"De parabel van de grote feestmaaltijd (Lc 14,1–24)," in: B. van Iersel and T. van Schaik e.a. (red.): *Parabelverhalen in Lucas. Van semiotiek naar pragmatiek* (133–67), Tilburg University Press, Tilburg 1987.
"De koning en de tien slaven (Lc 19,1–27)," in: B. van Iersel and T. van Schaik e.a. (red.): *Parabelverhalen in Lucas. Van semiotiek naar pragmatiek* (133–167), Tilburg University Press, Tilburg 1987.

"Matthew 27,3–10: An Intertextual Reading," in S. Draaisma (ed.): *Intertextuality in Biblical Writings, Essays in honour of Bas van Iersel* (159–74) Kok-Kampen 1989.
"Ideology and Text: John 15 in the Context of the Farewell Discourse," in P.J. Hartin and J.H. Petzer (ed.): *Text and Interpretation. New Approaches in the Criticism of the New Testament* (259–70), Brill-Leiden etc. 1991.
"Een joodse lezing van 1 Johannes 2,2: '... en Hij is verzoening voor onze zonden,'" in D. Akerboom e.a. (red.): *Broeder Jehosjoea. Festschrift voor B. Hemelsoet* (165–78), Kok-Kampen 1994.
"Wat deden de mensen in de dagen van Noë?," in G. Ackermans and P. Nissen (red.): *Kleine geschiedenissen. Een bundel van essays aangeboden aan Adelbert Davids bij gelegenheid van zijn vijfentwintigjarig dienstjubileum* (21–22) Katholieke Universiteit Nijmegen-Nijmegen 1995.
"Het scheppen van bijbelse verhalen," in P. Chatelion Counet and E. Eynikel (eds.): *Is het Grote Verhaal verloren? Het scheppen van bijbelse verhalen* (25–36) Kok-Kampen 1997.
"De mentale kosmografie van het Onze Vader," in G. Ackermans and A. Davids (eds.): *Voor de mens die er nog in gelooft. Overwegingen bij psalmen, liederen en gebeden, aangeboden aan L. Meulenberg* (98–103), Nijmegen 1998.
"Figures in Texts: An Application of Aspects from Gestalt Psychology to the Reading of Texts," in P. Joret and R. Remael (eds.): *Language and Beyond: Actuality and Virtuality in the Relations between Word, Image and Sound* (71–81), Rodopi-Amsterdam & Atlanta 1998.
"De geheimen van de geliefde leerling," in: A.-M. Korte, Fr. Vosman, and Th. de Wit (eds.): *De ordening van het verlangen. Vriendschap, verwantschap en (homo)seksualiteit in joodse en christelijke tradities* (27–44), Meinema-Zoetermeer 1999.
"Une lecture figurative des expressions en 'Je suis' dans l'évangile de Jean," in L. Panier (réd.): *Récits et figures dans la Bible* (145–77), Colloque d'Urbino-Profac Cadir, Lyon 1999.
"Drie manieren om de bijbel vast te houden," in P. Chatelion Counet and Sj. van Tilborg (eds.): *Speelse Spiritualiteit. Bundel opstellen aangeboden aan Huub Welzen bij gelegenheid van zijn afscheid als universitair docent* (55–57), Katholieke Universiteit Nijmegen 2000.
"The Women in John: On Gender and Gender Bending" (with a response by R. Bieringer: "The Johannine Women and the Social Code of the Time"), in J.W. van Henten and A. Brenner (eds.): *Families and Family Relations as Represented in Early Judaisms and Early Christianities: Texts and Fictions* (192–212; 213–19), Deo Publishing-Leiden 2000.
"Jezus temidden van de joden van het Loofhuttenfeest in Johannes 8," in H.J.M. Schoot (ed.): *Theologie en Exegese* (Jaarboek 2001, Thomas Instituut) (53–66), Utrecht 2002.

Articles

"A Form-Criticism of the Lord's Prayer," in: *Novum Testamentum* 14 (1972) 94–105.
"Luke 12,35–48: An Interpretation from the Ideology of the Text," in: *Neotestamentica* 22 (1988) 205–15.
"Language, Meaning, Sense and Reference: Matthew's Passion Narrative and Psalm 22," in: *Hervormde Teologische Studies*, 44 (1988) 883–908.
"The Gospel of John: Communicative Processes in a Narrative Text," Neotestamentica 23 (1989) 19–31.
"The Theology of the Johannine Gospel as an Imaginary-Narrative Reality," in *Europäische Theologie-Bulletin*, 5 (1994) 28–39.
"Metaphorical versus Visionary Language," in *Neotestamentica* 28 (1994) 77–91.
"MSC-Spiritualität einmal anders: eine buddhistische Interpretation," in: *Hiltruper Monatshefte* (1999) 78–83.

"That They Might Feel After Him and Find... (Acts 17:27)," in: *Hervormde Teologiese Studies*, 57 (2001) 86–104.
"Ongehuwd omwille van het Rijk der hemelen. Een uitleg van Mt 19,3–12," in: *Ons Geestelijk Leven*, 46 (1969) 30–36.
"Gods heerschappij: een juk en een onthulling," in: *Schrift*, 3 (1969) 90–93.
"Mattheus 19,3–12 en het onontbindbare huwelijk," in: *Annalen van het Thijmgenootschap*, 58 (1970) 23–34.
"With God on Our Side," in: *Schrift*, 8 (1970) 78.
"Bidden in de evangelies," in: *Schrift*, 16 (1971) 137–40.
"Volgens Mattheus," in: *Getuigenis*, 19 (1971/72) 227–36.
"Een landeigenaar ging uit om mensen te zoeken," in: *Getuigenis*, 16 (1971/72) 264–67.
"De Bergrede," in: *De Bijbel*, V, 73 (1972) 2334–35.
"De kameel en het oog van de naald," in: *Kruispunt*, 8 (1972) 22–24.
"'Neerdaling' en incarnatie: de christologie van Johannes," in: *Tijdschrift voor Theologie*, 13 (1973) 20–33.
"Exegetische notities bij de belangrijkste huwelijksteksten uit het Nieuwe Testament," in: *Alternatief Kerkelijk Huwelijksrecht, Annalen van het Thijmgenootschap* 62 (1974) 9–23.
"Jezus en Lazarus," in: *Ons Geestelijk Leven*, 52 (1975) 93–101.
"Afscheid van de Formgeschichte. Op zoek naar de verantwoording voor een andere manier van lezen," in: *Vox Theologica*, 46 (1976) 1–9.
"Historische mythevorming? En de rest...," in: *Praktische Theologie* 4 (1977) 380–82.
"Implicaties en evaluatie van drie teksten over Markus 2:1–12," in: *Wending* 33 (1978) 28–32.
"De materialistische exegese als keuze. Een uiteenzetting over intentie, reikwijdte en belang van de materialistische exegese," in: *Tijdschrift voor Theologie*, 18 (1978) 109–30.
"Als mens te midden van het geweld. Een uitleg van Mattheus 26:36–56," in: *Ons Geestelijk Leven*, 55 (1978) 132–39.
"Het lezen van de schrift. De persoonsgerichte schriftlezing als feit en mogelijkheid," in: *Praktische Theologie*, 5 (1978) 227–36.
"De schrift in goede handen? Materialistische exegese als maatschappelijk leerproces," in: *De Bazuin*, 61 (1979) nr. 15.
"Over de ideologie rond de Petrustekst in Mattheus," in: *Ons Geestelijk Leven*, 56 (1979) 4–15.
"Bevrijden en verlossen: twee werkelijkheden," in: *Schrift*, 63 (1979) 102–6.
"Medelijden als basis voor solidariteit: Mk 10:46–52," in: *Getuigenis*, 23 (1978/79) 265–70.
"Het structuralisme binnen de exegese: een variant van het burgelijke denken," in: *Bijdragen*, 40 (1979) 364–79.
"De arme spreekt op smekende toon, maar bars is het antwoord van de rijke. Notities bij een Braziliëreis," in: *Ons Geestelijk Leven*, 57 (1980) 50–54.
"'Als ik God zeg.' Een kritische beschouwing van Jacques Pohier's omstreden boek," in: *Ons Geestelijk Leven*, 57 (1980) 275–80.
"De farizeeërs als dragers van de staat," in: *Getuigenis*, 25 (1980/81) 101–6.
"De liefde in de havenstad Korinthe," in: *De Bazuin*, 64 (1981) nr. 10.
"Voortaan namens de leerlingen bij God, een materialistische lezing van Joh. 20 vers 1–18," in: *Rondom het woord, theologische etherleergangen*, 23 (1981) 72–77.
"Jezus in het krachtenspel van de wetsuitleg (Over Mt 5,17–48)," in: *Ons Geestelijk Leven*, 58 (1981) 282–94.
"Atomen, sterren en herders (Lk 2,13.14)," in: *De Bazuin*, 64 (1981) nr. 49/50.
"Taalfragmenten over het begin van de Jezus-beweging," in: *Tijdschrift voor Geestelijk Leven*, 37 (1981) 582–97.
"Burger en bijbel. Wie neemt wat in zijn handen en waartoe?," in: *De Bazuin*, 65 (1982) nr. 11.

"'God zal voor u strijden, zelf hoeft u geen vinger uit te steken.' Korte reflexies bij de strijd van het Filippijnse volk," in: *Ons Geestelijk Leven*, 59 (1982) 82–86.
"De schriftlezing in de liturgie," in: *Getuigenis*, 26 (1981/82) 244–50.
"Jezus en zijn vrienden. Homoseksualiteit als een goed voor iedereen," in: *De Bazuin*, 65 (1982) nr. 26.
"Verhalen van Jezus en van Marx," in: *De Bazuin*, 66 (1983) nr. 10.
"De overlevingskansen van de rijken, Lk 16:1–13," in: *Kommunikatieblad Pax Christi* (1979) 85–90.
"God is mijn wreker. Lukas over wreken en gewroken worden," in: *Schrift*, 89 (1983) 180–85.
"De kerken en het oprukkende machtsdenken," in: *De Bazuin*, 66 (1983) nr. 43.
"Het geding om de ervaring," in: *Opstand*, 10 (1984) 66–67.
"De koningszoon geeft het volk in overvloed te eten: een politieke lezing van Lucas 9:10–17," in: *School en godsdienst*, 38 (1984) 118–20.
"Jezus, koning in de naam van God: Joh 18,28–19,16," in: *Schrift*, 94 (1984) 143–47.
"Een politieke lezing van de bergrede," in: *Ons Geestelijk Leven*, 62 (1985) 170–78.
"Een vertaling van de parabel van de dagloners in de wijngaard. Een verantwoording," in: *Schrift*, 102 (1985) 220–23.
"Solidariteit met de armen in het kerkelijk perspektief van Lucas," in: *Kerugma*, 29 (1985/86) 2–9.
"Tussen trouw en barmhartigheid. Bij het begin van een chesed-groep," in: *Lijnen*, 3 (1986) 42–47.
"De betekenis van het Mattheüsevangelie na de shoah van de joden," in: *Schrift*, 108 (1986) 213–17.
"Hier woont God bij de mensen. Mattheus 5:3–11," in: *Ter Overweging*, KRO-Hilversum (1988) 5.
"Artemis in Efese, vrouwen als leidsters van de gemeenschap," in: *Faust Special, Liber Amicorum voor Johan Negenman* (41–45) Nijmegen 1988.
"De arme als beeld van God," in: *Kerugma*, 32 (1988/89) 2–11.
"Verhalen over het Rijk van God," in: *Geest en Leven*, 67 (1990) 63–70.
"Metaforen van de geest in het Johannesevangelie," in: *Schrift*, 130 (1990) 135–38.
"Teksten lezen zoals ze zijn," in: *Schrift*, 135 (1991) 83–87.
"Uitstel van betekenis. Het dekonstruktie-projekt in de literatuur-wetenschappen," in: *Bijdragen*, 52 (1991) 273–92.
"Visioenen van ondergang en geweld," in: *Jota*, 4 (1991) 58–93.
"Wanneer iemand hem als Christus belijdt," in: *Geest en Leven*, 69 (1992) 119–25.
"Efese en het Johannesevangelie," in: *Schrift*, 141 (1992) 79–111.
"God is liefde (1 Jo 4,9.16)," in: *Schrift*, 144 (1993) 147–50.
"De zelfpresentatie van Jezus in het Johannes-evangelie: een christologie tussen letterlijke en figuurlijke taal," in: *Tijdschrift voor Theologie*, 34 (1994) 128–154.
"De huisgemeentes van de 'johanneïsche' gemeenschap," in: *Schrift*, 173 (1997) 163–64.
"Het verhaal van Jozef van Arimatea," in: *Schrift*, 175 (1998) 25–26.
"In memoriam Bas van Iersel," in: *Tijdschrift voor Theologie*, 39 (1999) 288.
"Wie is de homo die gered wordt? De interpretatie van Genesis in documenten over homoseksualiteit vanuit de katholieke kerk," in: *Tijdschrift voor Theologie*, 41 (2001) 3–12.
"'Een God was het Woord': Theologen vóór Nicea over de proloog van Johannes," in: *Tijdschrift voor Theologie*, 41 (2001) 356–75.
"Verborgen stemmen en echo's in Johannes," in: *Schrift*, 200 (2002) 50–54.
"The Meaning of the Word Game, in Lk 14:20; 17:27; Mk 12:25 and in a Number of Early Jewish and Christian Authors," in: *Hervormde Teologiese Studies*, 58 (2002) 802–10.
"The Danger at Midday: Death Threats in the Apocalypse," in: *Biblica*, 85 (2004) 1–23.

INDEX OF AUTHORS

Abegg, M.G. Jr., 221, 223
Abma, R., 159, 171
Abrams, M.H., 171
Ackroyd, P.R., 116, 123, 152, 172
Agamben, G., 1
Albani, M., 33, 42
Albertz, R., 32, 42
Albrektson, B., 30, 42
Alexander, J.A., 47–49, 51, 53, 56, 62
Alexander, P., 238, 251
Allen, L.C., 71
Allwood, J., 127, 146
Alt, A., 134, 146
Anderson, R.D., 17, 173, 275–76, 284, 288
Arzt, P., 283, 288
Ashton, J., 2–3, 211, 223
Asmuth, B., 159–60, 171–72
Assmann, J., 26, 42
Auffret, P., 97
Aune, D.E., 239–40, 251, 275, 288
Austin, J.L., 269
Avemarie, F., 269–70, 272
Aycock, D.A., 199, 224

Bader, G., 100
Baird, W., 244, 251
Bal, M., 164–66, 172–73, 183, 194
Ball, D., 310
Ballhorn, E., 90, 93
Baltzer, K., 155–58, 162, 168, 172–73
Barbiero, G., 79, 93
Barth, H., 55, 63
Barthes, R., 210, 261
Bauer, W., 294, 310
Baumgart, N.C., 28, 42
Becker, J., 282, 288, 299, 310
Becker, U., 154, 156, 172
Beentjes, P., 111
Beex, H., 98, 104
Begrich, J., 81, 84, 92, 94
Berger, K., 263
Berges, U., 6, 14–15, 22, 34, 38, 41–42, 50, 53, 63, 80, 93, 172
Bergh, H.v.d., 166, 170–72

Berlin, A., 35–36, 38, 42
Bernard, J.H., 293, 310, 325
Betz, H.D., 275, 282–86, 288
Beuken, W.A.M., 15, 38, 42, 119, 121, 123–24, 160–62, 172
Bianchi, E., 324
Bieringer, R., 198, 223–24, 358
Billerbeck, P., 219, 225
Bjerkelund, C.J., 296, 310
Black, M., 293, 310–11
Blauert, H., 297, 310
Blenkinsopp, J., 47, 50, 55, 62
Blommestijn, H., 324, 332
Bodanis, D., 228, 251
Boer, M.C. de, 222–23
Boismard, M.-É., 294, 299–300, 304, 310–11, 313
Bonhoeffer, D., 100
Bonz, M.P., 177, 194
Bosshard-Nepustil, E., 46, 51, 63
Botha, J.E., 292, 295–96, 306–307, 309, 311
Bourguignon, E., 241, 251
Bovon, F., 177, 194
Boyarin, D., 220, 223
Braulik, G., 70, 79–80, 82, 87, 93–94
Braun, F.-M., 293, 311
Bremond, C., 259
Breuer, D., 262
Breytenbach, C., 262
Brink, A.P., 184–85, 187, 189, 194
Brinsmead, B.H., 275, 288
Broek, R. van den, 26, 42
Broer, I., 257
Bromboszcz, T., 294, 311
Brooke, A.E., 293, 311
Brown, R.E., 215, 223, 292, 311
Brown, S., 293, 311
Brown, W.S., 251
Bruce, F.F., 225, 284, 289
Brueggemann, W., 24, 43, 75, 156, 172
Brunert, G., 79, 93
Bryant, R.A., 280, 289

Bultmann, R., 257, 293, 298–99, 302, 311–12
Burney, C.F., 293, 304, 311
Bussmann, H., 297, 306, 311

Caron, G., 207, 223
Carr, D.M., 7, 154, 172
Carson, D.A., 303–304, 311
Casey, M., 293, 311
Cassian, John, 317–18
Chang, P.S.-C., 309, 311
Charles, R.H., 293, 311
Charlesworth, J., 219, 223, 251–52
Chatelion Counet, P., 1, 16, 133, 146, 223, 230, 253, 258, 270–71, 353, 357–58
Chatman, S., 165, 172
Childs, B.S., 47, 51, 62, 90, 93
Chilton, B., 218, 223, 225
Christensen, D.L., 70
Clark, G.R., 21, 42
Classen, C.J., 278, 289
Clements, R.E., 51, 62–63, 75
Clines, D.J.A., 2, 6, 21, 37, 42, 142
Cole, R.L., 79, 86, 93
Collins, J.J., 246, 251
Collins, R.F., 198
Colwell, E.C., 304, 311
Conrad, E.W., 3, 7, 116, 123, 339–40, 346
Conroy, C., 149, 172
Conzelmann, H., 269, 299, 311
Coppens, J., 293, 311
Courtès, J., 208, 224
Craffert, P.F., 17, 229, 232, 241, 249, 251
Craig, W.L., 225, 229, 251
Craigie, P.C., 81, 93
Creach, J.F.D., 78–79, 92
Credner, K.A., 309, 311
Crenshaw, J.L., 89, 93
Crossan, J.D., 230–31, 235, 251
Culler, J., 183, 194
Culpepper, R.A., 3, 198–200, 203, 205, 211, 216–19, 222–23, 295, 311

Dahood, M., 106
Danow, D.K., 184, 194
Davidsen, O., 259
Davidson, S., 253, 292, 311
Davies, M., 176, 195, 311
Davies, S.L., 245, 251
Davis, S.T., 229, 251
Dawson, A., 257

Day, J., 67
De Saeger, L., 289
Delabastita, D., 103, 153, 164–65, 171–72
Delitzsch, F., 47, 49–50, 62
Denaux, A., 306–308, 311
Derrida, J., 8–14, 197, 200, 223
Descartes, R., 233–34
Dietrich, F., 93
Dietrich, W., 25, 42
Dijk, T.A. van, 261
Dillmann, R., 256, 258
Dirven, R., 126–27, 146
Von Dobbeler, A., 265–68, 270, 273
Dobbs-Allsopp, F.W., 31, 32, 34, 41, 42
Doeker, A., 83, 93
Dohmen, C., 23, 42
Dormeyer, D., 17, 256–60, 262–63
Driver, G.R., 58, 62
Dschulnigg, P., 292, 294, 297, 302, 305–306, 314
Du Rand, J.A., 311
Du Toit, A.B., 289
Du Toit, W., 251–52
Duhm, B., 47–48, 50, 62
Duke, P.D., 295, 311
Dunn, J.D.G., 91, 14, 198, 207, 212, 223–24, 283–84, 287, 289

Eaton, J.H., 151–52, 162, 172
Ebeling, G., 282, 286, 289
Eco, U., 12, 308, 311
Egger, W., 258–59, 262
Ego, B., 74, 101
Ehrlich, A.H., 72
Elfferich, I., 253
Ellis, P.F., 304, 311
Emmerson, G.I., 116, 123
Engnell, I., 152, 172
Eriksson, A., 281, 289
Esler, P.F., 177, 194, 252
Essen, G., 41, 43
Evans, C.A., 215–16, 219, 223–25, 251
Exum, J., 2
Eynikel, E., 15, 66, 358

Fauconnier, G., 127, 131–33, 146, 148
Faure, A., 298, 312
Feldmann, F., 47, 62
Felton, T., 297, 312
Festugière, A.-J., 296, 312
Fischer, G., 257
Fischer-Lichte, E., 9

INDEX OF AUTHORS

Fisher, R.W., 121, 123
Fitzmyer, J.A., 177, 194
Flacius, M., 292, 309, 312
Fokkelman, J.P., 15, 97, 99–101, 103, 105, 108–109, 112
Follingstad, C.M., 128–29, 131, 133–35, 142, 146
Fortna, R.T., 294, 299, 302–304, 312
Fowler, R., 3, 326
Frankemölle, H., 257
Freed, E.D., 303, 309, 312
Frey, J., 205, 224, 292, 296–97, 299–305, 312
Frickenschmidt, D., 257
Friedlaender, M., 62–63
Friedman, R.E., 75
Füglister, N., 80, 90, 93
Fumagalli, G., 261

Galindo, F., 263
Gallagher, W.R., 50, 63
Gärdenfors, P., 127, 146
Genette, G., 183–84, 186–89
Gerhard, J., 309, 312
Ghesquiere, R., 103, 153, 164–65, 171–72
Gillman, N., 24, 43
Girard, M., 24, 26, 43
Girard, R., 24, 43
Glassius, S., 292, 309, 312
Glasson, T.F., 309, 312
Goguel, M., 293, 312
Görg, M., 23, 43
Gorp, H. van, 103, 153, 164–65, 171–72
Gosse, B., 116, 123
Goulder, M., 79, 83, 94
Granskou, D., 213, 224
Green, J.B. 177–78, 194, 233, 235, 240, 251
Greimas, A.J., 4, 26, 43, 208–10, 221, 224
Gressmann, H., 70
Griffiths, G.J., 134, 146
Grilli, M., 256
Groenewald, A., 2, 15, 80, 87, 94
Grol, H. van, 102
Grosheide, H.H., 161, 172
Grosjean, J., 292, 312
Gross, W., 25, 43, 70
Guerike, H.E.F., 292, 312
Guigo II, 18, 324–25, 327–28
Gülich, E., 258, 263
Gunkel, H., 81, 84, 92, 94, 134, 146

Haag, H., 151, 172
Hadot, P., 242, 252
Haenchen, E., 263, 265–67, 269, 272, 294, 299, 301, 304–305, 312
Hagner, D.A., 216, 224
Haldimann, K., 312
Hall, R.G., 282, 289
Halpern, B., 75
Hamilton, N.Q., 246, 252
Hanson, N.R., 249–50, 252
Häring, H., 25, 43
Hartke, W., 248, 312
Hayes, J.H., 50, 63
Heekerens, H.-P., 292, 297–98, 300–301, 312
Hehn, J., 68
Hempfer, K.W., 259
Henderson, I.H., 308, 312
Hengel, M., 302, 312, 314, 316
Herion, G.A., 25–26, 29, 43
Hermisson, H.-J., 56, 62, 150, 153, 157, 159–62, 172
Hesse, E., 70
Heßler, E., 153–54, 162, 172
Hildegard of Bingen, 18, 335, 341–42
Hirsch, E., 293–94, 297, 299, 301, 313
Hirsch, J., 50, 53, 62, 293
Hitzig, F., 47, 50, 63
Holtzmann, H.J., 292, 313
Horst, P.W. van der, 246, 253
Hossfeld, F.-L., 79, 81–94
House, P.R., 159, 162, 171–72
Houtman, C., 68, 134, 138, 147
Howard, D.M., 78, 79, 94
Howard, W.F., 293, 302, 313
Hübner, H., 275, 289
Human, D.J., 90, 94
Hunt, R.B., 303, 312
Hurtado, L., 219, 224
Huwyler, B., 95, 142, 147

Ingremeau, Chr., 26, 43
Irvine, S.A., 50, 63
Isaac, E., 239, 252
Iser, W., 261

Jacquier, E., 293, 313
Jahnow, H., 53, 63
Jakobson, R., 104, 185
Janowski, B., 59–60, 63, 77, 94
Janzen, J.G., 97
Jastrow, M., 48, 63
Jeremias, J., 44, 293, 297, 302, 313

Jervell, J., 269-70
Johnson, B., 199, 220, 224, 251
Jong, A. de, 33, 44-45, 49
Jong, M. de, 47
Jonge, H.J. de, 215, 224
Jonge, M. de, 310, 314, 357
Joüon, P., 47, 63
Jüngel, E., 41, 43, 172

Kaiser, O., 47, 63
Kaiser, T.P.C., 313
Kamp, A.H., 74, 130, 134, 142, 147
Kassel, M., 262
Kayser, W., 153, 172
Kee, H.C., 239, 252
Kennedy, G.A., 275, 282, 289, 315
Kenney, W., 182, 194
Kern, P.H., 17, 275-76, 289
Kikawada, I., 70
Kingsbury, J.D., 190, 194
Klauck, H.J., 262
Kleer, M., 90, 94
Knight, J., 178, 194
Köckert, M., 172
Koenen, K., 79, 94
Koester, H., 298, 313
König, E., 50, 63
Koole, J.L., 56, 63, 161, 172
Korpel, M.C.A., 102, 121, 123
Kowalski, B., 306-308, 313
Krahe, S., 23, 43
Krasovec, J., 73, 75
Kratz, R.G., 162, 172
Kremendahl, D., 283, 289
Krieger, K.-S., 25, 43
Kriel, J.R., 233-34, 236, 252
Kroeze, J.H., 142, 147
Kutscher, E.Y., 48, 63, 121, 124
Kysar, R., 203, 224

Laato, A., 116, 124
Labahn, A., 53, 63, 172
Lagrange, M.-J., 293, 313
Lamouille, A., 294, 299-300, 310-11, 313
Landes, G.M., 67, 69
Lang, B., 59, 246, 252
Langacker, R.W., 127-29, 131, 147
Lange, S.G., 292, 313
Lategan, B.C., 261
Laughlin, C.D., 241-43, 252
Lawson, S.J., 73
Leach, E.R, 199, 224
Lee, N.C., 24, 43

Leene, H., 84, 94, 159-63, 165, 169, 172-73
Lentzen-Deis, F., 259
Léon-Dufour, X., 313
Lewis, C.S., 100
Lieu, J., 198, 224
Lindemann, A., 311
Lindström, F., 82, 95
Link, C., 25, 42
Lipton, D., 134, 142, 147
Loader, J.A., 147
Lohfink, N., 24, 29, 43, 70, 79, 94-96
Lommel, P. van, 249, 253
Longenecker, R.N., 283, 289
Lorenzini, E., 293, 313
Lotman, J.M., 183-84, 194-95
Louw, J.P., 292, 313
Lowe, M., 205, 224
Ludwig, A.M., 249, 252
Lugt, P. van der, 105
Luthardt, E., 292, 313
Luxemburg, J. van, 165-66, 173
Lyons, J., 189, 195

Maas, F., 324
Maatje, F.C., 164, 166, 173
Machinist, P., 157, 172
MacLaury, R.E., 148
Malatesta, E., 219, 224
Malina, B.J., 232, 238, 252
Marcus, D., 66-68
Marcus, M., 95
Martin, D.B., 229, 232-34, 237-40, 246, 252
Martyn, J.L., 197-98, 214-15, 224, 279, 286, 289
Mayer, W., 32, 43
Maynard, H., 313
Mays, J.L., 90, 95
McCann, J.C., 79, 95
McEvenue, S., 62, 70, 121, 124
McGrath, J., 219, 224
McHugh, J., 198, 215, 224
Mcknight, E.V., 13, 259, 262
Meeks, W., 204, 219, 224
Meier, J.P., 190, 195
Menken, M., 211, 224
Menoud, P.-H., 293, 302, 313
Merwe, C.H.J. van der, 142, 148
Merz, A., 259
Meyers, V., 253
Michie, D., 261
Miggelbrink, R., 25, 43
Migne, J.P., 321

INDEX OF AUTHORS

Millard, A.R., 134, 147
Millard, M., 79, 90, 94–95
Miller, A., 41, 43
Miscall, P.D., 156, 173
Mlakuzhyil, G., 309, 313
Moloney, F.J., 311, 313
Moody, R.A., 249, 252
Moore, S.D., 1–2, 7, 96, 178, 180–81, 195
Mora-Paz, C., 258
Morgen, M., 313
Morgenthaler, R., 297, 313
Morris, L., 10, 309, 313
Mosis, R., 85, 95
Moulton, J.H., 293, 313, 316
Mowinckel, S., 151–52, 162, 173
Muilenburg, J., 123, 153, 155, 162, 173
Müller, P.-G., 297, 313
Muraoka, T., 47, 63
Mussner, F., 279, 289

Naudé, E., 82, 95
Naudé, J.A., 142, 147
Neirynck, F., 294, 304, 313–14, 316
Nel, P.J., 83, 95
Newberg, A.B., 241, 252
Newman, B.J., 335
Newman, C., 220, 224
Neyrey, J.H., 193, 195, 238, 252
Nicol, W., 294–95, 298–99, 309, 314
Nielsen, H.K., 314
Niemeyer, C.Th., 79, 95
Nissen, P., 291, 314, 324, 358
Noack, B., 294, 297, 314
Noll, K.L., 145, 147
Noort, E., 24, 43, 95
Nordland, O., 241, 252
Norris, K., 100
Nötscher, F., 70

O'Day, G.R., 295, 314
Oepke, A., 283, 286, 289
Olsson, B., 296, 314
Oosterhuis, H., 24, 99
Oswalt, J.N., 47–51, 56, 63

Paganini, S., 154, 162, 167, 173
Parrot, A., 134, 147
Peleg, Y., 75
Penna, A., 47, 63
Person, R.F. Jr., 304, 314
Pesch, R., 263, 265, 268, 270
Petersen, N.R., 181, 184–85, 195, 262

Pfister, M., 159–60, 165, 167, 173
Pilch, J.J., 246, 252
Pirson, R., 130–31, 147
Plümacher, E., 256
Pollefeyt, D., 198, 223–24
Popp, T., 309–310, 314
Porter, B.N., 145, 147, 251
Poythress, V.S., 304, 314
Prince, G., 188, 195
Prince, R., 252
Prinsloo, W.S., 77, 90, 95
Pritchard, J., 70
Pury, A., 134, 147–48

Quinn-Miscall, P.D., 156, 173

Rad, G. von, 134, 147, 220, 224
Radl, W., 256–57
Raible, W., 258, 263
Rakotoharintsifa, A., 314
Ranke, H., 70
Reedijk, W., 317–18
Reinhartz, A., 198, 215, 224
Reiser, M., 257
Resseguie, J.L., 177, 193, 195
Rhoads, D., 261
Richard, E., 304, 314
Richardis of Stade, 338, 341, 344
Ricoeur, P., 185, 195, 260, 262
Riesner, R., 257, 314
Rimmon-Kenan, S., 183, 188, 195, 210, 225
Ringgren, H., 151–52, 162, 173
Rissi, M, 215, 225
Ro, J.U., 80, 84, 95
Roberts, J.K., 283, 289
Rochais, G., 311
Roloff, J., 257, 263, 265, 267–70
Roscher, W.H., 72
Rose, M., 134, 143, 148, 223
Rösel, Ch., 79, 95
Rosenberg, A.J., 49–50, 53, 56, 63, 74
Rowland, C., 198, 244, 252
Ruckstuhl, E., 292–95, 297, 300–302, 305–306, 314
Rudzka-Ostyn, B., 147, 148
Russel, D.S., 239, 240, 252
Ruusbroec, Jan van, 320

Saler, B., 234, 253
Sanders, E.P., 177, 195
Sanders, J., 133, 148
Sarna, N., 134, 148
Sasson, J., 69, 72, 74–76

Saussure, F. de, 4–5, 8–9, 12, 307, 311
Schelling, P., 79, 85, 95
Schenk, W., 294, 314
Schlier, H., 283, 289
Schmidt, N.F., 83, 95
Schmidt, W.H., 85, 95
Schmithals, W., 292, 314
Schnackenburg, R., 299, 314
Schneider, G., 123–24, 269
Schneider, W., 168–69, 173
Schnelle, U., 257, 292, 295, 297, 300–303, 315
Schnider, F., 277, 279, 289
Scholtissek, K., 198, 219–20, 225, 295, 315
Schoon-Janßen, J., 275, 289
Schoors, A., 47, 63
Schröten, J., 79, 95
Schulz, S., 292, 297–98, 301–303, 315
Schulze, J.D., 292, 315
Schwager, R., 24, 43
Schweizer, A., 298, 315
Schweizer, E., 293–94, 300, 302, 305, 309, 313
Scoralick, R., 21, 23, 43
Searle, J.R., 260
Sedlmeier, F., 92, 95
Segal, A.F., 243, 252
Segal, B.J., 68
Seim, T.K., 186, 190, 195
Seitz, C.R., 154–55, 162, 173
Seyffarth, T.A., 292, 315
Sherwood, Y., 74
Simon, U., 71, 76
Ska, J.L., 165, 173
Smalley, S.S., 315
Smit, J., 275, 289
Söding, Th., 257, 259
Sommer, B.D., 173
Speiser, E.A., 134, 148
Spieckermann, H., 78, 95
Spieckermann, H., 21–22, 29, 44
Spitta, F., 293, 315
Spurrett, D., 234, 236, 252
Stacey, W.D., 162, 173
Staley, J.L., 295, 315
Steggink, O., 320, 324
Stenger, W., 277, 279, 289
Sternberg, M., 165, 173, 180–81, 183–84, 195
Sternberg-el Hotabi, H., 29, 44
Strack, H., 219, 225
Strauss, D.F., 302, 315

Stronck, C.W., 292, 315
Sweeney, M.A., 7, 50, 55, 63
Sweetser, E., 127, 131–32, 148

Talbert, C.H., 246, 252
Talstra, E., 5, 169, 173
Tannehill, R.C., 185–86, 189, 191, 195
Tarelli, C.C., 315
Tart, C.T., 242, 253
Tate, M.E., 81, 95
Taylor, C., 148, 235–36, 253
Taylor, J.R., 126, 129, 148
Teeple, H.M., 294, 315
Telford, W., 219, 225
Temple, S., 229, 315
Thatcher, T., 297, 312
Theissen, G., 257, 259
Thielman, F., 292, 315
Thompson, J.M., 298, 316
Thornton, C.J., 256
Thyen, H., 295, 300, 316
Tiede, D.L., 178, 195
Tilborg, Sj. van, 14–16, 21, 23, 40–42, 44, 60, 77, 112, 115, 124–25, 133, 146, 148–49, 171, 173, 179–80, 195, 198, 223, 225, 230, 235, 253, 258, 270–71, 273, 288, 291–92, 296, 310, 314, 316, 318, 351, 358
Tillmans, W.G., 329–31
Timmins, N.G., 309, 316
Todorov, T., 262
Tolmie, D.F., 17–18, 203, 210, 225, 275
Tomson, P., 198, 220, 225
Toorn, K. van der, 23, 32, 44
Trible, F., 67
Trible, P., 75
Turner, N., 146, 293, 316
Twelftree, G.H., 245, 253

Ulfgard, H., 218, 225
Ungerer, F. & Schmid, H.-J., 127, 148
Ungnad, A., 70
Untergassmair, F.G., 316
Uspenski, B., 181–82, 184, 194–95
Utzschneider, H., 149, 158–59, 162–64, 174
Utzschneider, U., 307, 316

Van Aarde, A., 16–17
Van Belle, G., 298–99, 302–303, 308–309, 313, 316

INDEX OF AUTHORS

Van Hecke, P., 130, 134
Vandecasteele-Vanneuville, F., 198, 223-24
Vandermoere, H., 184, 195
Vaux, R. de, 209, 225
Vawter, B., 67
Veenhof, K.R., 32, 44
Vervenne, M., 24, 44, 124, 172
Vincent, J.M., 151, 158, 162, 173, 357
Vitringa, C., 48, 63
Volmar of Disibodenberg, 338, 341, 344
Volz, P., 27, 44
Vorndran, J., 92, 95
Vorster, J.N., 180, 233, 238-39, 253
Vos, J.S., 282, 284, 289

Waaijman, K., 320, 324-25, 328, 332, 334
Wahlde, U.C. von, 203, 211-12, 225, 298, 304, 316
Walsh, R., 249, 253, 325
Watts, J.D.W., 47-49, 63, 116, 124, 155-58, 162, 173
Wead, D.W., 295, 316
Weber, B., 79, 82, 88-89, 92, 95
Weber, M., 27, 44, 292, 316
Weder, H., 312
Wees, R. van, 253
Wegscheider, J.A.L., 292, 316
Weippert, M., 48, 63
Weiser, A., 269
Wellhausen, J., 293, 316

Wendt, H.H., 293, 298, 316
Werlitz, J., 150, 161, 173
Werth, P.N., 148, 315
Westermann, C., 25, 44, 119, 124, 134, 148
Weststeijn, W.G., 164-66, 173
Wette, W.M.L. de, 292, 311
Whybray, N., 79, 95
Whybray, R.N., 25, 44
Wieringen, A.L.H.M. van, 16, 118-19, 121, 124
Wildberger, H., 48, 50, 54-55, 58-59, 63, 343
Wilks, J.G.F., 149, 473
Williamson, H.G.M., 121, 124
Wils, J.-P., 40, 44
Wilson, G.H., 79, 95
Wiseman, D.J., 71
Wolde, E.J. van, 16, 127, 130, 133-34, 146-48
Woude, A. van der, 16, 162, 173
Woude, A.S. van der, 71
Wright, M.R., 238, 253
Wright, N.T., 229, 253

Yri, K.M., 130, 134, 148

Zapff, B.M., 29, 44
Zeller, D., 292, 316
Zenger, E., 25, 40, 44, 78-90, 92-96, 100-101
Ziener, G., 299, 316
Zimmerli, W., 79, 86, 173, 343
Zumstein, J., 199, 203, 225

www.ingramcontent.com/pod-product-compliance
Lightning Source LLC
Chambersburg PA
CBHW031542300426
44111CB00006BA/149